Matthew Feldman, Karim Mamdani (eds.)

Beckett / Philosophy

Foreword by Alexander Gungov

Matthew Feldmann, Karim Mamdani (eds.)

BECKETT / PHILOSOPHY

Foreword by Alexander Gungov

ibidem-Verlag
Stuttgart

Bibliografische Information der Deutschen Nationalbibliothek
Die Deutsche Nationalbibliothek verzeichnet diese Publikation in der Deutschen Nationalbibliografie; detaillierte bibliografische Daten sind im Internet über http://dnb.d-nb.de abrufbar.

Bibliographic information published by the Deutsche Nationalbibliothek
Die Deutsche Nationalbibliothek lists this publication in the Deutsche Nationalbibliografie; detailed bibliographic data are available in the Internet at http://dnb.d-nb.de.

Cover design: Aglika Gungova

Excerpts from Samuel Beckett's unpublished works: © The Estate of Samuel Beckett, reproduced with kind permission of the Estate of Samuel Beckett c/o Rosica Colin Limited, London. For detailed information see bibliographical references in the text.
Excerpts from letters of Samuel Beckett: Martha Dow Fehsenfeld, Lois More Overbeck, George Craig, Dan Gunn (eds.): The Letters of Samuel Beckett, Vol. 1, 1929–1940 (2009), © The Estate of Samuel Beckett 2009, published by Cambridge University Press, reproduced with kind permission. For detailed information see bibliographical references in the text.

∞

Gedruckt auf alterungsbeständigem, säurefreien Papier
Printed on acid-free paper

ISBN-13: 978-3-8382-0641-7

© *ibidem*-Verlag

Stuttgart 2015

Alle Rechte vorbehalten

Das Werk einschließlich aller seiner Teile ist urheberrechtlich geschützt. Jede Verwertung außerhalb der engen Grenzen des Urheberrechtsgesetzes ist ohne Zustimmung des Verlages unzulässig und strafbar. Dies gilt insbesondere für Vervielfältigungen, Übersetzungen, Mikroverfilmungen und
elektronische Speicherformen sowie die Einspeicherung
und Verarbeitung in elektronischen Systemen.

All rights reserved. No part of this publication may be reproduced, stored in or introduced into a retrieval system, or transmitted, in any form, or by any means (electronical, mechanical, photocopying, recording or otherwise) without the prior written permission of the publisher. Any person who does any unauthorized act in relation to this publication may be liable to criminal prosecution and civil claims for damages.

Printed in the EU

In memoriam
Sean Lawlor (1948–2011)

The day that is darkest
Is the day without laughter

(Nicolas-Sébastien de Chamfort
via Samuel Beckett's *"Long After Chamfort,"* trans. Sean Lawlor)

Acknowledgments

The editors would like to thank, first and foremost, Alexander Gungov for his unflagging support of this project – from initial appearance in the Sofia Philosophical Review V/1 (2011) to his encouragment and assistance with an extended version, published via the kind offices of Sofia University Press under the title Beckett/Philosophy (2012). We would also like to gratefully acknowledge the assistance of David Addyman and Tania Mühlberger for their pivotal assistance in final preparations of this text for press, as well as to all invited contributors for their goodwill and forbearance in the process of publication. The editors would also like to thank Christian Schön, Valerie Lange and their colleagues at ibidem Press for committed and enthuiasistic support in the re-publication of this volume.

Excerpts from Samuel Beckett's unpublished "Whoroscope Notebooks"; "Human Wishes Notebooks"; "Philosophy Notes" and "Interwar Notes"; and letters to Mary Hutchinson and to Barbary Bray, all © The Estate of Samuel Beckett, reproduced by kind permission of the Estate of Samuel Beckett c/o Rosica Colin Limited, London.

Table of Contents

Acknowledgments	7
Table of Contents	9
Alexander L. Gungov Foreword to the ibidem Press Edition	13
Alexander L. Gungov Foreword: Is This the Right Time to Ponder Beckett and Philosophy?	15
Matthew Feldman Introduction to Beckett/Philosophy	23
Matthew Feldman "I am not a philosopher." Beckett and Philosophy: A Methodological and Thematic Overview	35
Donald Phillip Verene On Vico, Joyce, and Beckett	51
Erik Tonning "I am not reading philosophy": Beckett and Schopenhauer	75
David Addyman "Speak of Time, without Flinching… Treat of Space with the Same Easy Grace": Beckett, Bergson and the Philosophy of Space	103
Peter Fifield "Of being—or remaining": Beckett and Early Greek Philosophy	127

Matthew Feldman

Samuel Beckett, Wilhelm Windelband
and Nominalist Philosophy — 151

Chris Ackerley

Monadology: Samuel Beckett
and Gottfried Wilhelm Leibniz — 185

Steven Matthews

"The Books are in the Study as Before": Samuel Beckett's Berkeley — 211

David Tucker

Beckett's "Guignol" Worlds:
Arnold Geulincx and Heinrich von Kleist — 235

P.J. Murphy

Beckett's Critique of Kant — 261

Dirk Van Hulle

"Eff it": Beckett and Linguistic Skepticism — 279

Emilie Morin

Beckett, Samuel Johnson, and the "Vacuity of Life" — 299

Charlotta Palmstierna Einarsson

Beckett and Abstraction — 325

Kathryn White

"I can't go on, I'll go on": Beckett's Form of Philosophy — 341

Mireille Bousquet

Beckett and the Refusal of Judgment:
The Question of Ethics and the Value of Art — 359

Karim Mamdani
Conclusion: Beckett in Theses					379

Information about the Authors and Editors		395

Index of Names							397

Foreword to the *ibidem* Press Edition

*Alexander L. Gungov (Sofia University and
Sofia Philosophical Review)*

In Beckett's enigmatically appealing universe, a philosophical touch shows through, born of imaginary conversations and indirect disputes with philosophers. The authors in this volume have studied in depth the philosophical sources of the Irish sage's *oeuvre*, revealing his responses to the love of wisdom from various angles. The editors, Matthew Feldman and Karim Mamdani, have demonstrated the uniqueness of the contributions and their significance for the field, so they have released me from this duty. What I wish to do is to try to hear and share some notes from the philosophical sonority of Beckett's work amid the current human predicament.

Hope is ever more and more lacking today. Beckett's writings call for hope in spite of or due to their seeming obscurity and uncanniness edged with absurdity. His first publication on Joyce's *Work in Progress* had seminal impact on his later development. As Donald Phillip Verene points out in his essay included in this volume, Beckett did not pay special attention to the humorous aspect of Joyce's style. Nevertheless, he absorbed its influence, often deflecting it into ironic twists. Irony is Vico's fourth trope, which, unlike metaphor, is not a part of the poetic language of the heroic age but rather dominates in the following mediocre age, which is focused on attending to one's mundane concerns. For the twentieth and twenty-first centuries, however, irony is too week a tool; even satire proves short of vigor in coping with its unprecedented reality. The mode that matches the extraordinary demands of the present is the grotesque, which fully captures the world falling apart, masterfully conveying its innermost essence of decay.

Yet Beckett's grotesques are not just images of decline and destruction. The speculative impetus of Benedetto Croce's Vico has passed into Beckett's dealing with the plain nonsense of ambient life. The "paradoxically productive impasses"[1] are not simply examples of a deadlock into which the author brings his figures but the speculative circles of genuine infinity, not a mathematical infinity but Hegel's cunning, creative kind. Hopelessness and the vain tensions of seemingly blocked circumstances allude to the escape of sublation. This supreme faculty of reason is achieved with the decisive help of imagination embodied in a "Critique of Pure Imagination."[2] Beckett comes close to the Kantian/Lyotardian sublime in which the imagination is engaged in the impossible effort to provide visibility to an Idea. The successful conclusion of this hopeless task is only a lure; the real goal is the endless strife. Lyotard's *differend*—an assignment that, by definition, cannot be fulfilled—recalls the same situation but without the majestic delusion common to the sublime.

The speculative tendency in Beckett aiming at a new reality via a regenerated sense goes beyond the noble impotence of the sublime and the doomed *differend*. It assists us not only to recognize the marionette theater of our contemporary age—which is not its worst misfortune – but to face soberly the transformation of human beings into statistical units. The overwhelming ontology of statistics is opposed by "an autonomous grace in a frozen figure, a trembling tension, once again, between philosophy and image."[3] The irreplaceability of human warmth is awareness "yet to come"; but a piece of good news has already been announced, and it is my ardent wish that *Beckett/Philosophy*, now in **ibidem** Press' edition, spreads it against the dominating hyperreality of financial ledgers and statistical reports.

---

[1] Karim Mamdani, "Conclusion: Beckett in Theses," in this volume, 389.
[2] Ibid., 391.
[3] Ibid., 390.

Foreword

Is This the Right Time to Ponder Beckett and Philosophy?

Alexander L. Gungov (Sofia University, Bulgaria)

Why Bulgaria, and why Sofia University Press? What does Bulgaria have to do with philosophy, let alone with Beckett? The only Bulgarian philosopher renowned worldwide, St. Cyril, dates from the ninth century (fortunately A.D.) and the only prominent contemporary philosopher with a Bulgarian name, Julia Kristeva, happens to be French. Bulgaria—a Wonderland where people shake their heads to say "No" and nod to say "Yes," where the King *de jure* becomes the Prime Minister *de facto*; a low-budget deficit state where the principal qualification for one to be appointed Finance Minister (dedicated to fighting the soaring *foreign* debt) is that person's *foreign* citizenship, and whose most substantial element of national security is a doner kebab shop shield. In spite of, or perhaps because of this, Samuel Beckett is prominent in the academic circles of this country and enjoys a following among the wider reading/theatergoing public.[1] By thematizing and undermining the everyday confidence in common sense and axiomatic truths, Beckett inculcates a non-standard attitude toward the world and the self—one in keeping with the experience of stepping onto Bulgarian soil or taking in the news coming from this part of the globe. Indeed, Beckett's Nobel Prize "for his unremitting

---

[1] For Beckett's reception in the former Soviet Bloc countries, see Octavian Saiu, "Samuel Beckett behind the Iron Curtain: The Reception of Samuel Beckett in Eastern Europe," in *The International Reception of Samuel Beckett,* eds. Mark Nixon and Matthew Feldman (London: Continuum, 2009).

explorations of 'the degradation of humanity,'"[2] turned out to be a gesture prophetic of the later warm welcome of the Irish writer in Bulgaria and in the whole of Central and Eastern Europe.

During "real socialism"—a time when nothing exciting would or could happen in this country and in the other fraternal Warsaw Pact nations—*Waiting for Godot* seemed to speak directly to socialist laborers. Now, in the post-totalitarian transition period, the entire Beckettian *oeuvre* seems perfectly tailored to all sorts of job market players, still crying (and therefore living) retirees, mute (but nevertheless also alive) totally independent drug addicts and prostitutes, downsized former employees, the newly homeless freed from the oppressive state and Communist Party tutelage, not forgetting the optimistic army of tomorrow's unemployed alumni and their worshipping scholarship professors.

As the present collection of essays shows, there are many aspects and many senses of the relationship between Beckett and philosophy. Indeed, Beckett's writings are permeated by the intellectual mood of their time but they also seem to foresee a bleak human destiny. Beckett was, of course, a witness to many of the major events of the twentieth century, including both the end of the Cold War (unique in the annals of warfare in that no official winners were declared and no casualties counted) and the birth of the post-1989 New World Disorder. Beckett passed away on December 22, 1989, on the final day of the so-called Romanian Revolution—the only bloody event in the velvet Central and Eastern European autumn; just three days before the Ceauşescu couple's trial and execution—itself seemingly staged according to a script by another giant of the theater of the absurd, Romanian-born Eugène Ionesco.

The eagerly hoped-for, radiant happiness of utopia, which was scientifically predicted to last *ad infinitum* with the end of history,

---

[2] Quoted in Matthew Feldman, "'I am not a philosopher.' Beckett and Philosophy: A Methodological and Thematic Overview," in *Sofia Philosophical Review*, IV/2 (2010), 19. See also chapter 1 in this volume for a greater exposition on this point.

turned out to be an ongoing disaster—"to him who has nothing it is forbidden not to relish filth"—shared by the civic electorates (devoted civil consumers) on both sides of what once was the Iron Curtain. The metal of this awe-inspiring partition was symbolically melted in a truly Beckettian mode to produce a rather palpable income. Businessminded citizens of undisclosed ethnic origin, who had broken for good with the oppressive totalitarian past, started collecting various metal items for scrap purposes throughout the liberated former Communist Bloc—and in Bulgaria in particular. National electric grid cables, sewage manhole covers, streetcar/train rails and bronze memorials of different sizes and shapes went to scrap; no surprise, then, that some entrepreneurs had to be taken care of by hospitals and the last rites/rights institutions. These endeavors accompanying the acquisition of semi-miraculous skills became emblematic of the New Europe: receiving a wage in the hundreds but facing bills in the thousands; being paid only quarterly or biannually; coping with laws changing on a weekly basis, etc.—all of this turned out to be quite contagious for the rest of Europe. An eloquent illustration of this pestilential tendency occurred just a moment ago, as I was writing this Foreword: Henry Moore's £500,000 *Sundial* has been stolen from the author's estate-museum. It was reported that the robbery was made not to fence the sculpture on the black market (as hardly anybody could instantly command such a price) but simply to sell it for scrap—the copper in the bronze is estimated to fetch £1,500. Moreover, the news provided no details about the suspects being New Europe's free citizens and not Her Royal Majesty's own subjects.

Or to play a variation on the same theme, a conversation concerning Bulgaria's recent accession into the EU with two visiting faculty members from Ireland's prestigious Milltown Institute comes to mind. As our eyes were glued to horse carts edging their way through the traffic jams on the busy Sofia boulevards, I warned my colleagues to expect those carts in downtown Dublin soon, ridden by cheerful fellows of bronze complexion (naturally to become paler in time). Whether my prediction has already come true I am not sure, but in the pan-European distress felt so strongly in the EU (and in the soon to be EU), sooner or later it will.

The deterioration of the human condition Beckett writes about belongs to the society of producers and its sequel, the society of consumers. In both ages, as Zygmunt Bauman justly observes, everyone must sell oneself as a labor commodity (in the way only certain professions used to do in pre-industrial times). Leading the life of a commodity—leading to, of course, the longing for other commodities—does not make much sense, no matter how colorful and seductive the surrounding masquerade. In the age of Consumerism, Camus' feeling of absurdity goes beyond all deception and delusion in pleading for a serene, Stoic admission of hopelessness. Such a sense of absurdity is the brave admission of the dead end in which one has to live, of the absolute impossibility of finding a way out. Beckett's own literary dead end is of a different sort: an absolute imprisonment in the issueless human predicament; in the processes of one's consciousness, language, even stories. Beckett's solution thus differs from Camus' Stoicism but is no less philosophical—one might dare say it is even more so. Beckett relies upon the imagination not just as an artistic tool, but as a genuine philosophical faculty.

For a long time now, the imagination has been more than simply a psychic phenomenon; it is a central philosophical concept. We would do well to remember the social ontology constructed upon the imagination by the Renaissance Humanists; its contradictions in Descartes' disdainful but simultaneously respectful attitude to the imagination; Vico's praise of the imagination as the source of the social world supported by Providence; Kant's vague root of all experience we are usually unaware of; Fichte's interplay between intellectual intuition and the imagination; Hegel's recollection presupposed by the speculative thinking;[3] Bentham's untimely fictions; Husserl's free variations of phantasy; Heidegger's reaffirmation of Kant's ontological imagination; Sartre's existential imagination; or Bachelard's poet-

---

[3] Donald Phillip Verene, *Hegel's Recollection: A Study of Images in the Phenomenology of Spirit* (Albany: SUNY Press, 1985).

ic imagination; to mention only a few. Within these philosophies of the imagination, Beckett occupies a dignified place because he is positive that life itself could not be human without imagination. For him, the imagination is a powerful consolation for the human predicament rather than an instrument for utopia-building. While the Irish sage clearly and distinctly admits to a permeating and all-encompassing absurdity, he constantly suggests that the imagination is applied to absurdity in a striving to imagine the unimaginable: "imagination dead imagine."

Within philosophical discourse, imagining the unimaginable is sometimes referred to as the sublime. For Kant, the sublime pointed out to an awareness of the limits of the imagination and of the primacy of reason. According to Hegel, the imagination is sublated into speculative reason. For Jean-François Lyotard it is a painful and, at the same time, pleasant struggle to present what is unpresentable. To put this in social terms, it is the painful attempt to achieve justice when justice is impossible or, in Beckett's perspective, it is the making of sense when the absurd reigns supreme. For this purpose Lyotard introduced the term *differend*. This term is capable of shedding some light upon Beckett's struggle with human absurdity no less than upon Beckett's legacy in the current epoch of Post-Consumerism. Although Bauman would not agree, the plague of consumerism no longer prevails. We are stepping into an era when not the consumer but the statistical unit becomes of prime importance. The world divides into a vast majority of statistical units and a tiny segment of the few chosen to manipulate these units. The laws of the game are designed by and for those whose work it is to manipulate; the others are entrapped in the situation of a *differend*. In such an absurd situation, the law-abiding plaintiff cannot prosecute his or her claim—for that person is outside the legal framework by definition. No litigation could be held in such Kafkaesque circumstances, where the only option is to exercise one's *inalienable fundamental right to die*. To go beyond the *differend* one needs an amalgam of imagination and reason or, to echo Beckett, "a reason-ridden imagination" that is *sui gen-*

eris. It distantly resembles Hegel's speculation but is summoned to face the bewildering challenges of globalized humankind. This is a painful business, no doubt. Whether it also brings any pleasure is another question entirely. In any case, Beckett's disposition to imagine the unimaginable might be summarized as: "I can't go on, I'll go on." It is a kind of medicine. Is it intended just for palliative care or for an etiological treatment too? Who knows? . . .

* * *

Most of the present essays were published in the Sofia Philosophical Review's recent Special Issue, entitled Beckett/Philosophy, vol. V, No. 1, 2011 through the generous support of the Irish Embassy in Sofia, and with H.E. Mr. John Rowans' decisive encouragement. To this Special Issue, two chapters have been added to round out this collection: "On Vico, Joyce and Beckett" by the leading figure in the new philosophical humanism, Donald Phillip Verene, and "'I am not a philosopher.' Beckett and Philosophy: A Methodological and Thematic Overview" by the literary historian, Matthew Feldman. The first was already published in Sofia Philosophical Review's vol. V, No. 2, 2011 and the second—in vol. IV, No. 2, 2010. Further to these additions, the volume's co-editor, Karim Mamdani, has added a paragraph on Verene's submission in his "Conclusion."

The original idea for compiling this volume came from Mamdani who suggested it to Feldman. The latter was immediately inspired and both started working on identifying and contacting the prospective contributors. By December 2010 all abstracts had been collected and June 2011 was set as the deadline for completing the essays. By 21 October, 2011, a Special Issue launch was organized at Sofia University under the auspices and active participation of the Irish Embassy, and in particular, of its Cultural Section Director, Ms. Ina Grozdanova. Following a welcome by the Irish Embassy's Chargé d'Affaires, two insightful speeches were given—by Matthew Feldman and Nicolas Johnston of Trinity College, Dublin; they were followed by an enlightening presentation on Beckett's reception in China by Mr. George Wu, a doctoral student at the Graduate Program in Philosophy Taught in English at Sofia University. The audience was aware of being in attendance at one of the most splendid celebrations of Beckett's intellectual heritage in Bulgaria. Regrettably, Karim Mamdani could not attend but we hope he is coming for the SUP book on *Beckett/Philosophy* launch.

Shortly thereafter, Donald Verene kindly informed me about Emory University's Beckett Project where a volume containing scores of Beckett's previously unpublished letters was being compiled. In a real coincidence à la Vico, the launch of *The Letters of Samuel Beckett: Volume 2, 1941–1956* coincided with the launch of *SPhR*'s *Beckett/Philosophy* special issue. Meanwhile, Feldman and Mamdani were eager to publish the *Sofia Philosophical Review*'s Beckett edition in a separate, expanded volume. Their proposal was enthusiastically endorsed by the Sofia University Press Editor in Chief, Mrs. Margarita Krumova; its Director, Mr. Dimitar Radichkov; as well as by Mrs. Parka Atanasova, who was to become the SUP Editor in charge of the *Beckett/Philosophy* publication. The SUP, on behalf of these editors, Matthew Feldman and Karim Mamdani as well as myself, applied to the Bulgarian Ministry of Education for funding. The Ministry proved to be most responsive in wholeheartedly granting their support. H.E. Mr. Joan Rowan also kindly offered the support of the Irish Embassy in Bulgaria for the new volume. The Faculty of Philosophy at Sofia University decided to get involved financially too. Its pledge, however, due to a technical misunderstanding did not materialize until the very last moment (how not to recall yet again Vico's pattern of providential misfortune!?) when their support, too, was confirmed. Beckettian maybe, but also a sublime way to emphasize "Beckett Studies" in Bulgaria and, we collectively hope, further afield.

Introduction to Beckett/Philosophy

Matthew Feldman (Teesside University, UK)

Closed place. All needed to be known for say is known. There is nothing but what is said. Beyond what is said there is nothing. What goes on in the arena is not said. Did it need to be known it would be. No interest. Not for imagining. Place consisting of an arena and a ditch. Between the two skirting the latter a track. Closed place. Beyond the ditch there is nothing. This is known because it needs to be said. Arena black vast. Room for millions. Wandering and still. Never seeing never hearing one another. Never touching. No more is known.[1]

There can be little doubt, then, as Dermot Moran has recently suggested, that such a "stark Beckettian world cries out for philosophical interpretation."[2] Yet at the same time, in acknowledging the pitfalls facing any facile linking of Beckett's (or any other modernist's) literature with philosophical ideas—in no small measure due to the challenging opacity of Beckett's (especially postwar) literature—*Beckett/Philosophy* charts a narrow course. That is to say, the contributions to this collection examine specific philosophical interventions (or "slashes," as suggested by this volume's title), in Beckett's development and expression as a literary writer. Western philosophy is therefore selectively engaged here through the lens of Beckett's en-

---

[1] Samuel Beckett, "Closed Place," in *Texts for Nothing and Other Shorter Prose 1950–1976*, edited by Mark Nixon (London: Faber and Faber, 2009), 147.

[2] Dermot Moran, "Beckett and Philosophy," in *Samuel Beckett: 100 Years*, edited by Christopher Murray (Dublin: New Island, 2006), 94. Despite merely seeing many philosophical allusions in Beckett's work as simply "a kind of arbitrary collection or *bricolage* of philosophical ideas," Moran nonetheless astutely continues: "Beckett's relation to philosophy is difficult to complex. He was not a philosopher; if he had been, he would not have needed to engage with art" (94).

gagement with a particular thinker, doctrine or theme, as registered across his published prose, drama, and poetry, as well as in manuscripts, letters, and reading notes.

Moreover, in publishing this groundbreaking collection through the kind offices of the *Sofia Philosophical Review*, the cumulative implications throughout are that, first, Samuel Beckett was a particularly philosophically-minded writer; second, his knowledge of philosophy was extensive, perhaps more so than any other leading modernist author (save T.S. Eliot[3]); and finally, different philosophical concepts are repeatedly invoked and explored across an *oeuvre* lasting fully six decades. These suggestions thus open Beckett's engagement with, and deployment of, Western philosophy for a distinctly philosophical readership for the first time. As such, the editors of this volume greatly hope academic philosophers might take up the baton offered by the present collection from (mostly) literary critics, in order to further the work undertaken here by considering Beckett's work from a philosophical perspective—perhaps via the starting points advanced by the individual chapters that ensue.

Such a fruitful exchange might depart from a question literary-minded scholars should probably do well to avoid: just how accurately, or knowledgeably, did Beckett understand and employ philosophical ideas? Amongst the tributaries forked out by what is now a sub-discipline of Beckett Studies in its own right, "Beckett and philosophy," this stream has yet to be pursued. To date, in fact, it is notable for its absence. To be sure, however, many other streams have been traversed by "Beckett and philosophy"; often departing from Lance

---

[3] T.S. Eliot received postgraduate training in philosophy, like Beckett's friend Brian Coffey, and unlike most modernist authors. See comments on the latter in §2 of my contribution to this volume, and on the former, see Manju Jain, *T.S. Eliot and American Philosophy: The Harvard Years* (Cambridge: Cambridge University Press 1992); Rafey Habib, *The Early T.S. Eliot and Western Philosophy* (Cambridge: Cambridge University Press, 1999); and Donald J. Childs, *From Philosophy to Poetry: T.S. Eliot's Study of Knowledge and Experience* (London: The Athlone Press, 2001). Such book-length analyses are notable for their absence in Beckett Studies.

St. John Butler's comment that "[i]n spite of all protestations to the contrary, Beckett is working the same ground as the philosophers."[4] This contention will be considered by the present introduction, while the conclusion to this volume reflects individually upon the fifteen chapters published here for the first time. It therefore marks a racing start toward interdisciplinary collaboration, not least as *Beckett/Philosophy* represents the most extensive discussion in English yet of Beckett's relationship with philosophy. This is striking for at least three reasons.

First of all, Beckett seems the most philosophical of writers in both his "early" and "mature" (or postwar) work. His first essay from 1929, in praise of Joyce's then unfinished *Finnegans Wake*, contained Giordano Bruno and Giambattista Vico in the title; in 1930, an award winning 98 lines of verse parodied the life of René Descartes; and in the next year, Beckett's only academic monograph, *Proust*, was so steeped in the philosophy of Arthur Schopenhauer as to distort the eponymous author's *À la recherche du temps perdu* ostensibly under examination.[5] Other philosophers name-checked across Beckett's subsequent work, to name only some of those discussed in ensuing chapters, include Thales of Miletus in the 1932 poem "Serena I" (later included in Beckett's 1935 poetry collection, *Echo's Bones*); idiosyncratically "windowless" Leibnizian monads feature in the novel *Murphy* from 1935–1936; a long-unpublished dramatic fragment from 1940, *Human Wishes*, is based around the life of Samuel Johnson; Immanuel Kant's "fruitful bathos of experience" is quoted in the Addenda to *Watt* from 1945; Arnold Geulincx appears in the short

---

[4] Lance St. John Butler, *Samuel Beckett and the Meaning of Being: A Study in Ontological Parable* (London: MacMillan, 1984), 2. A similar view is espoused in a more recent study by Beckett's long-time English publisher, John Calder's *The Philosophy of Samuel Beckett* (London: John Calder, 2002), which argues that "Beckett was the last of the great stoics" (1).

[5] See, respectively, "Dante...Bruno.Vico..Joyce," in *Disjecta*; "Whoroscope," in Samuel Beckett, *Selected Poems 1930–1989*, edited by David Wheatley (London: Faber and Faber, 2009); and Proust, reprinted in *"Proust" and Three Dialogues* (London: Calder & Boyers, 1970).

story "The End" and the first novel of the "Beckett Trilogy," *Molloy*, written over the next two years; Aristotle, "who knew everything," makes an appearance in the *Texts for Nothing* from 1951; one of Zeno's paradoxes opens the 1958 play *Endgame*; the Occasionalist philosopher Nicolas Malebranche is cited in "The Image" and *How It Is* two years later; and Bishop Berkeley's tag "esse est percipi" prefaces the 1964 arthouse (and Beckett's only) film, *Film*; while Fritz Mauthner "may be it" in *Rough for Radio II*, first published in 1975.[6] Needless to say, there are many more along the way, but these are important and suggestive references by a writer well-known for his meticulousness.

Secondly and no less notably, philosophers have themselves been quick to invoke Beckett's work for a variety of doctrines—as evoked by the title of Bruno Clément's article, "What the Philosophers do with Samuel Beckett." As registered in one volume alone—and even before receiving the Nobel Prize for Literature in 1969—

---

[6] The dates provided above are taken from Ruby Cohn's indispensable *A Beckett Canon* (Ann Arbor, University of Michigan Press: 2001); see also John Pilling's more biographical *A Beckett Chronology* (Basingstoke: Palgrave, 2006). Philosophical references correspond to the following: Thales in *Selected Poems 1930–1989*, 25; Leibniz in Samuel Beckett, *Murphy*, edited by J.C.C. Mays (London: Faber and Faber, 2009), 114; the *Human Wishes* fragment is reproduced in *Disjecta*; Kant's "das fruchtbare Bathos der Erfahrung" comprises entry 31 of the 55 Addenda items at the end of Samuel Beckett, *Watt*, edited by C.J. Ackerley (London: Faber and Faber, 2009), 222; Geulincx appears in "The End," in Samuel Beckett, *The Expelled/The Calmative/The End/First Love*, edited by Christopher Ricks (London: Faber and Faber, 2009), 49, and in Samuel Beckett, *Molloy*, edited by Shane Weller (London: Faber and Faber, 2009), 50; Aristotle appears in "Text for Nothing VIII" in *Texts for Nothing and Other Shorter Prose 1950–1976*, 35; Zeno's paradox offers the backdrop to the opening of *Endgame*, in Samuel Beckett, *Endgame*, preface by Rónán McDonald (London: Faber and Faber, 2009), 93; Malebranche "less the rosy hue the humanities" is cited in "The Image," in *The Complete Short Prose, 1929–1989*, 167, and retained in Samuel Beckett, *How It Is* (London: Calder, 1996), 33; Berkeley's "to be is to be perceived" heads the script for *Film*, in *The Complete Dramatic Works*, 323; and Mauthner is mentioned in *Rough for Radio II*, in ibid., 276.

Beckett was the subject of texts by Gabriel Marcel (1953, 1957), William Empson (1956), Maurice Blanchot (1959), Northrop Frye (1960), Claude Mauriac (1960), Raymond Williams (1961), Wolfgang Iser (1966), David Lodge (1968) in addition to a longer essay by Theodor Adorno entitled "Trying to Understand Endgame."[7] In the years since, longer works have appeared by Gilles Deleuze, Slavoj Žižek, Alain Badiou, and most recently Hélène Cixous.[8] Although this list appears decidedly weighted toward French philosophers, in many ways Beckett's international reception was defined by leading intellectuals both across and within nations—from the USA to China—(largely) following the surprise Parisian success of *Waiting for Godot* in 1953.[9] Even the famous evasion by Jacques Derrida—that Beckett's work was "too close" for him to write on—suggests that Beckett's work may be seen as co-evolving with or even anticipating

---

[7] See Bruno Clément, "What the Philosophers do with Samuel Beckett," translated by Anthony Uhlmann, in *Beckett After Beckett*, edited by S.E. Gontarski (Tallahassee: University of Florida Press, 2006); and *Critical Essays on Samuel Beckett*, edited by Lance St. John Butler (Aldershot: Scolar Press, 1993). For discussion of Adorno's work on Beckett, including a planned future essay on *L'Innommable* "at the end of a projected fourth volume" of his *Noten zur Literatur*, see Shane Weller, "The Art of Indifference: Adorno's Manuscript Notes on *The Unnamable*," in Daniela Guardamagna nd Rossana M. Sebellin, eds., *The Tragic Comedy of Samuel Beckett* (Rome: Laterza, 2009), 223.

[8] See, for example, Gilles Deleuze, "The Exhausted," in his *Essays Critical and Clinical*, translated by Daniel W. Smith and Michael A. Greco (London: Verso, 1998); Alain Badiou, *On Beckett*, edited and translated by Nina Power and Alberto Toscano (Manchester: Clinamen, 2003); Slavoj Žižek, "Beckett with Lacan," parts one and two online at: www.lacan.com/article/?page_id=78, and www.lacan.com/article/?page_id=102 (last accessed 8/12/11); and Hélène Cixous, *Zero's Neighbour: Sam Beckett*, translated by Laurent Milesi (Cambridge: Polity, 2010)

[9] See *The International Reception of Samuel Beckett*, edited by Mark Nixon and Matthew Feldman (London: Continuum, 2009).

some of the major themes in contemporary philosophy (such as phenomenology or even Derrida's poststructuralist philosophy).[10]
Third and finally, right from the start Anglophone critics have interpreted Beckett's writings philosophically. In fact, the conventional starting point for "Beckett Studies," a 1959 Special Issue of the academic journal *Perspective*, contained essays with titles such as "The Cartesian Centaur" (Hugh Kenner) and "Samuel Beckett's *Murphy*: A Cartesian Novel" (Samuel L. Mintz). Moreover, as David Pattie deftly summarizes this first period of Beckett criticism in English:

> The *Perspective* issue identified Beckett as an important figure in English literature; and moreover, it introduced the notion that the Beckettian universe was governed by rules that were, at bottom, philosophical [....] English criticism in the 1960s linked Beckett not only to existentialism, but to Schopenhauer, Kierkegaard, Wittgenstein, and, most decisively of all, to the work of the seventeenth-century French philosopher René Descartes and his philosophical disciples.[11]

Similarly telling titles were to follow over the next decade, from a 1962 chapter by Martin Esslin—later of "theater of the absurd" fame—in the collection *The Novelist as Philosopher*, and Ruby Cohn's 1965 "Philosophical Fragments in the Works of Samuel Beckett" to John Fletcher's "Beckett and the Philosophers" two years later; all capped by David Hesla's remarkable "history of ideas" approach, and the first full-length study of Beckett and philosophy in

---

[10] Derrida, cited in *Acts of Literature*, edited by Derek Attridge (London: Routledge, 1992), 60. For a variety of recent phenomenological approaches to Beckett, see *Beckett and Phenomenology*, edited by Ulrika Maude and Matthew Feldman (London: Continuum, 2009); and for well-known discussions of Beckett's work in light of poststructuralism, see Steven Connor, *Samuel Beckett: Theory, Repetition, Text* (Oxford: Basil Blackwell, 1988); Leslie Hill, *Beckett's Fiction: In Different Words* (Cambridge: Cambridge University Press, 1990); and, most recently, Anthony Uhlmann, *Beckett and Poststructuralism* (Cambridge: Cambridge University Press, 1999).

[11] David Pattie, *The Complete Critical Guide to Samuel Beckett* (Abingdon: Routledge, 2000), 105.

English, his 1971 *The Shape of Chaos: An Interpretation of the Art of Samuel Beckett*. Readers of Beckett in English, by this time, should they have wished to consult literary criticism to divine meaning from Beckett's texts, would doubtless have been struck by the philosophical consistency in approaching a writer famed for his protestations of "ignorance" and "impotence."[12] The view taken in this early period, despite the many nuances of this first period of Beckett criticism in English, is shorthanded by a chapter entitled "The Human Condition" in *The Testament of Samuel Beckett*: "The whole of Beckett's work moves relentlessly towards the answering of one question: What is existence? or, What is man?"[13]

From this initial period of Beckett Studies, furthermore two philosophical readings emerged: the existential and the Cartesian. The first, largely a product of its time, found in Beckett a fictional exponent of existentialism *par excellence*: "From its inception, existential thought has felt itself at home in fiction. Because of its intense 'inwardness' and the 'commitment' of its proponents, it has expressed itself more strikingly in imaginative writing than in fictional treatises."[14] Yet existential thought—for all its very Beckettian emphasis on

---

[12] As Ruby Cohn's thoughtful "Philosophical Fragments in the Works of Samuel Beckett" puts it: "Beckett's heroes not only deny that they are philosophers; they flaunt an inviolable ignorance [.... But] they nevertheless continue to examine, propounding the old philosophical questions that have been with us since the pre-Socratics; on the nature of the Self, the World, and God," reprinted in *Samuel Beckett: A Collection of Critical Essays*, edited by Martin Esslin (Engelwood Cliffs: Prentice-Hall, 1965), 169. See also "Samuel Beckett," in *The Novelist as Philosopher: Studies in French Fiction 1935–1960*, edited by John Cruickshank Westport: Greenwood, 1962); John Fletcher, "Beckett and the Philosophers," in *Samuel Beckett's Art* (London: Chatto & Windus, 1967); and David H. Hesla, *The Shape of Chaos: An Interpretation of the Art of Samuel Beckett* (Minneapolis: University of Minnesota Press, 1971).

[13] Josephine Jacobsen and William R. Mueller, *The Testament of Samuel Beckett* (London: Faber and Faber, 1964), 109.

[14] Edith Kern, *Existential Thought and Fictional Technique* (London: Yale University Press, 1970), viii. Comparable existential perspectives underwrite Ramona Cormier and Janis L. Pallister's *Waiting for Death: The*

solitude, alienation and "intense self-consciousness"[15]—did not seem able to account for Beckett's artistic preoccupation with frailty, constraint and not knowing; or as he put it in conversation with James Knowlson: "he found the actual limitations on man's freedom of action (his genes, his upbringing, his social circumstances) far more compelling than the theoretical freedom on which Sartre had laid so much stress."[16] As for existentialism, so too for Cartesianism—at one point, the *de rigueur* philosophical interpretation of Beckett's work[17]—which may well be a red herring. Without doubt "Whoroscope," Beckett's first published poem in 1930, centered upon the life of René Descartes, and demonstrated some knowledge of Cartesian philosophy. However, this was inductively applied to a reading of Beckett's work as a whole, creating the misleading impression that, as both online sources and the *Encyclopaedia Brittanica* have it, Descartes was "Beckett's favourite philosopher."[18] Having had their say

---

Philosophical Significance of Beckett's En Attendant Godot (Tuscaloosa: University of Alabama Press, 1979); and L.A.C. Dobrez, *The Existential and Its Exits* (London: The Athlone Press, 1986).

[15] Hannah Copeland, *Art and the Artist in the Works of Samuel Beckett* (The Hague: Mouton and Co., 1975), 42–43.

[16] Cited in my "Beckett, Sartre and Phenomenology," in *Limit(e) Beckett*, 0 Issue, online at: www.limitebeckett.paris-sorbonne.fr/zero/feldman.html (last accessed 8/12/11).

[17] To note only the major accounts of Beckett and Cartesianism, see Edouard Morot-Sir, "Samuel Beckett and Cartesian Emblems," in *Samuel Beckett and the Art of Rhetoric*, edited by Edouard Morot-Sir (Chapel Hill, NC: University of North Carolina, 1976); Michael Mooney, "*Molloy*, Part 1: Beckett's Discourse on Method," in *Journal of Beckett Studies* 3 (1978); and Roger Scruton, "Beckett and the Cartesian Soul," in his *The Aesthetic Understanding: Essays in the Philosophy of Art and Culture* (Manchester: Carcanet Press, 1983).

[18] For some of Beckett's sources in the construction of "Whoroscope," see Francis Doherty, "Mahaffy's *Whoroscope*," in *Journal of Beckett Studies* 2/1 (1992). For an argument that Cartesian influence upon Beckett is largely circumstantial, and better recast in terms of a wider engagement with Western philosophy, see my "René Descartes and Samuel Beckett," in *Beckett's*

for so long over the past years, neither existentialism nor Cartesianism is given a chapter in this volume. Given this longstanding tradition of reading Beckett's explicit references, impulses and writings philosophically, it is thus surprising that an expansive collection in English has taken so long. Notwithstanding the scattergun approach taken by the recent *Beckett and Philosophy*—including essays on Beckett and everyone from Friedrich Nietzsche and Martin Heidegger to Jürgen Habermas and Michel Foucault—critics have largely neglected P.J. Murphy's call in his 1994 "Beckett and the Philosophers": "The whole question of Beckett's relationship to the philosophers is pretty obviously in need of a major critical reassessment."[19] Yet better late than never and, in this spirit, *Beckett/Philosophy* attempts just such a "critical reassessment" of Samuel Beckett's relationship with Western philosophy. This is undertaken in two distinct ways: the empirical and the thematic.

In terms of the empirical, the first twelve chapters are concerned with the "meat and potatoes" of Beckett's engagement with philosophy. It is now clear to scholars that Beckett's substantial readings in and note-taking from Western philosophy occurred during a period of systematic self-education across the 1930s. Beckett read widely and took detailed notes from a number of key philosophers during this period, as is demonstrated by the ensuing contributions. While Beckett's

---

Books: A Cultural History of Samuel Beckett's "Interwar Notes" (London: Continuum, 2008).

[19] See *Beckett and Philosophy*, edited by Richard Lane (Hampshire: Palgrave, 2002); and P.J. Murphy, "Beckett and the Philosophers," in *The Cambridge Companion to Samuel Beckett*, edited by John Pilling (Cambridge: Cambridge University Press, 1994), 222. Some recent exceptions on the subject of Beckett and philosophy include Anthony Uhlmann's *Samuel Beckett and the Philosophical Image* (Cambridge: Cambridge University Press, 2006); Garin V. Dowd, *Abstract Machines: Beckett and Philosophy after Deleuze and Guattari* (New York: Rodopi, 2007); Shane Weller, *A Taste for the Negative: Beckett and Nihilism* (Oxford: Legenda, 2005); and Simon Critchley, "Lecture 3: Know Happiness—on Beckett," in his *Very Little ... Almost Nothing* (London: Routledge, 1997).

philosophical indebtedness has long been recognized—particularly since the 1996 publication of James Knowlson's unrivalled biography, *Damned to Fame: The Life of Samuel Beckett*—a systematic treatment of leading "Beckettian" philosophers has been heretofore missing.[20] Those thinkers assembled in the first portion of *Beckett/Philosophy* may therefore be seen to represent the current "canon" of philosophical influences upon Samuel Beckett. While some of the names are to be expected (Arthur Schopenhauer, Immanuel Kant, Bishop Berkeley, Arnold Geulincx), others are not (Henri Bergson, Gottfried Leibniz, Wilhelm Windelband, and the early Greeks); and still others push at the boundaries of philosophy itself (in different ways, Samuel Johnson and linguistic skeptics like Fritz Mauthner). By moving chronologically through Beckett's interwar apprenticeship in philosophy, the first ten chapters here collectively represent the leading, demonstrable debts to philosophy accumulated between the writing of his only academic monograph in 1930, *Proust*, via *More Pricks than Kicks* and *Murphy*, to the start of the wartime novel *Watt*.

Although many of the ten initial essays trace the influence of particular philosophers and doctrines in Beckett's postwar writings, key "Beckettian" themes comprise the final trio of essays in *Beckett/Philosophy*. These philosophical themes, in turn, may be said to be at the forefront of Beckett Studies—Beckett's philosophical approach to literary aesthetics; ethics; and abstraction—as reflected by a number of recent studies.[21] Beyond pointing to the complexity of Beckett and/with/via philosophy, it is hoped that this connection of the empirical and thematic in *Beckett/Philosophy* shows that differing

---

[20] For a discussion of Beckett's philosophical readings during the 1930s, see James Knowlson, *Damned to Fame: The Life of Samuel Beckett* (London: Bloomsbury, 1996), especially chapters 6 to 11; and Feldman, *Beckett's Books*, chapter 2.

[21] See, respectively, Andrea Oppo, *Philosophical Aesthetics and Samuel Beckett* (Oxford: Peter Lang, 2008); *Beckett and Ethics*, edited by Russell Smith (London: Continuum, 2009); and Erik Tonning, *Samuel Beckett's Abstract Drama: Works for Stage and Screen, 1962–1985* (Bern: Peter Lang, 2007).

methodological approaches to Beckett's engagement with philosophy need not be an either/or affair. Rather, Beckett's early readings in philosophy are precisely the "scaffolding" for later key philosophical themes and concerns (such as Arnold Geulincx's influence on Beckettian ethics); or in Knowlson's recent formulation: "he does not attempt to reach firm conclusions. Concepts provide him rather with contrasting images, both verbal and visual, which he takes pleasure in weaving into intricate dramatic patterns."[22] And it is, finally, these "dramatic patterns" that keeps both readers and critics alike returning to the vexed, yet uncannily beautiful, terrain of Beckett and philosophy. Speaking of which, let's get moving, for

> ... time is limited. It is thence that one fine day, when all nature smiles and shines, the rack lets loose its black unforgettable cohorts and sweeps away the blue for ever. My situation is truly delicate. What fine things, what momentous things, I am going to miss through fear, fear of falling back into the old error, fear of not finishing in time, fear of revelling, for the last time, in a last outpouring of misery, impotence and hate. The forms are many in which the unchanging seeks relief from its formlessness. Ah yes, I was always subject to the deep thought, especially in the spring of the year. That one had been nagging at me for the past five minutes. I venture to hope there will be no more, of that depth.[23]

---

[22] Cited in James Knowlson, "Samuel Beckett's *Happy Days* Revisited." I am grateful to Prof. Knowlson for allowing me to consult this forthcoming, as yet unpublished, text.

[23] Beckett, *Malone Dies*, edited by Peter Boxall (London: Faber and Faber, 2010), 23.

"I am not a philosopher." Beckett and Philosophy: A Methodological and Thematic Overview*

Matthew Feldman (Teesside University, UK)

§1

Some eight years after his artistic breakthrough with the Parisian staging of *En attendant Godot*, and some eight years before receiving the 1969 Nobel Prize for his unremitting explorations of "the degradation of humanity," Samuel Beckett, unusually, consented to be interviewed. A now-famous exchange with *Nouvelles Littéraires* journalist Gabriel d'Aubarède cast longstanding doubt upon Beckett's engagement with philosophy:

> Have contemporary philosophers had any influence on your thought?
> I never read philosophers.
> Why not?
> I never understand anything they write.
> All the same, people have wondered if the existentialists' problem of being may afford a key to your works.
> There's no key or problem. I wouldn't have had any reason to write my novels if I could have expressed their subject in philosophic terms.[1]

---

* An earlier draft of this essay appeared in the *Sofia Philosophical Review*, IV/2 (2010), and is presented here with the kind permission of Prof. Alexander Gungov.

[1] The announcement of Beckett's 1969 Nobel Prize for Literature can be found online at www.nobelprize.org/nobel_prizes/literature/laureates/1969/press.html (all websites last accessed on 11/8/10); Beckett's interview with Gabriel d'Aubarède of 16 February 1961 is available in Lawrence Graver and Ray-

Yet the "novel" published by Éditions de Minuit only the month before, *Comment c'est*—tripartite in structure, unpunctuated in presentation, and notoriously difficult to digest—seemed at the same time to belie Beckett's claims of philosophical ignorance.[2] Some pages after name-checking the famous Presocratic thinker, Heraclitus the Obscure, and some pages before the same treatment is meted out to the obscure Malebranche (an Occasionalist follower of Cartesianism), the following passage occurs in the ensuing English translation, entitled *How It Is*:

> mad or worse transformed à la Haeckel born in Potsdam where Klopstock too among others lived a space and laboured though buried in Altona the shadow he casts[3]

Amongst the madness and mud and misery and tin-can openers, the phrase is but one of many betraying what must, *surely*, be considered "philosophic terms"; if not a suspiciously detailed philosophical knowledge.

However, in Beckett Country—or in the "Beckettian" world if one prefers adjectives to nouns in describing this unique terrain—little is as it seems. Interpretations of his work founder precisely because "surely," as above, is shorthand for reading into Beckett whichever theme, theory, or critical approach one fancies. And they have

---

mond Federman, eds., *Samuel Beckett: The Critical Heritage* (London: Routledge and Kegan: 1997), 217.

[2] As Ruby Cohn's *A Beckett Canon* (Ann Arbor: University of Michigan Press, 2004) makes clear, a likely source for the setting of *How It Is* can be found in the fifth circle of Dante's *Inferno*. Also in her work in terms of the tripartite structure employed in *How It Is*, consider Beckett's statement to his friend, the BBC Radio producer Donald McWhinnie: "The work is in three parts, the first a solitary journey in the dark and mud terminating with discovery of a similar creature known as Pim, the second life with Pim both motionless in the dark and mud terminating with departure of Pim, the third solitude motionless in the dark and mud. It is in the third part that occur the so-called voice 'quaqua,' its interiorisation and murmuring forth when the panting stops" (255–256).

[3] Samuel Beckett, *How It Is* (London: Calder, 1996), 47.

all been tried: gender, politics, psychology, you name it: sometimes with great merit.[4] But a problematic point remains; that is, given the challenging and slippery nature of the master's work, Beckett Studies contains no theoretical graveyards. A Rorschach Test is a fitting analogy.[5]

Yet at the same time, the interviewer had not misheard in February 1961, nor had the interviewee misspoken. For the sentiment was to be repeated that very summer, just as Beckett was commencing the arduous self-translation of *Comment c'est* into English as *How It Is*:

> One cannot speak anymore of being, one must speak only of the mess. When Heidegger and Sartre speak of a contrast between being and existence, they may be right, I don't know, but their language is too philosophical for me. I am not a philosopher. One can only speak of what is in front of him, and that now is simply the mess.[6]

And yet, avers the narrator in Part Three of *How It Is*, "nothing to be done in any case we have our being in justice I have never heard

---

[4] In terms of the important (and contested) areas of gender, politics, and psychology, respectively, see influential texts in Beckett Studies by Mary Bryden, *Women in Samuel Beckett's Prose and Drama: Her Own Other* (Basingstoke: Palgrave, 1993); Terry Eagleton, "Political Beckett?", in *New Left Review* 40 (July-August 2006); and J.D. O'Hara, *Samuel Beckett's Hidden Drives: The Structural Uses of Depth Psychology* (Gainesville, FL: University of Florida Press, 1998).

[5] In his seminal *Beckett/Beckett* (London: Souvenir, 1990), Vivian Mercier recounts a fascinating exchange between academic "experts" and audience members following a performance of *Waiting for Godot*: "the most effective contribution was made by a member of the audience who asked the panel the rhetorical question, 'Isn't *Waiting for Godot* a sort of living Rorschach [inkblot] test?' He was clapped and cheered by most of those present, who clearly felt as I still do that most interpretations of that play—indeed of Samuel Beckett's work as a whole—reveal more about the psyches of the people who offer them than about the work itself or the psyche of its author" (vii).

[6] Beckett's interview with Tom Driver of Summer 1961 is also reprinted in *Samuel Beckett: The Critical Heritage*, 219.

anything to the contrary."[7] So which is the real Samuel Beckett? The interviewee who repeatedly disclaimed any familiarity with philosophy—despite referring to both "philosophical terms" and famous philosophers in doing so—or the avant-garde artist who clearly, if nevertheless opaquely, incorporated aspects of Western philosophy into his writings?

§2

To some extent, that vexing question had already been addressed in the earliest critical responses to Beckett, such as the groundbreaking 1959 Special Issue of *Perspective*, containing titles like "Beckett's *Murphy*: A 'Cartesian' Novel." Other voices, also writing during Beckett's lifetime, similarly took those sporadic references to Western philosophers and ostensibly philosophical *mise en scène* as key clues to the unravelling of his work.[8] Yet the detailed, archival spadework was left for biographers in the first instance after Beckett's death; far and away most importantly in the expansive *Damned to Fame* of 1996. Only then were philosophical themes in Beckett's art properly *substantiated*, rather than *supposed*. This was largely due to an enormous corpus of manuscripts, letters and notes made available to Beckett's authorized biographer, James Knowlson, themselves joining the burgeoning Beckett Collection at the University of Reading for consultation by scholars exactly thirty years after its 1971 establishment in Reading, UK (now the home of the Beckett International Foundation).[9]

---

[7] How It Is, 135.
[8] Good examples are David H. Hesla, *The Shape of Chaos: An Interpretation of the Art of Samuel Beckett* (Minnesota: University of Minnesota Press, 1971) and the chapter "Beckett and the Philosophers," in John Fletcher, *Samuel Beckett's Art* (London: Chatto & Windus, 1967), 121–137.
[9] For a catalogue of materials at the University of Reading, see John Pilling, ed., *The Ideal Core of the Onion* (Reading: Beckett International Foundation, 1992). Materials unpublished during Beckett's lifetime include his first novel, *Dream of Fair to Middling Women*, and a play written just before *Waiting for*

For a number of contemporary critics, the task now is to separate *substantiated* from *supposed*. By way of contribution, the following chapters comprising *Beckett/Philosophy* provide unrivalled scope and empirical depth, in particular, by comprehensively demonstrating Beckett's knowledge of philosophy; by highlighting his intensive self-education process over the 1930s, and revealing the extent to which Beckett was acquainted with some canonical philosophers. In here presenting a "taster" of this discussion through a snapshot of Beckett's earliest textual philosophical engagement from 1929, pausing to raise an early methodological caution is in order first. While individual contributors to this collection may not recognize, let alone endorse, the falsifiable methodology I have elsewhere set out as a template for broaching the nettlesome matter of Beckett and philosophy, this methodological issue seems to me vital, and merits broaching here.[10] This is especially relevant to approaching Beckett's work for, as noted above, the very opacity of his art is such that all theories may be "verified" in writing that often has no subject, no place, no material referent.

At issue, ultimately, is the matter of evidence. In our (apparently) postmodern world, it would seem that Sir Karl Popper's great injunctions about the value of deductive logic have been lost in the ether of intellectual relativism. Perhaps nowhere has this phenomenon been more enthusiastically endorsed and applied than in philosophical approaches to literature. Whether in literature, or science, or politics, or psychoanalysis, as Popper has reminded us, evidence is not ephemeral, but integral to the human advancement of knowledge:

Godot, entitled *Eleuthéria*. For Beckett's reading notes on literature, psychology and philosophy, see the informative catalogue comprising the first 200 pages of *Samuel Beckett Today/Aujourd'hui* 16 (2006).

[10] See my "Beckett and Popper, or, 'What stink of artifice': Some Notes on Methodology, Falsifiability and Criticism in Beckett Studies," in *Samuel Beckett Today/Aujourd'hui* 16.

A Marxist could not look at a newspaper without finding verifying evidence of the class struggle on every page, from the leaders to the advertisements; and he also would find it, especially, in what the paper failed to say. And a psychoanalyst, whether Freudian or Adlerian, assuredly would tell you that he finds his theories daily, even hourly, verified by his clinical observations. But were these theories testable? Were these analyses really better tested than, say, the frequently 'verified' horoscopes of the astrologers? What conceivable event would falsify them in the eyes of their adherents? Was not every conceivable event a 'verification'? It was precisely this fact—that they always fitted, that they were always 'verified'—which impressed their adherents. It began to dawn on me that this apparent strength was in fact a weakness, and that all these 'verificationists' were too cheap to count as arguments. The *method of looking for verifications* seemed to me unsound—indeed, it seemed to me to be the typical method of a pseudo-science. I realized the need for distinguishing this method as clearly as possible from that other method—that is, the method of criticism, the *method of looking for falsifying instances.*[11]

A fine example of the former, "verificationist" approach is provided by essays on Samuel Beckett and Michel Foucault, Jürgen Habermas and other of their philosophical contemporaries in Richard Lane's edited book from 2002, *Beckett and Philosophy*. One exemplar must suffice here, from Steven Barfield's chapter, as an example of a recent intellectual linking that simply cannot be refuted: "In this chapter I argue that the texts of Beckett and Heidegger have an uncanny and unsettling relationship to one another, which shows similar preoccupations but does not necessarily mean any influence of one to the other."[12] In my judgment, a simple litmus test may be carried out by adding the word *not* to a methodological sentence like the one above, which looks uncannily like it would reveal just as much about Beckett and Heidegger by arguing the exact inverse; namely, "that their texts [*do not*] have an uncanny and unsettling relationship to one

---

[11] Karl Popper, *Realism and the Aims of Science*, edited by W.W. Bartley III (London: Hutchinson, 1985), 162–163.

[12] Steve Barfield, "Beckett and Heidegger: A Critical Survey," in Richard Lane, ed., *Beckett and Philosophy* (Basingstoke: Palgrave, 2002), 156.

another." In fine, Heidegger betrays some "Beckettian" themes, while Beckett is construed in a "Heideggerian" light. But does this, ultimately, tell us anything beyond Barfield's interest in Heidegger, or the books on the former's bookshelf? Put another way, how does this advance knowledge of Samuel Beckett?

What makes the latter approaches successful or otherwise is largely indebted to the rhetorical skill of the author, and to a much lesser extent, I believe, to the methodological guidelines for establishing *why* such a fusing of radical intellectuals should, or should not be, justified in terms of Popper's two great criteria for falsification: relevance and explanatory power. In effect, exhorts Popper, "falsificationists or fallibists [argue] that what cannot (at present) in principle be overthrown by criticism is (at present) unworthy of being seriously considered." As Popper naturally counted himself amongst this group, one of his major achievements in the history of science was in offering a template for constructing theories—not a theory itself (at least "theory" as this is normally construed by all but radical skeptics like Gorgias of Leontini, and perhaps the more counterfactual of postmodern critics). In a word, Popper has reminded our discipline of literary studies that it is always preferable to theorize from a position of empirical accuracy rather than to do otherwise, or to simply ignore facts that do not conform to one's preferred reading:

> And while the verificationists laboured in vain to discover valid positive arguments in support of their beliefs, we for our part are satisfied that the rationality of a theory lies in the fact that we choose it because it is better than its predecessors; because it can be put to more severe tests; because it may even have passed them, if we are fortunate; and because it may, therefore, approach near to the truth.[13]

Having sketched these methodological points by way of negative example, to quote from Beckett's unpublished review, "Les Deux Besoins" ("The Two Needs"), reprinted in his collected criticism of 1984, *Disjecta*, "let's get on with falsifying." In that 1938 text, Beck-

---

[13] Karl Popper, "Truth, Rationality, and the Growth of Knowledge", in *Conjectures and Refutations* (London: Routledge, 2002), 336.

ett first advanced the view that was later to make him an icon, and his works a unique beacon of humility in our all-too-clever world: reason is inimical to the artistic process which derives, instead, from the need to create. Quite unlike his early mentor, James Joyce, it was the gaps in knowledge that were to motivate Beckett, not the reformulation of extant knowledge so masterfully compiled in *Finnegans Wake*.

For it seems to be with this realization—along with the critical shift to writing in French (both the unpublished "Les Deux Besoins" article and the "Petit Sot" series of poems date from 1938)—that Beckett returned full-circle to his position of ten years earlier: engaging with philosophy was superfluous to his artistic needs. However, the key difference between 1928 and 1938 was that Beckett had returned to this practice point from a position of knowledge instead of ignorance; or better still, through the embrace of what Nicholas Cusanus had centuries earlier called "learned ignorance." In short, manuscript evidence strongly suggests that the direct influence of philosophy upon Beckett was a short and intense affair. Of course, philosophical themes were to recur across Beckett's *oeuvre* again and again, right up to his death in 1989. But these were artistic reformulations of the work he had done in the pivotal decade leading to 1938. After that date, I want to suggest, Beckett's philosophical *development* ceased, and thereafter only philosophical *reinforcement* is in evidence—such as his re-reading of Schopenhauer in the late 1970s/early 1980s (again, as demonstrably, *falsifiably* evidenced in his "commonplace notebook" from the period, the so-called "Sottisier Notebook").[14] Put simply, the philosophical evolution of Beckett's art ended prior to WWII, halfway between the completion of *Murphy* in 1936 and the start of the wartime *Watt*.

---

[14] For insight into the "Sottisier Notebook," see Mark Nixon, "'Guess Where': From Reading to Writing in Beckett," in *Genetic Joyce Studies* 6 (Spring 2006), online at www.antwerpjamesjoycecenter.com/GJS6/GJS6Nixon.htm.

§3

In addition to its value in taking the measure of Samuel Beckett's decade-long philosophical auto-didacticism, turning to his earliest engagement with philosophy is instructive for at least four reasons. In his first published essay, written to support James Joyce's *Work in Progress* (later titled *Finnegans Wake*), the 1929 "Dante…Bruno.Vico..Joyce," Beckett revealed tendencies that were to resurface again and again in his study of philosophy across the 1930s. None of these are unusual, even if all might be considered at variance with the (inductive) idea of Beckett as a universal genius and devourer of Western learning on one hand, or a philosophical novice on the other.

The first point is that, despite taking a degree in Italian and French at Trinity College, Dublin, Beckett had no philosophical training upon taking up a two-year teaching post in Paris at the start of November 1928. As he recalled decades later for his first biography (which he neither "'helped" nor "hindered"), Beckett, in a letter of 24 October 1974, "stressed he did not study philosophy" prior to leaving Ireland: "Because he had not taken a philosophy course at Trinity College, which he felt was a serious defect in his education, he set out on what he thought was a systematic schedule of readings."[15] On closer inspection, however, these readings were to be anything but systematic.

The second, derivative point is that Beckett relied heavily upon friends to recommend philosophical books. In the case of his initial philosophical engagement upon arriving in France as an English *lecteur* at the École Normale Supérieure, Giambattista Vico seems to have acted as Beckett's introduction to philosophy. This was thanks to his relationship, or better, hero-worship, of James Joyce.[16] Joyce's

---

[15] Deirdre Bair, *Samuel Beckett: A Biography* (London, Picador: 1978), 96, 694.
[16] With respect to James Joyce, Beckett remarked that his was "heroic work, heroic being", cited in James Knowlson, *Damned to Fame: The Life of Samuel Beckett* (London: Bloomsbury, 1996), 105. Also prior to WWII, other friends

own use of Vico as a "trellis"[17] for *Finnegans Wake* was to act as a catalyst for Beckett's engagement with *La Scienza Nuova*; and more specifically, Vico's "division of the development of human society into three ages: Theocratic, Heroic, Human (civilized), with a corresponding classification of language: Hieroglyphic (sacred), Metaphorical (poetic), Philosophical (capable of abstraction and generalization)" in order to explain "the ineluctable circular progression of society."[18] While it may be tempting to see in this tripartite structure the makings of the later tripartite, circular structure of a text like *How It Is*, Beckett—though he could not have known it then, unknown and unpublished as he was at twenty-two years old—as he presciently warned against such inductive mapping in penning the essay's very first, justly famous sentence: "The danger is in the neatness of identifications."[19]

Third, Beckett's knowledge of Vico—and other philosophers in this nascent pattern—derived less from Vico's writings than from

---

of Beckett who gave philosophical advice included Jean Beaufret, Brian Coffey, and A.J. 'Con' Leventhal.

[17] Cited in H.S. Harris, "What is Mr. Ear-Vico Supposed to be 'Earing'?", in Donald Phillip Verene, ed., *Vico and Joyce* (New York: SUNY Press, 1987), 72. Relevant chapters in this collection bearing on Beckett's first publication also include Peter Hughes, "From Allusion to Implosion. Vico. Michelet. Joyce, Beckett.", and Donald Phillip Verene, "Vico as a Reader of Joyce." Another angle is provided by Hayden V. White, "What is Living and What is Dead in Croce's Criticism of Vico," in Giorgio Tagliacozzo and Hayden V. White, eds., *Giambattista Vico: An International Symposium* (Baltimore: Johns Hopkins UP, 1969).

[18] "Dante...Bruno.Vico..Joyce," in Our Exagmination Round His Factification for Incamination of Work in Progress (Paris: Shakespeare and Co., 1929), reprinted in Samuel Beckett, Disjecta: Miscellaneous Writings and a Dramatic Fragment, edited by Ruby Cohn (New York: Grove Press, 1984), 20. To date, the most extensive Anglophone discussions of Vico and Beckett available in print can be found in John Pilling, Beckett Before Godot (Cambridge: Cambridge University Press, 1997), 13–25; and, to a lesser extent, Massimo Verdicchio, "Exagmination Round the Fictification of Vico and Joyce," in James Joyce Quarterly, 26/4 (Summer 1989).

[19] "Dante...Bruno.Vico..Joyce," 19.

Joyce's suggestions, and less from both of these than from extant secondary sources; in this case, from Benedetto Croce's 1911 *La Filosofia di Giambattista Vico*. Despite explicitly disagreeing with Croce's definition of Vico as a "mystic" who was rendered, in R.G. Collingwood's 1913 translation, "contemptuous of empiricism," Beckett nevertheless mined this source exhaustively; for example, for the definition of Providence, or again, for Vico's understanding of myth as a primitive "historical statement of fact."[20] In short, this is Croce's conceit more than it is Vico's—let alone that of Niccoló da Conti, cited *en passant* by Beckett and in Croce's primer, but omitted in Vico's original, who defines myth as "history of such a kind as could be constructed by primitive minds, and strictly considered by them as an account of actual fact."[21]

Regrettably, space permits only two final, yet definitive, examples of this persistent pattern of secondary source "notesnatching"[22]—albeit one that has not been previously raised in Beckett Studies. In the first place, Beckett happily, if mistakenly, follows Vico's introductory "Idea of the Work" (§34) and calls Book II, namely "Poetic Wisdom," "the master key to the entire work" (Vico, instead, actually identifies the "origins both of languages and of letters" in "poets who spoke in poetic characters" as the "master key" of *The New Science*); the debt, yet again, is to Croce, not Vico.[23] Similarly,

---

[20] Ibid. R.G. Collingwood's translation of Benedetto Croce's *La Filosofia di Giambattista Vico* (Rome: Bari, 1911) was published as *The Philosophy of Giambattista Vico* (London: H. Latimer, 1913); here cited 78, 118–119, and 62–64.

[21] Ibid., 64.

[22] Beckett, letter of 25 January 1931 to Thomas MacGreevy, in reference to the former's reading of St. Augustine, cited in John Pilling, *Beckett's Dream Notebook* (Reading: Beckett International Foundation, 1999), xiii. Along with details of many other Western philosophers consulted by Beckett, a similar passage on "phrase-hunting" in Augustine's *Confessions* can be found in *The Letters of Samuel Beckett, Volume 1: 1929–1940* (Cambridge: Cambridge University Press, 2010), 62.

[23] Giambattista Vico, *The New Science of Giambattista Vico*, translated by Thomas Goddard Bergin and Max Harold Fisch (Ithaca: Cornell University

in "Dante...Bruno.Vico..Joyce" one finds the first reference to a well-known Beckettian tag (given in Italian in his essay): "the human mind does not understand anything of which it has had no previous impression." Yet Beckett's initial encounter with this phrase—he was later to transcribe it into his central commonplace book of the 1930s, the so-called "Whoroscope Notebook," when he encountered it again in 1936 in Léon Brunschvicg's 1923 *Spinoza et ses contemporains*—does not derive from the expansive Book II in Vico's *New Science*.[24] Had Beckett found the phrase in the latter, he doubtless would have cited the full sentence there: "What Aristotle said of the individual man is true of the race in general: *Nihil est in intellectu quin prius ferit in sensu.*" But no. This referent is 2,000 years too early. Instead Beckett tells us that, far from being Aristotle's, the phrase is instead a "Scholastics' axiom": "*niente è nell'intelletto che prima non sia nel senso.*" And this, in turn, derives from the idiosyncratic Croce, who also seems to have been playing fast and loose with Giambattista Vico on this point:

> Poets and philosophers may be called respectively the senses and the intellect of mankind: and in this sense we may retain as true the scholastic saying "there is nothing in the intellect which was not first in the senses." Without sense, we cannot have intellect: without poetry, we cannot have philosophy, nor indeed any civilisation.[25]

It again bears reiterating that, without such evidence as the above, it is impossible to advance falsifiable claims in Beckett Studies—or elsewhere, I would contend—nor indeed to substantiate em-

---

Press, 1981), 21–22. Compare Collingwood's translation of *La Filosofia di Giambattista Vico*, 62.

[24] For coverage of this important phrase from Beckett's 1930s commonplace book, see John Pilling's "Dates and Difficulties in Beckett's *Whoroscope* Notebook," in *Jounal of Beckett Studies* 13/2 (2005), 46. For Italian readers, the phrase given in "Dante...Bruno.Vico..Joyce" is "*niente è nell'inelletto che prima non sia nel senso*" (24). For more on the Italian angle in Beckett's first published text, see Andrea Battestini, "Beckett e Vico," in *Bolletino del Centro di Studi Vichiani* 5 (1975), 78–86.

[25] The Philosophy of Giambattista Vico, 49.

pirically-supported interpretations in literary criticism (like that argued here: Croce's Vico was of greater influence to Beckett than Vico himself).

Fourth and finally, the above passage also highlights the way in which Beckett transformed what he read philosophically into his art. Thus, fully a generation later, this phrase, now truncated and defaced, is placed by the narrator of *Malone Dies* into the beak of the "whoreson" Jackson's "dumb" parrot, Polly, which he "used to try and teach [...] to say, Nihil in intellectu, etc. These first three words the bird managed well enough, but the celebrated restriction was too much for it, all you heard was a series of squaks." This led to Jackson's nagging, Polly's retreat to the corner of his imprisoning cage, which "was even overcrowded, personally I would have felt cramped." But as so often in Beckett's art, there is an opaque depth to this comical moment. For the cage is not only for Jackson's parrot; it is also a metaphor for Malone's imprisonment in the "hallucinations" of the mind—the mind of whom, one might reasonably ask?—without the material (dis)comforts of the senses:

> And in the skull is it a vacuum? I ask. And if I close my eyes, close them really, as others cannot, but as I can, for there are limits to my impotence, then sometimes my bed is caught up into the air and tossed like a straw by the swirling eddies, and I in it. Fortunately it is not so much an affair of eyelids, but as it were the soul that must be veiled, that soul denied in vain, vigilant, anxious, turning in its cage as in a lantern, in the night without haven or craft or matter or understanding.[26]

---

[26] Samuel Beckett, *Malone Dies* (London: Faber and Faber, 2010), 44, 48–9.

§4

And so, in conclusion, what does this reveal about Samuel Beckett? Obviously, it would not be possible to simply label him a philosopher. Yet equally, it is doubtful that the "philosophical language" he famously decried in the 1960s went over his head—even as a young man. As with the entirety of Beckett's literary *oeuvre*, such distinctions smack of an artificial "neatness." For even in his earliest short story, "Assumption," also first published in the June 1929 issue of the "little magazine" *transition*, the first line announces: "He could have shouted and he could not."[27] While it may be that clear answers to Beckett's art are, in the final analysis, "unsayable," that is not to say the sources and allusions are. Of the latter, philosophy plays no small role, even in Beckett's earliest writings. To this end, it is hoped that the chapters comprising *Beckett/Philosophy* will illuminate many of these philosophical engagements, in the 1930s and beyond.

From this detailed perspective it may be, as John Calder has argued regarding "the attitudes, the thinking, and the intellectual background of Samuel Beckett the philosopher" means that "Beckett was the last of the great stoics."[28] In quite another view, instead, perhaps the tracks of literature and philosophy run in tandem through Beckett's art, as Lance St. John Butler influentially argued long ago. Or still again, as Bruno Clément would have it, the reformulation of Beckett's literature by philosophers—such as Badiou, Deleuze or Cixous most recently—explores a writing that can be profitably critiqued through recourse to philosophical concepts and language.[29]

---

[27] Samuel Beckett, "Assumption", in *The Complete Short Prose, 1929–1989* (New York: Grove Press, 1995), 3.

[28] John Calder, *The Philosophy of Samuel Beckett* (London: Calder, 2002), 1.

[29] See Lance St. John Butler, *Samuel Beckett and the Meaning of Being: A Study in Ontological Parable* (New York: St. Martin's Press, 1984), which argues that, despite "protestations to the contrary, Beckett is working the same ground as the philosophers", 2; see also Bruno Clément, "What the Philosophers do with Samuel Beckett," in S.E. Gontarski and Anthony Uhlmann,

Whichever path is taken, one can be sure that the "philosophical" in Beckett's work (whatever that may be) will remain a live issue for literary critics no less than for philosophers. In placing such questions on an empirically sound footing, the chapters to follow are intended to give added impetus to those probing questions Beckett asks of us, and invites us to ask of ourselves.

Right from the start, as this overview has aimed to show, those same questions—the bread and butter of great philosophy, no less than of great literature—have made, and will continue to make, Samuel Beckett our intellectual contemporary. His is a "timeless parenthesis." Even in the early, uncertain, and apprentice days of writing "Assumption" in 1929, that Western philosophy contributed to Beckett's brilliant asides in our mythic narrative of human "progress" remains, to date, all too obscured. In bringing these into focus, one can only make the hopeful assumption that explorations of Beckett and philosophy, in the broadest sense, will help to keep us, his readers, "irretrievably engulfed" in his challenging art:

> After a timeless parenthesis he found himself alone in his room, spent with ecstasy, torn by the bitter loathing of that which he had condemned to the humanity of silence. Thus each night he died and was God, each night revived and was torn, torn and battered with increasing grievousness, so that he hungered to be irretrievably engulfed in the light of eternity, one with the birdless cloudless colourless skies, in infinite fulfilment.[30]

---

eds., *Beckett After Beckett* (Gainesville, FL: University Press of Florida, 2006).

[30] "Assumption," 6–7.

On Vico, Joyce, and Beckett

Donald Phillip Verene (Emory University)

A personal remark

In planning what was to become a week-long international conference on Vico and Joyce, held in Venice, Italy at the Fondazione Giorgio Cini in June 1985, I wrote to Samuel Beckett to inquire whether he might participate.[1] To amplify my request I enclosed with my letter a postcard purchased in Dublin, Georgia, with a composite picture of several churches and the inscription, "Home of Beautiful Churches." It was one of several postcards of Dublin for sale there in a drugstore with a storefront sign: *Strange Drug Co.*, reflecting the proprietor, H. J. Strange, R.Ph. The postcards were of sufficient age that the sender was instructed to "Place one cent stamp here."

Vico appears on the first page of *Finnegans Wake* ("by a commodius vicus of recirculation") as does Dublin, Laurens County, Georgia, located on the Oconee River, founded by a Dubliner, Peter Sawyer ("topsawyer's rocks by the stream Oconee exaggerated themselse to Laurens County's gorgios while they went doublin their mumper all the time"). In 1926 Joyce sent to his benefactor, Harriet Weaver, a draft of the first lines of what was to become *Finnegans Wake*, including a key to its references; in it he claimed that the motto of Dublin, Georgia is "Doublin all the time."[2] Joyce had asked an American visitor, Julien Levy, to look up Dublin, Georgia for him; he

---

[1] A selection of the papers presented at this conference appears in Donald Phillip Verene, ed., *Vico and Joyce* (Albany: State University of New York Press, 1987).

[2] Letter to Harriet Shaw Weaver, 15 November 1926, in *Letters of James Joyce*, vol. 1, ed. Stuart Gilbert (New York: Viking, 1957), 247–248.

was anxious to know if it lay on a river.[3] Thus Joyce was able to double Dublin on the first page of the *Wake*, the old world in the new. I am happy to report that the visitor who may go by "the choicest and the cheapest from Atlanta to Oconee" (FW 140.35)[4] will discover that Dublin has upheld the motto Joyce assigned it, as its gorgios have doubled their number (their mumper) such that there now stands next to Dublin, across the Oconee River, an East Dublin.

Beckett sent a very brief but gracious reply from Paris, thanking me for the invitation and enclosed card but saying that to his regret he could not accept. The letter is in the hands of the Beckett Project at Emory University, which is editing and publishing Beckett's correspondence.[5] Beckett was introduced to Joyce when he arrived in Paris in November 1928. In December Joyce suggested he write an essay, and the topic to write it on, for *Our Exagmination*.[6] In June the essay appeared in *transition*, at Joyce's urging, set from the proofs of *Our Exagmination*. Beckett had just turned twenty-three. It was his first published essay.

It would have been interesting to know of any reflections Beckett might have had on the essay or its topic, more than fifty years later. In those years Beckett became a major literary figure in his own

---

[3] Richard Ellmann, *James Joyce*, rev. ed. (New York: Oxford University Press, 1982), 583n.

[4] James Joyce, *Finnegans Wake* (London: Faber and Faber, 1939). Here and hereinafter I have used the standard citation by page and line. I have consulted the new, critically emended edition of *Finnegans Wake*, edited by Danis Rose and John O'Hanlon (Dublin: Houyhnhnm Press, 2010), the pagination of which differs from the 1939 standard edition, but I have retained the page and line of the 1939 edition and its reprintings, since at present the latter is more accessible to most readers than FW_2.

[5] Samuel Beckett, *The Letters of Samuel Beckett, Volume 1: 1929–1940*, edited by Martha Dow Fehsenfeld and Lois More Overbeck (Cambridge: Cambridge University Press, 2009). Beckett's first letter in this volume, dated "23/3/29" concerns his essay for *Our Exagmination*. I would like to thank Lois Overbeck for kindly reading a draft of this essay.

[6] *Our Exagmination Round His Factification For Incamination of Work In Progress* (Paris: Shakespeare and Company, 1929). *Beckett's essay is pp. 1–22*.

right, receiving the Nobel Prize for Literature in 1969 and having his own works become a subject of interpretation. Putting aside the obvious reason not to accept my invitation—of making the trip to Venice to speak in the stuffy, artificial atmosphere of an academic conference—my guess is that Beckett preferred the views of his essay simply to stand. It is a classic of Joyce interpretation that has yet to be fully absorbed, as I wish to show.

In the remarks that follow I would like first to say something of my views of Vico's presence in *Finnegans Wake* and then, as an *appassionato* of Vico as well as of Joyce, to attempt to draw out some aspects of Beckett's essay that I think are well worth attention in the study of Vico's connection to Joyce. In so doing I wish to presuppose what I have worked out much more fully in my *Knowledge of Things Human and Divine: Vico's New Science and "Finnegans Wake"*. It is, to my knowledge, the only single-authored book-length study of the topic of Vico and Joyce.[7]

Vico and Joyce

Adaline Glasheen, in *Third Census of "Finnegans Wake"*, in identifying Vico as one of the citizens of the *Wake*, cites Joyce's comment that Vico's views gradually forced themselves on him through the circumstances of his own life. She then states: "Unfortunately, knowledge of this work has not forced itself on Joyceans, who by and large read it in an abridgement which omits much that matters in *FW*; and I find it generally supposed that *The New Science* is little more than an almost invisible scaffolding which encloses *FW* and is unnecessary to an understanding of *FW*. I don't agree and direct the

---

[7] Donald Phillip Verene, *Knowledge of Things Human and Divine: Vico's New Science and "Finnegans Wake"* (New Haven, Conn.: Yale University Press, 2003). The only other work which comes to mind is the curious small volume of juxtaposed quotations from Vico, Joyce, and others by Norman O. Brown, *Closing Time* (New York: Random House, 1973).

reader (for starters) to Samuel Beckett's essay in *Our Exagmination*.[8]

Joyce's well-known remark about Vico, made to his friend Padraic Colum: "I use his cycles as a trellis," is often quoted as an obvious explanation of Joyce's connection to Vico. It is in fact a subtle and precise remark. A trellis is a scaffold of latticework for support of climbing plants. But it is also possible to speak of "a trellis of interlacing streams"—one is reminded of the many rivers of the *Wake*. Etymologically, "trellis" is a fabric of coarse weave but specifically, *trilicius* (Vulgar Latin) is "woven with triple thread." "Trellis" as such has within it the sense of three (*tres*)—Vico's three ages of gods, heroes, and men, and his three principles (beginnings) of humanity—religion, marriage, and burial.

James Atherton's well-known *The Books at the Wake* acknowledges the *New Science* as one of the books but gives it no pride of place. Things have not become better among professional Joyceans; they have become worse. *The Cambridge Companion to James Joyce*, edited by Derek Attridge, has only the slightest mention of Vico.[9] The professors and critics (whom Joyce predicted his work would keep

---

[8] Adaline Glasheen, *Third Census of "Finnegans Wake": An Index of the Characters and Their Roles* (Berkeley and Los Angeles: University of California Press, 1977), 298. The abridgement of which Glasheen speaks is *The New Science of Giambattista Vico*, revised and abridged translation by Thomas Goddard Bergin and Max Harold Fisch (New York: Doubleday, 1961); reissued by Cornell University Press, 1970. Vico is also discussed in Stuart Gilbert's essay, "Prolegomena to Work in Progress" in *Our Exagmination*, 51–56, but in a more conventional way than Beckett's.

[9] Derek Attridge, ed., *The Cambridge Companion to James Joyce* (New York: Cambridge University Press, 1997). An exception to interpretations of Joyce that ignore Vico is John Bishop, *Joyce's Book of the Dark: Finnegans Wake* (Madison: University of Wisconsin Press, 1986), chap. 7. In this regard, see also Hugh Kenner, *Dublin's Joyce* (New York: Columbia University Press, 1987; 1956), chap. 18. William York Tindall's *A Reader's Guide to Finnegans Wake* (Syracuse, N.Y.: Syracuse University Press, 1969) also consistently calls the reader's attention to the places where Vico appears in the *Wake*.

busy for a long time)¹⁰ populating the Joyce industry in departments of English throughout the Anglo-American world publish works that approach Joyce from every conceivable angle except through his connections to Vico. One impediment is that barely any of them can approach Vico in the original Italian, as Joyce did and as Beckett did, although today they might consider reading the excellent full English translation of the *New Science* of Bergin and Fisch. It is, however, a difficult book, which I would rank alongside Kant's *Critique of Pure Reason* and Hegel's *Phenomenology of Spirit*.

Joyce's other philosopher is Giordano Bruno, "the Nolan" of Nola (near Naples). Beckett claims that when Joyce used the expression "the Nolan" in his early "The Day of the Rabblement," the local philosophers were unable to understand it, concluding finally that it was a reference to one of the more obscure Irish kings. Joyce links Vico and Bruno, as in the Latin passage of the classbook section of the *Wake*, where he writes "Jordani et Jambaptistae" (FW 287.24), recirculating the first letters of his own name, JJ (using the *I* of Latin in its elongated form). Both Bruno and Vico are philosophers of contraries.

In *Lo spaccio della bestia trionfante* (*The Expulsion of the Triumphant Beast*), Bruno writes: "the beginning, the middle, and the end, the birth, the growth, and the perfection of all that we see, come from contraries, through contraries, into contraries, to contraries."¹¹ In the *Wake* Bruno's title appears as "Trionfante di bestia!" (FW 305.15). This doctrine of the coincidence of opposites in Bruno is influenced by Nicholas of Cusa, who is presented in the *Wake* in terms of both Vichian *corso* and *ricorso* and Brunian contraries: "Now let the centuple celves of my egourge as Micholas de Cusack calls them,—of all of whose I in my hereinafter of course by recourse de-

---

[10] Joyce said he wrote *Finnegans Wake* in the way he did, "[t]o keep the critics busy for three hundred years." See Ellmann, *James Joyce*, 703.

[11] Giordano Bruno, *The Expulsion of the Triumphant Beast*, translated by Arthur D. Imerti (Lincoln: University of Nebraska Press, 1992), 90–91.

mission me—by the coincidance of their contraries reamalgamerge in that indentity of undiscernibles" (FW 49.33–50.1).

We find also "the learned ignorants of the Cusanus philosophism" (FW 163.16–17), a reference to Cusanus's *De docta ignorantia*. Joyce's principle of contraries appears on the first page of the *Wake* as "twone." Cusanus's doctrines of God as *maximum absolutum* and metaphysics of *coincidentia oppositorum* is the key source for Bruno's metaphysics, as Bruno himself makes clear, saying "the Cusan speaketh divinely."[12] But an understanding of Bruno or Cusanus has not even fared as well among the Joyceans as an understanding of Vico. Glasheen remarks in her census: "To my knowledge, no Joycean has yet read Nicholas of Cusa."[13] In the essays of the *Cambridge Companion* there is no mention of Cusa, and attention to Bruno is confined to a page and a half characterizing his career and addressing why he likely appealed to Joyce.[14]

To devise interpretations of Joyce and especially *Finnegans Wake* without knowing the languages in which Joyce was fluent, those of the countries of continental Europe in which he lived and wrote, Italy, Switzerland, and France, is to go on a fool's errand. Italian, German, French, and ability in Latin are required as a basis for Joyce interpretation.[15] The *Wake* constantly plays on these languages,

---

[12] Giordano Bruno, *On the Infinite Universe and Worlds*, translated by Dorothea Waley Singer in *Giordano Bruno: His Life and Thought* (New York: Schuman, 1950), 307. On the influence of Cusanus on Bruno, see J. Lewis McIntyre, *Giordano Bruno* (London: Macmillan, 1903), 140–148.

[13] Glasheen, 206.

[14] Attridge, ed., 57–59. In *How Joyce Wrote "Finnegans Wake": A Chapter-by-Chapter Genetic Guide*, ed. Luca Crispi and Sam Slote (Madison: University of Wisconsin Press, 2007), no mention is made of Nicholas of Cusa, although there are a few pages that mention *coincidentia oppositorum* and Bruno. Vico is mentioned a number of times, but largely in passing.

[15] In addition to these major languages, Joyce spoke Danish. He had ability in Modern Greek (but not ancient Greek), partly due to his early residence in Trieste. In a letter to Harriet Shaw Weaver, Joyce wrote, "I speak four or five languages fluently enough" (Ellmann, *James Joyce*, 512). Roland McHugh, *Annotations to Finnegans Wake* (Baltimore, Md.: Johns Hopkins University

as well as others. "Are we speachin d'anglas landadge or are you sprakin sea Djoytsch?" (FW 485.12–13). Also, to produce interpretations of the *Wake* that are not based on a real comprehension of the central sources to which Joyce himself pointed is to miss the lesson Beckett's essay teaches, and is additionally foolish. Vico describes the conceit of scholars as taking the unfamiliar and putting it into terms familiar to themselves. His remedy for this is his axiom that "doctrines should take their beginning from that of the matters of which they treat" (NS par. 314).[16]

Vico in Finnegans Wake

I would like to call attention to four aspects of Vico that are present in *Finnegans Wake*. The second and third of these are treated in Beckett's essay; the first and fourth do not appear in it as such. Vico is present in many ways within the *Wake*; the more one seeks these out, the more one finds those previously missed. These four are: Vico and H.C.E. are the same person; Bruno's contraries become Vico's cycles; Vico's "common mental language" is Joyce's language; and Vico's claim that "memory is the same as imagination" is Joyce's guiding principle.

Humphrey Chimpden Earwicker or H.C.E., "Here Comes Everybody" is both the modern family man and all of us that have ever been, are now, or ever will be. But in a very prominent and particular

---

Press, 1991), delineates use or plays on words or phrases in sixty-two languages or dialects (xiv–xv), but Italian, German, French, and Latin dominate.

[16] *The New Science of Giambattista Vico*, translated by Thomas Goddard Bergin and Max Harold Fisch (Ithaca, N.Y.: Cornell University Press, 1984). Here and hereinafter cited by the paragraph enumeration common to this English translation and most contemporary Italian editions, such as Giambattista Vico, *Opere*, 2 vols., ed. Andrea Battistini (Milan: Mondadori, 1990). Regarding the defects of the translation of the *New Science* by David Marsh (New York; Penguin, 1999), see Donald Phillip Verene, "On Translating Vico: The Penguin Classics Edition of the *New Science*," *New Vico Studies* 17 (1999): 85–107.

way, he is Vico. If *Finnegans Wake* is a rewriting of Vico's *Scienza nuova*, it is also a rewriting of Vico's *autobiografia*. Finnegan's fall and rise on the first page of the *Wake* is parallel to Vico's fall headfirst from a ladder and miraculous survival, described on the first page of his autobiography. Vico's fable of himself, his autobiography, is a series of seven falls and rises that comprise a providential pattern.[17]

Vico is the protagonist of *Finnegans Wake*. He is Earwicker. "Wick" is a row of houses, or village, and is derived from the Latin *vicus*, Vico's name. Vico is also the vicar, both in the sense of the custodian of divine knowledge and as the representative of the divine on earth—the agent of providence, the vicar of history. Vico is "the producer (Mr. John Baptister Vickar)" (FW 255.27). G.B. Vico is H.C. Earwicker. The initials of Earwicker can be derived from Vico's initials by cycling one letter forward in the alphabet, thus: G. → H. and B. → C. Vico is vic or "old vic" (FW 62.6) → wick. "W" is a double "v." The "v" is pronounced as "w" in classical Latin (*vicus*, pronounced "weekus"). Earwicker is Vico's name in English. We can hear Vico in "Earwicker."

In part 3, Joyce merges the identities of Vico and H.C.E. Vico becomes H.C.E.'s middle name:

> — Hail him heathen, heal him holystone!
> Courser, Recourser, Changechild
> Eld as endall, earth (FW 481.1–3).

Vico is the courser and recourser, the child of change. He is also the changeling, the child of circumstances left by fairies in the cycles of history. Joyce continues, "I have your tristich now; it recurs in three times the same differently" (FW 481. 10–11). Each of the three lines of this tristich (group of three lines of verse) begins with one of the initials of H.C.E., which also recalls each of Vico's three ages:

---

[17] Donald Phillip Verene, The New Art of Autobiography: An Essay on the "Life of Giambattista Vico Written by Himself" (Oxford: Clarendon, 1991), esp. chap. 1.

"—*Hail him heathen*" is the appearance of Jove to the giants of Vico's first age; the middle is Vico, as if he were a heroic figure of the second age; *Eld* is old age (Norwegian), the decline of the third age. In the recourse each age recurs "the same differently."

Earvico is the one who hears the thunder, who hears the presence of providentiality in history. Vico has the ear for it, "for you cannot wake a silken nouse out of a hoarse oar" (FW 154.9–10); "there's no-one Noel like him here to hear" (FW 588.27–28); "the old hayheaded philosopher . . . old Earwicker" (FW 47.01–15) in the Ballad of Persse O'Reilly; "the ear of Fionn Earwicker" (FW 108.21–22); "Ear! Ear! Weakear!" (FW 568.26); "Earwicker, that patternmind, that paradigmatic ear, receptoretentive as his if Dionysius" (FW 70.35–36). Vico has the mind that finds the providential patterns and the paradigmatic ear to hear them. Like "Dionysius's ear," the chamber in Dionysius's palace in Sicily through which he could overhear what his enemies were saying, Vico can hear the murmurings in history that others cannot. Vico can hear and see what others cannot. Vico is "earsighted" (FW 143.9–10).

Bruno's *coincidentia oppositorum*, as taken from the ontology of Cusanus, is the principle that the absolute maximum and the absolute minimum coincide. Cusanus approaches this idea through a number of mathematical examples. The one most quickly grasped is that, if a curved line is extended to form the widest curve possible, at its maximum its difference from a straight line is an absolute minimum. These contraries, then, coincide. If such absolute contraries coincide, then any set of contraries that are less than absolute coincide, each in its own way. Change is the mutation of opposites.[18] If we conceive this mutation in moral terms, as Bruno describes in *The Expulsion of the Triumphant Beast*, "we see that man, changing nature

---

[18] See the mathematical examples in Nicholas Cusanus, *Of Learned Ignorance*, translated by Germain Heron (London: Routledge and Kegan Paul, 1954), Latin and English opposed texts. Cf. Giordano Bruno, *Cause, Principle and Unity*, translated by Robert de Lucca (Cambridge: Cambridge University Press), 1998), 5th Dialogue, esp. 97–101.

and modifying his affects, from a good man becomes wicked, from a temperate man, intemperate; and, on the other hand, that from one who seemed to be a beast, he ends up by seeming to be another better or worse...."[19]

In the dream of the night world of *Finnegans Wake*, Joyce replaces cause in human affairs with coincidence, even with "cocoincidences" (FW 597.01). Although dreams can be causally analyzed, as in Freudian psychology, in the dream itself causality often plays little or no role. Coincidence and mutation of contraries reign.[20] In Joyce's "dreamoneire" (FW 280.01) of *Finnegans Wake*, all is connected by the transformation and juxtaposition of opposites, but the result is not chaos. The result is "every person, place and thing in the chaosmos of Alle" (FW 118.21). It is a kind of cosmos because a narrative is possible. The whole can be spoken through its parts, its particulars. In the dream of the *Wake*, any sense of scientific causality or historical progression is irrelevant and in fact impossible.

Louis Gillet wrote: "Of course, it is no longer a question of Time and Space in this indivisible duration where the absolute reigns. These two comrades, who did their cooking for so long on the scrap-iron stove of Kantian categories, find their pot knocked over by a kick from James Joyce. Their soup is spilled out—chronology disappears and all the centuries are contemporary."[21] In *Ulysses*, Stephen remarks: "Maeterlinck says: *If Socrates leave his house today he will find the sage seated on his doostep. If Judas go forth tonight it is to Judas his steps will tend*. Every life is many days, day after day. We walk through ourselves, meeting robbers, ghosts, giants, old men, young men, wives, widows, brothers-in-love, but always meeting

---

[19] Bruno, *Expulsion*, 78.
[20] Donald Phillip Verene, "Coincidence, Historical Repetition, and Self-Knowledge: Jung, Vico, and Joyce," *Journal of Analytical Psychology* 47 (2002): 461–480.
[21] Louis Gillet, *Claybook for James Joyce*, translated by Georges Markow-Totevy (London and New York: Abelard-Schuman, 1958), 66.

ourselves."[22] We may add, from *Finnegans Wake*, "As who has come returns" (FW 382.28).

When Bruno's coincidence of contraries is joined with Vico's cycles, the *corso* and *ricorso*, the three ages—gods, heroes, and men—of his *storia ideal eterna* (ideal eternal history), change becomes not only a metaphysical and moral transformation back and forth between opposites, but a process of historical repetition. History, in the Vichian and Joycean sense, however, is not the past providing a basis for and leading into the present, with the present looking toward the novelty of the future. History is memory. As the Florentine historian Francesco Guicciardini puts it: "All that which has been in the past and is at present will be again in the future. But both the names and the faces of things change, so that he who does not have a good eye will not recognize them."[23] Memory, Mnemosyne, is the mother of the Muses, and the Muses sing of what was, is, and is to come. And as Hesiod says, in so doing, they can sing both true and false songs: "Singalingalying. Storiella as she is syung" (FW 267.07–08). Or as in *Ulysses*: "Fabled by the daughters of memory. And yet it was in some way if not as memory fabled it."[24] Or as Joyce invites us, early in the *Wake*: "This the way to the museyroom. Mind your hats goan in! . . . This way the museyroom. Mind your boots goan out" (FW 08.09–10.22–23).

Finnegans Wake, like all books of wisdom, is a complete speech. It contains all that there is, and anything that it does not say does not lie outside it, because whatever is not explicitly in it can be reached through it. When Bruno's somewhat stable exchange of contraries is taken up in Vico's "wholemole millwheeling vicociclometer," everything is connected: "the dialytically separated elements of precedent decomposition for the verypetpurpose of subsequent recombination so that the heroticisms, catastrophes and eccentricities

---

[22] James Joyce, *Ulysses*, edited by Hans Walter Gabler (New York: Vintage, 1993), 175.1042–46.

[23] Francesco Guicciardini, *Ricordi* (Milan: Rizzoli, 1977), 131. My trans.

[24] Joyce, *Ulysses*, 20.7–8.

transmitted by the ancient legacy of the past, type by tope, letter from litter, word at ward, with sendence of sundance . . ." (FW 614.27–615.02). Then, "Of cause, so! And in effect, as?" (FW 615.11). Such is Joyce's literary metaphysics.

In several places in the *New Science*, Vico speaks of a "common mental language" (*lingua mentale comune*), a mental vocabulary (*vocabolario mentale comune*), or a "mental dictionary" (*dizionario mentale*) (NS pars. 145, 445, 527, 542), but he gives little description of it. His most informative statement regarding it is in axiom twenty-two: "There must in the nature of human things be a mental language common to all nations, which uniformly grasps the substance of things feasible in human social life and expresses it with as many diverse modifications as these same things may have diverse aspects" (NS par. 161; see also 32, 335, 482). He claims further that "This common mental language is proper to our Science, by whose light linguistic scholars will be enabled to construct a mental vocabulary common to all the various articulate languages living and dead. . . . As far as our small erudition will permit, we shall make use of this vocabulary in all the matters we discuss" (NS par. 162).

Since this is a mental language, it can never be spoken or written as such; it can never be a *characteristica universalis*. Yet such a mental language must exist or we could not identify any particular language as language. Since human nature is constant from nation to nation, there must exist in the human mind an order of meanings such that any particular language may be regarded as an attempt to draw these meanings forth in its own way, much as an orator draws forth his speech from topics or places, and the same places can be used to draw forth other speeches. If we work backward from the myriad of articulate languages, we should be able to reach commonalities that would most nearly represent this original mental language from which the world is made by the human mind.

Original speech, for Vico as it is to a great extent for Joyce, is onomatopoetic. Vico gives a powerful example of such in connection with the primordial experience of thunder: "When wonder [*mara-*

viglia] had been awakened in men by the first thunderbolts, these interjections of Jove should give birth to one produced by the human voice: *pa*!; and that this should then be doubled: *pape*! From this interjection of wonder was subsequently derived Jove's title of father of men and gods" (NS par. 448). The third paragraph of the first page of the *Wake* begins with "the fall," followed by Joyce's first hundred-letter thunderword. In it, along with many thunderwords from various languages, is the combination of thunder in Italian and English: "tuonnthunn" (*tuono*, Italian; "thunder," English)—the two languages combined in the title, "Finnegans" (*fine* with its *n* doubled, and "again").

As we shall see, the language of *Finnegans Wake*, that Beckett so expertly describes, in answering Rebecca West in his essay, is as close as we can come to grasping the common mental language as a language expressing the particular universals of humanity.[25] Vico points the way to this conception of language; Joyce enacts it. If we wish to know what Vico's common mental language is, we have only to immerse ourselves in the language of the *Wake*; when we do, language will never be the same for us. After any great literary production, the language in which it is written is never the same. After Joyce, language itself can never be the same.

Richard Ellmann reports that "Joyce accepted Vico's idea that the phantasmal faculty was essentially a function of memory: 'Imagination is nothing but the working over of what is remembered,'" and Joyce remarked to his friend Frank Budgen that "imagination is memory."[26] In his discussion of the true Homer, Vico states: *"la memoria è la stessa che la fantasia* [memory is the same as imagina-

---

[25] In addition to Beckett's remarks to the criticisms made by the novelist and literary critic Rebecca West, see William Carlos Williams, "A Point for American Criticism," in *Our Exagmination*, 173–185. See also the reprinting of West's 1930 article from the *New York Herald Tribune Books* in *James Joyce: A Literary Reference*, ed. A. Nicholas Fargnoli (New York: Carroll and Graf, 2001), 326–329.

[26] Richard Ellmann, *The Consciousness of Joyce* (New York: Oxford University Press, 1977), 3 and 135.

tion]" (NS par. 819). In claiming this, Vico is glossing Aristotle's line in his little treatise *On Memory*: "if asked, of which among the parts of the soul memory is a function, we reply: manifestly of that part to which imagination [*phantasia*] also appertains; and all objects of which there is imagination are in themselves objects of memory" (450a 17–19). Vico defines memory as a threefold function of the mind: "Memory thus has three different aspects: memory [*memoria*] when it remembers things, imagination [*fantasia*] when it alters or imitates them, and ingenuity [*ingegno*] when it gives them a new turn or puts them into proper arrangement and relationship" (NS par. 819).

Finnegans Wake is the theatre of memory of humanity. Joyce forces the reader, as he forced himself, to employ all three of these aspects at once. He forces us to recall all of ourselves and all of history, and as we recall this totality, his language alters and imitates what is recalled. Furthermore, everything is given a new turn such that we see the similarities in the dissimilar and a proper arrangement emerges. What otherwise seemed disconnected and discrete becomes part of the whole. Among Joyce's last words in *Finnegans Wake* is memory: "Us then. Finn, again! Take. Bussoftlhee, mememormee!" (FW 628.13–14). But softly. Remember me.

There is a modern view that the object of imagination is novelty—that its purpose is to create the novel. Vico and Joyce have demonstrated otherwise. An admirer of Joyce, and a man of letters in his own right, is Jorge Luis Borges. Borges is the other major literary figure besides Joyce to employ Vico in a text. (In this respect, however, one might also mention the use of Vichian themes in the novels of Carlos Fuentes, such as *Christopher Unborn*.) Borges has incorporated Vico and his discovery of the true Homer in "The Immortal." The protagonist says: "In 1729 or thereabouts, I discussed the origin of that poem [the *Iliad*] with a professor of rhetoric whose name, I believe, was Giambattista; his arguments struck me as irrefutable."[27]

---

[27] Jorge Luis Borges, "The Immortal," in *Collected Fictions*, translated by Andrew Hurley (New York: Penguin, 1998), 193.

The essay is introduced through an epigraph from Bacon's essay, "Of Vicissitude of Things." "Solomon saith: *There is no new thing upon the earth.* So that as Plato had an imagination, *that all knowledge was but remembrance*; so Solomon giveth his sentence, *that all novelty is but oblivion.*"[28] The wisdom the immortals know is "that over an infinitely long span in time, all things happen to all men. . . . No one is someone; a single immortal man is all men."[29] Novelty is an impossibility. It is only a name for something that we have not remembered or it is nothing at all because it did not enter memory. Memory is the heart of culture. We can agree with the poet Giuseppe Ungaretti, who tells us with complete clarity, *"Tutto, tutto, tutto è memoria* [Everything, everything, everything is memory]."[30]

Commentary on Beckett's Essay

I wish to conclude with some comments on Beckett's essay, made from a Vichian perspective. In such a short space I make no attempt to summarize the essay itself. Beckett had at his disposal the extracts from Joyce's work, whereas we readers today have the full, final text of *Finnegans Wake* that appeared a decade later.

1. Joyce said, of the twelve authors of the essays of *Our Exagmination Round His Factification For Incamination Of Work In Progress*: "I did stand behind those twelve Marshals more or less directing them what lines of research to follow."[31] The title is from a line in Joyce's work (FW 497.02–03). "Exagmination" is examination merged with Latin *agmen* (a mass of persons in movement, an army on the march, a stream). "Incamination" contains a play on the Italian verb *incamminare*—"to put on the right road" (the Vico road), also

---

[28] See Francis Bacon, *The Major Works*, edited by Brian Vickers (New York: Oxford University Press, 1996), 451.
[29] Borges, 191.
[30] Giuseppe Ungaretti, in a lecture on Vico in São Paulo, Brazil, in 1937. See *Vita d'un uomo: Saggi e interventi* (Milan: Mondadori, 1974), 345.
[31] Letters of James Joyce, vol. 1, 283.

"round" (the Vico road "goes round and round"), and *factum* (what is made, Vico's famous principle of *verum esse ipsum factum*, "the true is the made." Beckett speaks for himself but we can assume that he also speaks for Joyce.

2. Beckett's title is "Dante...Bruno.Vico..Joyce" with no dot or period after Joyce. Beckett discusses each of these four figures but gives no explanation in the essay of the structure of the title or its significance. As a reader, I have two thoughts on it; one is chronological; the other is linguistic. If one recalls the birth dates of Dante (1265) and Bruno (1548), a span of approximately three centuries intervenes; between Bruno and Vico (1668) a span of a century is involved; between Vico and Joyce (1882), two centuries. The reader is reminded of the sequence of these figures in history, with Joyce just now taking his place.

Linguistically, the title contains two sentences. The first contains the ellipsis between Dante and Bruno. What is omitted is how we comprehend the movement from Dante, the "Tuscan Homer," as Vico calls him, the summarizer of medieval Thomism, to Bruno, the philosopher-heretic who, as Joyce says through Stephen Dedalus, "was terribly burned."[32] The second sentence is incomplete because what Joyce is and how we are to understand him is not yet finished. The ellipsis between Vico and Joyce is only partial because the gap between Vico and Joyce is not great. Vico is recycled in Joyce.

The first sentence and the second "sentence" can be juxtaposed or "recoursed." Vico is the poetic-philosopher who carefully asserts that his views are for the greater glory of "our Christian religion," but his cyclic conception of history is wholly pagan, presided over by a providence that does not lead to a final day of Resurrection. Joyce is not a heretic but a permanently lapsed Catholic whose world, in *Finnegans Wake*, as Beckett explains, corresponds to Purgatory. The four figures reflect Joyce's tetralogical manner of thinking and his interest

---

[32] James Joyce, *A Portrait of the Artist as a Young Man*, edited by Seamus Deane (New York: Penguin, 1993), 271; cf. *Stephen Hero* (New York: New Directions, 1944), 170.

in the square and the circle. As he once remarked, instead of squaring the circle, he circled the square.

3. Beckett begins by calling attention to how Vico has folded philosophy and philology into each other as a single method. Vico says "philosophy undertakes to examine philology" (NS par. 7). Philosophy fails by half in directing its efforts toward the true (*il vero*) as the universal in human nature, and philology fails by half in directing its efforts toward the certain (*il certo*) that is composed of those particular acts, done by choice.

4. Beckett opposes Croce's view of Vico: "It pleases Croce to consider him as a mystic, essentially speculative, '*disdegnoso dell'empirismo.*'"[33] Croce's *La filosofia di Giambattista Vico* (1911) was the standard comprehensive interpretation of Vico's philosophy of the day.[34] The sentence in full is "Ora, l'ispirazione del Vico era genuinamente ed esclusivamente teoretica, punto pratica o riformistica; altamente speculativo il suo metodo a disdegnoso dell'empirismo; idealistico, e perciò antimaterialistico e antiutilitaristico, il suo spirito [Now, Vico's inspiration was genuinely and exclusively theoretical, not at all practical or reformulatory, his method was deeply speculative and distaining of empiricism; his spirit was idealistic and thus anti-materialistic and anti-utilitarian]."[35]

For Croce to claim Vico is "deeply speculative" is not the same as to claim that he is a mystic. Croce was a Hegelian and thus by "speculative" he is likely referring to Hegel's "*spekulativer Satz*" or "speculative sentence," upon which Hegel claims his manner of thinking is based, and he definitely has in mind Hegel's overriding contrast between speculation that is the thought of reason (*Vernunft*)

---

[33] *Our Exagmination*, 4.
[34] Benedetto Croce, *La filosofia di Giambattista Vico* (Bari: Laterza, 1965). Beckett could also have consulted Robert Flint, *Vico* (Edinburgh and London: Blackwood, 1884) that appeared as a volume of the series "Philosophical Classics for English Readers." The interpretation in it would have been more to Beckett's liking; perhaps he did not know of it. Joyce likely knew it at some point, as we find, in the *Wake*: "A chip off the old Flint" (FW 83.10).
[35] Croce, *La filosofia*, 77. My trans.

and thought based on reflection or understanding (*Verstand*).[36] By saying that Vico disdained empiricism, Croce means that Vico's method rejects the philosophical doctrine that all thought derives from sense impressions, as is to be found in Locke or Hume. In claiming this, Croce is not claiming that Vico disdains the empirical in human existence. For Croce, Vico was the Italian Hegel, having a philosophy of objective idealism, a view that led Croce to write a fictional account in which Hegel, at the end of his career, is introduced to the writings of Vico and endorses them as like his own.[37]

Where Beckett's understanding of Vico really divides from Croce's is in Beckett's grasp of the fundamental importance of Vico's conception of poetic characters or imaginative universals (*caratteri poetici o universali fantastici*). Beckett loosely cites Vico's line declaring that the discovery of this original form of language is *la chiave maestra* or master key to his Science that cost him a good twenty years to accomplish (NS par. 34). As Vico says: "the first science to be learned should be mythology or interpretation of fables" (NS par. 51).

5. Beckett characterizes Vico as "a practical roundheaded Neapolitan." This is a statement taken directly from Joyce. In *A Portrait* Stephen refers to his Italian teacher Father Ghezzi as "little roundhead rogue's eye Ghezzi."[38] Padraic Colum, the Irish poet and playwright, reported that on one of their walks in Paris in about 1927, discussing *Work in Progress*, Joyce referred to Vico in a similar fashion:

---

[36] See Hegel's *Vorrede* in *Phänomenologie des Geistes*, edited by Johannes Hoffmeister, 6th ed. (Hamburg: Meiner, 1952). On the difference between speculation and reflection, see Donald Phillip Verene, *Hegel's Absolute: An Introduction to Reading the "Phenomenology of Spirit"* (Albany: State University of New York Press, 2007), chap. 1.

[37] Benedetto Croce, "An Unknown Page from the Last Months of Hegel's Life," translated by James W. Hillesheim and Ernesto Caserta, *New Vico Studies* 26 (2008): 143–165.

[38] Joyce, *A Portrait*, 271.

"'He was one of those round-headed Neapolitan men,' Joyce told me. I forget whom he mentioned as another of them."[39] The other was quite likely Bruno of Nola, since Nola is part of the comune of Naples. In the *Wake*, at the beginning of the classbook section, in which all of Vico's terminology is glossed in its marginalia, is "Old Vico Roundpoint" (FW 260.15). "Roundhead" is not a term known to me, nor to the *O.E.D.*, except in its Cromwellian associations, which do not seem to fit, given Cromwell's treatment of the Irish. The Vico road goes round and round, but to derive "roundheaded" from this seems trite or at least not especially clever. In Beckett's context of criticizing what he takes to be Croce's view of Vico, the term seems to mean "hardheaded," empirically minded, thinking in relation to facts, and probably a bit stubborn. In a novel about academic life, *Matricide at St. Martin's* (1995), by the Dublin-born Ruth Dudley Edwards, appears the comment: "'You need the whistle-blowers and the people who don't mind being unpopular and the people with tunnel vision.' 'But not too many of them,' said the Bursar. 'They're almost all Roundheads.'"[40]

6. The term Beckett settles on, for Vico, is "Vico, the scientific historian."[41] A case can be made for this as a precise designation for Vico. Broadly speaking, Vico can be called a philosopher or a philosopher of history, but he is most correctly an advocate of his own "new science," which is made up of both philosophical reasoning and philological analysis. Beckett rightly insists that Vico's unique conception of Providence is fundamental to this science. Vico uses the

---

[39] Mary and Padraic Colum, *Our Friend James Joyce* (Gloucester, Mass.: Peter Smith, 1968; 1958), 82. Andrea Battistini, "Beckett e Vico," *Bollettino del Centro di Studi Vichiani* 5 (1975), regards "roundheaded" as *coined* by Joyce: "Riecheggiando persino degli stilemi tipicamente joyciani per i loro fantastici accostamenti—si pensi soltanto alla definizione del Vico come 'una specie di "testa tonda," di puritano partenopeo,' del tutto identica a quella coniata da Joyce," 79.

[40] Ruth Dudley Edwards, *Matricide at St. Martha's* (New York: St. Martin's, 1995), 167.

[41] Our Exagmination, 5.

word "Providence" in 120 lines in the *New Science* that are spread throughout the text of the work.[42]

The definition Beckett quotes in Italian is quoted by Croce in *La filosofia* from the last few paragraphs of the *New Science*.[43] Vico does not use "Providence" in this passage, but it is to the mind of Providence that he is referring. He says that the world of nations has been made by men themselves but that this world has issued from "a mind often diverse, at times quite contrary, and always superior to the particular ends that men had proposed for themselves; which narrow ends, made means to serve wider ends, it has always employed to preserve the human race upon this earth" (NS par. 1108; cf. pars. 342, 344). Croce, in the conclusion to *La filosofia*, claims that Vico's Providence, as the objective, logical order of history, is what Hegel formulated as the "cunning of reason" (*List der Vernunft*).[44] This claim is symptomatic of Croce's Hegelianizing of Vico.

Beckett is quite clear that Joyce adds a fourth age to the three ages—gods, heroes, and men—of Vico's *corso* and *ricorso* of ideal eternal history, that of Providence.[45] This point is missed by some Joyce scholars who, not having read Vico, speak of Vico's four ages, presuming that Joyce's cycle is taken over directly from Vico. They have not only missed what Vico said, they have also missed what Beckett said. As Beckett states: "Part 4 is the day beginning again, and corresponds to Vico's Providence, or to the transition from the Human to the Theocratic, or to an abstraction—Generation. Mr. Joyce does not take birth for granted, as Vico seems to have done."[46]

---

[42] See Principi di Scienza Nuova d'intorno alla Comune Natura delle Nazioni: Corcordanze e indici di frequenza dell'edizione Napoli 1744, ed. Marco Veneziani (Florence: Olschki, 1997), 629–630.
[43] Croce, *La filosofia*, 113.
[44] Ibid., 223.
[45] Beckett claims (4) that Vico derived his three ages from the report of Herodotus that the Egyptians had three kinds of writing (*Hist.* 2.36). Vico mentions this but is clear that his principal source is Varro's view of three ages, found in the odd little book of Censorinus, *De die natali*, sec. 21 (NS par. 52).
[46] *Our Exagmination*, 8.

Joyce's "Providentiality" is what holds together Vico's *corso* and *ricorso*.

Regarding the course and later recourse a nation undergoes, Beckett grasps Vico's sense of decline, which includes "a six-termed progression of motives: necessity, utility, convenience, pleasure, luxury, abuse of luxury."[47] Beckett is paraphrasing Vico's axiom sixty-six: "Men first feel necessity, then look for utility, next attend to comfort, still later amuse themselves with pleasure, thence grow dissolute in luxury, and finally go mad and waste their substance [*finalmente impazzano in istrapazzar le sostanze*]" (NS par. 241). Beckett says: "At this point Vico applies Bruno—though he takes very good care not to say so."[48] Change, for Vico and for Bruno, is a transformation of opposites. Vico cannot mention Bruno by name because Bruno is a heretic and the Inquisition was unofficially present in Naples.

Vico does mention Bruno indirectly but prominently in describing the proof that governs his science, claiming that the matters of his science "have been established by divine providence, the course of the things of the nations had to be, must now be, and will have to be [*dovettero, debbono e dovranno*] such as our Science demonstrates, even if infinite worlds were born from time to time through eternity, which is certainly not the case" (NS par. 348). This is likely an endorsement of Bruno's doctrine, such as can be found in his *De l'infinito universo et mondi* (*On the Infinite Universe and Worlds*), emphasized by declaring that such is "certainly not the case."

7. A fundamental aspect of Joyce's language on which Beckett does not remark is its intention to be humorous, to produce laughter. Joyce once told Jacques Mercanton: "I am nothing but an Irish clown, a great joker at the universe,"[49] and to a drinking companion he once corrected "*In vino veritas*" to "*In risu veritas*."[50] As the ballad of Tim

---

[47] Ibid., 5.
[48] Ibid., 5–6.
[49] Jacques Mercanton, "The Hours of James Joyce," in *Portraits of the Artist in Exile: Recollections of James Joyce by Europeans*, ed. Willard Potts (New York: Harcourt Brace Jovanovich, 1986), 229.
[50] Ellmann, *James Joyce*, 703.

Finnegan says: "Lots of fun at Finnegan's wake." Joyce speaks of Dante as "the divine comic Denti Alligator" (FW 44.06). The sense of the humorous pun guides the language of the "Litter" that concludes *Our Exagmination*. Since part of the purpose of the volume was to answer the critics of *Work in Progress* Beckett may have deliberately avoided mention of the humor of Joyce's work lest it become grounds for not taking seriously the greatness of Joyce's talent.

In responding to Rebecca West's criticisms of Joyce, Beckett instructs her and thus the reader in how to approach Joyce's use of language. We must put aside the distinction between form and content. In Joyce's speech the words used to speak about a thing become the thing itself. Joyce's speech is a series of what today philosophically can be called "performative utterances," in which what is said does not refer to some separate act but is the act itself. The words become what the words themselves are about. Beckett points out that such semiotics are not unknown in literature. They can be found, for example, in passages of Shakespeare and in Dicken's *Great Expectations*. Although there are precedents for this language use, what we should realize, I think, is that Joyce does not, in *Work in Progress* or in *Finnegans Wake*, *sometimes* use words in this hieroglyphic way— *he uses words in nothing but this way*. Thus his work requires a new science of reading and a new kind of reader.

Beckett draws a parallel between the Italian that Dante created in order to write the *Divina Commedia* and the English Joyce created in order to write *Work in Progress*. It is commonly said that Dante wrote in Florentine dialect, but Beckett points out that the Tuscan in which Dante writes was spoken by no one: "He did not write in Florentine anymore than Neapolitan. He wrote a vulgar that *could* have been spoken by an ideal Italian who had assimilated what was best in all the dialects of his country, but which was certainly not spoken nor ever had been."[51] Beckett adds, however, that whereas Dante's language derived from what was spoken, "no creature in heaven or earth ever spoke the language of '*Work in Progress*.'" But he adds: "It is

---

[51] *Our Exagmination*, 18.

reasonable to admit that an international phenomenon might be capable of speaking it."[52]

I find it difficult to imagine what this "international phenomenon" would be. What would it be like to be "sprakin sea Djoytsch?" What kind of "landadge" would it be? We would be communicating directly by means of Vico's *lingua comune mentale* within the theatre of memory that surrounds us, without the security of our categories and most especially with that of causality replaced by coincidence and cocoincidences.

---

[52] Ibid., 18–19.

"I am not reading philosophy": Beckett and Schopenhauer

Erik Tonning (University of Bergen, Norway)

I am reading Schopenhauer. Everyone laughs at that. Beaufret and Alfy etc. But I am not reading philosophy, nor caring whether he is right or wrong or a good or worthless metaphysician. An intellectual justification of unhappiness—the greatest that has ever been attempted—is worth the examination of one who is interested in Leopardi & Proust rather than in Carducci and Barrès.

— Samuel Beckett, letter to Thomas MacGreevy, c. 18 to 25 July 1930.[1]

Arthur Schopenhauer's influence on Beckett's thought and writing has been amply documented by a number of critics over the years.[2] Recently, publication of the first volume of Beckett's letters,

---

[1] Samuel Beckett, *The Letters of Samuel Beckett, Vol. 1: 1929–1940*, edited by Martha Dow Fehsenfeld and Lois More Overbeck (Cambridge: Cambridge University Press, 2009), 33.

[2] See Steven J. Rosen, *Samuel Beckett and the Pessimistic Tradition* (New Brunswick, NJ: Rutgers University Press, 1976); John Pilling, "Beckett's *Proust*," *Journal of Beckett Studies* 1 (1976): 8–29, and "*Proust* and Schopenhauer: Music and Shadows," in *Samuel Beckett and Music*, edited by Mary Bryden (Oxford: Clarendon Press, 1998), 173–178; James Acheson, "Beckett, Proust and Schopenhauer," *Contemporary Literature*, Vol. 19, No. 2 (Spring 1978), 165–179; J. D. O'Hara, "Where There's a Will There's a Way Out: Beckett and Schopenhauer," *College Literature*, Vol. 8, No. 3 (Fall 1981): 249–270, and *Samuel Beckett's Hidden Drives: Structural Uses of Depth Psychology* (Gainesville, FL: University Press of Florida, 1997); entries on Schopenhauer in C.J. Ackerley, *Demented Particulars: The Annotated Murphy*, second edition (Tallahassee, FL: Journal of Beckett Studies Books, 2004) and in *Obscure Locks: Simple Keys: The Annotated Watt* (Tallahassee, FL: Journal of Beckett Studies Books, 2005); Matthew Feldman, "'Agnostic Quietism' and Samuel Beckett's Early Development," in

cited above, registers what is probably the first impact of Schopenhauer in July 1930. That summer, Beckett also worked his way through *A la recherche du temps perdu* twice, in order to write his only academic monograph, *Proust* (finished by September 1930). It is well known that references to Schopenhauer pepper the marginalia of Beckett's edition of Marcel Proust's multi-volume novel, just as they permeate his entire critical approach to it. However, less attention has been devoted to Beckett's second major reading of Schopenhauer from early September 1937 when he was ill with gastric influenza.[3] He wrote to his friend, Thomas MacGreevy, on 21 September, that Schopenhauer "was one of the ones that mattered most to me"; furthermore, he reports, it is pleasurable to "begin to understand now why it is so," and also to find "a philosopher that can be read like a poet" (*Letters*, 550). The trouble for scholars has been that Beckett did not reveal any textual specifics about this later engagement with Schopenhauer; and at the same time, the immediately following period turned out to be unusually barren of creative work. Hence, tracing significant new details of this 1937 encounter has been difficult. This is all the more frustrating since Beckett by now had access to the complete works of Schopenhauer in five volumes in the original German (Leipzig: Insel Verlag, 1922–1923), bought during his German travels in 1937. However, a forthcoming monograph (2011) on Beckett's library by Dirk Van Hulle and Mark Nixon promises to

---

Samuel Beckett: History, Memory, Archive, edited by Seán Kennedy and Katherine Worth (New York: Palgrave, 2009), 183–200; Franz Michael Maier, *Becketts Melodien: Die Musik und die Idee des Zusammenhangs bei Schopenhauer, Proust und Beckett* (Würzburg: Königshausen & Neumann, 2006); and Ulrich Pothast, *The Metaphysical Vision: Arthur Schopenhauer's Philosophy of Art and Life and Samuel Beckett's Own Way to Make Use of It* (New York: Peter Lang, 2008). These studies contain far more detailed information about Beckett's knowledge and demonstrable uses of Schopenhauer than there is space to fully analyze in this essay; however, the argument here will draw upon this body of work as background for its broader claims about Schopenhauer's influence.

[3] See James Knowlson, *Damned to Fame: The Life of Samuel Beckett* (London: Bloomsbury, 1996), 238.

remedy this situation through a close examination of the actual Schopenhauer editions owned by Beckett until his death. A preliminary paper given in Rome in 2008 reproduces some marginalia, and their full case will certainly be fundamental to further manuscript analysis of the Beckett-Schopenhauer relationship. Testifying to a lifelong interest, furthermore, evidence in the *Sottisier* notebook (kept between 1976 and 1982) shows that Beckett returned to Schopenhauer yet another time in 1979 (although apparently without highlighting further passages in the volumes themselves).[4] In general, as Ulrich Pothast has emphasised in a recent full-length study, Beckett not only read "standard writings like *The World as Will and Representation* [1818/1819, Vol. 2 1844] and the essays of *Parerga and Paralipomena* [1851]" but also took the time to read, and, in 1979, re-read, the dry and technical early thesis *On the Fourfold Root of the Principle of Sufficient Reason* (1813). This, Pothast rightly concludes, makes for "a lifelong intellectual commitment, probably stronger and deeper than his contact with any other of the many philosophers whom he quotes or refers to in passing" (Pothast, 16).

Yet even this appraisal may understate the case: there simply *is* no comparable influence on Beckett's work, philosophical or otherwise. In extending this thesis, the intention here is to focus upon an aspect of Schopenhauer's influence that has only received scattered recognition to date; namely, Schopenhauer's remarkable *utility* for Beckett. Schopenhauer's place in Beckett's intellectual development is unique because he becomes a kind of conduit through which any number of related influences and imaginative impulses can pass. Moreover, those points where Beckett in fact moves beyond (but still *through*) Schopenhauer provide vital clues to the development of Beckett's aesthetic thought and fiction. As such, this essay will heed

---

[4] Mark Nixon and Dirk Van Hulle, "Beckett's Library: From Marginalia to Notebooks," in *Beckett in Rome*, edited by Daniela Guardamagna and Rossana M. Sebellin (Rome: Laterza, 2009), 68. Nixon and Van Hulle also state that Beckett first read Schopenhauer in Auguste-Laurent Burdeau's French translation in 1930.

Beckett's initial caveat from 1930, "I am not reading philosophy": for what is at stake for Beckett is ultimately not the veracity of any metaphysical system, but rather Schopenhauer's usefulness for his Beckett's own, distinctly literary, project.

* * *

It is in fact surprisingly rarely noted that Beckett's July 1930 letter to MacGreevy maps Schopenhauer onto four pre-established literary coordinates: Giacomo Leopardi and Marcel Proust versus Giosuè Carducci and Maurice Barrès. An overlooked context for his remarks in that letter may be found in some of Beckett's earliest extant writings, his student notes from four years earlier:

> Carducci, with all his erudition & complicated metres, was not a poet. His work is stamped with a desperate self-conscious effort. He is an elephant jumping ponderously through a hoop. [...] Carducci produced poetry by sheer force of intellect. [...] Carducci is an excellent university professor but an excessively bad poet.[5]

Beckett was thus strikingly well-prepared to receive Schopenhauer's doctrine that "the concept, useful as it is in life, serviceable, necessary, and productive as it is in science, is eternally barren and unproductive in art."[6] The background for this judgment is Schopenhauer's absolute contrast between the "principle of sufficient reason" (the realm of cause and effect, subject and object, time and space: the phenomenal world as a whole) and the Thing-in-Itself behind these distinctions, which he famously identifies as blind, non-rational striving, or Will. Art is in fact defined by Schopenhauer as *"the way of considering things independently of the principle of sufficient reason"*

---

[5] TCD MS 10965/32, cited in Matthijs Engelberts, Everett Frost and Jane Maxwell, *"Notes Diverse Holo": Catalogues of Beckett's Reading Notes and other Manuscripts at Trinity College, Dublin, with Supporting Essays* (Amsterdam: Rodopi, 2006), 60.

[6] Arthur Schopenhauer, *The World as Will and Representation*, Volume 1, translated by E. F. J. Payne (New York: Dover, 1969), 235. Further references to this work appear in parentheses within the text as *WWR1*.

(*WWR1*, 185; emphasis in original; cf. Beckett, *Proust*, 87[7]). For him, art allows for a direct perceptual encounter with "the Idea" (brutally appropriated here from Plato to denote a particular "grade" of the Will's self-objectification, through which the ever-passing array of individual phenomena are supposedly articulated). In such an encounter it is possible to "*lose* ourselves entirely" in contemplation of an object, indeed "we forget our individuality, our will, and continue to exist only as pure subject [...] so that it is as though the object alone existed without anyone to perceive it" (178). Accordingly, the metaphysical Idea is "never known by the individual as such, but only by him who has raised himself above all willing and all individuality" (234). The concept, on the other hand, is "the unity once more produced out of plurality by means of abstraction through our faculty of reason" (235); it proceeds from, and remains bound to, the phenomenal realm.[8] In *Proust*, Beckett pours scorn on the desperate self-conscious efforts of university professors[9] by adapting Schopenhau-

---

[7] "And we are reminded of Schopenhauer's definition of the artistic procedure as 'the contemplation of the world independently of the principle of reason'"; Beckett, "*Proust" and Three Dialogues with Georges Duthuit* (London: Calder, 1999), 87. As Pothast (37 n. 35) makes clear, Beckett is here translating from the French text rather than following any English translation.

[8] Beckett seamlessly integrates references to Schopenhauer's concept/Idea distinction into his own particular judgments of artworks he viewed while travelling in Nazi Germany for six months in 1936–37. This is recorded in his "German Diaries" at the time (26 December 1936 and 28 January 1937; and I must here admit to a transcription error in Tonning, *Samuel Beckett's Abstract Drama: Works for Stage and Screen, 1962–1985* [Bern: Peter Lang, 2007], 24 and 25, where "post sum" should in both cases read "post rem"). Schopenhauer writes, "The *concept*, on the other hand, is the unity once more produced out of plurality by means of abstraction through our faculty of reason; the latter can be described as *unitas post rem*, and the former [i.e. the Idea] as *unitas ante rem*" (*WWR1*, 235).

[9] In a letter to MacGreevy written before 5 August 1930, Beckett states that he is "looking forward to pulling the balls off the critical & poetical Proustian cock" (*Letters*, 36); whereas in *Proust* itself he is scathing about the "Heidelberg laboratory" of criticism and the idea of a "positive relativism" (85).

er's distinction to the analysis of voluntary versus involuntary memory:

> The most successful evocative experiment can only project the echo of a past sensation, because, being an act of intellection, it is conditioned by the prejudices of the intelligence which abstracts from any given sensation, as being illogical and insignificant, a discordant and frivolous intruder, whatever word or gesture, sound or perfume, cannot be fitted into the puzzle of a concept (*Proust*, 72).

In contrast, involuntary memory, the accidental return of a past sensation only subconsciously registered at the time, can evoke "the ideal real, the essential, the extra-temporal" (75)—in short, the Schopenhauerian Idea.

Beckett's mention of Carducci in his 1930 letter, then, alerts us to Schopenhauer's critique of the "concept," and thus to the anti-rationalist, even anti-philosophical[10] strain in the German's whole system, which Beckett eagerly embraced. His subsequent aesthetic thought would amplify this note to the point of dominance, insisting on the "incoherence" of character;[11] and five years later figuring lan-

---

[10] See also *WWR1*, 271, on ethics: "For here, where it is a question of the worth or worthlessness of existence, of salvation or damnation, not the dead concepts of philosophy decide the matter, but the innermost nature of man himself ..." A philosopher might reply that the correct description of that "nature" remains very much in question; this is relevant here because Beckett's procedure is very much to *assume* that Schopenhauer's picture of the blind Will as Thing-in-Itself is more or less true, and then to use that assumption to undermine the broadly philosophical effort of "clarification" on the (circular) grounds that reality itself is incoherent (on this, see for instance the "German Diary" entry of 15 January 1937, cited in Knowlson, 244). Art, by contrast, "has nothing to do with clarity, does not dabble in the clear and does not make clear"; Beckett, 1938 review "Intercessions by Denis Devlin," in *Disjecta: Miscellaneous Writings and a Dramatic Fragment*, edited by Ruby Cohn (London: Calder, 1983), 94.

[11] "The reality of the individual [...] is an incoherent reality and must be expressed incoherently" (Samuel Beckett, *Dream of Fair to Middling Women* [Dublin: Black Cat Press, 1992], 101).

guage itself as "a veil that must be torn apart"[12] in the oft-quoted "German Letter" from 1937. In turn, this phrase alludes to the Hindu veil of Maya, Schopenhauer's favorite image for the phenomenal world as perceptual illusion.[13] Beckett is thus "not reading philosophy" in the sense that he takes no interest in any rigorous critique of Schopenhauer's metaphysics.

Another significant Beckettian reaction hides behind the July 1930 mention of Barrès, known above all as a right-wing French nationalist, leader of the Patriot League, and author of the novel trilogy *Roman de l'énergie nationale* (1897–1902). Years later, Beckett would write to A. J. Leventhal on 21 April 1958 that Leopardi "was a strong influence when I was young (his pessimism, not his patriotism)."[14] Andrew Gibson's recent mini-biography of Beckett[15] has usefully re-emphasized his consistent anti-totalitarian assault on all shades of nationalist rhetoric, whether writing in France, Ireland or, later, in Nazi Germany. Beckett's reaction against the increasingly nationalist Catholic ethos in Ireland surely contributed to his decision to bolt from his job and temporarily escape the country in 1931; and his exasperation with the repressive policies of the subsequent de Valera government would figure prominently in his 1930s fiction and reviews.[16] Schopenhauer's pessimism was attractive to Beckett not least because it was a tonic against patriotism, inasmuch as "the history of the human race, the throng of events, the change of times, the many varying forms of human life in different countries and centu-

---

[12] Letter to Axel Kaun, 9 July 1937, English translation by Martin Esslin in *Disjecta*, 171.
[13] Feldman, "Agnostic Quietism," 192–97, is indispensable on Beckett's uses of the "veil of Maya" image, and my discussion here draws on that essay.
[14] Cited in C.J. Ackerley and S.E. Gontarski, *The Grove Companion to Samuel Beckett* (New York: Grove Press, 2004), 316.
[15] Andrew Gibson, *Samuel Beckett* (London: Reaktion Books, 2010).
[16] On Beckett's tense yet lingering relationship with Irish nationalist rhetoric in literature and politics, see Emilie Morin, *Samuel Beckett and the Problem of Irishness* (London: Palgrave, 2009), 21–54.

ries, all this is only the accidental form of the phenomenon of the Idea" (*WWR1*, 182).

Clearly in *Proust*, then, Beckett's analysis of "the Time cancer" (18) draws heavily on Schopenhauer. Proust's characters are "victims and prisoners" of Time (12–13), driven by an insatiable "thirst for possession" of objects of desire which, however, are inherently in flux and ungraspable (15). In Schopenhauerian terms, the will strives endlessly, and every temporary satisfaction either entails immediate transition to another desire or an interval of empty longing, *ennui* (*WWR1*, 260, cf. *Proust*, 19, on the "boredom of living"). Within the phenomenal world, the will is ever at war with itself (*WWR1*, 253), and this situation is not in the least affected by such accidents as the rise and fall of nations. A flurry of pessimistic conclusions follows: since all willing springs from lack, human life as such is suffering (196); in all conflicts, the will "in the fierceness and intensity of its desire [...] buries its teeth in its own flesh," and thus, "[t]ormentor and tormented are one" (354); indeed, the true sense of tragedy is that "what the hero atones for is not his own particular sins, but original sin, in other words, the guilt of existence itself" (254). As the epigraph to *Proust*, from Beckett's favorite Leopardi poem, "A sè stesso" (1834), has it, *e fango è il mondo*.[17] One of Schopenhauer's main uses for Beckett throughout his writing career is precisely this idea of existence as such being marked by "original sin." The motif itself is first quoted—nearly word for word—from Schopenhauer in *Proust*,[18] and it becomes something like a Beckettian emblem or identification-tag thereafter.[19]

---

[17] "The world is dirt." This epigraph unaccountably is dropped out of the John Calder text. For more on Beckett and Leopardi, see Daniela Caselli, "Beckett's Intertextual Modalities: The Case of Leopardi," in *Journal of Beckett Studies* 6.1 (Autumn 1996), 1–24.

[18] Cf. *Proust*, 67: "The tragic figure represents the expiation of original sin, of the original and eternal sin of him and all his 'socii malorum', the sin of having been born."

[19] To give just one example: "I was given a pensum, at birth perhaps, as a punishment for having been born perhaps"; Beckett, *The Unnamable*, edited by

Again, some biographical context is required here. Beckett was brought up as a Church of Ireland Protestant, in a family where religious education was largely the domain of his formidable and fervent mother, May. She demanded conformity to a rarefied Anglo-Irish Establishment propriety as well as to a staunchly low-church, evangelically tinted Protestantism.[20] Rebellion against this regime set in early. Furthermore, Beckett's biographer James Knowlson suggests that his acute sensitivity to suffering, and in particular his outrage at any attempt to justify suffering as potentially redemptive in terms of a larger cosmic scheme, may have been decisive in his eventual rejection of Christian faith. The poem "Ooftish" (1938), based in part on a sermon Beckett had disliked intensely in 1926, sums up his attitude with searing irony: "offer it up plank it down / Golgotha was only the potegg / cancer angina it is all one to us / cough up your T.B. don't be stingy [...] we'll make sense of it we'll put it in the pot with the rest / it all boils down to blood of lamb."[21]

What is at stake here is essentially an *ethical* impulse, one which Beckett adheres to uncompromisingly over the whole course of his writing career,[22] and one which he found strikingly and comprehensively "justified" in Schopenhauer:

Steven Connor (London: Faber and Faber, 2010), 21. Cf. Steven Connor, "Beckett and the Loutishness of Learning," in *Samuel Beckett Today/Aujourd'hui* 22 (2010), 271. Connor also (257) draws attention to the aggressively academic connotations of the word "pensum," which, as O'Hara notes (*Samuel Beckett's Hidden Drives: Structural Uses of Depth Psychology* [Gainesville, FL: University Press of Florida, 1997], 29), Beckett lifted from Schopenhauer, *Parerga and Paralipomena* II, ch.XII, § 157.

[20] For a penetrating account of Beckett's early Protestant upbringing see Seán Kennedy, "Yellow: Beckett and the Performance of Ascendancy," in *New Voices in Irish Criticism 5*, edited by Ruth Connolly and Ann Coughlan (Cork: Cork University Press, 2005), 177–86.

[21] Beckett, *Selected Poems 1930–1989*, edited by David Wheatley (London: Faber and Faber, 2009), 37. See Knowlson, *Damned to Fame*, 68, for the biographical background.

[22] For a fuller argument here, see Erik Tonning, "Beckett's Unholy Dying: From *Malone Dies* to *The Unnamable*," in *Beckett and Death*, ed. Steven

> For the rest, I cannot here withhold the statement that *optimism*, where it is not merely the thoughtless talk of those who harbour nothing but words under their shallow foreheads, seems to me to be not merely an absurd, but also a really *wicked*, way of thinking, a bitter mockery of the unspeakable sufferings of mankind. Let no one imagine that the Christian teaching is favourable to optimism; on the contrary, in the Gospels world and evil are used almost as synonymous expressions (*WWR1*, 326).

The last sentence returns us to Schopenhauer's highly polemical—even violent—appropriation of the term "original sin." Traditionally, the doctrine has been saturated with cosmic optimism: the God who is Love creates Man for eternal happiness, though with freedom to fall; after that fall, our nature is damaged permanently, and we cannot restore our relationship with God unaided; however, God sacrifices Himself in the person of his Son in order to redeem us from this stain of inborn sin (which is not at all *ontologically* "original"); we are thus never without access to Grace, or the hope of redemption; and a final victory over evil is guaranteed in advance. For Schopenhauer, by contrast, *to exist at all* is figured as "sin"; all "happiness" is merely temporary and depends on the more fundamental evil of want or desire (319). For him, finally, it would be better if there were Nothing (411–412).

In fact, Schopenhauer contrives to siphon off an authentically ascetic "Christianity" grounded in the world-denying passages from the Gospels, preaching complete resignation and death of the individual will—much like the Eastern mystics he admires (386–87). If only the arbitrary "Jewish" dogma of Creation by a benign deity could be expunged, this "Christianity" would make perfect sense (406 n. 72). Correspondingly, Beckett makes use of Schopenhauer's whole approach to "original sin" in two main ways. First of all, he consistently reproduces Schopenhauer's polemical attitude: it is safe to say that, wherever the word "sin" appears in Beckett, we find in its vicinity

---

Barfield, Matthew Feldman and Philip Tew (London: Continuum, 2009), 124–127.

some reaction to the idea of a loving Creator, capable of redeeming the world He has made. One example must stand for many:

> that notion of punishment ... for some sin or other ... or for the lot ... or no particular reason ... for its own sake ... thing she understood perfectly ... that notion of punishment ... which had first occurred to her ... brought up as she had been to believe ... with the other waifs ... in a merciful ... [*Brief laugh*] ... God ... [*Good laugh*] ...[23]

Secondly, Schopenhauer's attempt to construct an alternative, ascetic Christianity probably also influenced Beckett more subtly: giving him an incentive to explore Augustine, the Christian mystics and Thomas à Kempis—and eventually to imbibe the ethos of quietistic *humilitas*, less the dogmatic content.[24] Here, perhaps, aspects of his low-church background survive: for the Christian writers Beckett preferred were decidedly hostile to the World, betraying little of what Schopenhauer dubbed the "Pelagian insipidity" (406 n. 72).

* * *

The rough overview presented above does not, of course, even begin to do justice to Beckett's crucial encounters with this thinker. Indeed, pointing forwards, Schopenhauer's utility for Beckett is such that, once noticed, it becomes hard to discuss almost any passage in Beckett, or any aspect of his thought, without referring to this influence. However, such a vague sense of ubiquity has created something of a quandary for Beckett scholarship. Generalized explication of Beckett texts in terms of Schopenhauer's ideas can feel like a distinctly tired exercise: the ideas themselves grow overfamiliar, distinctions between individual Beckett texts begin to blur, and the entire *oeuvre* starts to resemble a ludicrously extended argument for a certain metaphysics. On the other hand, strictly limiting the discussion to docu-

---

[23] Samuel Beckett, *Not I*, in *Krapp's Last Tape and Other Shorter Plays* (London: Faber and Faber, 2009), 86–87.

[24] See C.J. Ackerley, "Samuel Beckett and Thomas à Kempis: The Roots of Quietism," *Samuel Beckett Today/Aujourd'hui* 9 (2000), 81–92; and Feldman, "Agnostic Quietism" (2009).

mented allusions risks seriously under-estimating the full impact of the relationship under study, not least because allusions generally are much fewer and often hard to identify in Beckett's post-war work. This is not to suggest that the alternative method of simply assuming that Beckett "must be" alluding to this or that Schopenhauer passage in a given instance is any improvement: specific information about Beckett's reading and verifiable usage of Schopenhauer remains indispensable—and guesswork remains guesswork.

Yet as a potential alternative, the general argument advanced here bears repeating: Schopenhauer becomes for Beckett *the* conduit through which any number of other influences are absorbed and reworked. The main consequence of this thesis for further study is that the object of scholarly investigation is thus no longer simply "Schopenhauer and Beckett," but rather an evolving tapestry of influences held together by Beckett's appropriations of Schopenhauer as a uniquely indispensable glue. The remainder of this essay will recount how, in the 1930s, Beckett began to think beyond Schopenhauer in various ways; partly by assimilating new intellectual influences, but partly also by stretching, adapting or revising key Schopenhauerian ideas. To be sure, this is the period in which Beckett's aesthetic thought and writerly problematic were decisively shaped; it was also the period in which Schopenhauer's continuing centrality as an interlocutor is most readily demonstrable. Once the sheer range and protean nature of Schopenhauer's influence in this period is recognized, it becomes easier to suggest methods of further study which might be able to capture the even subtler Schopenhauerian presence in Beckett's later writing as well.

* * *

In the first instance, if Schopenhauer's take on religion is one of the main attractions of his thought for Beckett, it is also an area where he differs instructively from the philosopher. In two conversations with Charles Juliet, his basic attitude is specified:

No, he hasn't read Eastern philosophers.
"They suggest a way out, whereas I felt there was none" (October 24, 1968).[25]
I observe that over the last four centuries, man seems to have endeavored to give a reassuring and gratifying image of himself. It is precisely this image that Beckett has been trying to tear apart.
He points out that Leopardi, Schopenhauer, and a few others preceded him along the way.
I go on with my argument.
"Yes," he admits, "perhaps with them there was still hope for an answer, for a solution. Not with me" (November 11, 1977).[26]

Schopenhauer's "solution"[27] to the problem of existence itself draws heavily upon the "way out" suggested by Eastern mysticism and asceticism. In Schopenhauer's reading, the ascetic suppresses all natural impulses, receives sufferings with indifference, and mortifies his own body so as to "gradually break and kill the will" (*WWR1*, 382). When such a person dies, "the inner being itself [...] is abolished" (382). From here can be glimpsed the "final goal" (411), the end of *everything*: "what remains after the complete abolition of the will is, for all those who are still full of will, assuredly nothing. But also conversely, to those in whom the will has turned and denied itself, this very real world of ours, with all its suns and galaxies, is— nothing" (411–412).

For his part, Beckett's skepticism toward any notion that such Nirvana-like transcendence of the phenomenal is actually achievable is evident from the outset. By 1930, the "Proustian solution" (*Proust*, 75) of involuntary memory as a form of mystical experience, for example, comes in for scathing critique, by means of a telling bit of biblical satire: "He is a Romantic in his anxiety to accomplish his mis-

---

[25] Charles Juliet, *Conversations With Samuel Beckett and Bram Van Velde*, translated by Tracy Cooke, Axel Nesme, Janey Tucker, Morgaine Reinl and Aude Jeanson (Champaign and London: Dalkey Archive Press, 2009), 16.

[26] Ibid., 39.

[27] Cf. the derogatory reference to any "solution clapped on problem like a snuffer on a candle," in Beckett, "Intercessions by Denis Devlin" (*Disjecta*, 92).

sion, to be a good and faithful servant" (81, cf. Matthew 25:23). In fact, as I have argued in more detail elsewhere, Beckett's vehement ethical resistance to the Christian "answer" of eschatological hope fundamentally colors his reading of both Eastern and Western mystical traditions,[28] as well as his reading of Romantic transcendent yearning, or "Sehnsucht."[29] Correspondingly, as Nicholas Zurbrugg and, more recently, C. J. Ackerley have shown,[30] Beckett's own characters, from the "dud mystic" Belacqua of *Dream* (186) onward, are always signally failing to attain transcendence. Beckett, then, may be said to accept the basic terms of Schopenhauer's description of the phenomenal world as a prison-house of being, a cycle of perpetual torture; he simply intensifies the philosopher's pessimism by insisting that there is *no* possible salvation or "way out."

To put the matter thus, though, is to present Beckett's stance almost like another philosophical argument, a rival position to that of Schopenhauer. But Beckett offers no such positive assertion. Nonetheless, his "feeling" that there is no way out underpins a distinctive mode of writerly engagement with Christianity, with mysticism, and with Romanticism, in a tremendous variety of forms across his career. While this claim is too large to defend in detail here, a quotation from Beckett's "Clare Street Notebook," dated 11 August 1936, offers an illustrative example, giving further credibility to the thesis that Schopenhauer remains the conduit for other influences—years after Beckett's initial encounter with his thought in 1930:

---

[28] See Tonning, "Nor by the eye of flesh nor by the other: Fleshly, Creative and Mystical Vision in Late Beckett," *Samuel Beckett Today/Aujourd'hui* 22 (2010).
[29] Tonning, Samuel *Beckett's Abstract Drama*, 179–185.
[30] Nicholas Zurbrugg, *Beckett and Proust* (Gerrards Cross: Colin Smythe, 1988), 145–172, 190–216; Ackerley, *Demented Particulars*, 29–30.

> There are moments where the veil of hope is finally ripped away and the eyes, suddenly liberated, see their world as it is, as it must be. Alas, it does not last long, the perception quickly passes: the eyes can only bear such a merciless light for a short while, the thin skin of hope re-forms and one returns to the world of phenomena. Hope is the cataract of the spirit that cannot be pierced until it is ripe for decay. Not every cataract ripens: many a human being spends his whole life enveloped in the mist of hope. And even if the cataract can be pierced for a moment it almost always re-forms immediately; and thus it is with hope.[31]

The "veil of hope" here clearly draws upon Schopenhauer's interpretation of the phenomenal world as "veil of Maya," and it is tempting simply to explicate this passage by quoting the following as a probable source:

> At times, in the hard experience of our own sufferings or in the vividly recognized suffering of others, knowledge of the vanity and bitterness of life comes close to us who are still enveloped in the veil of Maya. We would like to deprive desires of their sting, close the entry to all suffering, purify and sanctify ourselves by complete and final resignation. But the illusion of the phenomenon soon ensnares us again, and its motives set the will in motion once more; we cannot tear ourselves free. The allurements of hope, the flattery of the present, the sweetness of pleasures, the well-being that falls to the lot of our person amid the lamentations of a suffering world governed by chance and error, all these draw us back to it, and rivet the bonds anew. Therefore Jesus says: "It is easier for a camel to go through the eye of a needle, than for a rich man to enter into the Kingdom of God" (*WWR1*, 379–380).

This juxtaposition helps to highlight the continuous presence of Schopenhauerian categories in Beckett well beyond his 1931 *Proust*. Moreover, the citation above is a full year ahead of Beckett's second major reading of the philosopher in 1937, and comes after he had encountered a number of fresh influences through his study of philosophy and psychology between 1932 and 1936. Schopenhauer is in no

---

[31] This translation of Beckett's German is given in Tonning, *Samuel Beckett's Abstract Drama*, 184–185.

way superseded or displaced in this period: several allusions to Schopenhauerian concepts in his 1936–37 "German Diaries";[32] and further, in the letter to Axel Kaun from July 1937 (noted above, and to which we will return) also point to this conclusion.

Yet first, there is much more to be said about Beckett's notebook passage. Mark Nixon, who discovered it, draws attention to its heading—"Victoria Group"—which refers to Goethe's *Faust* Part II (lines 5407–5470) and the figure of the "Göttin aller Tätigkeiten [goddess of all activity]."[33] Beckett's comments about "hope" are directed against what he reads as a generically Romantic *Vorwärtsstreben*: "All the on and up [of *Faust* Part I] is so tiresome also, the determined optimism à la Beethoven, the unconscionable time a-coming. […] I can understand the 'keep on keeping on' as a social prophylactic, but not at all as a light in the autological darkness, or the theological."[34] To recall his earlier formulation in *Proust*,

---

[32] See note 10 above.

[33] See Mark Nixon, "'Scraps of German': Samuel Beckett Reading German Literature," in Engelberts et. al., *Notes diverse holo*, 271. Note also that Beckett's use of a passage from Schopenhauer (quoted in the text) as part of a critique of a German Romantic writer like Goethe would be perfectly congruent with his notes from Wilhelm Windelband's *History of Philosophy* on German Romantic philosophy (see Tonning, *Samuel Beckett's Abstract Drama*, 182–184). These contain aggressive stabs at thinkers like Fichte, Schelling, Schlegel and especially Schiller; when Windelband finally gets to Schopenhauer, Beckett reacts with extraordinary relief, in a passage wholly unique in his entire corpus of notes: "*Irrationalism* comes to full development in *Schopenhauer* by removal of religious element. With him the *Urgrund* and *Urzufall* became the *will-to-live* and TII [Thing-in-Itself]. Whereas this activity directed solely towards itself is with Fichte the autonomy of ethical self-determination and with Schlegel (pfui!), the ironical play of fancy, with dear Arthur it is the *absolute unreason of objectless will*. Creating itself alone and perpetually it is the never satisfied, the *unhappy* will; and since world is nothing but self-revelation (objectivation) of the will, it must be a balls aching world" (TCD MS 10967/v. 253, cited in Matthew Feldman, *Beckett's Books: A Cultural History of the "Interwar Notes"* [London: Continuum, 2008], 49–50).

[34] Beckett to Thomas MacGreevy, 19 August 1936 (*Letters*, 368). Dirk Van Hulle uses the term *Vorwärtsstreben* in "Samuel Beckett's *Faust* Notes," in

the Romantic seeks to "fulfil his mission, to be a good and faithful servant" (81). Where Beckett's passage moves beyond Schopenhauer is in its much more single-minded focus on how the hope for transcendent fulfillment of any kind *itself* chains consciousness to the world of phenomena. By way of comparison, in the quoted passage above, Schopenhauer uses the word "hope" only once—and in a much more straightforwardly utilitarian sense. However, Schopenhauer's invocation of the parable of the camel and the needle's eye may perhaps have directed Beckett's emphasis, for eschatological Hope is one of the theological virtues (alongside faith and charity). Again, I would argue that Romanticism and Christianity are being run together by Beckett to some extent, as paradigmatic promulgators of "hope." But it is also worth noting the sheer power that Beckett attributes to the *re*-formation of that "cataract" of hope. This corresponds to the constant drama within his own texts, between the assertion and merciless undermining of transcendent hope; in its Romantic inflection, *Krapp's Last Tape* offers perhaps the clearest example of this pervasive thematic, whereas *Waiting for Godot* and *Nacht und Träume* just as obviously draw upon explicitly Christian sources.[35] Here, then, is a major and lasting quarry of ideas for Beckett's art.

It may well be asked, though, whether Beckett's 1936 notebook passage does not still hold out the possibility of some momentary access to a Schopenhauer-style ascetic purification, sanctification and final resignation? For while Beckett's language seems starker than Schopenhauer's in its focus on a "merciless light" beyond *all* hope (all "solutions"), there is an implicit recognition here and elsewhere in Beckett that the very desire for Nothing remains yet another form of hope, as in the novel written during World War Two, *Watt*:

Engelberts et. al, *Notes diverse holo*, 294; he is commenting on Beckett's excerpt from *Faust I* (1092–93) in his notes: "Doch ist es jedem eingeboren, / dass sein Gefühl hinauf u. vorwärts dringt" (UoR MS 5004, 61).

[35] For more extended discussion of *Krapp's Last Tape* and *Nacht und Träume*, respectively, see Tonning, *Samuel Beckett's Abstract Drama*, 179–182 and 243–250.

> What had he learnt? Nothing.
> [...]
> But was not that something?
> He saw himself then, so little, so poor. And now, littler, poorer. Was not that something?
> So sick, so alone.
> And now.
> Sicker, aloner.
> Was not that something?[36]

Nonetheless, Watt's fervent question, "was not that something?", continues to reverberate throughout the countless invocations of the void across Beckett's writing, no less than his determined linguistic push *worstward*:

> No. Naught best. Best worse. No. Not best worse. Naught not best worse. Less best worse. No. Least. Least best worse. Least never to be naught. Never to naught be brought. Never by naught be nulled. Unnullable least. Say that best worse. With leastening words say least best worse. For want of worser worst. Unlessenable least best worse.[37]

There is perhaps no more obsessively orchestrated theme in Beckett than the "need to seem to glimpse"[38] what may be beyond the veil, "whether something or nothing."[39] However, the explicit identification of that "beyond" with philosophical language such as "Thing-in-Itself" or "Will" comes to seem less and less relevant: to introduce it explicitly into the late texts, in particular, only obstructs Beckett's writerly dynamic.

---

[36] Samuel Beckett, *Watt*, edited by C.J. Ackerley (London: Faber and Faber, 2009), 127.

[37] Samuel Beckett, *Worstward Ho*, in *Company/Ill Seen Ill Said/Worstward Ho/Stirrings Still*, edited by Dirk Van Hulle (London: Faber and Faber, 2009), 95.

[38] Beckett, "what is the word," in *Selected Poems*, 115.

[39] Letter to Axel Kaun, in *Disjecta*, 172.

* * *

Even where Beckett does employ a more philosophically flavored language, its purpose is still to set the stage for a set of problems that must finally be enacted through art, and art alone. More specifically, Beckett's many references to the "rupture of the lines of communication" between subject and object, or the "breakdown" of both terms (*Disjecta*, 70), serve to define an aesthetic criterion: artistic work that confronts this fundamental dilemma is valid, whereas that which evades it in some way is not. Here too, Beckett's primary source for this thematic is Schopenhauer; although importantly, the latter seems also to have been decisively filtered and fortified on this point through Jules de Gaultier's discussion of Schopenhauer in *From Kant to Nietzsche* (1900). The following note from Beckett's *Dream Notebook* summarizes this communicative "rupture" between subject and object, derived from a passage in de Gaultier:

> Curiosity focussed on relation between the *object* & its *representation*, between the *stimulus* & *molecular disturbance*, between *percipi* and *percipere*.[40]
>
> To propound the problem of Cognition means to wonder and be concerned for the first time about the relation between objects such as we perceive them and objects as they may be; it means suspecting for the first time that the *object* may differ from its *representation*. [...] With growing disquiet one comes to perceive that the molecular movement in the brain [...] is still no more than a means of perception, thus a new screen between the object and knowledge thereof. At what instant and how does the subject of knowledge itself arise? How is the subject opposed to the object, *percipere* to *percipi*?[41]

---

[40] Quoted in John Pilling, ed., *Beckett's* Dream *Notebook* (Reading: Beckett International Foundation, 1999), 165.

[41] Jules de Gaultier, *From Kant to Nietzsche*, translated by Gerald M. Spring (London: P. Owen, 1961), 13–14.

Gaultier further argues along broadly Schopenhauerian lines that

> one cannot conceive a state of knowledge without a state of representation, without a subject confronted by an object. Outside of these conditions the term *knowledge* is for the mind devoid of all meaning, all intelligibility. [...] On the other hand, it is impossible to attribute to the *Being in itself* the distinction into object and subject: that would be identifying it with the world as representation and would, therefore, amount to abolishing it.[42]

Accordingly, he concludes that "knowledge is not an apanage of Being, and that there is *an essential antinomy between existence and knowledge*" (emphasis in original, 75). Gaultier here in fact seems to push beyond Schopenhauer in questioning our ability to know anything at all about the Thing-in-Itself, pointing out that every "means of perception" and all attempts at gaining "knowledge" always *presuppose* the division of subjects and objects. Gaultier's "antinomy" means that identifying the noumenon with the Will would be dubious—for the mere reason that it *is* an inference, which affirms the subject-object bifurcation by enactment.

The picture emerging here is one of inherently unstable "subjects" completely unable to establish real contact with any "object" of desire, perception or knowledge. Any attempt to escape this situation (through some form of union with the Thing-in-Itself) must fail simply because it remains an act of will, requiring some degree of perception and knowledge. This is of course consonant with Beckett's feeling that there is no "way out" and no "solution." This provides the basic structure for what he would later call the "one theme" of his writing life,[43] pithily summarized in the 1976 poem "neither":

---

[42] Ibid., 74–75.
[43] In conversation with Morton Feldman, around 20 September 1976 (Knowlson, 631).

to and fro in shadow from inner to outer shadow from impenetrable self to impenetrable unself by way of neither[44]

The strict irresolvability of the movement between "self" and "unself" points to an area in which art can fruitfully function, by dramatizing attempts to establish subject-object links and their inevitable breakdown. This is Beckett's famous idea of an art of *failure*, or "incoherence," or still elsewhere, the "authentic weakness of being."[45]

Unflinching confrontation of the subject-object disconnect thus becomes the measure of authentic art for Beckett, as well as a benchmark for his own writing. It is worth noting that this Schopenhauerian aesthetics also directs Beckett's approach to an enormous range of painting and music,[46] two art forms which, in the 1930s, he took as models for his own incipient "literature of the unword":

> As we cannot eliminate language all at once, we should at least leave nothing undone that might contribute to its falling into disrepute. To bore one hole after another in it, until what lurks behind it—be it something or nothing—begins to seep through; I cannot imagine a higher goal for a writer today. Or is literature alone to remain behind in the old lazy ways that have been so long ago abandoned by music and painting? [...] Is there any reason why that terrible materiality of the word surface should not be capable of being dissolved, like for example the sound surface, torn by enormous pauses, of Beethoven's seventh Symphony, so that through whole pages we can perceive nothing but a path of sounds suspended in giddy heights, linking unfathomable abysses of silence?[47]

---

[44] Beckett, *Texts for Nothing and Other Shorter Prose*, edited by Mark Nixon (London: Faber and Faber, 2010), 167.

[45] For "authentic weakness," see Beckett to Lawrence Harvey, 1961 (Knowlson, 492). The classic Beckett text about "failure" can be found in *Three Dialogues With Georges Duthuit* (1949).

[46] In Tonning, *Samuel Beckett's Abstract Drama*, I focused on painting in this respect, especially the art of Karl Ballmer (22–27) and Paul Cézanne (43–47).

[47] Samuel Beckett, "German Letter of 1937," in *Disjecta*, edited by Ruby Cohn (New York: Grove Press, 1984), 171–172.

The letter to Axel Kaun is one of the most cited documents in Beckett criticism, and there is certainly good reason for seeing in it a blueprint for much of the experimental fiction and drama Beckett would go on to produce. But it, and Beckettian aesthetics generally, make little sense except against a Schopenhauerian background. For instance, Beckett's comments on music as a paradigm of art clearly relate to Schopenhauer's influential account of music in *The World as Will and Representation*, while again carving out an independent and even more pessimistic position. As Franz Michael Maier has argued, the central point at issue between Schopenhauer and Beckett here is "Zusammenhang," or "connectedness"—of melody in particular.[48] In Schopenhauer's theory melody, with its "constant digression and deviation from the keynote in a thousand ways," expresses "the many different forms of the will's efforts, but also its satisfaction by ultimately finding again a harmonious interval, and still more the keynote" (*WWR1*, 260). For Schopenhauer, it is the very completeness of melodic progression that makes music a copy of the Will, enabling this art to transcend the phenomenal realm by depicting desire and its attendant sufferings *sub specie aeternitatis*.

Beckett, by contrast, finds in some favored pieces—like Beethoven's Seventh Symphony—a principle of internal *dis*integration, one that may negatively project, but still fails to achieve, the incursion of a final Silence. Beethoven's Seventh is actually a characteristically assertive, heroic work; but what Beckett hears is the breakdown of that assertiveness, its hollowness, the "great black pauses" that disturb Romantic *Vorwärtsstreben*. Again, Beckett's focus is firmly placed upon the drama of breakdown and failure enacted in and through a particular artistic language. His own projected "literature of the unword" would attempt to "dissolve" the "word surface"

---

[48] Maier, in *Becketts Melodien*, provides an impressive scholarly account of Beckett, Schopenhauer and music covering Beckett's entire career. See also Pilling, "*Proust* and Schopenhauer: Music and Shadows."

by putting a "mocking attitude towards the word" into words via a systematic "dissonance between the means and their use".[49]

* * *

It would seem that, far from being a tired or exhausted subject, the real range and complexity of Schopenhauer's influence upon Beckett is only now beginning to be understood. After James Knowlson's seminal 1996 biography and the general turn toward a more documentary approach within Beckett Studies thereafter, it has become possible to trace the development of Beckett's reading and thought in impressive detail. However, if the view presented here of Schopenhauer as a conduit for that development as a whole is accepted, it follows that we have only scratched the surface of this research. While much excellent work has been done on Beckett's reading of philosophy from about 1932 onward, it is arguable that Beckett's fundamental philosophical (or anti-philosophical) position had already been formed through his first encounter with Schopenhauer.[50] Thus, Beckett's interest in, say, the respective "nothings" of Democritus and Arnold Geulincx (so central to *Murphy*),[51] or the *esse est percipi aut percipere* of Bishop Berkeley,[52] or Fritz Mauthner's critique of language,[53] or G. W. Leibniz's monadology,[54] can all be

---

[49] *Disjecta.*, 172–173.
[50] One of the most revealing passages here comes from *Dream of Fair to Middling Women*, the terms of which recur essentially unchanged in the Kaun letter despite all Beckett's intervening reading activities: "I was speaking of something of which you have and can have no knowledge, the incoherent continuum as expressed by, say, Rimbaud and Beethoven. [...] The terms of whose statements serve merely to delimit the reality of insane areas of silence, whose audibilities are no more than punctuation in a statement of silences" (102).
[51] See entries on these philosophers in Ackerley, *Demented Particulars*.
[52] See Tonning, *Samuel Beckett's Abstract Drama*, chapter 3, for a discussion of Beckett's use of Berkeley in *Film*.
[53] See Feldman, *Beckett's Books*, chapter 5, for more information on Fritz Mauthner's influence.

seen as filling out the finer details in a picture already substantially composed. This matters because Beckett's pre-established thematic often determines which points are of interest in the subsequent philosophers he studied; consistently coloring his idiosyncratic appropriations of their thought in his own writing.

A similar point can be made about Beckett's readings in psychology and psychoanalysis (most intensively during his psychotherapy with Wilfred Bion in 1934–35). Space only allows for a short illustration here; and the link between Schopenhauer, Beckett and psychoanalysis has in any case been made in Beckett studies previously.[55] Freud's concept of the death drive, taken from the 1920 "Beyond the Pleasure Principle," underlies images of the yearning to return to the mineral world in Beckett's writing.[56] In terms of the unrelenting trope of "onwardness" that recurs throughout his *oeuvre*, relevant Schopenhauerian backgrounds here include the essay "On Death and Its Relation to the Indestructibility of Our Inner Nature,"[57] and in general the idea that corporeal existence as such expresses the Will at war with itself:

---

[54] See Tonning, *Samuel Beckett's Abstract Drama*, chapter 6, for an extended treatment of Beckett and Leibniz.
[55] See O'Hara, *Samuel Beckett's Hidden Drives*.
[56] See the entry on "geology" in Ackerley and Gontarski, *The Grove Companion*, 219–220.
[57] Dirk Van Hulle draws attention to the importance of this essay (and of Schopenhauer on suicide and death generally) to Beckett's work in *Manuscript Genetics: Joyce's Know-How, Beckett's Nohow* (Gainesville, FL: University Press of Florida, 2008), 146–148.

Therefore the parts of the body must correspond completely to the chief demands and desires by which the will manifests itself; they must be the visible expression of these desires. Teeth, gullet, and intestinal canal are objectified hunger; the genitals are objectified sexual impulse; grasping hands and nimble feet correspond to the more indirect strivings of the will which they represent. Just as the general human form corresponds to the general human will, so to the individually modified will, namely the character of the individual, there corresponds the individual bodily structure, which is therefore as a whole and in all its parts characteristic and full of expression (*WWR1*, 108).

Even Freud's Id/Ego/Superego model transcribed by Beckett[58]—wherein the personality emerges from constant internal struggle and defensive responses to a series of traumas inflicted upon the organism since its conception—seems somewhat tame beside his German precursor's language. Beckett clearly recognized this type of common ground,[59] and the assimilation into his work of the fashionable Freudian Otto Rank's concept of the "trauma of birth" as the origin of all subsequent anxiety appears almost foreordained given his established fascination with Schopenhauer's idea of the "original sin" of having been born.[60] Further examples are Beckett's excited reading of the Marquis de Sade's *120 Days of Sodom* in 1938, when he felt a "metaphysical ecstasy"[61] clearly linked to a metaphysics in which

---

[58] Beckett made detailed notes on Id/Ego/Superego from his reading of Freud's *New Introductory Lectures on Psycho-analysis* (see Feldman, *Beckett's Books*, 30–31).

[59] Beckett felt a much stronger affinity with Freud than with Jung (who was "in the end less than the dirt under Freud's nails"; letter to MacGreevy, 8 October 1935, *Letters*, 282); I would maintain that Beckett preferred Freud's Schopenhauer-influenced pessimism to Jung's mystic teleologies.

[60] For treatments of Rank and Beckett, as well as the "fatal pleasure principle," see Phil Baker, *Beckett and the Mythology of Psychoanalysis* (New York: Palgrave Macmillan, 1997), 64–144; and Matthew Feldman, *Beckett's Books*, 107 and 111–115. See also Tonning, *Samuel Beckett's Abstract Drama*, 131–146.

[61] Letter to MacGreevy, 21 February 1938, *Letters*, 607; see also 604–605.

"tormentor and tormented are one" (*WWR1*, 236);[62] or even his extended work on Samuel Johnson between 1937 and 1940 which, as the following quotation from *The Idler*, no. 89 (noted by Beckett)[63] suggests, is not unrelated to that "intellectual justification of unhappiness" which drew Beckett to Schopenhauer in the first place:[64]

> How evil came into the world; for what reason it is that life is overspread with such boundless varieties of misery; why the only thinking being of this globe is doomed to think merely to be wretched, and to pass his time from youth to age in fearing or in suffering calamities, is a question which philosophers have long asked, and which philosophy could never answer.

* * *

While this essay has adopted an impressionistic approach to showcase the sheer variety of ways in which Schopenhauer's influence colors Beckett's thought, reading and writing, future scholarship in any of the areas highlighted above will need to become more systematic. As mentioned before, vital information about Beckett's Schopenhauer editions is forthcoming; and the remaining volumes of the *Letters*, covering the period from 1941 to 1989, will hopefully follow soon. This information needs to be correlated with Beckett's texts in the usual way; but scholars will also do well to examine how the Schopenhauerian presence is being *inflected* in a particular work via other, related influences. Once again, the object of study should be

---

[62] On the Sade influence, see Shane Weller, "Orgy of false being life in common: Beckett and the Politics of Death," in *Beckett and Death*, ed. Steven Barfield, Matthew Feldman, and Philip Tew (London and New York: Continuum, 2009), and "The Anethics of Desire: Beckett, Racine, Sade," in *Beckett and Ethics*, ed. Russell Smith (London and New York: Continuum, 2009), 102–117; and also Elsa Baroghel, "From Narcissistic Isolation to Sadistic Pseudocouples: Tracing the Genesis of *Endgame*," in *Samuel Beckett Today/Aujourd'hui* 22 (2010).

[63] UoR MS 3461/2, 94; quoted in Tonning, "Beckett's Unholy Dying," 119–120.

[64] See Tonning, "Beckett's Unholy Dying," for an extended treatment of Beckett's uses of Johnson in *Malone Dies* and *The Unnamable*.

considered a shifting conglomerate, with Schopenhauer as glue: and this requires alert and evidence-based mapping, grounded in the formative years of the 1930s, but also pointing beyond that period to the middle and later Beckett.

It is still true that as Beckett's later work becomes more abstract, allusions become harder to identify: yet against the background of a more detailed map, it does become possible to pinpoint, as it were, the region of references underlying particular tropes or images. To take one final example, my own recent article "'Nor by the eye of flesh nor by the other': Fleshly, Creative and Mystical Vision in Late Beckett" argues that one of Beckett's early notes on William Inge's *Christian Mysticism* (1899), on the "right eye" of the *Theologia Germanica* (fixed on eternity rather than on creatures) was worked into an abandoned play draft from 1980 and into the 1979–1980 *Ill Seen Ill Said*—a text obsessed with eyes and failing vision. This is then related back to Beckett's recurring trope of "liberated eyes" (from the "Clare Street Notebook") in the 1930s and beyond, and to Beckett's uses of Schopenhauer on mysticism. My present point is simply that Schopenhauer would be basic to any wider attempt to unpack the multiple, complex images of eyes across Beckett's *oeuvre*:

> But the world as representation, with which alone we are dealing with here, certainly begins only with the opening of the first eye, and without this medium of knowledge it cannot be, and hence before this it did not exist. But without that eye, in other words, outside of knowledge, there was no before, no time (*WWR1*, 31).

What is characteristic about late Beckett, indeed, is that the simplest-seeming image or situation can be a distillation of a lifetime's thought and imaginative effort. Our task as critics is to trace that effort as conscientiously as possible, using what evidence is available to us, in order to get as close to the creative tensions at work in the texts as possible. I have suggested here that for such a task, Schopenhauer remains uniquely indispensable.

"Speak of Time, without Flinching... Treat of Space with the Same Easy Grace":[1] Beckett, Bergson and the Philosophy of Space

David Addyman (University of Bergen, Norway)

Bergson was rare among Beckett's philosophers in that he was one of the few that the author appears to have read first hand, rather than read *about* in synopses; he was also rare in being the only twentieth-century philosopher that Beckett read until his brush with Sartre's and Mauthner's work in the spring of 1938.[2] There are a number of explicit references to Bergson in Beckett's writings—particularly in the so-called "grey canon"—which, in consequence of a renewed interest in this corpus in recent years, have been referred to more often.[3] However, although Beckett's work has been compared to the philosophy of Henri Bergson since the earliest Anglophone studies,[4] there has never been an attempt to move beyond mere comparison, to establish the relationship on a firm empirical footing. In recent years a number of studies take Beckett's reading of Bergson to date from

---

[1] Samuel Beckett, *The Unnamable*, edited by Steven Connor (London: Faber and Faber, 2010), 108.
[2] See Matthew Feldman, "Beckett, Sartre and Phenomenology," *Limit(e) Beckett*, 0 issue (2010), www.limitebeckett.paris-sorbonne.fr/zero/feldman.html; last accessed 06/12/2011.
[3] However, Bergson is a surprising omission from many works; Richard Lane's *Beckett and Philosophy*, for example, makes no reference; Richard Lane, ed., *Beckett and Philosophy* (Basingstoke: Palgrave, 2002).
[4] The oldest study is Ruby Cohn, *Samuel Beckett: The Comic Gamut* (New Brunswick: Rutgers University Press, 1962); a more recent work in the comparative vein is Shane Weller, *Beckett, Literature and the Ethics of Alterity* (Basingstoke: Palgrave Macmillan, 2006); see in particular Chapter 3, *passim*.

before his 1930 monograph *Proust*, something which would be highly significant, since it would mean that Bergson was Beckett's first philosopher, perhaps read even before Descartes and Schopenhauer. However, the available evidence indicates that Beckett's reading of Bergson came later than is normally assumed. The aim here, then, is to examine the extent of Bergson's influence, how Bergsonian imagery appears—but also, crucially, how it does not appear—in Beckett's early works and beyond. This contribution to *Beckett/Philosophy* will argue that Beckett's postwar work is fundamentally opposed to Bergson's: Beckett conceives of identity as bound up with space in a way that would have been simply inconceivable to Bergson.

No Time for Space

One of the problems for scholars considering the influence of Bergson on Beckett's work is that it is not known when Beckett first read Bergson. Yet a critical commonplace holds that he did so before he wrote *Proust*, and that the latter's influence can be discerned in that monograph.[5] The source of this claim appears to be John Pilling's *Beckett Before Godot*,[6] which argues that Beckett "had certainly read [Bergson's] *Creative Evolution*" before writing *Proust* (39). However, Pilling provides no evidence for this. It is true that both during his time as an undergraduate at Trinity College, Dublin (1923–

---

[5] Anthony Uhlmann says that "Beckett was well aware of the links that had been made between Bergson and Proust as well as the different understandings of time each developed": Anthony Uhlmann, "Beckett and Philosophy," in Linda Ben-Zvi and Angela Moorjani, eds. *Beckett at 100: Revolving it All* (Oxford: Oxford University Press, 2007), 85–86. Gontarski writes that "The Bergson connection in *Proust* is not often acknowledged by Beckett": S.E. Gontarski, "Recovering Beckett's Bergsonism," in Ben-Zvi and Moorjani, 96. Ulrika Maude claims that "Beckett's early interest in Bergson's ideas is evidenced ... in *Proust*": Ulrika Maude, *Beckett, Technology and the Body* (Cambridge: Cambridge University Press, 2009), 175.

[6] Shane Weller at least cites Pilling as his source. See Shane Weller, *A Taste for the Negative: Beckett and Nihilism* (Leeds: Legenda, 2005), 35.

1927), and his time as an exchange lecturer at the École Normale Supérieure in Paris (1928–1930), Beckett may have been exposed to Bergson's thought. To be sure, Brigitte Le Juez claims that Beckett read Proust in his third year at Trinity.[7] Given the dominance of Bergsonian readings in the early days of Proust scholarship—a trend that Proust himself lamented[8]—it might be fair to assume that any tuition at Trinity adopted this perspective. Certainly, Suzanne Guerlac argues that French literary criticism was generally Bergsonian in outlook,[9] and this critical perspective may have reached Trinity through Beckett's tutor and mentor, Thomas Rudmose-Brown, described in a preface to one of his works as having "anticipated the direction of much contemporary French and English criticism."[10] However, Rudmose-Brown taught poetry, and according to John Pilling, the Trinity College Yearbook does not show a course offered on Proust while Beckett was a student there. Nevertheless, under the tutelage of Rudmose-Brown, Beckett did at one stage plan to write a thesis on a school of French poetry called Unanimism, which Anthony Uhlmann claims derived its ideas from Bergson (84). Beckett got as far as writing a research essay on the movement in the Summer of 1928, and according to Beckett's biographer, James Knowlson, "looked ... closely into the theories and ideals" of the school.[11] However, the connection with Bergson is extremely distant and it is unlikely that Beckett would have got much Bergson from his preparatory reading.

---

[7] Brigitte Le Juez, *Beckett Before Beckett*, translated by Ros Schwartz (London: Souvenir Press, 2009), 12.

[8] In an interview with Élie-Joseph Bois which appeared in *Les Temps* on 13 November 1913. See Jacques Bersani, *Les Critiques de notre temps et Proust* (Paris: Garnier, 1974), 66.

[9] Suzanne Guerlac, *Thinking in Time: An Introduction to Henri Bergson* (Ithaca and London: Cornell University Press), 183.

[10] Cited in Samuel Beckett, *The Letters of Samuel Beckett, Volume 1: 1929–1940*, edited by Martha Dow Fehsenfeld and Lois More Overbeck (Cambridge: Cambridge University Press, 2009), 46 n. 7.

[11] James Knowlson, *Damned to Fame: The Life of Samuel Beckett* (London: Bloomsbury, 1997), 76.

This leaves the École Normale. According to Guerlac, the all-pervasiveness of Bergsonian thought was only just beginning to be shaken off at the time of Beckett's stay in Paris. Regarding the ubiquity of the philosopher's ideas, Guerlac cites François Mauriac, for whom Bergson was "the philosopher we listened to," and the Binet report of 1908 on the teaching of philosophy in schools, which concluded that "Bergson's ideas prevailed over all others among both faculty and students."[12] Even as late as 1930–1931 at the École Normale, Maurice Merleau-Ponty felt that Bergsonism offered an alternative to the Neo-Kantian academic philosophy of his tutor, Léon Brunschvicg.[13] As part of this French intellectual culture, Beckett's friends Jean Beaufret and Alfred Péron would undoubtedly have been well-versed in Bergsonism. Péron shared a study with Sartre and his classmate Paul Nizan,[14] and Guerlac describes the former (one year above Merleau-Ponty at the École Normale) as "steeped in Bergson."[15] This presumably also applies to Beaufret, who like Sartre and Merleau-Ponty, was a *normalien*. This intellectual culture may explain why Beaufret and "Alfy" (Péron) laugh when Beckett tells them that he is reading Schopenhauer in July 1930 (*Letters*, 33).

Péron was at Trinity as exchange *lecteur* from the École Normale from 1926–28, and according to Knowlson, Beckett shared

---

[12] Guerlac, 11–12. For accounts of Bergson's place in early twentieth-century French thought see: Mark Antliff, *Inventing Bergson: Cultural Politics and the Parisian Avant-garde* (Princeton: Princeton University Press, 1993); A. E. Pilkington, *Bergson and His Influence: A Reassessment* (Cambridge: Cambridge University Press, 1976); and Romeo Arbour, *Bergson et les lettres françaises* (Paris: José Corti, 1955).

[13] See James Schmidt, *Maurice Merleau-Ponty: Between Phenomenology and Structuralism* (New York: St. Martin's Press, 1985), 17.

[14] C.J. Ackerley and S.E. Gontarski, *The Faber Companion to Samuel Beckett: A Reader's Guide to His Works, Life and Thought* (London: Faber and Faber, 2006), 431.

[15] Guerlac, 5 n.15. Dermot Moran notes that the first philosophical writer that Sartre read was Bergson during 1923–1924, his year of *khâgne* (the final year of preparation for École Normale): Dermot Moran, *Introduction to Phenomenology* (London: Routledge, 2004), 364.

many talks with him (Knowlson, 154). The content of these talks may be reflected in the character Chas' discourse on Bergson in *Dream of Fair to Middling Women* (written 1931-1932). Chas was partly based on Péron, and if an autobiographical element to *Dream* can be assumed, as Knowlson suggests, conversations with Péron availed Beckett of many key Bergsonian concepts. As the protagonist, Belacqua, apparently stands back and listens, Chas holds forth on Bergson to a group of attending students:

> The difference, then I say, between Bergson and Einstein, the essential difference, is the difference between a philosopher and a sociologist [...] And if it is the smart thing nowadays to speak of Bergson as a bit of a cod ... it is that the trend of our modern vulgarity is from the object ... and the idea to sense ... and REASON.[16]

This not only shows an awareness of the Einstein-Bergson controversy of the early 1920s, but also knowledge of the move away from Bergson in French thought.[17] However, as evidence that Beckett encountered Bergson's work before *Proust*, the passage is inconclusive: on the one hand, the novel appears to relate events from the late 1920s, but on the other hand, it was written after *Proust*, making it difficult to say whether the ideas reflect Beckett's knowledge of Bergson at the earlier period or, as is more likely, the later.

So far, then, it has been impossible to demonstrate conclusively that Beckett read Bergson before he wrote *Proust*. Nevertheless, S. E. Gontarski and Shane Weller, amongst others, have quoted passages from that work which they consider exhibit a Bergsonian influence (see Gontarski, "Recovering," 96, and Weller, *Negative*, 35). The difficulty with this argument, though, lies in separating Proust's thought from Bergson's—in identifying whether an idea comes to Beckett from Proust or from Bergson. Despite his protestations, Proust had considerable contact with Bergson's thought, and there are clear par-

---

[16] Samuel Beckett, *Dream of Fair to Middling Women*, edited by Eoin O'Brien and Edith Fournier (Dublin: Black Cat, 1992), 212.

[17] Bergson had a public disagreement with Einstein over the notion of time in the latter's theory of relativity. See Guerlac, 13.

allels between the two *oeuvres*. After graduating in law in March 1893, and after acting as best man at Bergson's wedding (Guerlac, 9), Proust attended his lectures in Paris.[18] As Guerlac points out, both writers describe two forms of memory, and these bear more than a passing resemblance. For Bergson, one of these forms of memory is identified with habit and "remains dependent upon our will [*volonté*]," while the other is more "capricious."[19] This corresponds to Proust's differentiation between "voluntary" and "involuntary" memory, on which Beckett writes in *Proust*.[20]

In order, then, to demonstrate that what we see is the influence of Bergson on *Proust* rather than of Bergson on Proust, it would need to be demonstrated that Beckett read *À la recherche du temps perdu* in a way that was more Bergsonian than Proustian—to show, in other words, that a dependence on Bergson led Beckett to a distorted or erroneous reading. John Pilling has pointed out some key points at which Beckett over-reads his own interests into Proust's work, and indeed Beckett later admitted as much,[21] but it is also possible to discern an interest that Pilling or other commentators have not identified: Beckett's reading of the novel is temporocentrist in the extreme, almost to the total exclusion of space, something which seems consistent with the influence of Bergson, but which is inconsistent with certain key passages in Proust's novel. In order to elaborate this difference it is necessary to summarize Bergson's thought briefly.

This was characterized by its concern with a concrete rather than a theorized conception of time. As Guerlac summarizes,

---

[18] See Sheila Stern, *Landmarks of World Literature: Marcel Proust: Swann's Way* (Cambridge: Cambridge University Press, 1989), "Chronology," unnumbered pages.

[19] Cited in Guerlac, 125.

[20] *Proust*, 29 ff. See also 18: "The laws of memory are subject to the more general laws of habit."

[21] Beckett admitted to Pilling, "[p]erhaps I overstated Proust's pessimism a little." John Pilling, "Beckett's 'Proust,'" *Journal of Beckett Studies* 1 (Winter 1976), 24 ff.

> Bergson [argues] that science gives us the world mediated through symbols, which deform our sense of reality to the extent that they immobilize what we experience as occurring in temporal flow. He [argues] that ordinary language only reinforces the worldview established by the formal languages of mathematics, and all of these modes of symbolic representation interfere with our ability to grasp the temporal nature of reality. They crush our sense of duration.[22]

Bergson suggests that the habit (and error) of Western metaphysics is to consider time statically, measured out as by a clock instead of as "pure duration," which is the form that, he argues, consciousness assumes when it is not seen as a succession, with past states separated from present, and set alongside them. Laying conscious states out to analysis in this way is to commit the fallacy of "spatializing" them, which destroys the pure experience of consciousness. By contrast, Bergson's emphasis is on inner experience or intuition, things that cannot be measured, and can only ever be experienced anew; they cannot be made identical to other things by wrapping them in language, or in an unchanging framework. Reality must be thought of as "mutual penetration," not as isolated states of succession. Duration should be seen as "ever the same and ever changing" as if we had "no idea of space."[23]

Bergson's emphasis on temporality and his exclusion of space helps to identify a rupture between his thought and Proust's. Though it may seem strange to suggest that a reading of a novel called *In Search of Lost Time* could ever be too concerned with the temporal dimension, there is a long tradition of space-focused studies of the novel. One of the earliest of these is José Ortega y Gasset's "Le Temps, la distance et la forme chez Marcel Proust," written in 1923 as a contribution to the obituary tribute to Proust in the *Nouvelle revue française*. There, Ortega y Gasset states at the outset: "What is involved [in the novel] is a new way of dealing with time and estab-

---

[22] Guerlac, 19.
[23] Henri Bergson, *Time and Free Will*, translated by F. L. Pogson (Mineola: Dover Publications, 2001), 100–101, 125; see also Chapter II, *passim*.

lishing a spatial dimension."[24] Some pages later, having discussed this temporal aspect, he writes, "[s]o much for what he [Proust] does with time. But more fundamental still, and more astounding, is his inventiveness where spatial relationships are concerned."[25] Presumably, what Ortega y Gasset finds astounding is for an author who comes out of a French tradition dominated by Bergsonian ideas to write about space. Other studies continuing to mine the rich vein of spatiality in the *Recherche* are Georges Poulet's *L'Espace Proustien* (1963) and, more recently, Jeff Malpas' *Place and Experience: A Philosophical Topography* (1999).[26]

By contrast, Beckett's temporocentrism is everywhere apparent in his account of Proust's novel. An initial indication can be got from his copy of the novel, held at the University of Reading. John Pilling has pointed out that Beckett made few if any marginal annotations to the sections most concerned with space: "Place Names: The Name" and "Place Names: The Place" ("Beckett's 'Proust,'" 16 n.21). In the monograph itself, the concern with time to the exclusion of space manifests itself in the opening paragraph: Beckett sets out to "examine in the first place that double-headed monster of damnation and salvation—Time".[27] Admittedly, Proust himself often elevates time over space. The ending of the novel, which Beckett quotes, is a fitting example:

---

[24] José Ortega y Gasset, "Le Temps, la distance et la forme chez Marcel Proust," in Leighton Hodson, eds., *Marcel Proust: The Critical Heritage* (London: Routledge, 1989), 222.

[25] Ibid., 224.

[26] Georges Poulet, *L'Espace Proustien* (Paris: Gallimard, 1963); Jeff Malpas, *Place and Experience: A Philosophical Topography* (Cambridge: Cambridge University Press, 1999).

[27] *Proust*, 11.

> I would describe men, even at the risk of giving them the appearance of monstrous beings, as occupying in Time a much greater place than that so sparingly conceded to them in Space, a place indeed extended beyond measure, because, like giants plunged in the years, they touch at once those periods of their lives separated by so many days—so far apart in Time. (cited in *Proust*, 12)

That time is subservient to space is also suggested in a letter written by Proust in 1912: "There is a plane geometry and a geometry of space. And so for me the novel is not only plane psychology but psychology in space and time"; though both space and time are evoked here, in the next sentence the former is eclipsed by the latter: "That invisible substance, time, I try to isolate."[28]

However, there are times in the novel when space is at least as important as time, if not more so, but Proust appears to overlook these passages in the ending to the novel, perhaps as a result of the prolonged and piecemeal composition of *À la recherche du temps perdu*.[29] In another passage (and one which Beckett quotes), the recovery of both time and space is crucial in the recovery of a loved one:

> We imagine that the object of our desire is a being that can be laid down before us, enclosed within a body. Alas! it is *the extension of that being to all the points of space and time* that it has occupied and will occupy. If we do not possess contact with such a place and with such an hour we do not possess that being. But we cannot touch all these points. (cited in *Proust*, 58; emphasis added)

The object of desire must be pursued in time and space, not time alone. However, Beckett refers to the passage—and to three others over pages 57 and 58 of his *Proust*—as an illustration of "the Goddess of Time." In his reading, the spatial element is absent: "No ob-

---

[28] Cited in Stephen Kern, *The Culture of Time and Space 1880–1918* (Cambridge, MA and London: Harvard University Press, 2003), 50.

[29] This aspect is something Beckett discussed four years later in "Proust in Pieces"; Samuel Beckett, *Disjecta: Miscellaneous Writings and a Dramatic Fragment*, edited by Ruby Cohn (London: Calder, 1983), 64–65.

ject prolonged *in this temporal dimension* tolerates possession, meaning by possession total possession, only to be achieved by the complete identification of object and subject" (57; emphasis added).[30] This "complete identification," Beckett has already told us, is frustrated by time, and time alone: "The aspirations of yesterday were valid for yesterday's ego, not for to-day's" (*Proust*, 13). He goes on to say that in a (hypothetical) moment in which the object of desire is gained, "the time-state of attainment eliminates so accurately the time-state of aspiration" (14). By contrast, for Proust, space is key in the pursuit and attainment (if such a thing is even possible) of the object of desire, and this is all the more true of the most important object of desire in the *Recherche*: the self.[31] As early as the fifth page of the novel, awaking disorientated in the middle of the night, the narrator says, "not knowing where I was, I could not even be sure at first who I was."[32] This is as clear a statement as we could want: identity is predicated on knowledge of one's location in space.[33]

This points, then, to something of a misreading on Beckett's part—and a misreading that appears to be in keeping with a Bergsonian perspective. So are we to conclude that Beckett's study of the *Recherche* is more Bergsonian than Proustian, by virtue of its being concerned more with time than with space, and that Bergson therefore influenced the composition of *Proust*? Plausible as this reading may seem, the evidence is overwhelmingly against it. Let us examine the facts as they are known.

---

[30] A few lines after the passage on page 57, and before the three passages from *À la recherche du temps perdu*, "time" becomes "time and space." Beckett speaks of "[a]ll that is active, all that is enveloped in time and space": in his account, at best there is no difference between time and space; at worst space is subordinate.

[31] This is something that Pilling notes, arguing that in Proust's work Beckett found an interest in a "radically new" subject, "what constitutes man's essential being" (Pilling, "Beckett's 'Proust'," 14).

[32] Marcel Proust, *Remembrance of Things Past, Volume 1*, translated by C.K. Scott Moncrieff and Terence Kilmartin (Harmondsworth: Penguin, 1989), 5.

[33] Oddly, none of the readings cited above which have explored the spatial element in Proust's work mention this passage.

First of all, the evidence that is usually given that Beckett used Bergson as the philosophical scaffold for *Proust* is Rachel Burrows' notes, taken when she was one of Beckett's students at Trinity in 1930–1931. Uhlmann and Gontarski both argue along these lines.[34] However, Pilling's *A Beckett Chronology* states that *Proust* was submitted to Chatto and Windus on 17 September 1930, but that Beckett did not begin lecturing until 15 October.[35] This does not exclude the possibility of Bergson's influence on *Proust*, but it does discount the main evidence given. Much more convincing is the evidence *against* such an influence. If Beckett were influenced by Bergsonian ideas, it might be expected that his marginal notes in his copy of the *Recherche* would reflect this. As Pilling shows, these offer an insight into Beckett's developing interpretation of the novel, quoting even Kant at one point, but they make no mention of Bergson ("Beckett's 'Proust'," 14). Furthermore, while Beckett's letters to Thomas MacGreevy over the Summer of 1930 offer a running commentary on his (lack of) progress on *Proust*, and make reference to his first reading of Schopenhauer, and to the fact that he is studying the German specifically in order to write the monograph (*Letters*, 26–46, *passim*), there is no mention of a similar recourse to Bergson. More revealing, though, is the letter that Beckett wrote on 14 October 1930 to Charles Prentice, senior partner at Chatto and Windus, the publishing house that had commissioned Beckett's *Proust*, confessing to having written the conclusion to *Proust* in a hurry, and asking:

> Would you let me add 5 or 6 pages to the last 9? Or would that make it too long? I would like to develop the parallel with Dostoievski and separate Proust's intuitivism from Bergson's.[36]

The key word here is "develop": it is the parallel with Dostoevsky, and not that with Bergson, which is to be elaborated *further—*

---

[34] See Uhlmann (85–86) and Gontarski (96).
[35] John Pilling, *A Beckett Chronology* (Basingstoke: Palgrave Macmillan, 2006), 27. See *Letters*, 48 n. 1.
[36] Ibid., 52).

i.e., more than it already is. By contrast, Bergson will seemingly become an awkward appendage, though this awkwardness is itself significant, testifying as will be seen below to a change in Beckett's perspectives.

Added to these considerations is the fact that Arnaud Dandieu, in his *Marcel Proust: sa révélation psychologique*—which, in his 1977 thesis, "Beckett as a Critic of Joyce and Proust," Terence McQueeny shows was Beckett's "chief secondary source"[37] for *Proust*—called a Bergsonian reading of Proust one of the key errors of previous analyses of the *Recherche*. In his avant-propos, from which Beckett "borrows" heavily, as McQueeny demonstrates, Dandieu mocks "les esprits 'sérieux'" [the serious minds] who see Proust as "nourri de Bergson" [fed on Bergson].[38] A few pages later Dandieu argues that the first eighty pages of the second volume of *Le Temps retrouvé* present a clear exposition of Proust's theoretical grounding, which should "couper court à tous les malentendus" [eliminate all misunderstanding]; specifically, those who see Proust as working under the influence of Bergson are committing a "méprise intellectualiste" [an intellectualist error], and will have to "rectifier leur erreur" [correct their mistake].[39]

More convincing still is the idea that the temporocentrism of *Proust* is derived not from Bergson but from other sources. This is apparent on page 63 of Proust, where, as McQueeny shows, Beckett paraphrases Dandieu closely[40]—with a subtle but significant difference: Dandieu, in some brief remarks on Proust's treatment of time, uses (despite his caution against Bergsonian readings of Proust) the phrase "durée concrète" [real duration][41] (Dandieu, 20–21), which cannot but evoke Bergson. However, in Beckett's gloss on this pas-

---

[37] Terence McQueeny, "Beckett as a Critic of Joyce and Proust," Ph.D Thesis, University of North Carolina, 1977, 93.
[38] Ibid., 94 ff.; see also Arnaud Dandieu, *Marcel Proust: sa révélation psychologique* (Paris: Firmin-Didot, 1930), 9.
[39] Ibid., 14.
[40] McQueeny, 94.
[41] Dandieu, 20–21.

sage, the Bergsonian element is absent; more, what sounds most Bergsonian is related to Dostoevsky:

> Proust's chronology is extremely difficult to follow, the succession of events spasmodic, and his characters and themes, although they seem to obey an almost insane inward necessity, are presented and developed with a fine Dostoievskian contempt for the vulgarity of a plausible concatenation.[42]

But the most damning evidence against the Bergsonian reading of Proust is that temporocentrism is a thoroughly Schopenhauerian attitude. In the present volume, Erik Tonning argues that "Beckett's analysis of 'the Time cancer' ... draws heavily on Schopenhauer."[43] This is supported by McQueeny's thesis, which shows the extent of the references to Schopenhauer (100 ff), tracing the derivation of certain key passages in *Proust* from Schopenhauer's work. In particular, he shows that Beckett summarizes Schopenhauer's views on music (100), and relies heavily on these in the concluding pages of *Proust*, taking from Schopenhauer the key pessimistic element that separates his (Beckett's) reading from Dandieu's. Crucially, Schopenhauer's theory of music is temporocentrist: McQueeny points out that "Schopenhauer holds that musical impressions are perceived through the form of time alone to the exclusion of space" (105–106); moreover, it is by spatializing the musical experience that the purity of that experience is lost: "Swann ... fails to appreciate the Sonata in itself, spatializes it by allowing the musical phrase to become the *entremetteuse* which links him with Odette, and by this reduction fails to achieve the will-less state of contemplation which provides a momentary escape from the sufferings of the world as will" (106). In the closing lines of the monograph, in his reading of this same passage, Beckett writes that Swann "identifies the 'little phrase' of the Sonata with Odette, spatializes what is extraspatial" (*Proust*, 72). It is clear how close the imagery here is to Bergson—who also writes on music—but

---

[42] *Proust*, 62.
[43] Erik Tonning, "'I am not reading philosophy': Beckett and Schopenhauer," 25.

McQueeny convincingly shows that the source is nonetheless Schopenhauer. We must therefore be skeptical when Gontarski claims that "[t]he passage does indeed summarize Schopenhauer, but it is a gloss on Bergsonian *durée* as well" ("Recovering," 98).

When we try to discern the longer-term influence of Bergson on Beckett's thought, a similar problem to the one we have encountered in *Proust* presents itself: that of demonstrating that the images and concepts in Beckett's work that seem Bergsonian are in fact just that, and not derived from another source. Gontarski sees the influence of Bergson extending into Beckett's drama of the 1950s, affecting particularly the treatment of movement in the postwar works. However, it seems more likely that the images he identifies come from Beckett's and Bergson's shared interest in the Pre-Socratics. For Beckett's part, references in the novel *Molloy* (written in French in 1947) and the play *Endgame* (written in French between 1954 and 1957) amongst others, attest to an enduring fascinating with these philosophers.[44] But this is no less the case for Bergson, who was profoundly influenced from the outset by early Greek thought. He lectured on the Pre-Socratics at Clermont-Ferrand in the mid-1880s, and later wrote a Latin thesis entitled "Quid Aristoteles de loco senserit," which rejected the Eleatic view of space in favor of the Aristotelian.[45] Connor J. Chambers argues that Bergson's philosophy began in reflections upon the paradoxes of Zeno, and indeed Bergson refers to the Eleatics constantly, seeing a parallel between nineteenth-century positivism's distortion of reality through scientific representation, and the similar dis-

---

[44] See Matthew Feldman, "Returning to Beckett Returning to the Presocratics, or, 'All their balls about being and existing,'" *Genetic Joyce Studies* 6 (Spring 2006); accessed online on 06/12/2011 at www.antwerpjamesjoycecenter.com/GJS6/GJS6Feldman.htm.

[45] Translated into French as "*L'Idée de lieu chez Aristote.*" At the time of writing the thesis has not been translated into English. Incidentally, none other than John Burnet, one of Beckett's sources on Greek philosophy, reviewed the book of the thesis in 1892; J. Burnet, Review of H. Bergson "Quid Aristoteles de loco senserit," *The Classical Review*, 6 (1892), 322.

tortion in Zeno's paradoxes, whose paradoxical element arises precisely out of a confusion of representation with reality.[46]

Again, though, we need to provide specific evidence that any of the apparent overlapping between Beckett's thought and Bergson's is just that, and not ideas derived from Beckett's reading about the Pre-Socratics. Gontarski cites a passage which he argues stands as an example of the former. Discussing the famous passage in *Endgame* (written 1954–1957, published 1957), in which the protagonist, Hamm, insists that his companion and servant, Clov, wheel him into the exact center of the stage, then loses his temper when he is not convinced that these instructions have been carried out to the letter, Gontarski insists on a Bergsonian reading, even in the face of Beckett's pronouncements to the contrary: "Beckett may have focussed on geometry and called Hamm's preoccupation [i.e., to be in the exact center of the stage] Pythagorean in his 1967 staging of the play, but it suggests a Bergsonian epistemology as well."[47] But Beckett had insisted that the imagery was derived from Pre-Socratic thought—albeit that of a different philosopher—on an earlier occasion. In response to a letter from Alan Schneider of 21 November 1957, inquiring as to whether Beckett had remembered the identity of the "old Greek" evoked by Hamm, Beckett makes it clear that the philosophical framework of the play comes from the Pre-Socratics:

---

[46] See Connor J. Chambers, "Zeno of Elea and Bergson's Neglected Thesis," *Journal of the History of Philosophy*, Volume 12, Number 1 (January 1974), 63–76.

[47] S.E. Gontarski, "There is No Outside the Image: Bergson on Movement," paper given at the Samuel Beckett: Debts and Legacies seminar series, Oxford, 11 June 2010; accessed online on 06/12/2011 at: http://backdoorbroadcasting. net/2010/07/stan-gontarski-there-is-no-outside-the-image-bergson-on-movement/

I can't find my notes on the pre-Socratics. The arguments of the Heap and the Bald Head (which hair falling produces baldness) were used by all the Sophists and I think have been variously attributed to one or the other. They disprove the reality of mass in the same way and by means of the same fallacy as the arguments of the Arrow and Achilles and the Tortoise, invented a century earlier by Zeno the Eleatic, disprove the reality of movement. The leading Sophist, against whom Plato wrote his Dialogue, was Protagoras and he is probably the "old Greek" whose name Hamm can't remember. One purpose of the image throughout the play is to suggest the impossibility logically, i.e. eristically, of the "thing" ever coming to an end.[48]

Hamm's efforts to place himself in the exact center of the stage thus suffer from the fate mentioned in the last sentence of Beckett's letter: the task can never be ended. It is thus the Pre-Socratics, not Bergson, that provide the imagery here.

It seems, then, that Beckett is unlikely to have used Bergson as the scaffolding of *Proust*—or indeed *Endgame*. It remains to be established precisely when Beckett actually encountered the philosopher's work, and the influence that this had on his own work. All that is known is that, as Rachel Burrows' notes show, Beckett mentioned Bergson often in his lectures at Trinity in 1930–1931, comparing writers such as Proust, Gide, Rimbaud and Dostoevsky to the philosopher.[49] This seems to suggest that the earliest known mention of Bergson—in the aforementioned letter to Prentice—came about as a direct result of Beckett's first encounter with the philosopher's work in the original, as he began to do his preparatory reading for his lectures after the completion of *Proust*. It seems plausible that, as a result of this encounter, Beckett then—and only then—became interested in the differences between Proust and Bergson, and wished to add—rather than develop—this point in proofs of his monograph on

---

[48] Samuel Beckett to Alan Schneider, in Maurice Harmon, ed., *No Author Better Served: The Correspondence of Samuel Beckett and Alan Schneider* (London: Harvard University Press, 1998), 23. See also Feldman, "Returning to Beckett."

[49] See Rachel Burrows' notes: Library of Trinity College Dublin, MIC 60.

Proust. Once he started to read Bergson in preparation for his teaching, he may well have realized that there are other parallels that he had overlooked—possibly something along the line of the notes that Rachel Burrows took from Beckett's lectures:

> Detached from Bergson's conception of time but interested in this opposition—instinct & conscious intelligence. Bergson insists on absolute time; Proust denies it. For Proust it's [i.e., time is] a function of too many things— local but not absolute reality.[50]

If Burrows' notes cannot be deployed, as they usually are, as evidence of Beckett's use of Bergsonian ideas in *Proust*, they are nevertheless significant in that they indicate that Beckett saw Bergson as a useful tool in the analysis of literature. For a brief period over the 1930–1931 academic year, it seems that he found the relevance of Bergson everywhere. It may be that a Bergsonian approach in his lectures was recommended to him by the Department at Trinity, and he had little control over the syllabus he taught. But this would not explain Beckett's wholesale and seemingly wholehearted adoption of Bergsonian ideas. In addition to the new approach to Proust that Bergson gave him, and the frequent references in the lectures—all to explain key points of a writer's thought—Beckett inserted a small but significant element of Bergson into the Trinity College Dublin Modern Language Society's play *Le Kid*, a spoof of Corneille's *Le Cid*, performed early in January 1931.

Knowlson reports that "the importance given to time" in *Le Kid* was Beckett's main contribution; it was his idea to take an alarm clock on stage, which he carried with him, and which interrupted (by design) one of his main speeches. The play also included the character of Old Father Time (Knowlson, 124). These temporal elements would not on their own be particularly interesting, were it not for the fact that, while the program described the *Le Kid* as "a Cornelian nightmare," Beckett described it to his friend as "Corneille & Bergson" (*Letters*, 68). Despite the charade that by all accounts the per-

---

[50] Ibid., 60.

formance turned into, Beckett appears to have had a serious purpose. As Knowlson points out,

> The classical unity of time, according to which all of the play's action occurs ... within a time span of twenty-four hours, was shown being observed literally by a "silent figure seated on a ladder and smoking a pipe [playing] Einsteinian tricks with time" [...] *Le Kid* was, as Pelorson himself recognised ... an intellectual *canular*, a product of the École Normale kind of mind: clever, avant-garde and rather Surrealistic, but with a mixture of the effete, the pretentious, and the puerile. (124–25)

The production suggests classical drama cannot reflect a post-Einsteinian world, but Beckett's contribution perhaps hints at a belief that Bergsonian ideas can revive drama for the twentieth century.

What seems to be the case, then, is that for a brief period Beckett turns constantly to Bergson as a support for his ideas.[51] He seems to have taken a lot more from Bergson than the "straws, flotsam, etc., names, dates, births and deaths" that he took from other philosophers.[52] Moreover, this connection with Bergson may have been lasting. Pilling argues that at the time of composing *Murphy* in 1935 and 1936, Beckett had not forgotten what he had told his students at Trinity about Bergson.[53] Certainly, in 1938 he wrote to MacGreevy saying that the latter's essay on Yeats would help people who "in the phrase of Bergson can't be happy until they have 'solidified the flowing'" (*Letters*, 599). Later still, John Calder reports having conversations

---

[51] However, what cannot be established is which Bergson texts Beckett read. Pilling suggests *Creative Evolution*. In any case, it is a characteristic of Bergson's work that its key themes remain relatively constant, meaning that the temporocentrism of *Time and Free Will* is still present in *Creative Evolution* (see Guerlac, 6). The latter work's idea of "continual elaboration of the absolutely new," for example, pervades Chapter III of *Time and Free Will*.

[52] Samuel Beckett, "German Diary," Notebook 4, 15 January 1937; cited in Knowlson, 244. See also, Samuel Beckett, "Philosophy Notes," Library of Trinity College Dublin, MIC 10967.

[53] John Pilling, "A Critique of Aesthetic Judgment: Beckett's 'Dissonance of Ends and Means,'" in S.E. Gontarski, ed., *A Companion to Samuel Beckett* (Chichester and Oxford: Wiley-Blackwell, 2010), 63.

with Beckett sometime between the mid-1950s and his death in 1989, on, amongst other things, Bergson, which "went on all night."[54] However, Beckett's brief but intense flirtation with Bergsonism seems to be waning by the time of the composition of Beckett's first novel, *Dream of Fair to Middling Women*. Begun in 1931, but written mostly over the summer of 1932, this novel contains the aforementioned passage in which the character Chas describes Bergson as a "bit of a cod." To be sure, the joke could be on those for whom speaking of the philosopher in this way is "the smart thing," but Beckett's growing interest in spatial matters—notably the representation of landscape in painting[55]—from this point in his career on is indicative of a turn away from the thought of Bergson.

Time for Space

Bergson's treatment of space is extremely troubled. He insists that *durée* be considered pure consciousness, without any contact with the outside world: "the fact is there is no point of contact between the unextended [*durée*] and the extended [space]" (Bergson, 70). But he struggles to explain the flow of conscious impressions without a space that would allow things to happen: events must *take place* somewhere. Bergson's constant use of spatial imagery, though, suggests that *durée* cannot do without space; Bergson simply finds it impossible to keep space out of his discussion. In a passage which cannot but recall Beckett's 1938 phrase "solidify the flowing," Bergson says that "[w]e instinctively tend to solidify our impressions in order to express them in language" (130); a page earlier he has explicitly equated solidification with homogeneous space.[56] Bergson cannot conceive any other spatialization but the geometric. He cannot

---

[54] John Calder, *The Philosophy of Samuel Beckett* (London: Calder, 2001), 109.
[55] See Beckett's famous comments on landscape painting in the so-called "Cézanne letters" of September 1934 (*Letters*, 222–223, 227).
[56] Fluid inner states are first isolated then "solidified in homogeneous space" (Bergson, 129).

see that, just as "clock time" differs from "lived time," there may also be something we might call "map space" which differs from what Maurice Merleau-Ponty calls *"l'espace vécu"* or *"l'espace anthropologique"* [lived space].[57] Part of the problem is that Bergson has no word for this second type of space. Although again and again he needs to refer to a space other than geometrical, spatialized space, he uses the same term "space" for both: within a few pages he speaks of "an objective cause situated in space," and of things existing "[o]utside of me, in space"; he says, "[t]here is a real space," then cryptically asserts that "[s]pace contains only parts of space" (106, 108, 110, 111).

By contrast, Beckett's work is profoundly concerned with space—or rather, with what he more often calls "place," perhaps in order to avoid the problem of terminology that dogs Bergson's work. While there are a number of instances in the letters and journalism of the 1930s of Beckett speaking of place alongside Bergsonian terminology,[58] the concern with place is most obvious apparent in the

---

[57] Maurice Merleau-Ponty, *Phenomenology of Perception*, translated by Colin Smith (London: Routledge & Kegan Paul, 1962), 340. It is called "l'espace agissant" [lively space] by André Masson, in an article which Beckett and Duthuit discussed in the second of the *Three Dialogues* (*Proust*, 112): André Masson, "Divagations sur l'espace" [Divagations on space], *Les Temps modernes* 44 (1949), 962. Contemporary phenomenologists call this alternative space "lived place" or simply "place:" see Malpas, *Place and Experience*, and Edward S. Casey, *The Fate of Place: A Philosophical History* (Berkeley: University of California Press, 1997). Alternatively, the British anthropologist, Tim Ingold calls this dimension the environment: Tim Ingold, *The Perception of the Environment: Essays in Livelihood, Dwelling and Skill* (London: Routledge, 2000). In the last analysis, though, Casey says "the exact choice of term does not matter" (212).

[58] See, for example, the "Cézanne letters," and the 1936 review of Jack B. Yeats' *The Amaranthers*: in the latter, Beckett defends the work as "art, not horology" (Samuel Beckett, *Disjecta: Miscellaneous Writings and a Dramatic Fragment*, edited by Ruby Cohn [London: Calder, 1983], 89). So far so Bergsonian, but as the review progresses the temporal imagery is often blended with the spatial: "The moments are not separate, but concur in a single process: analytical imagination. Not first the old slum coming down, then

postwar fiction. Written in 1964, *All Strange Away*, in its opening lines, retrospectively makes what seems like a clear statement of the ubiquity of place in Beckett's postwar fiction:

> A place, that again. Never another question. A place, then someone in it, that again. Crawl out of the frowsy deathbed and drag it to a place to die in. Out of the door and down the road in the old hat and coat *like after the war*, no, not that again.[59]

The phrase "like after the war" can be read as a reference to Beckett's postwar work: the image of crawling out of a frowsy deathbed and dragging it to a place to die in is the basic narrative trajectory of many of the works of this period, both the most famous ones—the "Trilogy" of *Molloy*, *Malone Dies* (written in French 1947–8) and *The Unnamable* (written in French 1949–1950)—as well as lesser known texts such as *Four Novellas* and *Mercier and Camier* (written in French 1945–196) and *Texts for Nothing* (written in French 1951). This suggests that, in these works too, there was "never another question" than place. However, this concern with place does not take the form of a simple rejection of geometric space in the style of Bergson, or *Proust*, but sees space as bound up with the sense of self, as in Proust's work. Unable to gain a command of their environment, Beckett's characters are unable to gain a sense of self.

This is most apparent in *Texts for Nothing*, which announces a concern to establish a robust sense of self: "With perseverance I'd get

---

the new slum going up, but in a single act slum seen as it is and other" (89). The description of moments as "a single process," with the slum of the past as tangible as the slum of the present seems very close to passages throughout *Time and Free Will*: at one point in that work Bergson says that *durée* "refrains from separating its present state from its former state ... but forms both ... into an organic whole" (100), and something similar seems to be happening here, the old and new slum melted together. However, the subtle but key difference here is that Beckett is speaking of *places* melted together, as well as moments.

[59] Samuel Beckett, *Texts for Nothing and Other Shorter Prose, 1950–1976*, edited by Mark Nixon (London: Faber and Faber, 2010), 73; emphasis added.

at me in the end" (26). Crucially, this knowledge of self is to be "got at" by recourse to place: the narrator will list all the "tried and trusty places"—"those places *where there was a chance of my being*, where once I used to lurk" (29, emphasis added): the sea, mountains, the forest, the city, the plain, various rooms (5). But when the narrator is tempted to locate his self in those places—in the South Eastern Railway Terminus, or if not then in a two-stander urinal on the corner of Rue d'Assas—he berates himself, "tut there I am far again from that terminus and its pretty neo-Doric colonnade, and far from that heap of flesh, rind, bones and bristles waiting to depart it knows not where [...] that lump is no longer me and should be made elsewhere" (30, 46, 30–31). His attempt to locate self in place yields nothing, and he must resign himself to "reporting me missing and giving up" (29). The "high hopes of a habitable earth" (28) that he holds ultimately come to nothing.

It is striking just how close this project of seeking the self in the places it has occupied is to Proust's. At one point, the narrator of *Texts for Nothing* describes his very cells as dispersed across space: "What can have become [...] of the tissues I was, I can see them no more, feel them no more, flaunting and fluttering all about and inside me, pah they must be still on their old prowl somewhere, passing themselves off as me" (26). As noted above, Proust writes, in a passage which Beckett quotes, that beings are extended in the time and space which they have occupied, meaning that "If we do not possess contact with such a place and with such an hour we do not possess that being. But we cannot touch all these points" (cited in *Proust*, 58). Echoing this, the narrator of *Texts for Nothing* asks, "[h]ow is it that nothing is ever here and now?", and, again: "What elsewhere can there be to this infinite here?" (25, 26). In a highly significant move, the passage from Proust's *Recherche* that Beckett earlier read from a temporocentrist perspective is transformed in *Texts for Nothing* into spatial terms.

There is still another key instance where Beckett's earlier temporocentrism leads him to overlook a conception of place in Proust's work, one close to that which will appear in his own postwar work. Mentioned above is the passage in which Proust says that knowledge of *where one is* is vital to a sense of *who one is*. If we look at the passage in its context, we see that it supplies a key image for Beckett's later work.

> ... when I woke in the middle of the night, not knowing where I was, I could not even be sure at first who I was; I had only the most rudimentary sense of existence, such as may lurk and flicker in the depths of an animal's consciousness; I was more destitute than the cave-dweller; but then the memory—not yet of the place in which I was, but of various other places where I had lived and might now very possibly be—would come like a rope let down from heaven to draw me up out of the abyss of not-being. (*Remembrance*, 5–6)

The image of waking without knowing at first to what, and groping to find out where (and thereby who) one is appears in "Ceiling" (written in 1981). In a passage which has clear echoes of the above excerpt, the narrator has

> No knowledge of where gone from. Nor of how. Nor of whom. None of whence come to. Partly to. Nor of how. Nor of whom. None of anything. Save dimly of having come to. Partly to. With dread of being again.[60]

In both *Remembrance of Things Past* and "Ceiling," a lack of knowledge about one's location is bound up with a lack of knowledge about one's identity: command of place seems to go hand-in-hand with command of the environment. Significantly, this passage is not marked in Beckett's copy of the novel—indicating that Beckett's later work comes to a more nuanced understanding of Proust's thought than that presented in his 1930 monograph. Importantly this is an understanding that moves him far away from any sympathy with Bergson. Indeed, it moves him towards the Proustian pole of the dichotomy that Burrows noted: away from Bergson's insistence on absolute

---

[60] Samuel Beckett, *Company/Ill Seen Ill Said/Worstward Ho/Stirrings Still*, edited by Dirk Van Hulle (London: Faber and Faber, 2009), 129.

time, toward *local*—emplaced—reality. It seems that just as where geometry was concerned, Beckett was a Protagorean before he was Bergsonian, where place was concerned, he was more Proustian than Bergsonian.

"Of being—or remaining": Beckett and Early Greek Philosophy

Peter Fifield (St. John's College, University of Oxford, UK)

The contours of Beckett's substantial debt to early Greek philosophy have been emerging with increasing detail for over forty years, not least spurred on by the reluctant benediction of the author himself. Offering direction to Lawrence E. Harvey in 1962, he proposed that "if he were a critic setting out to write on the works of Beckett (and he thanked heaven he was not), he would start with two quotations, one by Geulincx: 'Ubi nihil vales ibi nihil velis,' and one by Democritus: 'Nothing is more real than nothing.'"[1] He gave the same response to the enquiry of Sighle Kennedy in 1967, noting that the quotations were "both already in *Murphy* and neither very rational."[2] This has given to both Geulincx and Democritus a critical standing unlike any other figures in the field, including interpretive mainstays such as Schopenhauer, Johnson and Descartes; not only allowing scholars to work from a rich body of documentation, but to follow something like an authorial preference.

The expansion of the so-called "grey canon" has encouraged an empirical reawakening in the study of Beckett. His relationship to Greek philosophy from the seventh to the fourth century BC is central to this. The availability of the extensive "Philosophy Notes" (TCD MS 10967) in particular has issued an invitation to weigh-up existing scholarship afresh, as well as to move in new directions.[3] If many

---

[1] Lawrence E. Harvey, *Samuel Beckett: Poet and Critic* (Princeton, NJ: Princeton University Press, 1970), 267–268.

[2] Samuel Beckett, *Disjecta: Miscellaneous Writings and a Dramatic Fragment*, edited by Ruby Cohn (London: Calder, 1983), 113.

[3] Although all references are given to the manuscript numbers at Trinity College Dublin, all citations of Beckett's "Philosophy Notes" go by way of the

readings in the area have torn their insights from the jaws of an influential Cartesian view of Beckett, future readings will, I suggest, increasingly depart from the ongoing critical preference for *Murphy* and Democritus, to consider the relations of other works and thinkers. This article thus aims to demonstrate that the still unfolding richness of the empirical resources encourages both a richer empirical and thematic digestion of Beckett's works. Examination of this material reveals the nature of Beckett's engagement with early Greek philosophy as a varied and sizeable body of thinkers and texts rather than a handful of prominent figures or conceptual highlights. This essay reviews existing scholarship before considering Beckett's note-taking and a newly identified source. It then broaches an assortment of correspondences less frequently explored between Beckett's work and philosophers including Thales, Hippokrates, Parmenides and Anaximander, before considering briefly the life of the early Greeks in contemporary intellectual culture.

Traces of these philosophers can be found in the three main sets of manuscript notes from the 1930s, and indicate the depth and persistence of Beckett's interest in the area. Notes on Robert Burton's "Democritus to the Reader," from *The Anatomy of Melancholy*, which Beckett read in its entirety, can be found in the "*Dream* Notebook," notes that John Pilling dates to September 1931.[4] References derived from this source can be found in *Dream of Fair to Middling Women*, *More Pricks than Kicks* and beyond. Appearing amidst the various subjects covered in the polyglot "*Whoroscope* Notebook" (RUL MS 3000) are entries on Pythagoras, Hippasus of Croton and other Greek philosophers, which were used in the composition of *Murphy*, as well as further quotations from Burton.

---

appendix to Matthew Feldman, *"Sourcing Aporetics": An Empirical Approach to the Philosophical Development of Samuel Beckett's Writings*. Unpublished PhD., Oxford Brookes University, 2004.

[4] Samuel Beckett, *Beckett's* Dream *Notebook*, edited by John Pilling (Reading: Beckett International Foundation, 1999), xviii.

Evidence of a more systematic reading program can be found in the "Interwar Notes," covering more than five hundred sides, two hundred and sixty-seven of which treat of ancient philosophy, and have become known as the "Philosophy Notes."[5] These were most likely composed between mid-1932 and mid-1934, and provide the most substantial body of notes on early Greek philosophy in the "grey canon." They are drawn principally from John Burnet's *Greek Philosophy: From Thales to Plato*, Wilhelm Windelband's *A History of Philosophy* and, to a lesser extent, Archibald Alexander's *A Short History of Philosophy*, although other sources were clearly used in a more sporadic fashion. The extent to which Beckett deviated from his two main sources, the identity of those texts, likely reasons for his doing so, and the effect on his work is only now becoming apparent.

Before considering these manuscript resources it is worth considering those critical works written before their availability to scholars. These texts thus follow Beckett's direction to consider Democritus and *Murphy*, and together form something of an interpretive "pseudocouple" in their own right. Alice and Kenneth Hamilton's book *Condemned to Life*, which includes their essay "The Guffaw of the Abderite: Samuel Beckett's Use of Democritus," consider Democritus' relevance to a selection of works including *More Pricks than Kicks*, "Enueg I" and, most substantially, *Murphy*. The congruence includes anecdotal similarities between the philosopher and various characters in Beckett's *oeuvre*, as well as the illustration of an assortment of Democritean tenets, including the unreliability of the senses, and the belief that bestowed the title of the "laughing philosopher," whereby "cheerfulness must arise from within us and have its source in indifference to outward misfortune."[6]

Sylvie Debevec Henning's similarly-titled "The Guffaw of the Abderite: *Murphy* and the Democritean Universe" sees *Murphy* as a

---

[5] Matthew Feldman, *Beckett's Books: A Cultural History of Samuel Beckett's "Interwar Notes"* (London: Continuum, 2006).

[6] Alice and Kenneth Hamilton, "The Guffaw of the Abderite: Samuel Beckett's Use of Democritus," *Mosaic* 9/2 (1976), 5.

Menippean satire of philosophy, rather than a philosophy *per se*; a "farrago of philosophical systems"[7] as opposed to an illustration of a particular metaphysics. The object of this satire is no individual philosopher but "monism" more widely, whose perpetrators include Parmenides and Leibniz. Opposing "the belief in the possibility of ultimate totalization and identity" (5), Henning argues that, in *Murphy*, "Democritean Atomism thwarts any attempt to synthesize the dyad or make its elements completely complementary" (7). Democritus is the figure alongside whom Beckett works to "accommodate the mess,"[8] in defiance of diverse systems that seek to neutralize, expel or deny the chaotic.

C.J. Ackerley's annotations to *Murphy*, entitled *Demented Particulars* (1998, rev. 2004), show the almost incalculable richness of reference to the philosophers, and again afford Democritus some prominence. He casts the Greek philosophers in a particularly important role in *Murphy*, where the Atomists are the "microbes in the [Cartesian] ointment."[9] Ackerley affords these intruders the novel's literal last laugh, stating that the "end of *Murphy* is a huge Democritean guffaw" (19), and follows Henning by suggesting that "Beckett found in the Atomists (Leucippus, Democritus, Epicurus and Lucretius) an ironic anticipation" of a world chaotic, "unclear and indistinct—in a word, absurd" (18). In the course of his annotations Ackerley also enumerates the particularly extensive debt to Pythagoras and his disciples, the most prominent gesture to which is Neary's Pythagorean Academy in Cork, of which Murphy is a former pupil.

David H. Hesla's *The Shape of Chaos* employs ancient philosophers in a more diffuse fashion, supplying chapter epigraphs from a variety of figures, including Empedocles and the source text of Diogenes Laertius' *Lives of Eminent Philosophers*. These and others take

---

[7] Sylvie Debevec Henning, "The Guffaw of the Abderite: *Murphy* and the Democritean Universe," *Journal of Beckett Studies* 10 (1983), 20.

[8] Lawrence Graver and Raymond Federman, eds., *Samuel Beckett: The Critical Heritage* (London: Routledge and Kegan Paul Ltd., 1997), 219.

[9] C.J. Ackerley, *Demented Particulars: The Annotated* Murphy (Tallahassee, FL: Journal of Beckett Studies Books, 2004), 21.

their place within a reading of Beckett's work that draws substantially on the history of philosophy, with the earliest philosophers taking an important position. Hesla's versatile reading sees Beckett inhabiting the spirit of early Greek philosophy as Beckett's "art is a Democritean art, energized precisely by the interplay of opposites—body and mind, the self and the other, speech and silence, life and death, hope and despair, being and non-being, yes and no."[10] Bearing in mind the appreciation of the broader philosophical narrative it is with some frustration that we might see the recourse to Democritus again, especially considering the enduring currency of oppositional thought among the Greek philosophers. It is with the benefit of hindsight that we can now see that Beckett included such lists of binary terms not in his notes on Democritus but on the Eleatics and the Pythagoreans.

Moving into studies that make explicit use of the "Philosophy Notes," in "'Gnawing to be Naught': Beckett and Pre-Socratic Nihilism"[11] Shane Weller conducts a re-examination of Beckett's engagement with nihilism and the nothing in the light of his notes of the 1930s, unavailable to previous commentators on the subject. Concentrating on *Worstward Ho* and, of course, *Murphy*, he stresses the importance of Archibald Alexander's particular translation of Democritus' "Naught is more real than nothing,"[12] the interplay between "naught" and "nothing" giving so much material to Beckett's explorations of negation. Opening one of the many underexamined relations, Weller goes on to consider the importance of the Sophist Gorgias of Leontini. Beckett's denial of the charge of nihilism to Goffried Büttner is pitted against his debt to the "cosmological" nihilism of Gorgias' three-pronged attack on the possibility of existence,

---

[10] David H. Hesla, *The Shape of Chaos: An Interpretation of the Art of Samuel Beckett* (Minneapolis, MN: University of Minnesota Press, 1971), 10–11.

[11] Shane Weller, "'Gnawing to be Naught': Beckett and Pre-Socratic Nihilism," in Matthijs Engelberts, Danièle de Ruyter, Karine Germoni and Helen Penet-Astbury, eds., *Des éléments aux traces/Elements and Traces. Samuel Beckett Today/Aujourd'hui* 20 (2008): 321–33.

[12] Archibald B. D. Alexander, *A Short History of Philosophy* (Glasgow: Maclehose, Jackson & Sons, 1907), 39.

knowledge and communication. Weller situates Beckett as nihilism's fellow-traveller rather than devotee, led by its "Pre-Socratic" manifestations.

And finally, in *Beckett's Books* Matthew Feldman surveys a large quantity of empirical material on Greek philosophy, including that behind *Murphy*, adding his weight to the theses of "Mooney, Henning and the Hamiltons [who] are more right than they know: *Murphy* is much less a Cartesian novel than a Presocratic one," refining this to "a Democritean one shaped by Beckett's notes."[13] He also traces Democritus' presence through a wide range of other works, from *Malone Dies* to *The Lost Ones*, but, significantly, demurs from the suggestion that Beckett is "obsessed by Democritus" (62), demonstrating the extensive use of Heraclitean and Pythagorean philosophy in *Murphy*. He also advances the more significant—and more nebulous—idea of "Beckett's *general* indebtedness to philosophical themes and debates, as opposed to defining his artistic evolution by virtue of one philosopher or movement" (66).

At this point, a note must be made here on convention. This article consciously departs from the habit, near universal in Beckett studies, of referring to the early Greek philosophers as the "Presocratics." This is for two significant reasons. The first is the difficulty of providing a definition of what constitutes "Presocratic." As is habitually observed by classical scholars, the grouping implies a chronological boundary that is not obeyed by the usual selection of "Presocratic" philosophers, which includes figures contemporary to and longer-lived than Socrates, such as Democritus. Do the Sophists belong in this group? The whole debate is beyond the task of this essay, but may be sidestepped by avoiding the term entirely. More significant for this article, Beckett's own sources barely use the term: Alexander and Windelband use it once each and it is never used by Burnet. In Beckett's other established sources it is not used above half a dozen times. If empirical research can teach us at least one thing here, it would be to pay attention to the detail of Hamm's lacunar reference

---

[13] Feldman, *Beckett's Books*, 59.

to "that old Greek,"[14] who was for Beckett precisely an "old Greek" rather than a Presocratic. Dispensing with this term eases the question of definition, as Beckett follows the structure and groupings of his various sources, including Alexander, Windelband and others. His "Philosophy Notes" on the early Greeks thus run from Thales of Miletus to Democritus of Abdera and Plato. They cover the major "schools" of the ancient Greek Mediterranean settlements, including the Milesians, Pythagoreans, Eleatics, Pluralists, Atomists, Sophists and Cynics. These are the terms used by Beckett throughout the notes, and the ones that should guide future readings of Beckett and early philosophy. Discussing the thinkers as a group, the term "early Greek philosophers" provides an openness suited to a group of thinkers whose interests include poetry, astronomy, astrology, medicine, ethics, metaphysics, religion, the afterlife, politics and general conduct, and who stretch over several centuries.

Having gestured toward the substantial body of commentary on both *Murphy* and Democritus, it is important to consider other facets of Beckett's Greek connections. This is neither to challenge nor to dismiss the superlative importance of Beckett's early novel as a "laboratory of ideas,"[15] nor to evict Democritus from his central position, but to address some of Beckett's less sustained, and less examined, engagements with Greek philosophy. For what much writing on Beckett and the early Greek philosophers has done—and not without significant merit—is seek a coherent theoretical account, whether from manuscript evidence or more intuitively, of Beckett's writing that necessarily excludes the more idiosyncratic and incidental use of their writings. In doing so, Beckett studies has itself adopted a method common to most commentators on the philosophers, including Beckett's own sources. The synthetic tradition in philosophical interpretation is lengthy and hardwearing, and ties centuries of diverse

---

[14] Samuel Beckett, *Endgame*, preface by Rónán McDonald (London: Faber and Faber, 2009), 42.
[15] Feldman, *Beckett's Books*, 67.

Greek philosophy into a single, enduring quest for the *Weltstoff*; the very notion that heads and organizes Beckett's "Philosophy Notes."

The true texture of early Greek philosophy, it ought to be recalled, is rather more like Beckett's reading notes themselves. It is a patchwork of secondary sources within which anecdote and doctrine jostle, the essential and incidental become indistinguishable, major sources are joined by minor ones, all while the particular compiler acts to select, frame and represent his sources according to a singular purpose and context. That early Greek philosophy is almost exclusively reconstructed from fragments, reportage, or imaginative—as well as interested—projections such as those in Plato's dialogues, sits at odds with the taste for coherence native to academia. To reflect this fundamental aspect of these sources, we may consider the persistence of the fragment form itself in Beckett's corpus to be one of the most striking inheritances from the Greeks. To consider merely the titles that allude to an incomplete form, one can list the "Rough for Theatre" (*"Fragment de théâtre"*) and "Rough for Radio" pieces, the *Foirades* (*Fizzles*), the *"mirlitonnades," Ends and Odds*, and the various abandoned works, published or otherwise. Alternatively, we may consider the descent of the philosophical "fragment" in its more usual sense of citation, so that the beliefs of Thales are preserved as fragments quoted in Aristotle. This economy of reference recalls Beckett's *How It Is,* which is made of ambiguous quotations: "I quote [...] I say it as I hear it"[16]—the boundaries and origins of which are ambiguous, just as is normally the case in the classical sources themselves. At the very least, this article seeks to indicate some of the variety and unpredictability in Beckett's philosophical debts. Beckett is no more a devotee of Thales than he is of Leucippus, Hippokrates, or Democritus and yet he draws on these and many others in his writing.

Turning to the "Philosophy Notes" themselves, it is clear that empirical and interpretive legwork remains to be done. Everett Frost and Jane Maxwell, in their catalog of the manuscripts held at Trinity

---

[16] Samuel Beckett, *How It Is,* edited by Édouard Magessa O'Reilly (London: Faber and Faber, 2009), 3.

College, Dublin, mention at least one text not treated by Feldman's rigorous *Beckett's Books*. And yet, perhaps constrained by the rubric of their task, they do not trace the impact of Friedrich Ueberweg's 1871 *History of Philosophy: From Thales to the Present Time*. It is therefore worth observing, for example, that when Dirk van Hulle recognizes in the Anaximander fragment "[a]ll things must in equity again decline into that whence they have their origin" (TCD MS 10967/7) an important pre-echo of Beckett's favored phrase "dust thou art,"[17] Beckett's source is Ueberweg's text rather than any of the better documented histories. Beckett writes,

> Primal substance the <u>Indefinite, Infinite</u>. His soul, like that of Anaximenes, aeriform. Occupies intermediate position between Thales & Anaximenes.
> 'All things must in equity again decline into that whence they have their origin, for they must give satisfaction & atonement for injustice, each in the order of time.'
> 'Definite individual existence constitutes an injustice & must be atoned for by extinction.'
> His 'infinite' as vague as Hesiod's chaos, something intermediate between water & air, or air & fire
> (TCD MS 10967/7r.)

All of these entries derive from Ueberweg, whose translation "[a]ll things must in equity again decline into that whence they have their origin" Beckett reproduces verbatim. Ueberweg goes on to note of Anaximander that "he posits a matter, undetermined in quality (and infinite in quantity) [...] Anaximander is said to have described the soul as aëriform."[18] After a discussion of determining the historical dates for Anaximander's life, where he does indeed place him between Thales and Anaximenes, he continues "([d]efinite individual existence, as such, is represented as an ἀδικία, injustice, which must

---

[17] Dirk Van Hulle, *Manuscript Genetics: Joyce's Know-How, Beckett's Nohow* (Gainsville, FL: University Press of Florida, 2008), 162.

[18] Friedrich Ueberweg, *History of Philosophy: From Thales to the Present Time*, Vol. 1: *History of the Ancient and Mediaeval Philosophy* (New York: Charles Scribner's Sons, 1889), 35.

be atoned for by extinction)" (36). This provides one of the most strikingly Beckettian phrases in the notes and it is interesting to see the intervention that slightly changes Ueberweg's expression. In place of Ueberweg's "represented," which distances the historian from his source, Beckett chooses "constitutes," as if voicing Anaximander himself. In the act of notation it appears that Beckett endorses the view that extinction is scripted into existence as a just facet of individual being. As such, it is worth returning to this quotation later.

Feldman has suggested that the "earliest of many direct borrowings taken from Beckett's notes on the history of philosophy"[19] is to be found in "Serena I." The poem's "our world dead fish adrift / all things full of gods"[20] is lifted almost directly from Beckett's notes on, appropriately, the earliest philosopher, Thales. Here they read

> His primal substance water. Earth afloat (dead fish) on surface of primal substance.
> All things are full of gods.
> (TCD MS 10967/5r.)

As Frost and Maxwell identify, this derives from Ueberweg rather than Alexander, Burnet or Windelband, and confirms his *History of Philosophy* as Beckett's first source on Thales, Anaximenes and Anaximander. Following "[a]ll things are full of gods"—also cited by Burnet—Beckett notes "[m]agnet animated because it attracts iron" (TCD MS 10967/5), which comes from Ueberweg (35), who quotes his sources with greater frequency than any of the other historians of early Greek philosophy. This habit, and the substantial scholarly apparatus detailing the sources cited, may be at the root of Beckett's use of the text while finding his bearings in the earlier part of his reading. Furthermore it is this tendency to give substantial citations that clarifies a link inexplicably missed by Frost and Maxwell. They suggest that the dead fish image of "Serena I" does not derive from either

---

[19] Feldman, *Beckett's Books*, 35.
[20] Samuel Beckett, *Selected Poems, 1930–1989*, edited by David Wheatley (London: Faber and Faber, 2009), 25.

Ueberweg or Alexander but from a still unidentified source. However, Ueberweg, whose extensive citation of Aristotle relates that Thales was "the originator of such philosophy" and who took "water for his principle" (35), which is to say his *Weltstoff*, does in fact provide the answer. He goes on to say that "Aristotle reports that Thales represented the earth as floating on the water. It is possible that the geognostic observations (as of sea-shells in mountains) also lay at the bottom of Thales' doctrine" (34). Beckett's dead fish, on source evidence, is therefore a sea-shell.[21]

This discovery opens a certain ambiguity between manuscript- and publication-based readings of "Serena I." Based on the source, Beckett's dead fish would unmistakably be the remains of marine crustaceans found in the mountains due to tectonic movements and, one assumes, thought by Thales to have been transferred by the currents presumably flowing between the world-water and its supporting fluid. But even in identifying this point of origin, this remains a less convincing reading than the more obvious use of a dead fish as a metaphor for the world afloat. While the obscurity of the sea-shell image certainly chimes with the allusiveness and difficulty of Beckett's poetry at this period, it does not have the clarity or vividness of the im-

---

[21] The true extent to which Beckett makes use of Ueberweg's work is beyond the scope and purpose of this essay and indicates the substantial work still to be done in this area. It seems likely, I suggest, that Beckett was still using this text later in his reading as an occasional point of reference. Collecting information on the Cynic Antisthenes of Athens, for example, he begins with the description of him as the "Rousseau of antiquity" (TCD MS 10967/67). With no such suggestions in Alexander, Windelband or Burnet, we might consider the claim of Ueberweg, who, in his chapter on Antisthenes, relates that "[h]e demands that men return to the simplicity of a natural state" (93), and trumpets the philosopher's supreme belief in man's virtue. Intriguingly, when Ueberweg moves on to a description of Antisthenes' Cynical accomplice, Diogenes of Sinope—still under the heading of Antisthenes—he notes "[a]s tutor of the sons of Xeniades, at Corinth, he proceeded not without skill, on the principle of conformity to nature, in a manner similar to that demanded in modern times by Rousseau" (94). If this is the source for this note, it appears to be an error on Beckett's part, attributing to Antisthenes what Ueberweg states of Diogenes.

age of the world as a lifeless creature, which itself possesses a certain liquid appearance. The play of light on the scales of a dead fish, its smooth lines and curves, suggest a fluidity of movement—even in death—and implies a unity of substance between the world and its supporting medium; a unity not evoked by the calcitic solidity of the shell embedded in mountain rock. This does, however, draw attention to the question of Beckett's specifically *poetic* activity with regard to the composition of "Serena I." For while the image is, in a certain sense, drawn directly from Ueberweg, Beckett's note-taking has introduced an important degree of ambiguity; the latter perhaps noticing that the Aristotelian "evidence" for the world's being afloat is also its image-in-waiting.

This is consonant with other examples from the notes, where Beckett's note-taking, so often performed verbatim from the source text, introduces a foreign element. On several occasions, like the example above, Beckett sees fit to deploy the briefest of images that are not to be found in any of his identified source texts. Thus, on Anaximenes, Beckett writes, "[e]arth born aloft like a leaf or a bird on primal substance. Earth breathing. Soul is air. His earth flat & round like a plate" (TCD MS 10967/6r). The image of the planet breathing derives from Alexander, who writes that "[t]he world is a huge animal which breathes just as man does" (Alexander, 16) and the plate comes from Ueberweg, who writes "[t]he earth, which is flat and round like a plate, is supported by the air" (37). But the other images—the leaf and bird—appear to be Beckett's own. Similarly, when Beckett notes Anaximander's belief in a plurality of worlds, he alters Burnet, who has "[e]ach world is a sort of vortex in a boundless mass,"[22] to "bubbles in the boundless mass" (TCD MS 10967/7r). These are, in themselves, tiny alterations amidst a body of notes that follow the source texts faithfully for page upon page. Yet they do affect our understanding of Beckett's note-taking. These show that, rather than the persistence of word-perfect transcription indicative of "academic habits of

---

[22] John Burnet, *Greek Philosophy, Part I: Thales to Plato* (London: Macmillan, 1914), 23.

mind,"[23] Beckett's most systematic reading also had a distinctly writerly dimension, no matter how modest in scope. This recasts the notebook as an imaginative, perhaps even a compositional space, as well as one in which Beckett could exercise "the old demon of notesnatching."[24]

In a similar manner, Beckett repeatedly takes visible pleasure in turns of phrase used by his sources, noticing, for example, that Burnet's style has a dryly humorous tone quite different from that of Windelband. Thus Beckett switches round—whether by accident or design is unclear—Burnet's wry comment on Thales' floating-earth doctrine, "[i]t was something to get the earth afloat" (21), to "[t]o get the earth afloat was something" (TCD MS 10967/5r). More convincingly, Thales' renunciation of worldly wealth by means of predicting the harvest is taken from Burnet's "[h]e is said to have foreseen an abundance of olives and made a corner in oil" (18), and turned into "[f]oresaw a scarcity in olives and made a corner in oil" (TCD MS 10967/5r). Retaining Burnet's elegant phrase, with its hints of colloquialism, Beckett, in contrast to both Burnet and his source, Diogenes Laertius' *Lives of Eminent Philosophers*, sees a shortage where there was an alleged glut. Logically speaking, either situation would allow an enterprising citizen to make a lot of money. Thus Beckett is not rectifying or introducing an error but apparently expressing a certain preference for lack above abundance. While the phrase does not feed into his published works as such, it represents a neat presentiment of the later, and iconically Beckettian, art of negation in the midst of a body of notes which themselves suggest an aesthetic of unrestrained accumulation.

Beckett's tendency to move between verbatim transcription, such as the swathes of Burnet and Windelband, and a more creative or synthetic use of the texts also makes the establishment of his

---

[23] John Pilling, "From a (W)horoscope to *Murphy*," in John Pilling and Mary Bryden, eds., *The Ideal Core of the Onion: Reading Beckett Archives* (Reading: Beckett International Foundation, 1992), 19.

[24] Beckett, *Beckett's* Dream *Notebook*, xiii.

sources more difficult, although by no means impossible. For example, the previously unidentified source for Beckett's initial notes on Zeno (TCD MS 10967/14r - 10967/15v) is Johann Eduard Erdmann's 1866 *History of Philosophy* Vol. 1 *Ancient and Mediaeval Philosophy*. Beckett begins by noting that Zeno is:

The Diogenes of Eleaticism, in sense that he is its apologist. Inventor of dialectic of negation, disproof by reduction ad absurdum.

> Considers Plurality, Becoming, & Motion in antithesis to Unity, Being, Persistence, & exposes contradictions inherent in ["latter" scored through] former concepts, in the celebrated fallacies:
> 1. Race between Achilles (Hound) and Hector (Tortoise). Relying on infinite subdivision of space.
> 2. Flying arrow always in state of rest. Relying on successive occupations of points in space.
> 3. Impossibility of plurality. Relying on sum of unities having no quantity.
> (TCD MS 10967/14r.)

With a little reworking by Beckett, these notes derive from Erdmann, who writes "the perfection of the formal side of his philosophizing, which makes Zeno into the Diogenes of Apollonia of his school."[25] He goes on to observe that "he is the inventor of dialectic as the art of discovering contradictions; but ... his dialectic only leads to negative results" (44). Supplying a little context for Zeno's thought, Erdmann writes that "[w]hile Parmenides had only attributed truth to the Unity excluding all Plurality, the Being negating all Becoming, the Persistent devoid of all Motion, Zeno's aim is rather to show that all who assume Plurality, Becoming and Motion involve themselves in contradictions" (45). On this point, it is interesting to notice that Erdmann's clarity is fudged by Beckett who, in removing the association of the former properties with Parmenides, mistakes them for Zeno's before correcting his error.

---

[25] Johann Eduard Erdmann, *History of Philosophy*. Vol. I *Ancient and Mediaeval Philosophy*, translated by Williston S. Hough. (London: Swan Sonnenschein & Co., 1890), 44.

Although Beckett's numbering departs from that on Erdmann's list of fallacies, it is clearly his source. Erdmann writes,

> Of the four proofs of this which Aristotle mentions as due to Zeno, the first two again rest upon the infinity produced by the infinite divisibility, in the one case of the space to be passed through, and in the other of the start which Hector (or the tortoise) has as regards Achilles (or the hound). The third proof first takes for granted that the flying arrow at every moment is at a point (i.e. at rest), and then draws from this the inevitable conclusions.
> (45)

The identification of Hector with the tortoise and Achilles as the hound is a curious one, and an explicit identifying marker for Erdmann's text. In relating the paradox in question, Aristotle mentions neither Hector nor a hound, nor even a tortoise, while the inclusion of the first two elements in the tale is equally novel among philosophical commentaries on the early Greeks. The final version of the paradox condenses a broader description of Zeno's challenge to the notion of plurality, which must, Erdmann asserts, rest upon a contradiction. He writes that the proof for this

> consists in showing that on the supposition of the reality of plurality one and the same thing would be definite and yet indefinite, and rests upon the fact that all plurality is a definite thing, i.e. number, and yet contains an infinity i.e. of fractions. […] The Many, too, would be infinitely great as containing an infinite number of things, and at the same time infinitely small, as consisting of nothing but infinitely minute particles.
> (45)

A substantial distilling process is brought to bear on Erdmann here, but taken together these examples are highly significant. For this is the earliest version in Beckett's notes of the paradoxical thought that later features in *Endgame*, which disputes the possibility of completion: "Finished, it's finished, nearly finished, it must be nearly finished. [*Pause.*] Grain upon grain, one by one, and one day, suddenly, there's a heap, a little heap, the impossible heap" (6). This would, as Ackerley points out in *The Grove Companion to Samuel Beckett*, find precise expression in Windelband's allusion to the sorites paradox of Eubulides of Miletus—"Which kernel of grain by being added makes the heap? Which hair falling out makes the bald head?"[26] But Beckett, following Windelband (89), claims Zeno as the origin of all of these infinity-based paradoxes: "Euclid's adherents Eubulides and Alexinus were famous for a series of such catches, among which the Heap (which kernel of grain by being added makes the heap?) and the Baldhead (which hair falling out makes the head bald?), were fundamental thought [*sic*] far back to Zeno, who used it to [prove—added above] that the composition of magnitudes out of small parts is impossible" (TCD MS 10967/42). As such, if Ackerley is right that "[t]he philosopher is less important than the paradox,"[27] it is significant to note that Beckett's first extant reference to these paradoxes derives from Erdmann.[28]

Turning toward Beckett's published writing, it is clear that he continued to use his notes on Greek philosophy after 1945, a period often understood to be marked by his removal of specific references to other texts. Yet some references remain explicit, such as the comment by the narrator of "The Expelled," who asks, "[w]ould you like me, I said, without thinking for a single moment of Heraclitus, to get down in the gutter?"[29] This comes from Beckett's "Philosophy

---

[26] Wilhelm Windelband, *A History of Philosophy*, translated by James H. Tufts (New York: Macmillan, 1901), 89.

[27] C.J. Ackerley and S.E. Gontarski, *The Grove Companion to Samuel Beckett* (New York: Grove Press, 2004), 661.

[28] The role that Erdmann's text played in Beckett's "notesnatching," like that of Ueberweg, is difficult to measure. It is highly likely that it was used in conjunction with Alexander to compile the organizing structure that heads the philosophy notes themselves. Cross referencing the contents pages of the two texts, Beckett produces a synthesis that combines the three sections of Alexander—Physical World, Moral Period and Systematic Period—with distinctive references to the "Pure Physiologers" (Erdmann, xviii), and groupings close to those in Erdmann.

[29] Samuel Beckett, *The Expelled/The Calmative/The End & First Love*, edited by Christopher Ricks (London: Faber and Faber, 2009), 8.

Notes," where the author follows Ueberweg's "[w]e step down a second time into the same stream and yet not into the same" (38). Thus, rather than the more familiar step *into* the stream, for Beckett's Heraclitus "it is not possible to step *down* twice into the same stream" (TCD MS 10967/24; emphasis added). As such, the parallel that Beckett draws in his 1946 short story depends upon the particular formulation in Ueberweg's syntheses, with their felicitous spatial arrangement, as much as on the ideas of Heraclitus themselves.

There are less prominent allusions to be found also. For example, in *The Unnamable*, the narrator's lament that "I alone am man and all the rest divine"[30] is a direct challenge to Hippokrates' statement, related by Burnet and noted by Beckett: "Nothing is more divine or human than anything else, but all things are alike and all divine" (Burnet, 33/TCD MS 10967/8.1). Unlike the 1932 "Serena I," the original note is transcribed accurately from Burnet but contested by Beckett much later; during the composition of *The Unnamable* in 1949–1950. This observation questions the pantheism—or "polite atheism" (Burnet, 33)—of the Orphic religion; a faith consonant with the Thales quotation from "Serena I" that "all things full of gods" (Burnet, 33). A belief in the transmigration of souls, whereby each soul works toward escape from embodiment into eternal, godly existence suggests "that all creatures were fundamentally the same in kind, inasmuch as they are hosts to the same souls."[31] For the Unnamable to assert his exception from this system is not to critique Orphicism as such, but to render it the very vehicle for his sufferings. The process of climbing through embodiment would posit an eventual liberation from that condition, whereas the Unnamable is a thing set apart from this all-embracing divinity. Indeed, the Unnamable's uncertainty about his embodiment—"I don't feel a mouth on me, nor a head, do I feel an ear, frankly now, do I feel an ear" (*The Unnamable*, 100)—

---

[30] Samuel Beckett, *The Unnamable*, edited by Steven Connor (London: Faber and Faber, 2010), 10.
[31] Jonathan Barnes, *Early Greek Philosophy* (Harmondsworth: Penguin, 1987), 37.

indicates his uneasy position somewhere between embodied and disembodied experience. The inability of the novel's narrator to maintain a single identity, shifting between ever more tortured avatars, means that the system of death and rebirth, which would bring elevation and eventual release, is closed to him. Neither alive nor dead, this is, at times, a question of some complexity, demanding external verification.

> That qua sentient and thinking being I should be going downhill fast is in any case an excellent thing. Perhaps some day some gentleman, chancing to pass my way with his sweetheart on his arm, at the precise moment when my last is favouring me with a final smack of the flight of time, will exclaim, loud enough for me to hear, Oh I say, this man is ailing, we must call an ambulance! Thus with a single stone, when all hope seemed lost, the two rare birds. I shall be dead, but I shall have lived [...] (56)

Held apart from the structured world of embodiment, life, death and metempsychosis, such reason would not itself be sealed against the efforts of the Unnamable's determined skeptic, whether Greek or Cartesian. The chance remains, as the narrator is keen to point out, that the gentleman may be the "victim of a hallucination" (56). This, then, might be seen as the other side to Anaximander's "[d]efinite individual existence constitutes an injustice & must be atoned for by extinction" (TCD MS 10967/7); for the Unnamable—for the most part—has no such distinct being, and no assurance of eventual death.

This direct reference is followed by a more general evocation of philosophical enquiry as to the nature of the primal substance, so that *The Unnamable*'s narrator turns to a prime candidate for the *Weltstoff*, asking: "Air, the air, is there anything to be squeezed from that old chestnut?" (10). Bringing an empirical bent to the enquiry, he is keen to test whether apparently denser air in the distance is "in reality [...] the enclosure wall, as compact as lead" (11). Acquiring a stick, "I would dart it, like a javelin, straight before me and know, by the sound made, whether that which hems me round, and blots out my world, is the old void, or a plenum" (11); those two well-used terms in Greek philosophy and in Beckett alike.

Places where the influence of the ancient Greeks can be felt in spirit more than in letter include *Krapp's Last Tape*. When consulting the dictionary for "viduity" Krapp reads: "State—or condition—of being—or remaining—a widow—or widower."[32] Holding his attention first of all are the verbs used: "[*Looks up. Puzzled.*] Being—or remaining?" (7). The weight of the concept of existence appears to strike Krapp still more sharply than any characteristic dependent upon that Being, even the curious ornithological association with the "vidua-bird." The question of permanence and change strung between "being" and "remaining" is a long-lived philosophical preoccupation. Indeed, Krapp's puzzlement can be set usefully alongside Parmenidean logic, where Being is "a self-evident postulate [but] Non-being cannot be and cannot be thought" (TCD MS 10967/11r). As such, for Parmenides, Being is "homogenous, without beginning or end, unchangeable, complete, limited and definitive" (TCD MS 10967/11r). From this perspective, therefore, the conditions of being and remaining would be identical for Parmenides; change impossible, and a plurality of existents "scarcely even an illusion" (TCD MS 10967/12v) masking the uninterrupted unity of everything.

If such a world-view speaks to Krapp's puzzlement, it is at an ambiguous remove. On the one hand we might see Krapp as evidence of the inevitability of change, whereby the tapes give evidence of his aging, disappointment and decline. On the other, such change might also be understood as mere illusion, in both a strong Parmenidean and a weaker, metatheatrical, sense. In the case of the latter, it must be remembered that the audience is faced with a scenario that represents change as an illusion achieved with the stagecraft of pre-prepared vocal agility, make-up and acting prowess: there is no true change, but only an apparent one. But in a stronger sense, independent of theatrical trickery, we may also observe that the drama functions by assum-

---

[32] Samuel Beckett, *Krapp's Last Tape and Other Shorter Plays*, preface by S.E. Gontarski (London: Faber and Faber, 2009), 7.

ing an instantly recognizable unity between the recorded and the visible Krapp. That is, for all of the change in the timbre of the voice, the stage is the space where all change is resolved into identity; these are shown to be aspects of the fixed substance present on stage.

Thinking of other approaches, one might also consider the claims of early Greek thought upon the Trilogy's very rhetoric of contradiction—"affirmations and negations invalidated as uttered" (*The Unnamable*, 1)—which finds its echo, as Feldman argues, in the oppositional world-view of various Greek philosophers. Beckett tabulates extensive sets of opposing concepts in Pythagoras and Empedocles, including Limited and Non-limited, Odd and Even, Light and Darkness, and Feldman is certainly correct in suggesting that such structures are "ill-suited to Cartesian mind-body interactions" and ought instead "to be subsumed into that larger dialectical thinking first advanced by the Presocratics" (*Beckett's Books*, 72–73). While the transit from oppositional states to the rhetoric of contradiction might be contested, Feldman's wider assertion draws our attention toward the explicit use of such oppositional structures within Beckett's *oeuvre*.

In looking to the "closed space" prose pieces, such as *All Strange Away* and "Imagination Dead Imagine," a more literal depiction of these competitions between opposing forces can be observed. The periodic but measured shifts in the enclosed environments appear to be governed by a logic of necessity consonant with the world-view of a number of the early Greek philosophers.

> Emptiness, silence, heat, whiteness, wait, the light goes down, all grows dark together, ground, wall, vault, bodies, say twenty seconds, all the greys, the light goes out, all vanishes. At the same time the temperature goes down, to reach its minimum, say freezing-point, at the same instant that the black is reached, which may seem strange.[33]

---

[33] Samuel Beckett, "Imagination Dead Imagine," in *Texts for Nothing and Other Shorter Prose, 1950–1976*, edited by Mark Nixon (London: Faber and Faber, 2010), 87.

The distinctive rotunda of "Imagination Dead Imagine" subsequently makes the return journey to settle momentarily back at white and heat, as if to equalize its venture. Although we are told that the "extremes alone are stable" (88), they are not so stable that the site fails to make its periodic passage between these two polar conditions. Unpredictability enters the system only in the pattern of transition: the "variations of rise and fall, combining in countless rhythms" (88). This recalls the battle of oppositions that Beckett notes of the Eleatic and Pythagorean philosophers, but may again be seen to relate to the judicial logic advanced by Anaximander noted above. For within these shifting conditions—indefinite if not infinite as Anaximander asserts of the *Weltstoff*—the two figures have a form that "[s]weat and mirror not withstanding [...] might well pass for inanimate but for the left eyes" (89). Instead of joining the all-changing constitution of their abode, becoming part of indefinite being, they are distinct from it: "Between their absolute stillness and the convulsive light the contrast is striking" (89). Indeed, the recognition of their sweating and breathing asserts a certain resistance to the forces of change that characterize their environment. Thus, instead of becoming wholly one with this shifting system they emerge from it as inhabitants, as definite beings in an environment of unpredictable and inhospitable flux. The price of such emergence from the swamp of the indefinite, however, is eventual elimination. Thus, where the narrator of "Imagination Dead Imagine" intends to "[l]eave them there, sweating and icy" preferring the "better elsewhere" (89), he decides instead that "life ends and no, there is nothing elsewhere" (89). Instead of life continuing infinitely within an equally endless space, the fact of their living demands an active limit on both duration and extension. That is to say, the possibility of delivering even the briefest of narrations of two such living creatures appears to be predicated upon their inevitable elimination and the circumscription of their residence. Viewed in this way, the logic of "Imagination Dead Imagine" is governed by an Anaximandrean logic, which finds its final cause in a notion of justice, whereby "[d]efinite individual existence constitutes an injustice

& must be atoned for by extinction" (TCD MS 10967/7r). Considered in this manner, the justice of suffering and death may be based upon the oppositional metaphysics of early Greek philosophy just as much as the Judeo-Christian and psychoanalytic rationales that have been previously advanced in Beckett studies.[34]

Beckett's debt to early Greek philosophy is extensive in depth and range. References can be found from *Dream of Fair to Middling Women*, written in the summer of 1932, to *Ill Seen Ill Said*, published in 1981; from Thales of Miletus (c. 624 BC-546 BC) to Diogenes of Sinope (412 BC-323 BC). This system of reference is supplemented by the openness to philosophical reading of Beckett's writing, as has been abundantly demonstrated with existentialism, phenomenology and poststructuralism, but which equally invites interpretation based on atomism, Eleaticism and Pythagoreanism. Beckett's proximity to the continental tradition has also, however, posed a query for Greek philosophical readings. Quotations such as *The Unnamable*'s "all their balls about being and existing" (63), as Feldman points out, may be assumed to refer to the distinction drawn by the contemporary phenomenologies of Martin Heidegger and Jean-Paul Sartre or the philosophy of the early Greek thinkers.[35] Without being able to resolve this particular debate, it is essential to note the significance of the Greek thinkers in either case. Twentieth-century phenomenology, with its focus on questions of being and existence, was born of the work of Hegel, Nietzsche and Heidegger, all of whom were also animated by readings of early Greek philosophy. Indeed, Heidegger saw the turn to the question of being as a recovery of the early Greek philosophical tradition, which had been abandoned, damaged or obscured by later thinkers. If *The Unnamable*'s interest in being and ex-

---

[34] For an account of the latter variety, see Erik Tonning, *Samuel Beckett's Abstract Drama: Works for Stage and Screen, 1962–1985* (Bern: Peter Lang, 2007), 141.

[35] Matthew Feldman, "Returning to Beckett Returning to the Presocratics, or, 'All their balls about being and existing'" *Genetic Joyce Studies* 6 (Spring, 2006), available at www.antwerpjamesjoycecenter.com/GJS6/GJS6Feldman.htm.

isting rings out most clearly as a reference to the continental philosophy of the period, this is because those works are themselves conscious echoes of Parmenides, Anaximander and Heraclitus. Thus, in Heidegger's *Introduction to Metaphysics*, first published in 1935, and reissued in 1953, the same year as Beckett's *L'Innommable*, he would extol the supreme virtue of Parmenides' writing:

> What we still possess of Parmenides' didactic poem fits into one slim volume, one that discredits the presumed necessity of entire libraries of philosophical literature. Anyone today who is acquainted with the standards of such a thinking discourse must lose all desire to write books.[36]

Beckett's reference in *The Unnamable*, alongside other such ambiguous allusions, belongs to its own time precisely insofar as early Greek thought wielded renewed influence on philosophy and literature. Presenting the poem of Parmenides, who lived in the early fifth century BC, as the essence of contemporary philosophy is as dynamic a move on Heidegger's part as the acknowledgement of "[a]ll their balls" by Beckett. Seen in this light, moreover, the reawakening of Beckett's "old Greeks" constitutes not only a central strand of Beckett's aesthetic, but an animating force in a broader intellectual current. Indeed, it is this most ancient of Beckett's debts that characterizes and propels his modernity.

---

[36] Martin Heidegger, *Introduction to Metaphysics*, translated by Gregory Fried and Richard Polt (New Haven, CT: Yale University Press, 2000), 102.

Samuel Beckett, Wilhelm Windelband and Nominalist Philosophy

Matthew Feldman (Teesside University, UK)[1]

§1

I know of no work that presents so clearly in their succession the main problems of past thought, or brings out so connectedly and concentratedly the preparation that was made by the ancient philosophy for the introduction of Christianity, or that exhibits more justly the relations between it and the Christian thought of the first Christian centuries. It is gratifying to follow a writer so thoroughly imbued with the principles of his own science, and so controlled by them, and who recognizes […] the progress of philosophy, and who does not claim for the latter more than its just due in the shaping of ecclesiastical dogmas. The book deserves the attention of all who would learn how thought has come to be what it is, and who would themselves "learn to think".

– 1893 review of *A History of Philosophy*[2]

---

[1] I am grateful to the Bergen Research Foundation and the University of Bergen, Norway, for a Senior Research Fellowship with the 'Modernism and Christianity' project facilitating the completion of this text. I also gratefully acknowledge permission to quote from Samuel Beckett's "Interwar Notes" from Mr Edward Beckett, the Estate of Samuel Beckett, and the Beckett International Foundation at the University of Reading, UK. Portions of this text were first presented at the June 2011 "Samuel Beckett: Out of the Archive" conference at the University of York; I am grateful to the conference organisers, Peter Fifield, Bryan Radley and Lawrence Rainey, for inviting me to organise the "Beckett and Philosophy" panel there, and for the helpful feedback received from delegates on my discussion of Windelband and nominalism. Finally, I would also like to extend my thanks to Erik Tonning, James Knowlson, John Pilling, and David Addyman for discussing, reading and commenting upon the ideas presented here; however, any mistakes are my own.

Professor Wilhelm Windeband's 681-page overview of Western philosophy, breathlessly endorsed in the contemporaneous review excerpted above, was not only useful to readers "who would themselves 'learn to think.'" In the case of Samuel Beckett, famously and on the contrary, his interest was nearly the opposite. Rather than knowledge, what he increasingly viewed as "the loutishness of learning"—already decried in his 1934 poem, "Gnome"—is more likely to have motivated Beckett's extensive note-taking from *A History of Philosophy* in the early 1930s.[3] In the same spirit, he informed Anne Atik some four decades later, "you have to get back to ignorance"; put another way, even at the outset of his literary career, Beckett sought to "unlearn to think."[4] Given the genocidal disasters brought about by twentieth-century thinking, to which he was an engaged and traumatized witness, Beckett's reminders of human ignorance are refreshingly heretical. However, it remains the case that both "learn[ing] to think" and "unlearning to think" necessitated a prior knowledge of Western thought. That is to say, for systematic thinking to be turned on its head in characteristically Beckettian fashion, knowledge of systematic thought—in this case, of Western philosophy from the ancient Greeks to Friedrich Nietzsche—was an essential precursor.

Whether for "learned ignorance" or in pursuit of "the progress of philosophy," it is clear above all that Beckett's engagement with, and employment of, Wilhelm Windelband was both extensive and profound. This is so much so, I want to suggest here, that the latter ought to be included in that "canon" of philosophers exerting the greatest influence upon Beckett's crucial development in the years before his postwar breakthrough. When Beckett first encountered

---

[2] Egbert C. Smyth, "Brief Notice of Important Books," in *The Andover Review: A Religious and Theological Monthly* 114 (Nov./Dec. 1893), 776.

[3] Samuel Beckett, "Gnome," in *Selected Poems: 1930–1989*, edited by David Wheatley (London, Faber and Faber: 2009), 9.

[4] Quoted in Anne Atik, *How It Was: A Memoir of Samuel Beckett* (London, Faber and Faber: 2001), 121.

Windelband in (likely) mid-to-late 1932, perhaps nowhere else were the "evolution of the ideas of European philosophy" in terms of *"the history of problems and conceptions* [....] as a connected and interrelated whole" more succinctly and accessibly presented than in *A History of Philosophy*.[5] Furthermore, many of those frequently recognized as "Beckettian" philosophers—Arnold Geulincx, Bishop Berkeley, Gottfried Leibniz and several others—were first encountered in the revised, second edition of *A History of Philosophy* from 1901. Before going on to explore some of the philosophical debts to this text, however, a moment's pause over the context and corpus of Beckett's note-taking during this period is in order.

During his years of self-education across the 1930s, Beckett took notes on a striking range of subjects. As James Knowlson's imperative biography makes plain, this was a period of dejection, directionless travel, and uncertainty. On one hand, the death of Beckett's father in June 1933 led him to two years of thrice-weekly analysis with the trainee psychotherapist Wilfred Bion between Christmastime 1933 and Christmastime 1935; but there were also panic attacks, psychosomatic illnesses, and a growing desire to leave the constraints of Ireland for the continent—or indeed anywhere, as suggested by letters to the Soviet filmmaker, Sergei Eisenstein, or applications for a lectureship in South Africa at this time.[6] Adding to Beckett's frustrations, furthermore, was a lack of success for his fiction, ranging from the failure to publish his first novel, *Dream of Fair to Middling Women* to literally dozens of rejection letters from publishers prior to Routledge's publication of *Murphy* in 1938.[7] Comparatively more successful at this time were Beckett's poems (notably the 1935 col-

---

[5] Wilhelm Windelband, *A History of Philosophy*, 2 vols., translated by James H. Tufts (New York, Harper Torchbooks: 1958), ix-x.

[6] See Samuel Beckett, *The Letters of Samuel Beckett, vol. 1: 1929–1940*, edited by Martha Dow Fehsenfeld and Lois Overbeck (Cambridge: Cambridge University Press, 2009), 317, 523–528.

[7] For insightful accounts of both of these publishing fiascos, see Mark Nixon ed., *Samuel Beckett and Publishing* (London: The British Library, 2011), especially chapters 1 and 3.

lection *Echo's Bones*) and freelance criticism (collected in the 1984 *Disjecta*), but this provided neither enough income to live on, nor enough plaudits to convince him that he was, at that time, what he was to become after 1945: a groundbreaking artist; a literary genius; and for some, the very conscience of the last century—or, to use a phrase from the 1969 Nobel Presentation Speech, "a miserere from all mankind, its muffled minor key sounding liberation to the oppressed, and comfort to those in need."[8]

Long before that infamous pessimism and stoicism earned Beckett the Nobel Prize for Literature, then, were the far less celebrated, but no less important, "years of wandering" also announced in the quatrain "Gnome." As a number of critics in Beckett Studies have established over the last generation, this period of intellectual gestation was vital for the breakthrough achieved in the "frenzy of writing" between 1945 and 1950—a period producing *Waiting for Godot* and "The Trilogy" of novels (*Molloy, Malone Dies* and *The Unnamable*), amongst others. Considering that his 1996 authorized biography, *Damned to Fame*, largely sparked this empirical turn toward Beckett's formative years, it is hard to disagree with the conclusion regarding Beckett's postwar creative burst offered there: "the ground was well prepared."[9] Nowhere are his provisions for an unsettled present and unknown future—captured by Beckett's reflexive question in his "German Diary" entry of 13 December 1936, "What is to become of me?"[10]—better revealed than in the "Interwar Notes" compiled between the late 1920s and late 1930s. As sketched out by the 2006 catalogue published in *Samuel Beckett Today Aujourd'hui* 16, these reading notes extend to psychology, art history, the histories of German and English literature, Irish and European history; as well as

---

[8] "Nobelprize.org," available at: http://nobelprize.org/nobel_prizes/literature/laureates/1969/press.html (last accessed 20/5/11).

[9] James Knowlson, *Damned To Fame: The Life of Samuel Beckett* (London: Bloomsbury, 1996), 353.

[10] Cited in Mark Nixon, *Samuel Beckett's German Diaries 1936–1937* (London: Continuum, 2011), 125.

notes on specific writers as divergent as Dante and d'Annunzio; Mauthner and Mistral; Augustine and Ariosto.[11]

Far and away the largest corpus portion of these extant notes comprise the 266 pages, mostly recto and verso (with a few blank sides scattered throughout), forming what I have called Beckett's "Philosophy Notes." These were taken from a variety of sources, including John Burnet's 1914 *Greek Philosophy, Part I: Thales to Plato*, J. Archibald Alexander's 1907 *A Short History of Philosophy* and—as most recently identified by Peter Fifield—selected entries from Friedrich Ueberweg's 1871 two-volume *History of Philosophy: From Thales to the Present Time*.[12] Alongside Windelband, these sources—and bits from potentially others, such as the *Encyclopaedia Britannica*, or an as-yet unidentified French text—were used to cover the origins of Western philosophy. These origins were, as Beckett duly noted, to be found in the "Philosophy of the Greeks—from the beginning of scientific thought to the death of Aristotle (600–322 B.C.)." This first section—numbered "1.", following Windelband's "General Classification"—was clearly of greatest interest to Beckett. In fact, typed and handwritten entries covering these initial three centuries of Western philosophy form fully 40 percent of the entire corpus of "Philosophy Notes"; that is, nearly as much as that taken from the ensuing six eras set out in Windelband's Table of Contents.[13]

Despite being passed over in silence across Beckett's published texts or letters from the time, *A History of Philosophy* accounts for

---

[11] *"Notes diverse holo"*: *Catalogues of Beckett's reading notes and other manuscripts at Trinity College Dublin, with supporting essays*, in *Samuel Beckett Today Aujourd'hui* [hereafter *SBT/A*] 16 (Amsterdam: Rodopi, 2006), 29–172.

[12] For further details of Beckett's engagement with "early Greek philosophy," see Peter Fifield's groundbreaking essay in this collection.

[13] The subsequent periods identified by Windelband, and transcribed verbatim by Beckett in structuring his notes, were "Hellenistic-Roman Philosophy"; "Mediaeval Philosophy"; "Philosophy of the Renaissance"; "Philosophy of the Enlightenment"; "The German Philosophy"; and seventh, "Nineteenth Century Philosophy" (TCD MS 10967/1a).

more than three-quarters of the entire "Philosophy Notes." Windelband is one of (at least) four sources on Ancient Greek philosophy, but one of the only two sources employed in section two, "Hellenistic-Roman Philosophy"—with typed entries steadily decreasing until Beckett apparently tired of Alexander's wearying prose with "Origen (185–254)."[14] Thereafter, the final five sections are taken from only one source, namely Windelband. The rest of Beckett's "Philosophy Notes," covering the remaining 1,600 years of Western philosophy, are derived entirely from *A History of Philosophy*. Put another way, the 266 folios comprising TCD manuscript 10967 may be largely seen as a corpus made up of two halves: the first part is a wide-ranging study of classical Greek philosophy (and to a much lesser extent, classical Roman thought); the second is Windelband's account of everything since. Before turning to the outstanding features of this second half of Beckett's "Philosophy Notes," however, a few final observations on the "Philosophy of the Greeks" are relevant for what follows.

Evidence for Beckett's attraction to early Greek philosophy is underscored by the multiple sources used in what he later called, in a 1957 letter to Alan Schneider on *Endgame*, "my notes on the pre-Socratics." Much care was taken in the construction of these notes, with passages from Alexander typed out, those from Burnet entered in red ink, and notes from Windelband made in blue or black ink.[15] Moreover, these two hundred or so typed and handwritten sides of "notes on the pre-Socratics" help to date the composition of Beckett's "Philosophy Notes," with the earliest explicit reference to them oc-

---

[14] TCD MS 10967/145r.
[15] Beckett's letter to Schneider of 21 November 1957 is reprinted in Maurice Harmon, ed., *No Author Better Served: The Correspondence of Alan Schneider and Samuel Beckett* (London: Harvard University Press, 1998), 23. Apparently the only critic to have been given access to the original manuscripts of the "Philosophy Notes" is Everett Frost. Despite a number of howlers (exemplified by the mistranscription of the volume's title), Frost's overview of the color coding of TCD MS 10967 can surely be accepted; see *"Notes diverse holo"*, 67.

curring in the poem "Serena I," which John Pilling authoritatively dates to Autumn 1932:

> scarlet beauty in our world dead fish adrift
> all things full of gods

This reference corresponds perfectly to Beckett's notes on the first recorded Western philosopher, Thales of Miletus: "Earth afloat (dead fish) on surface of primal substance. All things are full of gods."[16] The last opaque allusion to these "notes on the pre-Socratics" in Beckett's art, interestingly, comes nearly half a century later in the 1981 *Ill Seen Ill Said*, in relation to another ancient Greek philosopher, Empedocles of Agrigentum:

> Slow systole diastole. Tightening and loosening their clasp. Rhythm of a labouring heart. Till when almost despaired of a gently part. Suddenly gently.
> In the beginning, the Sphere which Love keeps the "roots" is solution. Strife enters, drives Love to centre, and separates elements (cf. concept of world breathing). Until reverse process begins (systole - diastole), Love expanding and Strife expelled. (E. was the first to formulate theory of flux and reflux of blood to and from heart).[17]

Parenthetically, instead of a Cartesianism all too often asserted rather than shown, Beckett's interest in many familiar philosophical debates and dialectics—such as mind and body interactions, the role of consciousness, and methodological doubt, to name but three—may thus be cast as perennial issues in Western thought, commencing with the Presocratics rather than, two millennia later, with René Descartes. It is thus not the case that it is a "Cartesian system that underlies the

---

[16] See "Serena I," in *Selected Poems 1930–1989*, 25, corresponding to TCD MS 10967/5r. John Pilling dates the commencement of this poem to 12 September 1932 in *A Samuel Beckett Chronology* (Basingstoke: Palgrave, 2006), 39. As Peter Fifield has shown, this reference is actually taken from Ueberweg; see his chapter in this collection for discussion.

[17] Samuel Beckett, *Ill Seen Ill Said*, in *Company/Ill Seen Ill Said/Worstward Ho/Stirrings Still*, edited by Dirk Van Hulle (London: Faber and Faber, 2009), 60, corresponding to TCD MS 1096730v.

whole of Beckett's work," let alone that Descartes "was Beckett's favourite philosopher."[18] Rather, it was the contours and development of Western philosophy as a whole, starting in Ancient Greece, which were under central consideration in the "Philosophy Notes."

The utility of these notes as a whole, especially those on the Ancient Greeks, is thus manifest across virtually the entirety of Beckett's writing life; as evidenced in his plays, poetry, prose and even nonfiction alike. This was a corpus of reading notes to which Beckett seems to have returned, again and again. Beckett's notes on what Windelband characterized as the "Philosophy of the Greeks" consist of some fifty thousand words, extending from folio 1r to 109v. Beckett's use of (at least) four sources for these notes on classical Greek philosophy—of which *A History of Philosophy* is, here too, most frequently in evidence, followed by Burnet's *Greek Philosophy*, Alexander's *A Short History of Philosophy*, and fragments from Erdmann's *A History of Philosophy*—conclude with the following handwritten passage on Aristotle:

---

[18] For these canonical discussions of Beckett and Descartes, see respectively, John Fletcher, *Samuel Beckett's Art* (London: Chatto & Windus, 1967), cited 129; and Roger Scruton, "Beckett and the Cartesian Soul", in *The Aesthetic Understanding: Essays in the Philosophy of Art and Culture* (Manchester: Carcanet Press, 1983), 230. For a counter-argument positing Beckett's more general indebtedness to Western philosophy, see my *Beckett's Books* (London: Continuum, 2008), chapter 3.

> Reason develops, partly as rational action, partly as rational thought; as perfection on one hand of character, on the other of the faculty of intelligence. Thus excellence of rational man is compound of the <u>ethical</u> and <u>intellectual</u>, or <u>dianoetic</u> virtues. A. gave up the Socratic intellectualism, which made the determination of the will by rational insight stronger than the desire arising from defective knowledge [.
> …] Knowledge of these, the full unfolding of the "active reason", is a "beholding" and with this beholding of the highest truth man gains participation in that <u>pure thought</u>, the essence of deity, and thereby in the eternal <u>blessedness</u> of the divine self-consciousness. For this beholding, existing only for its own sake without ends of will or deed, this wishless absorption in the perception of the highest path, is the blessedest and best of all. Tra-la-la-la.

Like roughly half of these two hundred recto and verso sides, this passage is taken from *A History of Philosophy*.[19] Notwithstanding

---

[19] TCD MS 10967/109r-109v, corresponding to *A History of Philosophy*, 151, 154. When placed alongside Windelband's original, Beckett's summary gives a useful and representative insight into his method of taking summative notes from this source:
As in the animal soul impulse and perception were to be distinguished as different expressions, so, too, the reason develops itself, partly as rational action, partly as rational thought; as perfection, on the one hand, of the character or disposition, on the other, of the faculty of intelligence. Thus there result, as the excellence or ability of the rational man, the *ethical* and the *intellectual* or *dianoetic virtues*.
The ethical virtues grow out of that training of the will by which it becomes accustomed to act according to right insight. It enables man, in his decisions to follow practical reason, i.e. insight into what is correct or proper. With this doctrine Aristotle transcends the principles of Socrates,—with evident regards to the facts of the ethical life: not that he assigned to the will a psychological independence as over against knowledge; the point, rather, is, that he gave up the opinion that the determination of the will arising from the rational insight must itself be stronger than the desire arising from defective knowledge [(151)….] But knowledge of these, the full unfolding of the "active reason" in man, is again designated by Aristotle as a "*beholding*"; and with this beholding of the highest truth man gains a participation in that *pure thought*, in which the essence of the deity consists, and thus, also, in the eternal *blessedness* of the divine self-consciousness. For this "beholding" which exists only for its own sake and has no ends of will or deed, this wishless ab-

his seeming rejection of Windelband's interpretation with one of his—exceedingly rare—interpolative comments, the above represents yet another of the many instances of Beckett's subsequent use of material gleaned from the "Philosophy Notes." In this case, as Chris Ackerley has indicated, Aristotle's apex of virtue is traceable to *Watt*.[20] That which brings "complete happiness" for Aristotle forms Arsene's memorable three laughs, or "modes of ululation," corresponding to the "successive excoriations of the understanding." Yet, far from representing supreme truth, virtue or happiness, Windelband's meaning is wholly inverted in Arsene's "short speech":

> The hollow laugh laughs at that which is not true, it is the *intellectual* laugh. Not good! Not true! Well well. But the mirthless laugh is the *dianoetic* laugh, down the snout—Haw!—so. It is the laugh of laughs, the *risus purus*, the laugh laughing at the laugh, the *beholding*, the saluting of the highest joke, in a word the laugh that laughs—silence please—at that which is unhappy.[21]

The entry cited above, finally, raises a number of questions relating to the "Interwar Notes" generally, and to the "Philosophy Notes" in particular: Beckett's recourse to laconic and lapidary summaries from secondary sources; his repeated transformation of these reading notes into his art; and not least, his undeniable knowledge and use of Western philosophy across his published work. Amongst these extant reading notes, furthermore, *A History of Philosophy* emerges as, by far, the most significant of Beckett's selected texts on Western philosophy. It is from here, for example, that much of the dialogue in *Murphy* is drawn, even down to the famous epigraph for

---

sorption in the perception of the highest truth, is the blessedest and best of all (154, all emphasis in original; Windelband's numbering and use of Greek terminology is excluded both here and in Beckett's "Philosophy Notes").

[20] C.J. Ackerley, *Obscure Locks, Simple Keys: The Annotated* Watt (Tallahassee, FL: Journal of Beckett Studies Books, 2005), #48.3, 73–74.

[21] Samuel Beckett, *Watt,* edited by C.J. Ackerley (London, Faber and Faber: 2009), 39–40, emphasis added on "intellectual", "dianoetic" and "beholding".

chapter 6 on Murphy's mind.[22] In fact, Beckett's extant Windelband notes are more extensive than those relating to any other author—Dante, St. Augustine, or Arnold Geulincx. So just who was he?

At the time of writing *A History of Philosophy* in *fin de siècle* Germany, Windelband had ascended the heights of academic philosophy as a leading exponent of neo-Kantianism. In fact, Windelband's own motto was a shorthand for an understanding of the neo-Kantianism championed throughout his forty-five-year career: "to understand Kant is to go beyond him." Insofar as this became something of a working program, Windelband's *Badische* or Southwest-German school of philosophy—of which he remained the acknowledged leader from the late nineteenth century until the outbreak of the Great War—emphasized the importance of "objective norms [...] as an attempt to dispense with Kant's dualism." This would be undertaken by focusing upon epistemology and methodology; upon value theory as against the then-fashionable positivism; and, finally, upon the "rational will" over and above philosophical scepticism and relativism.[23] So much was this the case that Windelband identified transcendental norms as the "central concept of the critical philosophy".[24] Quite simply, as he claimed elsewhere, philosophy itself was nothing more than "a system of norms."[25]

To use a different terminological register, Windelband championed the philosophy of "realism," against its age-old opponents, the "nominalists"—the latter remaining highly unlikely to write systematic histories of philosophy "as an interconnected whole." Yet this dia-

---

[22] The corresponding entry used for the epigraph to chapter 6 of *Murphy* can be found in a footnote in *A History of Philosophy*, 410.

[23] "Wilhelm Windelband: Philosophy as the Science of Values," in Thomas E. Willey *Back to Kant: The Revival of Kantianism in German Social and Historical Thought, 1860–1914* (Detroit: Wayne State University Press, 1978), 134–139.

[24] Lanier R. Anderson, "Neo-Kantianism and the Roots of Anti-Psychologism," *British Journal for the History of Philosophy*, 13/2 (May 2005), 314.

[25] Cited in Frederick C. Beiser, "Normativity in Neo-Kantianism: Its Rise and Fall," *International Journal of Philosophical Studies* 17/1 (2009), 14.

lectic between realism and nominalism stretches back to the very origins of Western philosophy. For the question also vexed Plato and his disciple Aristotle, and reached boiling point in the late medieval debate over Universals; quite literally for philosophers facing the stake for endorsing a nominalist position regarding, for example, the doctrine of the Trinity and of transubstantiation. In a word, it is hugely ironic that perhaps Beckett's greatest debt to *A History of Philosophy* was precisely Windelband's discussion of nominalism, to which this essay will now turn.

§2

> I am not interested in the "unification" of the historical chaos any more than I am in the "clarification" of the individual chaos, & still less in the anthropomorphisation of the inhuman necessities that provoke the chaos. What I want is the straws, flotsam, etc., names, dates, births and deaths, because that is all I can know. Pas l'onde, mais les bouchons [....] Whereas the pure incoherence of times & men & places is at least amusing. Schicksal = Zufall, for all human purposes [e.g. fate equals coincidence ....] the expressions "historical necessity" & "Germanic destiny" start the vomit moving upwards.[26]

Beckett famously and repeatedly claimed that he was not a philosopher. But he was also a lifelong reader and intellectual, leading Ruben Rabinovitz to rightly note by way of response: "Samuel Beckett says in interviews that he knows little about philosophy; but his little could easily be another man's abundance."[27] Following this point, I want to suggest that Beckett's relative philosophical "abundance" during his "years of wandering", in large measure, specifically revolved around the doctrine of nominalism. Insight into this view is given by Beckett's fascinating confession to his German Diary, cited

---

[26] All English passages from Beckett's German Diary entry of 15 January 1937 are taken from Knowlson, *Damned to Fame*, 244–245.

[27] Rubin Rabinovitz, "*Watt* from Descartes to Schopenhauer," in Raymond J. Porter and James D. Brophy eds., *Modern Irish Literature: Essays in Honor of William York Tindall* (Iona College Press: New York, 1972), 261.

above. It was not only the racial "norms" inside Nazi Germany that Beckett was reacting against on 15 January 1937; he was also putting forward a much broader philosophical preference.[28] This may be summarized as a rejection of universals in the wake of the abortive *Dream of Fair to Middling Women*—that "ideal core of the onion" announced in his 1930 academic monograph *Proust*[29]—via his initial encounter with *A History of Philosophy*. Instead, what *Murphy* memorably dubbed "demented particulars" better represent Beckett's philosophical outlook at this time.[30] It is also worthwhile to recall here a less-quoted portion of the 1937 "German Letter" to Axel Kaun: tearing at the "veil of language" and advocating the literary equivalent of "Beethoven pauses" was a goal to be achieved, for Beckett, through recourse to "nominalist irony."[31]

As this suggests, of especial significance is the backdrop of Beckett's interwar maturation and intellectual development; of his autodidactic approach to Western philosophy; and, of course, the archival turn in Beckett Studies sensitive to this material and its historical context—one that has been flowering over the past fifteen years in the wake of Knowlson's aforementioned biography. By way of a contribution to these areas, two considerations shall be pursued in this and the following section. The central point concerns locating Beckett's interest in nominalism, as both first encountered in, and wholly mediated by, Windelband's *A History of Philosophy*. Secondly, Beckett's continued pursuit of this philosophical thread may also be seen in other, subsequent notebooks, jottings and sources across the

---

[28] For discussion of Beckett's claims not to understand philosophy, see my "'I am not a philosopher'. Beckett and Philosophy: A Methodological and Thematic Introduction," in the *Sofia Philosophical Review* 4/2 (2010).

[29] Samuel Beckett, *Proust*, in *"Proust" and Three Dialogues* (London: John Calder, 1970), 29.

[30] Samuel Beckett, *Murphy*, edited by J.C.C. Mays (London: Faber and Faber, 2009), 13.

[31] Samuel Beckett, "German Letter of 1937," cited in *Disjecta: Miscellaneous Writings and a Dramatic Fragment*, edited by Ruby Cohn (New York: Grove Press, 1984), 51–55, translated on 171–73.

1930s, testifying to a sustained engagement with nominalist philosophy. Yet before undertaking this triangulation of philosophy, interwar note-taking and Beckett's philosophical—and, by implication throughout, literary—development, a final philosophical pause is needed.

It bears restating that, as a neo-Kantian interested in transcendental norms and supra-factual values, Windelband could hardly be further from nominalist thinking. Quite aside from his normative philosophy, additional evidence suggests that Windelband was no advocate of nominalism. In fact, in the only other book of his currently available in English—Joseph McCabe's 1921 translation of *An Introduction to Philosophy* (published in German the year before his death), Windelband addresses nominalism in roughly one out of 346 pages—or, to be more "particular," a term that shall be pressed into important service shortly—using 427 words in a book containing some 128,000 of them. This matters because *An Introduction to Philosophy* is thematic, and treats a variety of contemporaneous philosophical debates around issues like Truth, Value, Morality, Aesthetics, History and Religion. Yet the passage in question, useful as a working summary, recounts the medieval debate between "realists" and "nominalists" as briefly as possible (and is the only reference to "nominalism" given in the index):

> [...] in antiquity and also in the Scholastic movement, there developed the antithesis of the two points of view on the theory of knowledge which we call Realism and Nominalism. Realism (*universalia sunt realia*) affirms, in the terms of Plato, that, as our knowledge consists of the concepts and must be a knowledge of reality, the contents of the concepts must be regarded as copies of being. This Realism is maintained wherever our views recognise in reality a dependence of the particular on the general. Hence the knowledge of laws of nature is the chief form of Realism in this sense of the word. But from the time of Plato onward the serious difficulties of Realism arise from the fact that it is impossible to form a satisfactory conception of the sort of reality that ideas can have, or of the way in which they condition the other reality, that of the particular and corporeal. These difficulties have driven thought in the opposite direction, into

the arms of Nominalism, which regards the concepts as intermediate and auxiliary constructions in the reflecting mind, not as copies of something independent of the mind and existing in itself. Their importance is still further reduced if they are supposed merely to be common names of similar objects (*universalia sunt nomina*). Nominalism will freely grant that the particular elements of our perceptive knowledge have a direct relation (either as copies or in some other way) to reality, but it declares it inconceivable that the results of conceptual reflection, which is a purely internal process of the mind, should have an analogous truth-value. It must, however, concede that this purely internal reflection is actually determined by the contents which it combines in its entire movement and its outcome, and that, on the other hand, the process of thought which its concepts leads in turn to particular ideas which prove to be in agreement with perception. It therefore finds itself confronting the problem, how the forms of thought are related to those of reality: whether they, as belonging to the same total system of reality, point to each other and are in the end identical, or whether, since they belong to different worlds, nothing can be settled as to their identity or any other relation. We thus see that in the last resort it is metaphysical motives which must pronounce in the controversy about universals. All the forms of worldview which we describe as Henistic or Singularistic are from the logical point of view Realistic; whilst all forms of Individualism must have a Nominalistic complexion.[32]

By contrast, Windelband was unable to get away from the discussion of medieval nominalism in his chronological, two-volume *A History of Philosophy*, for this earlier text was intended to cover "the evolution of the ideas of European philosophy," from antiquity to the late nineteenth century.[33]

Prior to considering Windelband's much more substantial treatment of nominalism in *A History of Philosophy*, a sketch of this doctrine is merited here. At its most basic, holds Zoltán Szabó, nominalism contests the "status of mind-independent entities" called "universals"; the doctrine of "realism" thus "posits that we are aware of them

---

[32] Wilhelm Windelband, *An Introduction to Philosophy*, translated by Joseph McCabe (London, Unwin: 1921), 186–187.

[33] *A History of Philosophy*, ix.

[universals] not by sense itself but by reason." "Nominalism is nothing more than the thesis that there are no abstract entities," a doctrine which "does away with so many kinds of putative entities that the ontology it yields may not even be properly described as a desert landscape." Realist opponents of nominalism, Szabó continues, "suspect that nominalism is indeed much like a desert: an uncomfortable place whose main attraction is that it is hard to be there." This is due to conventional renderings of nominalist doctrine stressing "the extent to which rejection of all abstract entities flies in the fact of common sense." By this, Szabó means that, both in philosophical debates and everyday interactions, nominalists still make use of abstract concepts, such as number, colour or, *pace* Windelband, normative values. Such a paradox, of course, reeks of Beckett Country, for such a position seems to be "self undermining":

> Suppose that a nominalist—call him Nelson—just told you that there are no abstract entities. How should Nelson describe what he did? Did he say something? Certainly not, if saying something amounts to expressing a proposition. Did he utter something? Clearly not, if uttering something requires the articulation of a sentence type. Did he try to bring you to share his belief? Obviously not, if sharing a belief requires being in identical mental states [....Yet] there is a nominalistically acceptable way of describing what happened: he produced meaningful noises and thereby attempted to bring you into a mental state relevantly similar to one of his own. There is not mention of propositions, sentences, or shareable beliefs here, and still, in an important sense, we are told precisely what was going on.[34]

It is not for nothing that readers familiar with Beckett's *Watt* might see in this explanation of nominalism the vexed conversation between the eponymous Watt and Sam, the novel's narrator: "These were sounds that at first, though we walked face to face, were devoid of significance to me," laments Sam, unable to grasp the tale of

---

[34] Variously quoted in Zoltán Szabó, "Nominalism," in *The Oxford Handbook of Metaphysics*, eds., M. J. Loux and D. Zimmerman (Oxford: Oxford University Press, 2003).

Knott's house until Watt's linguistic inversions and meaningless sounds were repeated enough for Sam to make sense of them: "But soon I grew used to these sounds, and then I understood as well as ever, that is to say fully one half of what won its way past my tympan" (*Watt*, 144). It is no surprise, therefore, that Chris Ackerley's authoritative annotations for *Watt, Obscure Locks, Simple Keys*, contains fully a dozen references to nominalism. Ackerley's examples range from the opening pastiche on Scholasticism—debating the classification of a rat having eaten a consecrated wafer—to the memorable experiences of "unintelligible intricacies" with the Galls father and son, to the arbitrary naming of a "famished dog," Kate, for the eating of Mr. Knott's leftovers.[35] Right across the narrative of *Watt*, the failure of language is intertwined with the failure of naming, as with the example of Mr. Knott's various pots refusing to conform to the universal Idea of a generic "Pot":

> It was in vain that it answered, with unexceptionable adequacy, all the purposes, and performed all the offices, of a pot, it was not a pot. And it was just this hairbreadth departure from the nature of a true pot that so excruciated Watt. For if the approximation had been less close, then Watt would have been less anguished. For then he would not have said, This is a pot, and yet not a pot, no, but then he would have said, This is something of which I do not know the name [....] a thing of which the true name had ceased, suddenly, or gradually to be the true name for Watt. For the pot remained a pot, Watt felt sure of that, for everyone but Watt. For Watt alone it was not a pot, any more. (*Watt*, 67–68)[36]

---

[35] See *Obscure Locks, Simple Keys*, 289, with references corresponding to pages in *Watt* on Scholasticism (22–23); the Galls father and son (60ff, quoted 80); and on the "famished dog" (75ff; quoted 80).

[36] Ackerley writes of the passage "Pot, pot": "Beckett in the galleys (G26) was particular about this capitalization, the two 'forms' intimating the Idea and the particular, the latter evading by a hairbreadth the nature of a true Pot," contributing to "Watt's awareness of the pot as pot, as individual and not as a class," entry #81.2, 99.

Nominalism thus assumes the imprecision of language. One can only "fail better," as it were, when employing language to link concrete objects or entities through "analogies," "semantic paraphrase"; in a word, through metaphor. "The nominalist refuses to construe abstract terms as names of entities distinct from individual things," writes Dena Shottenkirk, for "so-called universals are terms or signs standing for or referring to individual objects and sets of objects, but they themselves cannot be said to exist as mind-independent entities."[37] Nominalism may then be said to reject the one-to-one correspondence of abstract terms and concrete things as nothing more than a linguistic sleight of hand by realism. There is consequently no mileage in the identification of categories like genera and species with linguistic representations of them—considerations that reach back to Aristotelian categories, Platonic Ideas and, before them (at least for Beckett, as we shall see below), ancient Greek debates over the world's underlying essence (or otherwise), termed *"weltstoff"* by *A History of Philosophy*.[38]

---

[37] Dena Shottenkirk, *Nominalism and Its Aftermath* (London: Springer, 2009), p. 5, which continues: "to summarize, the first problem with universals for the nominalist is that no sense can be made of what exactly these universals are; their existence can't be accounted for in the way that something is normally said to exist in space and time. Secondly, the exact way that they come to participate in the separate entity of the participating particular is likewise inexplicable, the account usually remaining on the metaphorical level with the use of words such as 'instantiating', 'inhering in', 'partaking in', etc. None of these terms are description of the mechanism of the relationship between the two different ontological entities; in other words, they are no explanations but merely attempts at analogies."

[38] *A History of Philosophy*, 32. Regrettably, space does not permit a discussion of these classical Greek debates here, except to note Shottenkirk's insightful point *en passant*: "While the debate between those who maintained the existence of mind-independent universals and those who argued against such entities presented itself from the earliest of pre-Socratic philosophy—framed as the One and the Many—and while this continued throughout ancient Greek writings in the examples of both Plato and Aristotle, it is in two other separate time periods that this issue comes to dominate much of philosophical

Beckett's introduction to nominalism via *A History of Philosophy* duly noted the wide-ranging medieval debates over the "problem of universals." As emphasized above, by this point Beckett's "Cliff's Notes" on the history of philosophy—itself remarkably consistent in seeking out that flotsam of "names, dates, births and deaths" noted in his German Diary entry of 15 January 1937—was fashioned from one source, that is, Wilhelm Windelband's rendering of the sixteen centuries of Western philosophy from classical Rome to Nietzsche. Across this period, the amount of attention Beckett paid to the sections on nominalism is striking, not least given the cursory notice taken of sections on either side of Windelband's main discussion of nominalist philosophy. Beckett raced through Chapter 1 of Part III on the "First Period" of Medieval Philosophy until reaching Section 23, "The Controversy over Universals." Importantly, there, Windelband is at pains to stress that the medieval debate over general and particular "had influence in the succeeding development of philosophy until long past the Middle Ages."[39] Yet as Beckett carefully noted, the more important direction of influence was not forward, but backward to the ancient Greeks:

> This possibly the same problem as that at the centre of first Greek period. After Socrates had assigned to science the task of thinking the world in conceptions, the question how the class-concepts, the generic conceptions, are related to reality became, for the first time, a chief motiv [sic] of philosophy. It produced the Platonic doctrine of Ideas, Aristotelian logic. The mediaeval dispute worked in Paris schools, has its counterparts only in the debates at Athens.[40]

Building upon his expansive notes on early Greek conceptions of reality in the preceding "Philosophy Notes," Beckett's interest seems to have been truly piqued by the medieval debate between nominalism and realism. A few pages later—in both the "Philosophy

---

writing: in the medieval period and in the mid-twentieth century" (*Nominalism and Its Aftermath*, 5).

[39] *A History of Philosophy*, 285.

[40] TCD MS 10967/153v, corresponding to *A History of Philosophy*, 288.

Notes" and *A History of Philosophy*—Beckett prominently entered the word "NOMINALISM" in the margins. Quite beyond nominalism's connection to ancient Greek individualism and scepticism, Windelband argues that this doctrine was "repressed and stifled" during the medieval period, meaning that little written by the Nominalists themselves survives. Windelband reckoned that this had much to do with medieval Catholic dogma: "Realism in its theory of universals found an instrument for establishing some of the fundamental dogmas, and therefore rejoiced in the approbation of the Church. The assumption of a substantial reality of the logical genera [...] seemed to make possible a rational exposition of the doctrine of the Trinity," amongst other medieval Christian ideals, including "inherited sin" and "vicarious satisfaction."[41]

These features of nominalism appear to have been enough for Beckett to pay close attention to Windelband's ensuing pages. The following is a summary of Beckett's summary of Windelband's summary:

---

[41] Ibid., 295–296.

> The source of Nominalism is the Aristotelian logic, in particular the De Categoriis. In this individual things of experience were designated as true "first" substances [....] it seemed to follow that universals could not be substances. What then? The comprehension of many particularities in one numen [name] vox [voice ...] defined by Boethius as "the motion of the air produced by the tongue". Here all the elements of extreme nominalism are given: universals are nothing but collective names, sounds (flatus vocis) serving as signs for a multiplicity of substances or their accidents [....] Attached to this—sensualism, since the individual is that given by the world of sensible reality [....] This doctrine became moments thro [sic] its application to theological questions by Berengar of Tours and Roscellinus. The one contested, in doctrine of Sacrament, the possibility of transubstantiation of substance while the former accidents were retained; the second reached the consequence that the three persons of divine Trinity were to be looked on as 3 different substances.[42]

Aside from being a suppressed and near-heretical doctrine that Beckett first encountered in Windelband, the ideas of "extreme nominalism" appear to be an ideal stomping ground for a modern artist fascinated by the iniquities of language. For what Szabó calls nominalism's use of "semantic paraphrase," and Willey terms "analogies" is little more than the idea that individual things are not properly reflected by general categories of names or things. This medieval turn toward language in eleventh- and twelfth-century Europe later took on the perfectly Beckettian name "terminism"—which is found underlined in the margin of this portion of the "Philosophy Notes," even though Windelband only discusses the subject properly some forty pages later. It was this linguistic aspect of "extreme nominalism" that is best represented by William of Occam—he of Occam's Razor fame—the fourteenth-century scholastic and champion of the doctrine Beckett later evoked in his famous 1937 letter to Axel Kaun, in which the Joycean method is associated with the universalizing tendencies of Realism, while Beckett's preference was for a "literature of the

---

[42] TCD MSS 10967/156r-10967'156v, corresponding to *A History of Philosophy*, 296–298.

unword" taking the form of a "Nominalist irony"; that is, nominalism "(in the sense of the Scholastics)."[43]

Some five years before penning the "German letter of 1937," Beckett had noted that "Nominalism reappeared as Terminism which regarded concepts (termini) as subjective signs for really existing individual things."[44] As this suggests, it was not only Fritz Mauthner who raised the specter of linguistic ineffability for Beckett: six centuries earlier a very similar idea was advanced by the "extreme nominalism" of "Terminism." This key section of *A History of Philosophy*, headed "Problem of Individuality," also specifically uses a term Beckett first encountered in Schopenhauer's philosophy to describe the "principle of individuation," which is systematically obscured by the "veil of Maya": "with the increase of intellectualism the universalistic tendency increased also, the counter current was necessarily evoked all the more powerfully, and the same antithesis in motives of thought which had led to the dialectic of the controversy over universals now took on a more real and metaphysical form in the question as to the ground of existence in individual beings (*principium individuationis*)."[45] (In this light, it is unsurprising that Schopenhauer, one of Beckett's favourite philosophers, is categorised by *A History of Philosophy* under the heading "Doctrine of Irrationalism." Beckett mischievously concludes his summation of Windelband's overview of Schopenhauer's ideas with "Dear Arthur's" view that "it must be a balls aching world."[46])

Terminism is then discussed by Windelband at greater length, and closely followed in Beckett's "Philosophy Notes." The following is again noted from *A History of Philosophy*, and treats the "victori-

---

[43] Samuel Beckett, "German Letter of 1937," in *Disjecta*, 173.
[44] TCD MS 10967/159v, corresponding to *A History of Philosophy*, 342.
[45] *A History of Philosophy*, 337. For further discussion of Beckett, Schopenhauer and the "veil of Maya," see my "Agnostic Quietism and Beckett's Early Development," in *Samuel Beckett: History, Memory, Archive*, eds. Seán Kennedy and Katherine Weiss (New York: Palgrave, 2009).
[46] TCD MS 10967/252r. For discussion of Beckett's entry on Schopenhauer in the "Philosophy Notes," see *Beckett's Books*, 48–50.

ous development" experienced by nominalism in the second period of medieval philosophy:

> The Terminism of Occam proceeds from the logical theory of "supposition"; a class-concept or term (terminus) may, in language and logic, stand for the sum of its species, a species-concept for the sum of individual examples (homo = omnes homines), so that in operations of thought a term is a sign of its content. Individual things are represented in thought intuitively, without mediation of species intelligibles, but those mental representations are only signs for things represented, with which they have as little real similarity as any sign towards the object designation. This relation is that of "first intention". But as individual ideas stand for (supponunt) individual things, so general ideas supponunt individual ideas. This "second intention", in which general idea refers no longer directly to the thing itself, but primarily to the idea of the thing, is no longer nature, but arbitrary (ad placitum instituta).
> Upon this distinction Occam bases that between real and rational science, the former relating immediately or intuitively to things, the latter abstractly to the relations between ideas.
> For this Terministic Nominalism, knowledge of the world refers to the inner states excited by phenomena. Nicolas Cusanus, who committed himself absolutely to this idealistic Nominalism, taught that human thought possesses only conjectures, modes of representation corresponding to its own nature. This awareness of relativity of all positive prediction, this knowledge of non-knowledge, is the docta ignorantia.[47]

It is therefore clear that Beckett thus encountered a philosophical doctrine specifically treating the inadequacy of language after the completion of *More Pricks than Kicks* in late 1933, and before starting *Murphy* in mid-1935. While philosophical ideas are treated humorously, and largely superficially, in the more Joycean *Dream of Fair to Middling Women* and *More Pricks than Kicks*, they are put to greater structural use in *Murphy*, where Celia represents nominalism's "demented particulars," while her grandfather, Mr. Kelly, reflects the

---

[47] TCD MSS 10967/170r-10967/171v, corresponding to *A History of Philosophy*, 341-343.

universal norms of Realism. This philosophical dialectic is reflected in much of their dialogue, with Mr. Kelly telling Celia to be "less beastly circumstantial" in her detailed account of Murphy in Chapter 2, for example. In fact, Celia is herself introduced in dementedly particular terms; terms based upon the specific measurements of the Venus de Milo (*Murphy*, 9):

Age	Unimportant
Head	Small and round
Eyes	Green
Complexion	White
Hair	Yellow
Features	Mobile
Neck	13¾"
Upper Arm	11"
Forearm	9½"
Wrist	6"
Bust	34"
Waist	27"
Hips, etc	35"
Thigh	21¾"
Knee	13¾"
Calf	13"
Ankle	8¼"
Instep	Unimportant
Height	5' 4"
Weight	123 lb

In contrast, in the thirteenth and final chapter of *Murphy*, following the death of the eponymous "hero", Celia and Mr. Kelly go kite-flying at the Round Pond. Mr. Kelly's kite loses its particular features and comes to represent a timeline that "could measure the distance form the unseen to the seen, now he was in a position to determine the point at which seen and unseen met." This unseen is described in *Murphy* as "the historical process of the hardened optimists"—or, as Beckett confided to his "German Diary," noted above, by the Third Reich's rhetoric of "historical destiny." Thus, at the close of *Murphy*, "Mr Kelly let out a wild rush of line, say the industrial revolution" with a "pleasure" that was "in no way inferior to that conferred (presumably) on Mr Adams by his beautiful deduction of Neptune from Uranus" (157). Despite these and other undertones of nominalism in *Murphy*, however, it is only *after* that novel that Beckett appears to have returned to the doctrine more extensively—both in his notes and fiction.

§3

> These are most delicate questions. Watt spoke of it as involving, in the original, the Galls and the piano, but he was obliged to do this, even if the original had nothing to do with the Galls and the piano. For even if the Galls and the piano were *long posterior to the phenomena destined to become them*, Watt was obliged to think, and speak, of the incident, even at the moment of its taking place, as the incident of the Galls and the piano, if he was to think and speak of it at all, and it may be assumed that Watt would never have thought or spoken of such incidents, if he had not been under the absolute necessity of doing so. But *generally speaking* it seems probable that the meaning attributed to this *particular type* of incident, by Watt, in his *relations*, was now the initial meaning that had been lost and recovered, and now a meaning quite distinct from the initial meaning, and now a meaning evolved, after a delay of varying length, and with greater or less pains, from the initial absence of meaning.
> One more word on this subject. (*Watt*, 65–66; emphasis added)

One impetus for Beckett's return to nominalism after the completion of *Murphy* may well be through the aegis of fellow Irish poet Brian Coffey. Coffey, a friend from Beckett's Dublin days, had been studying in Paris under the renowned Catholic theologian Jacques Maritain. Although Coffey's doctorate concerned ideas of order in the medieval realism of St. Thomas Aquinas, this study may well have also authorized his recommendations for philosophical sources more generally. Beckett's recently-published letters show that, while preparing in Dublin for his six-month trip to Germany from late 1936 to early 1937, he spent much time with Brian Coffey, who recommended reading the philosopher Benedict de Spinoza. Beckett also read works by the "self-confessed nominalist" Bishop Berkeley at this time.[48] It is entirely plausible that, through this philosophically-minded friend, Beckett again took up the subject of medieval nominalism in 1936. This could, in fact, help to date the following English translation from vol. 1 of Joseph Gredt's 1926 *Elementa philosophiae Aristotelico-Thomisticae*, which Beckett typed out in the original Latin:

---

[48] Tom Stoneham, *Berkeley's World: An Examination of the* Three Dialogues (Oxford: Oxford University Press, 2002), 216. Stoneham adds (220, 221, 223–224): "Nominalism is a working assumption of Berkeley's philosophy. There is a strong connection between empiricism and nominalism [...in] that we never come across universals in our sense experiences [....] we can summarize Berkeley's reasons for agreeing with the 'universally received maxim' that everything which exists is particular: only minds and perceived ideas exists; minds are particulars and all perceived ideas are particulars." See also Steven Matthews' discussion of Beckett and Berkeley in this volume.

2. Nominalists: Heraclitus (+475 BC), Cratylus, Heraclitus' disciple, Antisthenes (+369), the Epicureans like Roscellinus (XI century) who was St Anselmus' adversary. The Empiricists, the Sensualists and the Positivists of the most recent periods: Hobbes (1588–1679), Locke (1632–1704), Hume (1711–1776), Condillac (1715–1780), August Comte (1798–1857), Stuart Mill (1806–1873), Spencer (1820–1903), Wundt (1832–1921). They give to "universality" only a mere denominational meaning. In fact, they deny concepts and preach that the term "universal" does not correspond in one's mind to a universal concept, but to a group of individuals already established.

Conceptualists. (the early Stoics, Conceptualists of XIV and XV centuries: William of Occam, John Buridanus, Petrus de Alliaco, Gabriel Biel and finally, Kant (1724–1804) and the Kantians). They admit universal concepts; however, they teach that concepts are a mere creation of our mind and that nothing in nature corresponds to them.

Realists believe that universals have a correspondence with the individual things of external reality. Nevertheless, once more we have two different positions: one which believes that the universal exists independently as such (exaggerated realism). The other instead, (i.e. Aristotle (384–322), Boethius (480–525), St Anselmus (1033–1109), St Thomas (1225–1274) and most Scholastics) teaches that we must distinguish two elements: the matter and what contains the universal concept, namely, nature and form. In fact, they teach that universality is present not only in the intellect but also in the singular object (moderate realism). From this position, as it has been acknowledged by the exaggerated realism, some thinkers believe that the universal as such can exist outside the intellect and outside the object. Others believe instead that the universal is outside the intellect but within the object. The first position is represented by Plato (428–347) who said that pre-existent ideas or forms of objects nevertheless participate to the matter in the same way as the transcendental, universal, and incorruptible eternal matter does.* Another position is the one of Guillelme de Champeaux (1070–1121), who thought that nature does not multiply herself within the same individual species, but there is one and only nature in everything and that individuals are different only in presence of accidents.

Neo-Platonics. Hegel (1770–1831), Schelling (1775–1854) thought that singulars are nothing more than phenomena of the universal nature.

* This is Plato's position as interpreted by Aristotle and the Scholastics. It must be added though, that some thinkers believe that the Platonic ideas are divine ideas or copies of objects. But whatever is the nature of the controversy, it is an established fact that Plato did not consider the forms of objects as immanent to the singulars but transcendental.[49]

This single page from Beckett's "Interwar Notes," in turn, is a strong candidate for the scholastic nominalism advanced as a potential literary method in Beckett's "German Letter of 1937." This is the most likely candidate, despite the fact that Beckett purchased the German edition of Windelband's two-volume *A History of Philosophy*—surprising, given that he had summarized most of it during 1932 and 1933—including *Geschichte der Philosophie* in one of his books posted home in December 1936 from Germany. Interestingly, Gredt includes the ancient Greek "weeping philosopher," Heraclitus, in his list of Nominalist philosophers, giving "to 'universality' only a mere denominational meaning," thus denying concepts and genera while holding "that the term 'universal' does not correspond in one's mind to a universal concept, but to a group of individuals already established."

Beckett's latest extant notes on philosophical nominalism are contained in his commonplace book, kept for most of the 1930s, called the "Whoroscope Notebook" (after Beckett's "title" on the notebook's cover). Although possibly started as early as 1934 or 1935, the bulk of entries date from the period after Beckett's return from Nazi Germany in April 1937. A year later, Beckett first encountered the Austrian language philosopher Fritz Mauthner, who advocated a form of radical nominalism that, like William of Occam's

---

[49] TCD MS 10971/6/37, corresponding to Joseph Gredt, *Elementa philosophiae Aristotelico-Thomisticae*, 2 vols. (Freiburg: Herder, 1926), 96–97; the translation, provided by Anna Castriota, is also available in my "Sourcing Aporetics: An Empirical Study on Philosophical Influences on the Development of Samuel Beckett's Writings" (Oxford Brookes University, Unpublished PhD. thesis: 2004), Appendix E.

scholastic terminism, argued that "Pure nominalism puts an end to thinking":

> the teaching that all concepts or words of human thought are only exhalations of the human voice is logically consistent nominalism, according to which the recognition of reality is just as much denied to the human brain as the make-up of a surface of stone, this pure nominalism, which despite all of the natural sciences still as easily despairs of understanding a fall or colour or electricity as an understanding of consciousness, this epistemological nominalism is not a provable world-view. It would not be nominalism if it pretended to be more than a feeling, than a disposition of the human individual facing the world.[50]

As Dirk Van Hulle's important article in the 2002 edition of *Text* makes clear—perhaps the only article in Beckett Studies containing Nominalism in the title, it might be added—Mauthner's discussion of nominalism occurs at the end of his third and final volume of the revised, 1923 edition of *Beiträge zu einer Kritik der Sprache* [*Contributions to a Critique of Language*]. Yet it is also in the second volume that Beckett copies large, verbatim transcriptions from Mauthner's opus, which holds that all language is but a poor metaphor for expressing empirical sensory experience. What van Hulle usefully calls Mauthner's "nominalist thesis" holds that, on account of its metaphorical nature, language is unable to convey concepts, ideas, and general principles. This position is made strikingly clear toward the end of his second volume, *Concerning Linguistics*, in a section fittingly entitled "History of Philosophy." Unlike Beckett's other eleven transcribed passages from Mauthner, however, the following, excerpted passage on the "Self-Destruction of the Metaphori-

---

[50] This entry in Beckett's "Whoroscope Notebook," 47v in UoR 3000/1, translated from the German by the late Prof. Detlef Mühlberger, is the first of 10 verbatim handwritten quotations taken from the 1923 edition of Fritz Mauthner's *Beiträge zu einer Kritik der Sprache*, 615. Windelband's subject discussed in this section is "Epistemological Nominalism." For a complete translation of these transcriptions, see "Sourcing Aporetics," Appendix D.

cal" is not hand-copied into the "Whoroscope Notebook," but stands alone as a four-page typescript:

> The coherent history of so-called philosophy starts first, however, with the ancient Greeks, who with enormous, bold, false analogies made—either something impossible to imagine, like xxxx, or one of the four elements—into a world view "determining" principle, the sole "of that which exists." This had therefore to be caused by itself, a senseless concept, even if it has dominated for a full two thousand years. That was recognised immediately by logical thinkers and made "that which does not exists" the cause for "that which exists," whereby the metaphor really makes the world turn a somersault. The Sophists undermined both concepts and made the human being into the standard of the world; one abused them because of that, and Socrates had to die for it. The reaction announced itself in his poetic pupil Plato, who was responsible for raising the over-estimation of metaphorical language to a highpoint which it has occupied for more than a millennium, indeed to the present. While he had learned from a predecessor the deceptiveness of the "reality picture" (everything is in a state of flux), he did not thereby—as did Socrates—confess to not knowing, but personified instead the abstractions of language, made ideas into the mothers of the world. Time is turned upside down, the last is termed the first; the concepts abstracted from "individual things" are called the cause of the singular thing.
> Aristotle was able to see through the enormity of this false analogy, which after all only made "that which does not exist" the basis for "that which exists" again. That is why he stated ideas as being immanent. One expressed this in the Middle Ages in the following fashion: that he replaced the Universals *ante rem* with Universals *in re*. It was a destruction of the "ideas metaphor." But with a much more dangerous, less easy to comprehend anthropomorphism he now made on his part the 'necessity concept' the causal factor for the world, for the soul, for the "form principle" of matter. To these ideas Christendom brought—along with the epigone schools of Greek philosophy which preceded it—the religious concept of God, and for centuries the scholastics wore their teeth out in chewing through the chain of these entwined metaphors. <u>The nominalism of the Middle Ages is the first attempt at a genuine self-destruction of metaphorical thinking.</u> Nominalism could not, despite all sorts of heresies, liberate itself from theology. In this connection Descartes also appears as a theologian who

> wore his teeth out. He solves many minor metaphors, but prays to the highest metaphor, God, who is now assigned a much more difficult role than in religion. [....]
> This continuity could be represented in such a schematic fashion that one could start the great division with Plato and Aristotle, and even more so with their one-sided interpreters; both intellectual direction want to make that does not exists the cause of all that exists. The Platonists' conceptual ideas, the Aristotelians' "essential concepts" of Scholasticism, which in its spread reaches down to Kant and Schopenhauer, is in all free thinkers an amazingly astute attempt to undermine Plato's teaching of ideas and to surmount the intellect-murdering "word realism." On the effectiveness of "essential concepts" not one of these series of thinkers really has any doubt, since Kant still constructs his practical philosophy on "essential concepts" and Schopenhauer also teaches the "monster" of an admittedly stupid, but still "purposeful-thinking" will in nature [.... This] critique of language has taught us that even the most concrete concept does not provide any experience, but only the appearance of experience, that therefore even the brilliant richness of pictures painted by a poet of thought cannot transcend the boundaries of language. A critique of pure reason cannot help here, but only the critique of reason in general, the critique of language. We only understand the world of reality when we act, only when we ourselves stand actively in the midst of reality, never when we just wish to confront it by thinking about it. Whatever the human may dare to do through superhuman strength in order to discover truth, he always finds only himself, a human truth, an anthropomorphic picture of the world.[51]

The proximity to medieval terminism is unmistakable, even if Mauthner's scepticism regarding the value of language *tout court* might be considered an even more extreme form of "extreme nominalism" than that ever ventured by medieval philosophy. Interestingly, following the last of Beckett's transcriptions from Mauthner's "epistemological nominalism" into his "Whoroscope Notebook"—so

---

[51] TCD MSS 10971/5/1-10971/5/4, a four-page transcription corresponding to Fritz Mauthner's second volume of *Beiträge zu einer Kritik der Sprache*. Translation provided by the late Prof. Detlef Mühlberger, and available in "Sourcing Aporetics," Appendix D.

dating from 1938, and thus ostensibly forming the final extant entry from his readings in philosophy—Windelband crops up yet again.[52] Thanks to his preparations for, and travels in, Germany during 1936 and 1937, Beckett was able to read difficult German passages in philosophy that he likely could not have understood four or five years earlier; that is, at the time of composing his "Philosophy Notes". The final excerpted transcription, while also focusing on the relationship of general to particular, does not come from *A History of Philosophy*, but from another of Windelband's thematic texts, *The Handbook of Philosophy* co-written by Windelband and Heinz Heimsoeth:

> The crucial exemplar for this philosophy of the human mind, for its idealist standpoint and its methodology (considerably differing in detail) is Kant, as creator of the three critiques. The realistic considerations, as well as the metaphysical backgrounds and ultimate intentions, of Kantian reflexion on reason and consciousness are shed, or rather interpreted away, throughout. "Critique" here becomes an excluding antonym [Gegenbegriff] of "metaphysics." Under the influence of the positivistic-agnostic resignation of the 19th century, Kant, and the task of philosophy to be taken over [or: borrowed] from Kant, are seen strictly in terms of "transcendental logic," which as pure self-reflection of the human mind should take the place of all ontology and metaphysics before and after Kant. The fundamental conviction is the absolutely insurmountable immanence of consciousness. All questions touching on the being beyond (or even this side of) consciousness, are to be rejected as "uncritical." The ground of consciousness—as of a spiritual [ideellen] "consciousness as such" constituting everything representational [alles Gegenständliche] in categories of thought and functions of meaning—is the basis for all preconditionless reasoning [Begründung] and thus for all scientific philosophy. The idealism of consciousness [Bewusstseinsidealismus] overcomes the dogmatism of the "scientific worldview" ["naturwissenschaftlichen Weltanschauung"] and demonstrates or: proves the autonomous laws of the mind as being preconditions of all apparently

---

[52] Beckett's transcriptions from Mauthner's *Beiträge zu einer Kritik der Sprache* conclude at 59r of the "Whoroscope Notebook," while that from Windelband/Heimsoeth, under Beckett's headed note "Philosophy in 20th century stresses problem of cognition," begins on 65r.

"given" reality and all encounterable determinations of being [vorfindbaren Seinsdeterminationen]. Consciousness is uninhibited; its spontaneity lies before all causality [Kausalgebundenheit]; the natural laws themselves are creations of the mind. The system of spiritual forms [ideellen Formen] to be researched philosophically lies ahead of all reality that can be experienced; all "being" is itself dependent on the methods of consciousness [....] It is the limitation and danger of this modern form of "idealism," that although it puts a stop to naturalism with the demonstration of autonomous laws and the superior significance of the mental (as of the human consciousness with its spiritual-meaningful forms which has to be assumed in all science and scientific worldview), reality, however, the representational realm of experience and the sciences, was split off from the mental-spiritual [vom Geistig-Ideellen]: so that on the one hand conscious and thinking, idea and value had to remain purely in the abstract of a "transcendental consciousness" removed from any question of reality, on the other hand, however, all concrete empirical amount of content [Gehaltsfülle], even for instance that of the psyche, was given over to the representational categories [Gegenstandskategorien] of causal thinking. Two worlds, an abstract spiritual and a concrete real, even though in a relation of encompassing, stand facing each other.[53]

Nominalism thus veritably snakes through the entirety of Beckett's "Interwar Notes," from the beginning of his "Philosophy Notes" in Autumn 1932 until his encounter with Mauthner, and return to Windelband, some six years later, in Spring 1938. That it was Windelband, decidedly no advocate of nominalism, who had introduced Beckett to the subject makes for a fascinating irony; yet that the latter continued to work on the concept—especially in relation to medieval philosophy—suggests something altogether less coincidental. For Windelband's writings effectively book-ended Beckett's philosophi-

---

[53] UoR MSS 300, "Whoroscope Notebook," 65r-66v; I am extremely grateful to Christian Egners for translation of this passage, corresponding to the section "Philosophy in the 20th Century," 574–576 of Wilhelm Windelband and Heinz Heimsoeth's *Lehrbuch der Geschichte der Philosophie. Billige Ausgabe. Mit einem Schlusskapitel "Die Philosophie im 20. Jahrhundert" und einer Übersicht über den Stand der philosophiegeschichtlichen Forschung.* (Tübingen: J.C.B. Mohr, 1935).

cal note-taking in the 1930s, and were responsible for the bulk of Beckett's readings on Western philosophy. Even if Beckett was to turn this kind of systematic knowledge on its head in *Watt*—and, more notably, in the "frenzy of writing" after 1945—in order to embrace a "docta ignorantia" worthy of Nicolas Cusanus and Fritz Mauthner, nominalism was a major stepping stone on the way to Beckett's artistically-employed linguistic scepticism. If originally derived from Windelband's systematic history of philosophy, comprising a portion of the "Philosophy Notes," Beckett took further notes on these ideas after the completion of *Murphy* and before starting *Watt*. From Watt's inability to name a pot to his general need of "semantic succor," Beckett's wartime novel may be considered the first to weave Nominalist—or better, terminist—ideas into its very fabric. And while I have not broached works written after 1945 here, what Enoch Brater has called Beckett's "minimalism" in the postwar work for stage and page, again, may be similarly read in the light of philosophical nominalism. For it is not for nothing that *Watt* also points forward to the mature works, concluding in good terministic fashion: "No symbols where none intended" (*Watt*, 223).[54]

---

[54] See Enoch Brater, *Beckett's Minimalism: Beckett's Late Style in the Theatre* (Oxford, Oxford University Press: 1987).

Monadology: Samuel Beckett and Gottfried Wilhelm Leibniz

Chris Ackerley (University of Otago, New Zealand)

Writing to Thomas MacGreevy in 1933, Samuel Beckett noted of his recent reading: "Leibniz a great cod, but full of splendid little pictures."[1] The reference is to the *Monadology* (1714), in Robert Latta's edition (1898). Beckett's judgment was not unlike that of Bertrand Russell, who had famously recorded in the Preface to his critical exposition of Leibniz his initial impression that the *Monadology* was "a kind of fantastical fairy tale, coherent, perhaps, but wholly arbitrary."[2] Beckett's opinion would not change substantially, yet his skepticism does not explain why he, like Russell, was attracted to the thought of Gottfried Wilhelm Leibniz, nor why he retained a deep respect for it, given its fundamental absurdity (above all, as it were, the claim that God *necessarily* exists). Once Russell had determined how Leibniz's metaphysics derived from a small set of coherent premises, the *Monadology* no longer struck him as arbitrary. Beckett's response was similar: a genuine respect for the Monad informs the "splendid little pictures" that manifest themselves (however ironically) in his prose works from *Dream of Fair to middling Women* to *How It Is* (indeed, into the later works for stage and screen), and by so doing dramatize the isolated "soul" (by which this essay understands the self conceived as an atomistic monad) as it accommodates itself (not always successfully) to a world that for Beckett—if not for Leibniz— was always contingent.

---

[1] Samuel Beckett to Thomas MacGreevy (5 December 1933), in Samuel Beckett, *The Letters of Samuel Beckett, Vol. 1: 1929–1940*, edited by Martha Dow Fehsenfeld and Lois More Overbeck (Cambridge: Cambridge University Press, 2009), 172.

[2] Bertrand Russell, *A Critical Exposition of the Philosophy of Leibniz* (Cambridge: Cambridge University Press, 1900), xvii.

The first of the "splendid little pictures" appears in *Dream* when Lucien, the philosophical alter-ego of Jean Beaufret, cites from the *Monadology* (§67 & §68)[3] a passage that "compares matter to a garden full of flowers or a pool of fish, and every flower another garden of flowers and every corpuscle of every fish another pool of fish."[4] Leibniz's fascination with new worlds opened up by Leuwenhock's microscopy underlies the paradox of his monads: infinite in number, but each reflecting the whole universe, an infinity of parts (consciousness may have, or may be perceived as having, this monadic quality). Later, Beckett dismisses the characters of *Dream* as "a collection of Kakiamouni wops, scorching away from their centres" with the reflection: "What would Leibnitz [*sic*] say?" (179).[5] Something, doubtless, about the affront to pre-established harmony (the paradox of accord, given the independent nature of substance) in a fictional *kosmos*, which, since its denizens refuse to work in unison, cannot be the best of all possible worlds.[6] Nemo is the most monadic (unknown, impenetrable) character in *Dream*, but his calculated plunge ("saltabat sobrius") at Leixlip (182) disputes with Leibniz the contention that Nature never makes leaps (Latta, 376).[7]

Motion is a primary monadic force that shapes much of Beckett's early work. *Dream* ends with Belacqua enjoined by a higher au-

---

[3] Robert Latta, *Leibniz: The Monadology and Other Philosophical Writings*, translated with Introduction and Notes by Robert Latta (Oxford: Oxford University Press, 1898), 256. Beckett's comment in his 1929 essay, "Dante...Bruno.Vico..Joyce," that "all things are ultimately identified with God, the universal monad, Monad of monads" (6), though echoed by Leibniz, was expropriated from Lewis McIntyre's *Giordano Bruno* (1903).

[4] Samuel Beckett, *Dream of Fair to middling Women* (Dublin: Black Cat Press, 1992), 47.

[5] "Kakiamouni" is a scatological variant of *Sakya-Muni*, Buddhist avatar of forgiveness and gentility; "wops" may imply the souls undone by death in Dante's *Inferno* (III).

[6] The narrator comments: "The only unity in this story is, please God, an involuntary unity" (132). The God of Leibniz would not be pleased.

[7] As in the classical tag, *Nemo enim fere saltat sobrius, nisis forte insani* [No-one leaps (*dances*) sober, unless he is insane].

thority to "move on" (241); in "Ding-Dong," he must be moving;[8] and the poem "Serena III" urges the cyclist to "keep on the move."[9] The solitary monad moves from *Murphy* into *Watt*, which offers (as *Murphy* does not) a sustained critique of Leibniz's central philosophical doctrine, pre-established harmony. My annotations of these two novels respected these matters, but a closer Leibnizian reading of them may complement other recent studies of Beckett and Leibniz: the *monade nue* in Garin Dowd's Beckettian baroque;[10] Windelband's "philosophy notes" as discussed by Matthew Feldman;[11] "Beckett's Leibniz" in Erik Tonning's study of the later works for stage and screen;[12] Katrina Wehling-Giorgi's application of Leibniz to Beckett and Gadda;[13] and my blueprint of the Monad in the Blackwell *Companion* to Beckett.[14]

The first principle of the *Monadology* is the doctrine of substance.[15] In his bachelor's dissertation, *De principio individui* (1663),

---

[8] Samuel Beckett, "Ding-Dong," in *More Pricks than Kicks*, edited by Cassandra Nelson (London: Faber and Faber, 2010), 31.

[9] Samuel Beckett, "Serena III," in *Samuel Beckett: Poems 1930–1989*, edited by David Wheatley (London: Faber and Faber, 2009), 29.

[10] Garin V. Dowd, "Nomadology: Reading the Beckettian Baroque," *Journal of Beckett Studies* 8 (1) (1998): 15–49; and Dowd, "Mud as the Plane of Immanence in *How It Is*," *Journal of Beckett Studies* 8 (2) (1999): 1–28.

[11] Matthew Feldman, *Beckett's Books: A Cultural History of Samuel Beckett's "Interwar Notes"* (London: Continuum, 2006).

[12] Erik Tonning, *Samuel Beckett's Abstract Drama: Works for Stage and Screen, 1962–1985* (Bern: Peter Lang, 2007).

[13] Katrin Wehling-Giorgi, "'Splendid Little Pictures': Leibnizian Terminology in the Works of Samuel Beckett and Carlo Emilio Gadda," *Samuel Beckett Today / Aujourd'hui* 22 (2010): 341–354.

[14] C.J. Ackerley, "Samuel Beckett and Science," in *A Companion to Samuel Beckett*, edited by S.E. Gontarski (Oxford: Blackwell, 2010), 143–164. Representations of the monad as described in this and the present chapter are located at: www.otago.ac.nz/english/staff/ackerley.html.

[15] Hereafter, with occasional wanderings into the Beckett country and other byways, I follow Latta's exposition of Leibniz's thought. Beckett's significant sources seem to have been Latta, Windelband, and Sorley on "Leibniz" in the *Encyclopaedia Britannica*.

Leibniz had defended the Nominalist position that individuality is constituted by the entirety or essence of a thing. This premise informs his definition of monads as the fundamental building blocks of the universe. Leibniz considered them simple substances and individual units of force, or motion, possessing neither parts, extension, nor figure: "They are metaphysical points or rather spiritual beings whose very nature it is to act."[16] This differentiated his monads from the indivisible units of Democritus, whose theory of atoms and the void had once "charmed his imagination" (Latta, 23); Leibniz would later find in the monad an essence, independent of the physical atom, without being stuck in the "idealist tar."[17] Leibniz tried to reconcile the notion of substance as continuous with the contrary notion of substance as consisting of indivisible elements (Latta, 21). The problem arose from an inadequate conception of substance, and his response was to affirm, in contradiction to Spinoza whose "[d]etermination is negation"[18] amounted to saying that substance can have no real parts (Latta, 22), and in opposition to the Atomists whose affirmation of the reality of material atoms was to deny the infinite divisibility of matter (Latta, 23)—that substance is non-quantitative. Thus, a "simple substance" has no parts (no quantitative elements) and yet must comprehend "a manifold in unity" (Latta, 27). Consider, again, the flowers and fish of *Dream*: each "monad" (flower or fish) is an entity, a simple substance (conceptually) that opens to disclose infinite worlds within.[19]

---

[16] William Ritchie Sorley, "Leibnitz," in *The Encyclopaedia Britannica* [Fourteenth Edition], vol. 13 (London & New York: Encyclopaedia Britannica, 1929), 886.

[17] Samuel Beckett, *Murphy*, edited by J.C.C. Mays (London: Faber and Faber, 2009), 69.

[18] Beckett cites "[d]eterminatio est negatio" in his commonplace book, the "Whoroscope Notebook," with no comment nor any attribution to Spinoza.

[19] Consider Ezra Pound's Image as "that which presents an intellectual and emotional complex in an instant of time" ("A Few Don'ts by an Imagiste," in *Poetry* 1 (1913); rpt. in *Ezra Pound*, ed., J. P. Sullivan (Harmondsworth: Penguin, 1970), 41. That "complex" reflects a unified monadic awareness that may be composed, nevertheless, of infinite *petites perceptions*. A similar

The problem was to find a unit of substance that reconciled or avoided the imperfections of the Cartesian and Atomist theories.[20] Spinoza's philosophy, Latta argues, asserts "the unity and continuity of the whole at the expense of the reality of the parts" (Latta, 22), whereas Atomism "endeavours to establish the reality of the parts at the expense of the whole" (Latta, 23). Enter the monads, as units of substance: "simple, percipient, self-active beings," but endowed with impulses of perception and appetition: "Every monad is a microcosm, the universe in little, and according to the degree of its activity is the distinctiveness of its representation of the universe" (Sorley, 886). Every monad, then, is a complete world: it has perception, but not necessarily as consciousness (Latta, 34); and appetition, an internal principle that produces change or passage from one perception to another (Latta cites the *Monadology*, §15), but not necessarily as conscious will or desire (Latta, 35). The major error of Descartes, Leibniz asserted, was that his insistence on "clear and distinct ideas" took no account of perceptions that were not apperceived (rendered fully conscious), "for it treats as non-existent those perceptions of which we are not consciously aware" (§14, 224). These are the *petites perceptions*, a term employed by Windelband in *A History of Philosophy*. Leibniz instanced the hundred thousand waves that together constitute the moaning of the sea, each in itself indistinguishable but together making up the unified whole (371).[21]

---

aesthetic underlies Bergson's *durée*, Proust's moment, Joyce's epiphany, Virginia Woolf's transparent envelope, and Beckett's "ideal real" as it persisted into his later stage images (these, for all their ironies, are grounded in an aesthetic that is ultimately Modernist).

[20] Compare the contemporary search for the Higgs boson.

[21] This finds frequent expression in Beckett as Zeno's *sorites* paradox: "Which kernel of grain by being added makes the heap? Which hair falling out makes the bald head?" In *Endgame*, this translates itself into human terms: at what point do the separate moments of existence mount up to a life? See C.J. Ackerley & S.E. Gontarski, *The Grove Companion to Samuel Beckett* (New York: Grove Press, 2004), 661, 175.

For Beckett, this point was crucial, for Leibniz's view that each monad acts as "a perpetual living mirror of the universe" could also be applied to the perceptual process. By demonstrating that consciousness is not the totality of mental reality, Feldman argues, Leibniz implied a link between philosophy and psychology (Feldman, 97). Since each monad is, with reference to others, a perfectly independent substance, the monad is not so much *physical* as *psychical* in its nature,[22] and the *petites perceptions* (for Leibniz, the infinitely small constitutive parts of the representative life of monads) may be identified with "*unconscious mental states*" (Windelband, 424; emphasis in the original). This insight facilitated Beckett's identification of the self as monadic, with every moment—however complex or confused its *petites perceptions* might be—constituting a unit of identity, without, however, committing him to either a physical or metaphysical Truth (until, that is, the *psychical* ground is further questioned, as in *Watt*).

In applying this formulation to Beckett's works, I first consider *Murphy*, rather than immediately pursue the *Monadology* toward its distant goals of pre-established harmony and best of all possible worlds (aspects of Leibniz that arise inexorably from the monad, but which elicited Voltaire's ridicule, Russell's bemusement, and Beckett's skepticism). One quality that distinguishes *Murphy* from *Watt*, despite their common matrix, is that the former enacts the Cartesian catastrophe of the solitary monad, whereas the latter rehearses the tragedy of the monad that tries to accommodate itself to the "establishment" (as Mr. Knott's Big House is called).

The origin of *Murphy* is indelibly grounded in the *Monadology*.[23] Although the novel is broadly a Cartesian satire (the failure to integrate body and mind) and/or an Atomist guffaw (the posthumous dispersal of Murphy's "body, mind and soul" in the "necessary

---

[22] Wilhelm Windelband, *A History of Philosophy*, translated by James H. Tufts (New York & London: Macmillan, 1901), 423.

[23] See my Introduction to *Demented Particulars: The Annotated Murphy* (1998, 2004; rpt. Edinburgh: Edinburgh University Press), 20–24.

house" [*Murphy*, 168]), the first entries in the "Whoroscope Notebook" relating to what would become *Murphy* concern the "Impetus" given by H (the horoscope) to X (later to become Murphy), "who has no motive, inside or out, available" (§1). This generates the "[d]ynamist ethic of X. Keep moving the only virtue" (§2). As H "acquires authority of fatality" it becomes no longer "a guide to be consulted" but "a force to be obeyed" (§3). There follows (§4) an explicitly Leibnizian comment:[24]

> X. and H. clarified side by side. Monads in the Arcanum of circumstance, each apperceiving in the other till no more of the <u>petites perceptions</u>, that are life. So that H., more and more organic, is realised in X. as he [via] it, and they must perish together (fire oder was).

This conceives the Monad as attempting to "realize" itself in the "arcanum" (secret wisdom) of "circumstance" (the contingent world), with the horoscope (as in the novel) a "motive" force to replace the 6 God and regulate the machinery of the Big World.[25] X is therefore set in motion, to transform the "petites perceptions" of confused ideas into the clear and distinct insights of apperception. This is in accordance with Leibniz's sense of the individual monad rising from virtual to actual as it realizes more of its potential; the tragedy being that as H and X become increasingly integrated ("clarified side by side" ... "more and more organic"), they reach a state of equilibrium (§3: "after stichomancy [X reading H] had given quietism oder was"), and

---

[24] Quoted from Beckett's "Whoroscope Notebook" (BIF 3000/1) as cited by Feldman, 64–65. I read Feldman's "If corpus of motives" as a "1/- corpus of motives" (i.e., the horoscope originally cost one shilling [later reduced to 6d]). Feldman's statement (65) that the phrase "petites perceptions" is not to be found in "standard translations of Leibniz's *Monadology*" is mildly misleading, as it appears throughout Latta's commentary (and the *New Essays*), though in the translated *Monadology* Latta prefers "little perceptions" (§21, for instance).

[25] Leibniz despised almost nothing, he said, "except judicial astrology and trickeries of that kind" (Latta, 154).

perish together, by fire or whatever,[26] consumed by the Will (Leibniz giving way to Schopenhauer?). This remains obscure, but Knowlson clarifies its tenor by citing from the German Diaries (18 January 1937) Beckett's sense of the "necessary journey" (for Murphy, "the Necessary Staying-Put"), which he relates to the "fundamental unheroic" and real "freedom of choice" (in the quiet zone of the microcosm, which Murphy has not attained) "when the fire comes."[27]

Another echo of Leibniz in Beckett's "Whoroscope Notebook" which is directly applicable to *Murphy* is a curious comment (in English) before the account (in French) of Dives and Lazarus (Luke 16:22–26): "Dives–Lazarus, prayer from virtual to actual in entelechy ... petites perceptions to be apperceived in monad–poem" (*Demented Particulars*, 39 [#5.7]). Yet the monad's presence can be "felt" (the pun enters the later making of Murphy's greatcoat) in several "splendid little pictures" through which the plot arises (from virtual to actual, if you wish). These include: (a) the hermetic sphere that contains Murphy's mind, (b) Murphy as Monad in motion, (c) pads and garrets of the Big World, and (d) Murphy's encounter with Mr. Endon. Despite their apparent diversity, these images are closely integrated.

Murphy's mind pictures itself as "a large hollow sphere hermetically closed to the universe without" (*Murphy*, 69). As such, it is a unit of autonomous substance, independent and self-sufficient, for "it excluded nothing that it did not itself contain" (69). A perpetual liv-

---

[26] Feldman, 68. Noting that Beckett initially structured "what becomes *Murphy*" around Leibnizian monads, Feldman usefully clarifies the fate of X and H by referring to Anaximander's concept of atonement, as mentioned in the "Whoroscope Notebook" [§6]: "Purgatorial atmosphere sustained throughout, by stress on Anaximander's individual existence as atonement"; and as clarified by Beckett in the arcanum of the "Philosophy Notes": the "doctrine that things must perish as an expiation for injustice presents the first dim attempt to conceive the cosmic process as ethical necessity and the shadows of transitoriness" (TCD MS 10967/7v). Feldman is the first to document these matters, and despite minor quibbles I am indebted to his account.

[27] James Knowlson, *Damned to Fame: The Life of Samuel Beckett* (London: Bloomsbury, 1996), 247. The "fire" is best understood in the Heraclitan sense, which consumes all (compare "The Circular Ruins" of Borges).

ing mirror of the universe, it contains within itself—both potentially and ideally—the world without: "Nothing ever had been, or would be in the universe outside it but was already present as virtual, or actual, or virtual rising into actual, or actual falling into virtual, in the universe inside it" (69). In a word, the little world of the mind is a *microcosm* of the Big World, or *macrocosm*, existing outside it. In thus picturing Murphy's mind, and despite copious inpourings from Spinoza, Descartes, Geulincx, Kant, and Schopenhauer,[28] Beckett follows Windelband's discussion (462–464) of Leibniz and the "*virtual innateness of ideas*." As this suggests, Murphy's mind differs crucially from that of Belacqua (*Dream*, 120ff), with which it is otherwise congruent, in that it is monadic—whereas Belacqua is far from apperceiving this potential.

The difference concerns "the conception of *unconscious representations or petites perceptions*" (Windelband, 462). Leibniz distinguishes between states in which the soul merely has ideas (*perception*) and those in which it is conscious of them (*apperception*). This intimates "the process by which unconscious, obscure and confused representations are raised into clear and distinct consciousness" (463). Simple substances with perception but not consciousness are Monads, or Entelechies; those in which apperception is "clear and distinct" he calls Souls (*Monadology* §19; Latta, 230). Sensuous perception is confused thought; knowledge develops from the soul's activity. All ideas are innate, rising from virtual into actual as conscious knowledge; and so, to the scholastic aphorism appropriated by Locke, *Nihil est in intellectu quod non prius fuerit in sensu* [Nothing is in the mind that was not first in the senses], Leibniz added: *nisi intellectus ipse* [except the mind itself] (Windelband, 464; this Latin phrase is recorded in Beckett's "Whoroscope Notebook" with the tag "Leibniz to Locke"). The aphorism shapes a splendid little picture in *Malone Dies*, when the dubious hero takes counsel of an Israelite (one Jackson, an avatar of Spinoza) who owns a pink and white parrot: the feathered biped can utter *nihil in intellectu*, but "the celebrated re-

---

[28] Ackerley, *Demented Particulars*, 116–130.

striction was too much for it, all you heard was a series of squawks."[29]

The monad is self-sufficient: "Each monad is with reference to the rest a perfectly independent being which can neither experience nor exercise influence"; their "windowlessness" is an expression of their "metaphysical impenetrability" (Windelband, 423).[30] The phrasing derives from Leibniz: "The monads have no windows, through which anything may go in or out" (*Monadology* §7; Latta, 219); hence the curious conceit in Part III of *Watt*, where Sam describes the "call" of their weather as yet reaching them, "in our windowlessness" (monadic insulation).[31] A still more obscure jest ends "The Expelled," when the narrator, trapped in a tiny cab—greatcoat and all—is "obliged to leave by the window";[32] unlike the narrator of *Company*, who remains alone in the dark: "The place is windowless."[33] Similarly, Murphy's desire is to retreat into the windowless little world, the third or dark zone of the mind where he is a missile without provenance amidst the tumult of non-Newtonian motion (*Murphy*, 72). To define this primarily in Atomist terms (*Demented Particulars*, 123–30) is not wrong, but it does not acknowledge the paradox of the monad as independent of the physical world while yet reflecting within itself all the elements of the macrocosm. What the Monad offers that the Atom does not, in short, is the synthetic unity of the manifold; or,

---

[29] Samuel Beckett, *Malone Dies*, edited by Peter Boxall (London: Faber and Faber, 2010), 44. This anticipates another "parakeet" jest, when Malone cannot finish his inventory: "a little bird tells me so, the paraclete perhaps, psittaceously named" (77).

[30] Beckett recorded these details in his "Philosophy Notes" (for example, in TCD MS 10967/191). See my *Obscure Locks, Simple Keys: The Annotated Watt* (2005; rpt. Edinburgh: University of Edinburgh Press, 2010), 147 [#152.1].

[31] Samuel Beckett, *Watt*, edited by C.J. Ackerley (London: Faber and Faber, 2010), 129.

[32] Samuel Beckett, "The Expelled," in *The Expelled/The Calmative/The End & First Love*, edited by Christopher Ricks (London: Faber and Faber, 2009), 15.

[33] Samuel Beckett, *Company*, in *Company, Ill Seen Ill Said, Worstward Ho, Stirrings Still*, edited by Dirk van Hulle (London: Faber and Faber, 2009), 42.

more prosaically, the self apperceived as Monad, in principle free of the demands of the Big World: the Monad is an elementary unit of awareness and being.

In the Blackwell *Companion* to Beckett, I map Beckett's conceptual world, not as it really was ("that would be an extravagance and an impertinence," as Beckett wrote in *Murphy* [69]), but as it might have pictured itself to be. This is cast as a three-dimensional computer representation, now available online, a model of the monad that reflects the paradox of a consciousness finally denied its metamorphosis into the light and so destined to return to the realm of the mineral from which it inexplicably arose.[34] This template may be useful as a guide to the dichotomies that shaped the conceptual world of *Murphy* and *Watt*, to convey something of the curious conceit (the Monad) that structures this inner world.

The self-sufficiency of that inner world is repeatedly tested in *Murphy*, and the outcome was not, perhaps, what Beckett expected when Leibniz first entered the "Whoroscope Notebook." *Murphy* may be read as a cautionary tale of one who tries to attain a state of self-sufficiency, but fails to achieve that goal. Images of Murphy as monad suggest why this might be. About to tread the Job-path, he asks Celia to give his coat "a bit of a dinge," which she does: "In vain, it filled out immediately, as a punctured ball will not retain an impression" (*Murphy*, 89). When Murphy leaves, irresolute, Celia hears him hissing, and his strange figure attracts derision from a group of boys playing football in the road. A football is the most common everyday embodiment of the Pythagorean dodecahedron, which of all solids "approaches most nearly to the sphere" (*Demented Particulars*, 71 [#47.9]). A curious image suggests itself: the Monad spiked by the

---

[34] The model may be accessed on the University of Otago (English Department) web-site: www.otago.ac.nz/english/staff/ackerley.html. My thanks to fellow monad, Karen McLean, for helping to design this splendid little picture.

exigencies of Job (allegiance to the Big World), with a hiss as the vital element of air escapes (142 [#143.1]).[35]

Murphy is an image of peripatetic motion, the monad as nomad. His greatcoat,[36] into the making of which much felt (sensation) and size (extension) has entered, allows no "vapours" (Cartesian or Occasionalist) to escape; he is completely self-contained (90 [#72.5]). Such is the idea he might form of himself, yet that image is undone not only by the exigencies of Job, but by his "deplorable susceptibility" (*Murphy*, 112) to Celia and ginger biscuits. These manifest the Proustian desire that undoes Neary quite; but, Murphy believes, they can be set aside. In chapter 10, when the Horoscope as a force to be obeyed (*oder was*) has led him to the Magdalen Mental Mercyseat, he believes (as the epigraph from Gide intimates) that, as one wishing to live "hors du monde" (99), he has found his kind.

In *Murphy*, the Beckettian monad assumes physical forms. Murphy's mew, in the beginning, is not among them, for the door hangs off its hinges and a telephone is still connected (6); these inhibit any attempt to enter the dark zone. Nor is Brewery Road much better, despite the "dream of Descartes" linoleum and walls distempered with a lucky lemon (42), for it is large (a word repeated), furnished, and subject to miscarriage; a cradle for the *vita nuova* of the body rather than the life of the mind. Small wonder, then, that the rocking-chair trembles. However, when Murphy is away Celia sits in his chair, and intimates something of the "larval" impulse (44), the stirrings of Leibniz's *monade nue*. Another room upstairs is rented by an "old boy" who spends his day "padding" to and fro (the motion of the monad). He has much in common with Murphy, and may even have attained a greater degree of monadic impenetrability (he is unknown, unknowable). His death upsets Celia, and after Murphy moves out she moves into his room, which is much smaller.

---

[35] C.J. Ackerley, "Samuel Beckett's Sibilants; or, Why does Murphy Hiss?" *Journal of Beckett Studies* 8.1 (1998): 119–120.

[36] No hyphen in "greatcoat," lest this violate the *monade nue* within.

Murphy, meanwhile, has found his place, in a genuine garret "twice as good" as one he had known in Hanover, because half as large (102). The "garret in Hanover" entered the text only after Beckett, on his necessary journey, visited on 5 December 1936 Leibniz's house in the Schmeidestrasse.[37] In a letter to Brian Coffey (in French, in homage to the original *Monadologie*) from the Leibniz-Haus, already an Arts and Crafts museum, Beckett noted that here, for fifty years, Leibniz "formed distinct ideas, or, worse, let them form in him" (*Letters*, 395).

More hermetic than the garret are the MMM's padded cells, which surpass all that Murphy could have imagined in the way of "indoor bowers of bliss" (*Murphy*, 113). These are "windowless, like a monad" (114); saving the shuttered Judas peephole, the "pads" are the visible embodiment of the ideal monad. And in one of them Mr. Endon abides. Drawn to Mr. Endon, "as Narcissus to his fountain" (116), Murphy cherishes the illusion that he has found his ideal other, "perfect in every detail." Their climatic chess game, however, has a calamitous consequence: Murphy, his pieces in disarray but poised to force Mr. Endon into a move that would finally make the latter acknowledge his opponent, lays down his "Shah" (153); he then looks long into the eyes of Mr. Endon, only to see "himself unseen by him" (156), in the latter's immunity from seeing anything but himself. In the 1964 *Film*, Beckett would return to *Murphy* for not only the Berkeleyan theme of *percipere* and the setting of the room as monad from which all perception is excluded, but also for the "angle of immunity"[38] from the anguish of perceivedness that arises from the failure to extinguish apperception (*Demented Particulars*, 201 [#250.2a]). Murphy, looking into Mr. Endon's eyes, sees that the latter does not

---

[37] This is more explicit in the French translation of *Murphy* (Paris: Bordas, 1947), 119, where the street is specified and Leibniz's death noted (*Demented Particulars*, 148 [#162.1]).

[38] Samuel Beckett, "Film," in *All That Fall and Other Plays for Radio and Television*, preface and notes by Everett Frost (London: Faber and Faber, 2009), 98. "Eh Joe," borrowing much from *Film*, improves upon that monad with a setting that is almost bare.

perceive his own existence, let alone that of another; then, with equal certainty, appreciates that the cost of such inner freedom is the abnegation of awareness, or in a word *insanity*. In an ultimate irony Murphy discovers, to his chagrin, that he is sane, and the loss of apperception is a price, he now understands, that he is not prepared to pay (202 [#250.3]).

The consequences are stark: if Murphy is sane, it follows that his attempts to attain self-sufficiency are misguided, and that his appropriation of Leibniz's Monad, for all its attractions (a bathysphere, perhaps christened "The Great Cod," in which to plummet the inner depths), is not so much cranky as crazy: given monadic awareness as an elementary unit of being, one cannot both extinguish apperception yet be aware of so doing. The immediate consequence, for *Murphy*, is a provisional return to Atomist convictions (for what follows can only be described as a Democritean guffaw) that accommodate, as the Monad cannot, the fundamental irrationality of the microcosm (to say nothing, for the moment, of the macrocosm beyond). What Beckett's flirtation with the *Codology* attains, then, is not consummation, however devoutly wished, but the ambiguous recognition that dalliance with monadic impenetrability is itself absurd. Beckett's fiction to come would engage this theme, in the (finally vain) attempt to penetrate the paradox.

Watt restates the monadic themes of *Murphy*, and the fate of its eponymous protagonist is equally a Cartesian catastrophe: the failure to reconcile an inner self to the contingencies of a contingent world.[39] Watt shares with Murphy not only his outer garb,[40] but the impulse to a self-sufficiency that cannot be sustained. Just as Hamm and Clov are Vladimir and Estragon, but further down the road, Watt is a Murphy figure *in extremis*. Unlike Murphy, however, he does not go out

---

[39] C.J. Ackerley, *Obscure Locks, Simple Keys: The Annotated Watt* (2005; rpt. Edinburgh: Edinburgh University Press, 2010), 14.

[40] On departure, however, Watt wears a waistcoat, which Murphy does not (it makes him feel like a woman), and a hat (which reminds Murphy of the caul).

with a bang, but has time to contemplate a rapprochement between his world and that of his master, Mr. Knott. This does him little good, for instead of enacting the rational consciousness that apperceives itself in rising to a clear and distinct understanding of the Monad of monads, Watt's *petites perceptions* become more confused, and finally drive him into the asylum. Whatever the monadic qualities of the mansions there, his is not obviously the best of all possible worlds.

Whereas Murphy endeavors to attain the freedom of the microcosm, Watt attempts to accommodate the monad to the macrocosm. Latta defines the difficulty: "if the universe consists of an infinity of Monads, each independent of the rest, impenetrable and unaffected by them, and each containing within itself the principle of all its changes, how is it possible for a change to take place in any one of them without destroying the continuity of the series?" (Latta, 40). To circumvent this philosophical objection, Leibniz famously invoked "the system of the pre-established harmony between substances" (Latta, 41). This doctrine holds that while the succession of changes in each monad is different from that in every other, all are in metaphysical harmony: "One Monad influences another ideally; that is to say, not *ab extra*, but through an inner pre-established conformity" (Latta, 42).[41] When the Expelled's head, for instance, reaches its maximum dimensions, his father says, "Come, son, we are going to buy your hat, as though it had pre-existed from time immemorial in a pre-established place" (*The Expelled*, 48). As in every monad each succeeding state is the consequence of the preceding, and the nature of every monad is to mirror or represent the universe, it follows that the perceptive content of each monad will be in "accord" with that of every other. This arises, Leibniz believed, from the very nature of the monads as percipient, self-acting beings, and not from an arbitrary determination by God: "The whole is potentially present and seeks its realisation in

---

[41] This is implicit in *Murphy* in the iterated conviction that "all things hobble together for the only possible" (*Murphy*, 141; *Demented Particulars*, 183 [#227.4]).

each of the parts. Consequently, the pre-established harmony is not arbitrary, but rational: no *Deus ex machina* is invoked" (Latta, 44).

Latta discusses two images that Leibniz used to illustrate this precept: clocks and choirs. Two clocks may keep perfect time in three different ways (Latta, 45). Firstly, they may be linked so that there is a mutual transference of the vibrations between them, resulting in perfect agreement; this corresponds, he suggests, to the Cartesian doctrine of *influxus physicus*, the interaction of the animal and vital spirits.[42] Beckett first read this in Windelband, where it is ascribed to Geulincx. The obvious difficulty of this position—that identifying *where* the transubstantiation takes place does not explain *how* it takes place—led two other post-Cartesian philosophers, Malebranche and Geulincx, among others, to a second option: the clocks are kept in time by the agency of an artisan. This requires the clockmaker's intervention at every moment, and hence a continuum (rational rather than incoherent, one piously assumes) of infinitesimal miracles that even the calculus of Leibniz could not integrate. In the 1960 *How It Is*, for example, the dog with a sudden yip sets off in perfect synchronicity with its master: "no reference to us it had the same notion at the same instance Malebranche."[43] Finally, the two clocks may have been so perfectly constructed that they keep time of themselves, without any mutual influence or assistance (Latta, 46). This was the option Leibniz advocated, from which it follows that the relations between the clocks or monads are metaphysical or ideal, thus intellectually apprehended. This image, Anthony Uhlmann believes, Beckett took from Geulincx, where it is more prominent.[44]

The better analogy, Latta argued, was Leibniz's comparison of the monads to independent musicians playing in perfect choral harmony: "a real harmony formed out of the complementary movements

---

[42] Murphy's conarium, having shrunk to nothing, affords no facility for the two to have commerce (*Murphy*, 6).

[43] Samuel Beckett, *How It Is*, edited by Édouard Magessa O'Reilly (London: Faber and Faber, 2009), 24.

[44] Anthony Uhlmann, *Samuel Beckett and the Philosophical Image* (Cambridge: Cambridge University Press), 78.

of several self-acting units" (Latta, 47). Watt, resting in the ditch en route to Mr. Knott's house, hears the sounds, indifferent in quality, of a mixed choir, voices that "really" seem to come "from without" (*Watt*, 26). The question as to whether such "voices" are internal (schizophrenic?) or external (divine?) recurs incessantly in Beckett's writings over the next thirty years. Other choirs are heard in the post-War prose, under like conditions of extremity, in *Mercier and Camier*, *Molloy*, and *Malone Dies*—each intimating a distant prospect of salvation (as in Goethe's *Faust*) immediately offset by a distrust or rejection of that promise. In *How It Is*, for instance, the considered possibility of a choir gives way to megaphones, prompting the comment: "something wrong there" (93).

The doctrine of pre-established harmony, with its consequent affirmation of optimism and the assertion that this is the best of all possible worlds, is, for the satirist, a sitting "runner-duck," as Voltaire (1757) had demonstrated in *Candide* ("che sciagura"), and Denis Diderot (1773) had confirmed in *Jacques le fataliste* ("comme il était écrit là-haut"). Arsene's "short statement" repeats the "celebrated conviction" that all is well, or at least for the best (31). He then refers to "Lisbon's great day," 1 November 1755 (All Saints' Day), when an earthquake struck at 9:40 a.m., when many were at church, wreaking devastation across Portugal. Like Voltaire and Diderot, Beckett could not accept this as part of a divine plan able to be explained by a principle of sufficient reason, however unclear that principle (from our limited and serial perspective) might seem. Nor could he see suffering as potentially redemptive, whatever Leibniz might argue. In Beckett's paraphrase of Leibnizian thought, taken from his "Philosophy Notes," 1932–1933 (his major introduction to post-Cartesian thought):[45]

---

[45] These notes are from Beckett's summary of Windelband (491–92) in the "Philosophical Notebooks" (TCD MS 10967/212); they are also cited by Tonning (213).

physical evil consequence of moral evil, which arises in finiteness of the creature (*metaphysical evil*); motives to sin in the petites perceptions of finite monad; problem of theodicy reduced to why did God permit evil? Answer: finiteness inseparable from conception of created beings, & imperfection from that of finiteness; a world of perfect beings is a contradiction in terms; thus world without sin unthinkable … impossible. But goodness of God reduces it to a minimum; world is contingent (i.e., may be thought other); of the infinite number of possible worlds variously evil, God has created the one with as little evil as possible; the world is not a metaphysical necessity, but a choice among possibilities made by the all-good will of God, & therefore the best; God's goodness would have welcome[d] a world without evil, but his wisdom, bound to metaphysical law, allowed him only the best among possible worlds.

Thus optimism, Windelband concludes, arises "from supposition of metaphysical necessity of evil" (213).

Watt (largely written during the brutal Nazi era) offers further "splendid little pictures" (rather, extended paradigms) to interrogate that metaphysical necessity. The parable of the famished dog, while mocking the pre-established harmony, identifies the conceptual crux at its heart (*Obscure Locks*, 108):[46]

---

[46] The discussion in *Obscure Locks* is more extensive, and indicates Leibniz as Beckett's target. References are changed to the Faber and Faber text (a new order), and I delete the craven "perhaps" that once qualified the final sentiment.

> This, the most outrageous parody of scholasticism in an impossible treatise, derives from the simple premise that if a dog's dish is put outside at evening full or partly so, and is brought in the next morning, empty, then someone or something must have wrought that change. A dog. A famished dog. A dog kept famished to eat the food. A family that owns the dog. A family that (necessarily) must breed dogs so that there is always a famished dog. And so on, each premise yet fresh premises begetting, until, from the simple statement that "it was necessary" that a dog from outside call at the house and several hypothetical propositions, there finally comes into being (95) an empirical declaration that the name of this dog "was" Kate, and that the family necessary for her being "was" the Lynch family (84). The reification of this is purely linguistic, Nominalist, but by the end of the sequence the image of Kate eating from her dish with the dwarfs standing by (99) *is* substantive: the conditional has become the indicative. In like manner, ~~perhaps,~~ have countless human societies reified their nominalist "gods."

Another perspective is offered by Arsene's moment in the sun—recounted in his "short statement"—when everything seemed to slip, the grains of sand accommodating themselves like monads to the movement of the whole. This testifies to the momentary sense of existence off the ladder (*Watt*, 36), an experience both real and ideal, and not an illusion, though Arsene is buggered if he can understand how it could have been anything else (37). Later in the novel, the meticulous paradigm of the Frog Song (117–118) exposes the transcendental machinery behind the experience: three frogs, Krak, Krek, and Krik (in principle, a Leibnizian choir), croak at intervals predetermined by the Fibonacci series (bars of 3, 5, and 8 respectively), beginning in unison and, after 120 bars, resolving the independent notes in a final chord. Were the intervals to be increased, by adding a fourth frog, Krok (intervals of 13), that resolution would take 1,560 intervals; add Kruk (intervals of 21) to the choir, and total harmony would require 32,760 intervals (*Obscure Locks,* 138 [#136.5]). Membership of the choir is open to all, but even if one assumes that (unlike those of *Dream*) the independent singers will behave the mathematics quickly become impossible.[47]

In like fashion, Part III of *Watt* ends with several paradigms of increasing complexity, with these "series" culminating in lists that are devoted to Mr. Knott's physical appearance. These derive from four simple categories {figure, stature, skin, hair}, each with three terms {fat, thin, sturdy}, {tall, small, middlesized}, {pale, yellow, flushed}, and {dark, fair, ginger}; but the exhaustive enumeration of the 81 sets covers two full pages (*Watt*, 181–182; *Obscure Locks*, 181–184 [#209.7]). Were the categories extended, as they might be infinitely (carriage, expression, shape, size; frail, stocky, freckled, bleached), there would not be room in the entire universe to list all possible variants. The process is obsessively rational, and logically represents the machinery of pre-established harmony, but in the end invites the question: is the pre-established harmony finally distinguishable from the "pre-established arbitrary"?

The latter term is used explicitly in *Watt* (114), after series of series concerning the coming and going of Mr. Knott's servants (he abides; they come and go),[48] the feeling of absurdity followed by that of necessity, and vice-versa (113–114). Bruno's identified contraries—as noted in Beckett's 1929 essay, "Dante...Bruno.Vico..Joyce"—suggest one resolution, maximal order (entropy) implying its identified contrary, total disorder (chaos); consequently, the greatest necessity (harmony) would be identical to the greatest absurdity (arbitrary), and all things ultimately identified with God, "the universal monad, Monad of monads."[49] This quickly becomes circular, but the paradox may be seen from two perspectives,

---

[47] Indeed, the figures given in *Obscure Locks* are wrong, and should be corrected.

[48] Windelband contends (73) that the central problem of Greek ethics, as of physics, concerned the relationship between the unchanging order of things (*ousis*) and the world of change (*genesis*).

[49] Samuel Beckett, "Dante...Bruno.Vico..Joyce," in *Our Exagmination Round His Factification for Incamination of Work in Progress* (London: Faber and Faber, 1929), 5.

from above and below (as it were), the two meeting in the middle, on the perceptual ground where the philosophical encounters the psychical.

As Latta notes (177), looking from above (as Mr. Knott might do):

> ... if God is one of the Series of Monads, it seems impossible to regard Him as the sufficient reason, as choosing to create the system of which He is an element. And on the other hand, if the essence of the Monads is to represent the Universe, and if He (*actus purus*) perfectly realises the universe within Himself, what place is there for a system of Monads apart from Him?

One response raises a further paradox of Berkleyan *percipi*, namely, that Mr. Knott cannot exist unless he is witnessed, the "place" of the Monads being to do precisely that. Yet that way greater madness lies. The other way, from the serial perspective of "Tom, Dick, and Harry" (*Watt*, 113–16), asserts that because the movements of Tom are not *dependent on* or *because of* those of Dick or Harry (each a separate monad, and cannot therefore affect the others), the very notion of the pre-established harmony entails an impossible contradiction. Richard Coe explains:

> For either Tom is temporal, in which case his whole existence is determined by his place in the series; or else he is a-temporal, a-spatial, and independent of the series–he cannot very well be both. *And yet* says Beckett, *this is precisely what he is.* Human existence is a logical impossibility. It belongs to the series and yet evades the series; it is at once in time and out of time.[50]

The "Tomness of Tom" (*Watt*, 116), and hence the Wattness of Watt, is an absurdity (in the strict sense of a rational incompatibility), leaving the individual in much the position Watt had earlier found himself, unable to reconcile (if only by a hairbreadth) a particular pot with the idea of Pot (67). Nor will Watt's enumeration of the *accidents* of his master define his *essence*: a gulf remains between the

---

[50] Richard Coe, *Samuel Beckett* (New York: Grove Press, 1967), 52.

particular and the universal, with the monadic mind so curiously constituted as to perceive itself on both sides simultaneously, but lacking a sure foothold on either. Where does this "logical impossibility" lead the enquiring mind, "always on the alert against itself"?[51] Into the Frogpond, perhaps, where a Leibnizian choir reconciles seriality with essentiality; but, as noted above, the mathematical harmonies quickly assume the lineaments of disorder. For even if one admits the experiential reality of the chord, a transcendental validation of its harmony does not necessarily follow (consider Arsene's "buggered" sunlit moment). One might endlessly rehearse this, or simply agree with the Ottolenghi in Beckett's short story, "Dante and the Lobster," when Belacqua annoys her with inquiries of similar metaphysical urgency: "Where are we ever? ... where we were, as we were."[52]

As Garin Dowd has argued, Beckett in the great works of his middle period returned to the *Monadology*, not systematically to work "a Leibnizian thematic" into his fiction, but rather to revisit "a conceptual detritus" in which "Leibniz's architechtonic resounds."[53] Malone, completing his inventory, acts as an archivist setting out to tabulate "those vaguely perceptible prolongations" of the series of which (dimly) he feels himself part (Dowd, 26). This anticipates *The Unnamable*, with its depiction of *l'homme larvaire* at the threshold that marks the distinction between the possession of mere consciousness (*petites perceptions*) and their translation into apperception. Worm (for it is he) embodies the *monade nue*, or "bare monad" of the *Monadology*, the naked or degenerate form at a low level of representation, invoked as being always "in a state of stupor," for "this is the state in which the bare Monads are" (*Monadology* §24; Latta 1898,

---

[51] Samuel Beckett, *From an Abandoned Work*, in *Texts for Nothing and Other Shorter Prose, 1950–1976*, edited by Mark Nixon (London: Faber and Faber, 2010), 59.
[52] Beckett, "Dante and the Lobster," in *More Pricks than Kicks*, 13.
[53] Garin V. Dowd, "Nomadology: Reading the Beckettian Baroque," 22–23.

231), and so denied his metamorphosis into the light.[54] The incompossible protagonist of Beckett's post-War *Trilogy*, unable to raise his little perceptions to the level of apperception and thus enter the clear zone, must instead "go on" in the dark.

Dowd continues this analysis into *How It Is*, with respect to what he calls the "vigilance of the threshold."[55] Offering the intriguing suggestion that the "archival subject" of *Krapp's Last Tape* represents Leibniz's God, Dowd considers *l'homme larvaire* of *How It Is* as bearing witness before the Tribunal of Reason ("Mud," 2). The mud is "an amorphous plane," apparently ordered from "above"; this raises the question of the ordering principle. Again, this is considered from the perspective of the *monade nue* ("Mud," 4), whose life in the mud is one of stupor, dimly lit by the stirrings of apperception. *How It Is* may therefore be viewed as representing a final attempt to break through the paradoxes of perception that had informed *Murphy* and *Watt*, but remained unresolved in *The Unnamable*; here, as in the novel's predecessors, the protagonist fails again (not even "better") in his attempt to break free, or, in the implicit Leibnizian terms, to realize within himself the *petites perceptions* that might lead into the light. The enterprise is doomed, for though he establishes with reasonable conviction that he is "sole elect" (*How It Is*, 9), such monadic certainty allows no escape from the prisons of language and being (equally the inconclusive conclusion of Beckett's *Texts for Nothing*).

Instead, in the third part of the narrative ("after Pim"), the protagonist considers the old conundrum of the "sacks"—"a possible thing in this world so little possible" (91)—in terms that again question Leibniz's pre-established harmony: "more sacks here then than souls infinitely" (97); and "if we are to be possible our couplings journeys and abandons need of one not one of us an intelligence

---

[54] Leibniz rejects metempsychosis, but offers metamorphosis as the way that the body of the substance, or soul, continually changes by gradual removal of or addition to its parts.

[55] Garin V. Dowd, "Mud as Plane of Immanence in *How It Is*," 1.

somewhere a love who all along the track at the right places according as we need them deposits our sacks" (120). Dowd identifies this loving intelligence with Leibniz's God and the "formula of monads" that expresses "the divinely ordained entirety of existence" ("Mud," 21). Dowd then shows why this conclusion must be finally unsatisfactory for the poor creature in the mud, who arrives at "another solution more simple by far and far more radical" (*How It Is*, 126). That is to say, as the narrator does, that "all this business of sacks deposited" (127) is "unthinkable"; that it is "all balls" (the monad's spherical perfection reduced to a fundamental sound). What remains is the mud, that "plane of immanence" finally "free of the plane of transcendence," one from which any loving intelligence is excluded ("Mud," 22): "no not even a sack" but "only me yes alone yes with my voice" (*How It Is*, 128).

Erik Tonning notes Beckett's "residual dream of a complete transcendence of the *principium individuationis* first formulated in *Proust*" (Tonning, 49). Simply put, though Leibniz was a great cod and that dream of transcendence "all balls," something enduring emerges from the detritus of the *Monadology*. In his later works for stage and screen, Tonning argues, Beckett used specific early sources, such as Leibniz, in "submerged form," as a kind of "scaffolding" that underlies narrative structure to create form (16). Leibniz allowed him to rework such topics as "the self's hermetic solitude, porous insubstantiality, and ineluctable involvement in an inhuman, non-rational system" (17–18), often unexpectedly. The legacy of the Monad, Tonning argues, referring to comments in the German Diaries about Karl Ballmer (22), was what Beckett called the *metaphysical concrete*, that element of abstraction without which there was only "photography" (18).[56]

Beckett relates the "metaphysical concrete" to the sense of the work as totally self-contained: "I think of Monadologie and my Vul-

---

[56] Tonning cites the "German Diaries" (23 January 1937), where Beckett states that the *will* to escape from abstraction is "senseless" (but the wish to indulge it totally even more so).

ture."[57] The "Extraordinary stillness" of the Expressionist painter Ballmer's work, he claimed, makes anything else irrelevant: "Thus Leibniz, monadologie, Vulture, are by the way." In a later Diary entry (24 March 1937), he further asked, with respect to Ballmer's sense of creating out of himself: "Where does this differ from the Monadology?" (Tonning, 24). These entries intimate that Beckett here conceived the artistic mind, and his own in particular, as monadic; its chief aim, he recorded in the Diaries (18 February 1937), was "light in the monad," by which is to be understood the aim of increasing within the soul-monad of the self the awareness of the ineradicable "dark zone" at its center (210). Beckett's poem "The Vulture" is the first of many works of stillness and the unsaid set within the skull, blending the metaphysical with the concrete "simplicity" of its being. This constitutes the lasting aesthetic legacy of Leibniz to Beckett,[58] more important even than the "closed space" settings of so many of the later writings or the more obvious images of the Monad and/or pre-established harmony in serial works such as "Quad" where characters (independent, unknowable) circle enigmatically about a center that might be the All or equally the Nothing (204).

Beckett acknowledged few eschatological certainties, but these included: the incoherent continuum; suffering as unredeemable; irrationality; chaos; nothingness; the senseless, issueless predicament of existence; and the conviction that there was finally no way out. All that could be known, he recorded in the German Diaries (15 January 1937), after his visit to the Leibniz-Haus, are the "straws" and "flotsam" of understanding, which "is at least amusing" (Knowlson, 244). Individual consciousness, in these terms, is an absurdity, an "epiphenomenon of this primary chaos" (Tonning, 33), which rejects Reason as the governing principle of reality. And yet, as Tonning insists,

---

[57] Details from the "German Diaries" (26 November 1936), as cited by Tonning (22) and Knowlson (240).

[58] Tonning indicates (215) that "so dark in his windowless self that no knowing whether light or day" (from the manuscripts of *Stirring Still*) "incontestably" references Leibniz; while "[n]o such thing as no light" (from *A Piece of Monologue*) implies virtual perceptions below the threshold of consciousness.

Beckett's intellectual and literary development was shaped by "a continuous *agon* with Christian beliefs," of which the Leibniz Monad was one of the more fascinating and formidable expressions. He notes the paradox implied by Beckett's attraction to Leibniz's world of teleology and theodicy: despite its radical difference from "philosophies that saw reality as at bottom incoherent, chaotic and utterly alien to the epiphenomenon of human consciousness" (205), let alone Beckett's intense dislike of anthropomorphism, Leibniz was for him a natural and even "obvious" point of resistance, with genuine affection and respect retained for the residua of beliefs that he could not bring himself to share.[59]

---

[59] Beckett's attraction to the Monad is like that to other systems (Dante, Descartes, Freud, Jung), which offer splendid little pictures that (like Christianity) finally will not do. A final frivolity: I am small, round, and bouncy; but occasionally I go flat, so they stick a needle in me and pump me up again. What am I? Answer: Diego Monadona.

"The Books are in the Study as Before": Samuel Beckett's Berkeley

Steven Matthews (Oxford Brookes University, UK)

The suggestion by Beckett's Dublin friend, Joseph Hone, that he read the *Commonplace Book* by the eighteenth-century Anglo-Irish philosopher George Berkeley, presumably came on the back of Hone's recent completion, along with the Italian scholar M.M. Rossi, of a critical biography of Berkeley. Beckett's response to his reading of the book, conveyed in a 1932 letter to Thomas MacGreevy, contains something of the intrigued interest he immediately felt for Berkeley's thought; but also something of his vehement resistance to it. The book is both "full of profound thought," and of "intellectual canaillerie, enough to put you against reading anything more."[1] Yet, that reading nevertheless (perhaps because of the violently dichotomized reaction it brought) seems to have proffered something of value for Beckett. He retained a copy of the *Commonplace Book*, in the 1930 edition by G.A. Johnston, in his library until his death; he also retained a copy of the 1926 edition, by A.D. Lindsay, of Berkeley's key philosophical writings from the earlier part of his career, gathered under the title *A New Theory of Vision and Other Writings*. Lindsay's volume collects, along with *A New Theory*, its successor, *A Treatise Concerning the Principles of Human Knowledge*, and the *Three Dialogues Between Hylas and Philonous*, in which Berkeley sought to defend the more original aspects of his philosophy against his several critics in London.[2]

---

[1] Letter to Thomas MacGreevy of 23 April 1932, in Samuel Beckett, *The Letters of Samuel Beckett, Volume 1: 1929–1940*, edited by Martha Dow Fehsenfeld and Lois More Overbeck (Cambridge: Cambridge University Press, 2009), 154.

[2] See Appendix A of F.N. Smith, *Beckett's Eighteenth Century* (London: Macmillan, 2002), 165.

Successive commentators upon the significance of Beckett's readings in Berkeley have noted the allusions which are made to him directly, in the novels from *Murphy* onward, as well as the tropic significance of some of Berkeley's key ideas within the later work and the drama.[3] The comprehensive article on George Berkeley in *The Grove Companion to Samuel Beckett*, for instance, points to the persistent presence of Berkeleyan tropes (principally concerning perception) from *Murphy*, through *Watt* and *The Unnamable*, to *Waiting for Godot*, *Endgame*, and *Film*.[4] More recently, commentators have referred to recently-released archival sources, and to Beckett's notebooks of the 1930s, in order to expand upon the origins of his interest in the earlier Anglo-Irish writer. This has not only added to our sense of the complexity of the verbal and comic processes with which Beckett contrived to integrate his learning into the novels. It has also brought new ways of considering the textual linkages which exist *between* those varied moments in the novels which relate to Berkeley, and so allows us to reconsider the inflections with which his influence is treated within Beckett's texts.

One example of this archival sourcing provides us, at the outset, with a handy delineation of the territory within which Beckett's difficult, and sometimes polarized, responses to Berkeley were centered. Amongst the best of these more recent interventions, C.J. Ackerley's *Demented Particulars: The Annotated Murphy* points to the reference to Berkeley in the "*Whoroscope* Notebook" in order fully to gloss the complexities and perplexities of the distinctions made in *Murphy*, Chapter Six. Ackerley focuses on these sentences: "This did not involve Murphy in the idealist tar. There was the mental fact and there

---

[3] See, for instance, David Berman, "Beckett and Berkeley," *Irish University Review*, Vol. 14 No. 1 (Spring, 1984), 42–45. Other relevant recent works relating to the two have included Benjamin Keatinge, "Beckett and Language Pathology," *Journal of Modern Literature*, Vol. 31, No. 4 (Summer, 2008), 86–101 and Ann Banfield's "Beckett's Tattered Syntax," *Representations*, Vol. 84, No. 1 (November 2003), 6–29.

[4] C.J. Ackerley and S.E. Gontarski, *The Grove Companion to Samuel Beckett* (New York, Grove Press, 2004), 49–50.

was the physical fact, equally real if not equally pleasant."[5] That this performs a witty reference to Berkeley is proven by Ackerley, via reference in the archive Notebook to Beckett's knowledge of the curious obsession Berkeley had in his later years with tarwater as a panacea (an obsession he passed on to, amongst others, the novelist Henry Fielding, from whom Beckett in turn gained his information).[6] This fairly standard labelling of Berkeley's philosophical stance, as an "idealist" who had little belief in the physical particulars of the world, is derisively attacked by being put into concatenation with, by being seen as being mired in, the risible "tar," which later in life Berkeley prescribed for all ills. The seemingly passing reference adds to the anecdotal and satiric tone with which the philosophizing in *Murphy* more broadly is treated, and suggests that Berkeley presents no lasting solution to the intractable dichotomies with which *Murphy* is broadly engaged—dichotomies between mind and matter, the material and the immaterial, crucially.

But the passing and punning allusion in Chapter Six also adds further to the terms of a subdued debate which have gone on across the novel. That debate casts the Berkeleyan background to the novel in more complicated lights. Such is the annotative nature of *Demented Particulars* that the fact that this reference to the "idealist tar" picks up on, and complicates, certain strains in the direct allusions to Berkeley earlier in *Murphy* is not noted by Ackerley. But it is clear that the Chapter Six presentation of Murphy's sanity, in his lack of "involvement" with "the idealist tar," is some form of response to Neary's mistakenly sympathetic outburst, amid the knockabout "philosophical" banter of Chapter Four: "'I don't wonder at Berkeley,' said Neary. 'He had no alternative. A defence mechanism. Immateri-

---

[5] Samuel Beckett, *Murphy*, edited by J.C.C. Mays (London: Faber and Faber, 2009), 69.

[6] C.J. Ackerley, *Demented Particulars: The Annotated Murphy* (Tallahassee, FL: Journal of Beckett Studies Books, 1998), 105. Ackerley does not give the precise source for his comment on Berkeley and tarwater in the "*Whoroscope* Notebook"; it appears on page 29 of the University of Reading MS3000 document.

alize or bust. The sleep of sheer terror. Compare the opossum'" (*Murphy*, 38). Neary's cod psychology hints at a more various understanding of Berkeley's situation, one at least open to the context which gave to his idealizing philosophy "no alternative," and which is haunted by the nightmare which encroached upon him. The dismissive final reference to the secretive animal (a sly smack at the contemporarily self-involved "possum," T.S. Eliot, perhaps?) does not hide the fact that, in Neary's view at least, there is more to say about the native philosopher whose inclinations ventured into the central territory of *Murphy*; namely, the relation of the mind to (a hostile) material or external world, and the possibilities or otherwise of release from it. Berkeley's "idealism," Neary signals, does not so much reject the material world, as defend itself against it, because there is no other possibility of conciliation.

Such complexity of response to Berkeley as that evidenced in these two, partially opposed, statements in *Murphy* seems evident also in the archival remains that Beckett left regarding him. Broadly, the perplexities of Berkeley's position, that of a seeming disbeliever in the external reality of the material world who consistently denies that to be the case ("the sun that I see by day is the real sun," as he has it in section XXXVI of his *Principles*[7]), are treated equitably if skeptically by Beckett. But such complexity is also a facet of the presentation of the philosopher in those books that we know Beckett dealt with, and retained on his shelves, regarding Berkeley, across the mature part of his own writing career. As is already evident from the *Murphy* instances, the kinds of complexity which Berkeley's writing engages, including the national one, go directly to the center of Beckett's own intellectual concerns.

And that includes the intellectual concerns embodied in, and concentrated by, Beckett's novels and drama, and as exemplified by the aesthetics which he openly discovered, as he moved toward the mature works of mid-career. My essay, therefore, will trace some-

---

[7] *A New Theory of Vision and Other Writings*, edited by A.D. Lindsay (London: J.M. Dent, 1926), 130.

thing of the context of Beckett's reception of Berkeley into his thought and writing, one which complicates the sense implied in *Murphy* that Berkeley was simply a deluded solipsist, one whose confusion of "the mental fact" with "the physical fact" made him easily dismissable within Beckett's continuing, and rigorously skeptical, preoccupation with the relation between these elements. Rather, as I will show toward the end of this piece, Berkeley's own compensatory awareness about the potential absurdities of his position—particularly as demonstrated in his *Three Dialogues Between Hylas and Philonous*—taught Beckett much in terms of his own aesthetic as it evolved in the years immediately after the Second World War.

That there was a national immediacy to Beckett's interest in Berkeley is everywhere evident in both Beckett's allusion to him, and in the context out of which that reading derives. For example, Neary's outburst is sparked by Wylie's anecdote about a "young Fellow of Trinity College"—Berkeley having written his key philosophical work while also being one such "Fellow," and Beckett having recently escaped the prospect of becoming another such. Beckett apparently told Lawrence E. Harvey that his own perpetual feelings about "being absent" from the everyday reality around him led him to associate directly with

> the idealist philosophy of Berkeley. Perhaps it was an Irish thing, basically a skepticism before nature as given, complicated by a skepticism about the perceiving subject as well.[8]

Neary's "defence mechanism" is here amplified into a national trait. And yet this is no random, if tentative, assertion on Beckett's part. The ambiguously Irish origination of Berkeley's thinking is directly taken up in those sources which first introduced Beckett to him.

The introductory essay by the poet W.B. Yeats appended to J.M. Hone and M.M. Rossi's *Bishop Berkeley: His Life, Writings, and Philosophy* had eccentrically and gleefully read into Berkeley's estab-

---

[8] Lawrence E. Harvey, *Samuel Beckett: Poet and Critic* (Princeton, NJ: Princeton University Press, 1970), 247.

lishment of a group of thinkers at Trinity (a group who had, in their turn, skeptically reviewed recent philosophical ideas), what Yeats calls "delight,"

> ...delight in that fierce young man...who established...a secret society to examine the philosophy of a 'neighbouring nation'; who defined that philosophy, the philosophy of Newton and Locke, in three sentences, wrote after each that Irishmen thought otherwise...[9]

The instigation for Yeats' comments would seem to be the closing pages of Berkeley's *Commonplace Book*, that seeming diary of his developing ideas which laid the ground for the philosophical works from *An Essay towards a New Theory of Vision* (1709) onward. In those closing pages of the *Commonplace Book*, Berkeley mounts a direct attack upon the refusal of such as Newton and Locke to give credit for what is evident before their eyes. (In contrast, Yeats describes Berkeley, in terms which would presumably find agreement from Beckett—as will become clear—as "idealist and realist alike" [xxiii]). Within Berkeley's extended peroration, the phrase "we Irishmen" achieves something of an incantatory quality of denunciation:

> There are men who say there are insensible extensions [i.e. of forms of matter]. There are others who say the wall is not white, the fire is not hot, &c. We Irishmen cannot attain to these truths.[10]

Such moments offer their own corrective to the notion, retailed as it is in *Murphy*, Chapter Six, that Berkeley's thinking amounts to little more than an unregenerate "idealism," a victory of mind over matter, and sealing of the mind against it. As Yeats intuits, Berkeley's insistence upon the immediate reality of the world as it is perceived marks the original energy of his ideas, in their determined contradis-

---

[9] W.B. Yeats, "Bishop Berkeley," *Bishop Berkeley: His Life, Writings, and Philosophy* by J.M. Hone and M.M. Rossi (London: Faber and Faber, 1931), xv.

[10] *Berkeley's Commonplace Book*, edited by G.A. Johnston (London: Faber and Faber, 1930), 111.

tinction to the distrust which contemporaneous *English* abstractionist science or philosophy had created toward the world. Berkeley's "attain to" in the above fragment is nicely snide; the Irish rightly cannot win themselves over to share the English delusion that "the fire is not hot &c." In the main text of *Bishop Berkeley*, Hone and Rossi point out that the nationalist impetus of the philosopher's writings had previously "escaped notice"; they locate it, however, within a telling and irresolvable paradigm of attachment which surely spoke to Beckett's own, if later, situation:

> Now so far as can be ascertained, Berkeley himself had no trace of pure Irish blood, and he belonged by association and religious sympathies to a comparatively recent English colonisation. (*Bishop Berkeley*, 29)

The value, according to them, to be found in Berkeley's peroration around "we Irishmen" is ultimately indecipherable, but also purely oppositional. It enables him further to establish distance from those recent philosophical innovations by such as Locke, innovations which had rapidly become seemingly unchallengeable conventions, and which therefore seemed to carry their own imperial force over the mind. Berkeley's "defence mechanism" is at least partly a way of preserving distinction, of asserting a version of the mind which resists complacent otherworldliness, as conceptualized by those from the "neighbouring nation."

Beckett would seem to have felt the implicit charge of the reorientation Berkeley sought to make against the abstractions of a Newton or Locke, in the way he noted down for himself the nature of that resistance. In one of the surprisingly rare interpolative comments in Beckett's "Philosophy Notes," this much seems conceded; it is related that, for Berkeley, "abstract ideas" are "a fiction of the Schools." Instead, for Berkeley as rendered in the "Philosophy Notes," it is the "sensuous idea" obtained from perception of the world which "provokes" ideas in the mind, and which, indeed, provides the "sole content of intellectual activity." Under the heading "Knowledge of the Outer World," a few pages later in the manuscript notebook, Beckett again writes that Berkeley attacked "the metaphysicians," who maintained that an "unknowable substance" "lay within perceived reality," as presenting an "unthinkable" "fiction," something "inexistent." Instead, Berkeley in this reading by Beckett in the "Philosophy Notes" favors the perspective offered by "the naïve consciousness," by "common sense," which locates ideas in the sensuous experience individuals have of "corporeal substance." As Beckett resonantly paraphrases the case, "the *esse* of body is its *percipi*."[11] Beckett's understanding here, as elsewhere throughout the "Philosophy Notes," remains close to one of his central sources for those Notes, *A History of Philosophy* by Wilhelm Windelband:

> For the naïve consciousness, for "common sense," whose cause Berkeley professes to maintain against the artificial subtlety of philosophers, bodies are just exactly what is perceived, no more and no less.[12]

Against Windelband's version of Berkeley's key idea, Beckett's use, in the "Notes," of the correct Latin terminology in the phrase "the *esse* of body is its *percipi*" suggests, however, that he was already familiar with the idea in Berkeley's original form, however now mediated in its explication by later commentary. Hone and Rossi render this key notion from the 1710 *Principles of Human Knowledge* as "*Esse est percipi*, to be is to be perceived—such is the celebrated axiomatical expression" (*Bishop Berkeley*, 36). But the intonation of Beckett's rendering is perhaps closer to the original version, given at the end of section III of Berkeley's book:

---

[11] Samuel Beckett, "Philosophy Notes," TCD MS 10967/203r and 10967/2087r.
[12] Wilhelm Windelband, *A History of Philosophy*, translated by James H. Tufts (London: Macmillan, 1893), 470. Windelband had earlier provided Beckett with the terms about Berkeley's resistance noted above: "Abstract ideas ... are a fiction of the schools; in the actual activity of thought none but sensuous particular ideas exist" (453).

> For as to what is to be said of the absolute existence of unthinking things without any relation to their being perceived, that seems perfectly unintelligible. Their *esse* is *percipi*, nor is it possible they should have any existence, out of the minds or thinking things which perceive them.
> (*Vision*, 114)

"[O]r thinking things" is a nice corrective which opens the kind of Beckettian irresolution and imaginative possibility, in his response to Berkeley, with which my essay is concerned. "Idealist *and* realist" is a logical impossibility; "or" is the displacing crux. "Minds" are both active principles and mechanisms unconnected with the reality they register. That this is the core original understanding in Berkeley's philosophy, although he nowhere else puts it so directly or eloquently using these Latin words, could not be missed by Beckett, since it is emphasized by each of the commentators on that philosophy with which he was familiar. To Hone and Rossi's "celebrated axiomatical expression" should be added G.A. Johnston's "[t]his is the essence of Berkeley's theory" (*Commonplace Book*, xiv) and A.D. Lindsay's declaration of it as Berkeley's "one great philosophical principle" (*Vision*, vii). Johnston, however, and immediately after his statement on "essence," explores the full purport of the observation, one potent for the Beckettian reader, in implying that the perceiver of "unthinking things" in turn must be granted an existence from somewhere other than itself:

> The whole existing order depends on mind. The determinate existence of the world is due to the fact that it is an object of thought or perception. Hence the source of existence must be in that on which existence depends, and that is consciousness. Existence, we may say, is of two kinds; it is either 'perceiving' or 'being perceived'. The universal and comprehensive truth is *esse est aut percipere aut percipi*.
> (*Commonplace Book*, xiii-xiv)

In making this extension of the basic conception by Berkeley into something comprehensive, and of perception, Johnston seems to be giving priority to aphorism 426 in the *Commonplace Book*: "Existence is percipi, or percipere, [or velle, i.e. agere]. The horse is in the stable, the Books are in the study as before" (47). "Perceiving" is equated, in Berkeley's brief aside confirming his existential status quo, with "willing" and "doing" ("velle," "agere"), the desire or action of the mind as it seeks to encounter the world external to it.

Perceiving is what the living consciousness does, rendering the external world existent, in Johnston's emphasis. But this implies a crucial tension to which Beckett's sympathies were creatively attuned. It is a tension as to how far the establishment of "unthinking things" in the mind might be translated also, into a proving, through God-as-perceiver, of the existence of "thinking things"—the individual minds *per se*. And does Johnston's version of this crux imply the *necessity* of a God for Berkeley at all? Does it not relate to all (human) consciousness in relation to "other" consciousnesses? My essay will return to this point continually, in the meantime noting that, for Beckett, "the *esse* of body is its *percipi*" seems almost casually included in the complications of all perceptual being. As Beckett's *How It Is* later conceives it, "the eyes try and see another to whom of whom to whom of me of whom to me or even a third."[13]

Aphorism 426 offers, then, an important crux in Berkeley's thinking, as it is highlighted in the edition of the *Commonplace Book* which Beckett owned. It is a crux which will become key to Beckett's many considerations of the relation of mind to matter, of the physical to the metaphysical, considerations which will receive literal embodiment and dramatic currency in works such as *Waiting for Godot* and *Endgame*. This aphorism 426, given pithy reality in the abbreviations of the *Commonplace Book*, contains, in fine, Berkeley's comprehensive consideration of the same thoughts, given in section CXXXIX of the *Principles*:

---

[13] Samuel Beckett, *How It Is*, edited by Édouard Magessa O'Reilly (London: Faber and Faber, 2009), 93.

> What I am myself, that which I denote by the term I, is the same with what is meant by *soul* or *spiritual substance*. If it be said that this is only quarrelling at a word, and that since the immediate significations of other names are, by common consent, called *ideas*, no reason can be assigned, why that which is signified by the name *spirit* or *soul* may not partake in the same appellation. I answer, all the unthinking objects of the mind agree, in that they are *entirely passive*, and their existence consists only in being perceived; whereas a soul or spirit is an active being, whose existence consists not in being perceived, but *in perceiving ideas* and thinking. (*Vision*, 185–186)

Herein lies the extension of his ideas which Berkeley, in the seventeenth century, was able to make, but which Beckett, in the twentieth, could not, although *Godot* and the other plays make frustrated dramatic action and interchange out of the possibility.

Wilhelm Windelband concluded the section of his *A History of Philosophy* on the Enlightenment, the section in which his comments on Berkeley appear, by noting that "the tendency of the Enlightenment philosophy [was] toward *establishing the universal, 'true' Christianity by means of philosophy*. True Christianity is in this sense identified with the *religion of reason*" (487). Quite to the contrary, Hone and Rossi call the expansion of Berkeley's speculations into consideration of such things as "spirit," a "metaphysical leap," *un*reasoning. They conceive the notion that God is necessary within Berkeley's philosophical panorama, God as the creator who oversees the finite perceivers of the unthinking objects in the world, as a "difficulty" founded upon "vague" and under-articulated concepts (*Bishop Berkeley*, 87, 88). That this is a difficulty partly associated in Beckett's mind with Berkeley continues to be proven in the mangled rant of Lucky in *Waiting for Godot*:

> ... what is more for reasons unknown but time will tell to shrink and dwindle I resume Fulham Clapham in a word the dead loss per caput since the death of Bishop Berkeley being to the tune of one inch four ounce per caput approximately ...[14]

That Berkeley's death brought a "dwindling" to be calculated, and calculated with, "per caput," suggests an unexpectedly central place for the philosopher within the play's paradigms. Behind Estragon, Berkeley's Hylas (meaning "matter"), perhaps. Behind Vladimir, Philonous ("love of mind"), within the *"Dialogue"* which the play engages, in its temporizing in the absence of that God who put these entities into creation at the beginning.

Several things further might immediately be noted, however, about the impossible "leap" in Berkeley as described by Hone and Rossi, things which would seem to keep the issue as originally conceived by him at the center of Beckett's debates with himself through his writing from the outset. The first is that, as established in section CXXXIX of the *Principles*, the issue for Berkeley involved in the "leap" from physics to metaphysics is largely one brought about by the belated intransigence of the language itself. If the "immediate significations of other names are by common consent called *ideas*," then, even when dealing with more complex and less immediate "appellations" ("spirit," "God'"), Berkeley's assumption is that there must be a similar chance or hope of "signification." A thread through all of his philosophy is the encounter with, and resistance against, an English language which had become degenerate, and lost its expressive powers. This is a preoccupation of the Introduction to the *Principles*:

---

[14] Samuel Beckett, *Waiting for Godot*, edited by Mary Bryden (London: Faber and Faber, 2010), 41.

> If any one shall join ever so little reflexion of his own to what has been said, I believe it will evidently appear to him that general names are often used in the propriety of language without the speaker's designating them for marks of ideas of his own, which he would have them raise in the mind of the hearer.[15]

Against (English?) "propriety," what is "evident," are "marks of ideas," which, if properly expressive, "mark" the "mind of the hearer." They also establish true identity upon a speaker ("his own"), one established against the polite vagaries of that "propriety." Aphorism 178 of the *Commonplace Book* had seen Berkeley in anguish at "[s]peech metaphorical more than we imagine; insensible things, & their modes, circumstances, &c. being expression for the most part by words borrow'd from things sensible ... Hence many-fold mistakes" (*Commonplace Book*, 19). In the shift from "signification" to "metaphor," the essential reality in the equation of words ("ideas") and things is dissipated—"intelligible" qualities merely "borrow" a reality from the more immediately experienced "sensed" ones, they do not *own* it.

Similar distinctions and preoccupations underwrite also a plethora of decisions about the translation of a world into writing, which were taken by Beckett across his career, decisions which he was alert to from the beginning. Three years before first reading this fret by Berkeley, about the drift of language into metaphor, Beckett had occasion, in "Dante...Bruno.Vico..Joyce," to remark that "no language is so sophisticated as English. It is abstracted to death. Take the word 'doubt': it gives us hardly any sensuous suggestion of hesitancy."[16] That words enact physical mimesis, and that they should so communicate to their hearers (leave their "mark"), is a perception shared by Beckett and Berkeley. For the former, however, the physical is a condition towards which language must be brought; for Berkeley, that

---

[15] *Vision*, 108. A similar point is made in section 120 of *A New Theory of Vision* itself (68).

[16] Samuel Beckett, *Disjecta: Miscellaneous Writings and a Dramatic Fragment*, edited by Ruby Cohn (London: Calder, 1983), 28.

proximity can be a condition of despair that "ideas" can ever be fully expressed. Beckett's wry launching of the little word "doubt" against the iconic "sophistication" of "English," is, of course, a proleptic version of that "complication" which he later raised with Lawrence E. Harvey; that is, a "skepticism" about and within "the perceiving subject" which, as emblematic of a Berkeleyan aesthetics in Beckett, I will raise at the end of this piece.

At the heart of the "difficulty" in translating experience into language, the difficulty which Berkeley engages is the recurring problem of expressiveness, of finding a hearer to hear the contents of the individual mind, and then of making her or him hear them so as to leave their "mark." Hone and Rossi encompass the "difficulty" which, for them, generates the "metaphysical leap" in Berkeley:

> On the road to the New Principle it is then impossible to avoid the peril of solipsism, i.e. of affirming that our mind, and our mind *only*, is real.
> (*Bishop Berkeley*, 61)

"God" is, in Berkeley's thought as rendered by Hone and Rossi, the entity which redeems the individual from a windowless and unconfirmed mind as the *only* "reality." Windelband, having described the Cartesian implications of a dependence of the material world upon mind, as conceived in his view by Berkeley, draws this conclusion:

> If ... the whole corporeal world is only an idea in the mind, every individual is ultimately certain only of his own existence; the reality of all else, all other minds not excluded, is problematical and cannot be demonstrated. This doctrine was at that time designated as *Egoism*; now it is usually called *Solipsism*. (*A History of Philosophy*, 471)

Beckett asks himself the crucial question in the "Philosophy Notes," presumably having read at least the Windelband extrapolation of the seemingly unfortunate implication of Berkeley's original thinking: "Body therefore is a *complex of ideas*—nothing real. What remains when the real qualities are abstracted? Nothing."[17] What is extremely and thrillingly the case, however, is that such an absolute contemplation, as encouraged at least partially by Berkeley, unleashes an imaginative possibility in Beckett which underwrites the nature of that contemplation rendered through a large number of his characters of the post-Second World War career. This is true, even from the time of *Murphy*, which is seemingly the first direct fictional involvement with these possibilities. Against Neary's sense that the "solipsistic" condition is the "sleep of sheer terror," there is Murphy's famous consideration of the encounter with Mr. Endon during the game of chess:

> ... Murphy began to see nothing, that colournessness which is such a rare postnatal treat, being the absence (to abuse a nice distinction) not of *percipere* but of *percipi*. His other senses found themselves at peace, an unexpected pleasure. Not the numb peace of their own suspension, but the positive peace when the somethings give way ... (*Murphy*, 154)

"Numb" autistic "peace" might give way to a "positive," if accompanied by something of that "reflection" upon the self that Berkeley continually encourages ("so little reflection of his own"). Lurking somewhere behind this is a humor like that of Dr. Johnson, who, Boswell reports, greeted the retreat of someone who had been praising the "ingenious" philosophy of Berkeley with the raillery "don't leave us; for we may perhaps forget to think of you, and then you will cease to exist."[18] It is the hilarious nightmare confronted by O in *Film*, the seeking of "inexistence" via invisibility; in a minor key, it is the "colourlessness" of the whitened eyes of Hamm in *Endgame*.[19]

---

[17] Samuel Beckett, "Philosophy Notes," TCD MS 10967/207r.
[18] James Boswell, *Life of Johnson*, edited by R.W. Chapman (Oxford: Oxford University Press, 1980), 1085.
[19] Samuel Beckett, *Endgame* (London: Faber and Faber, 2009), 7. Beckett's one-off *Film* is, of course, beloved of critics who try to think through the paradigms from Berkeley in Beckett's work—hence it will not be treated at length here. A comprehensive statement of the case is offered by Ruth Perlmutter, "Beckett's *Film* and Beckett and Film," *Journal of Modern Literature*, Vol. 6 No. 1 (February 1977), 83–94.

Berkeley had a specific figural method of contemplating the solipsistic "peril" (as Hone and Rossi saw it) of his inductive philosophy, a figure which would seem to have left its own particular mark on Beckett. In proof of the greater "certainty" of "ye existence and reality of bodies" which he claims to hold over Locke's abstractions, in the *Commonplace Book* Berkeley suggests that "any one" might experience "solidity": "put a flint between his hands and he will know" (8)—almost in itself an anticipatory refutation of Johnson's notorious kick in refutation of Berkeley's idealism. "To restore silence is the role of objects," as the speaker in *Molloy* spells it out.[20] But the sequence of thoughts which the *Commonplace Book* enacts will posit a more distinctive and absolute potentiality:

> 594. A good proof that Existence is nothing without or distinct from perception, may be drawn from considering a man put into the world without company. (71)

Such a solitary "man" meanders through the middle third of the *Commonplace Book*, as he will become the ironic "hero" of Beckett's later fictions. For Berkeley, such a man is primarily victim of the inability of words to get through ("I have no idea of Existence, or annext to the word Existence. And if others have that's nothing to me" [81]—the Beckettian intonations abound). As such, therefore, words rapidly reach their tautological extreme:

> 598. 'A stone is a stone.' This a nonsensical proposition, and such as the solitary man would never think on. (71)

It could never be "thought on," because such tautologies render the world (and its thinker) "inexistent," with "nothing" to think. The Cartesian "Cogito ergo sum" is, for Berkeley, just another "Tautology. No mental proposition answering thereto" (91). Paradoxically, and nonsensically, tautologies only "make sense" in and between "company," "ideas," as Berkeley has it, "being incommunicable by

---

[20] Samuel Beckett, *Molloy*, edited by Shane Weller (London: Faber and Faber, 2009), 68.

language." Molloy, solitary, seeking to calculate the incalculable, does not make the same kind of "nonsense" as that contemplated in aphorism 598.

> I took advantage of being at the seaside to lay in a store of sucking-stones. They were pebbles but I call them stones. (*Molloy*, 69)

Berkeley's questioning is, then, essentially as to what kind of company the solitary would have to make, with her- or himself and with "others," in order to be able to think of her- or himself as an "I" (as in "I took advantage … I call them"):

> 613 *Qu.* whether the solitary man would not find it necessary to make use of words to record his ideas, if not in memory or meditation, yet at least in writing—without which he could scarce retain his knowledge. (*Commonplace Book*, 73)

That "at least in writing" is compelling: writing as final recourse, neither "memory or meditation" in itself, but simple retainer of "knowledge" or the experience of having been in the world as a thinking being. "Memory is obviously conditioned by perception," as Beckett had understood via *Proust* in 1931.[21] Berkeley's creatures are similarly as conditioned by the circumstance of "Time":

> 206. *Qu.* Wherein consists identity of person? Not in actual consciousness; for then I'm not the same person I was this day twelve-month but while I think of wt I then did. Not in potential; for then all persons may be the same, for ought we know. (*Commonplace Book*, 22)

"The same," presumably, because ultimately and testingly "solitary." Under such an aegis, writing emerges as both the record and the "mark" of solitariness, not a guaranteed puncturer of the solipsistic ectoplasm. And out of some such paradox arises the Beckettian career.

---

[21] Samuel Beckett, *"Proust" and Three Dialogues With Georges Duthuit* (London: Calder, 1965), 30.

More intriguing, perhaps, because less hubristic, is Berkeley's encounter, in the *Commonplace Book* and elsewhere, with his own first discipline, mathematics:

> 657. Wt would the solitary man think of number? (78)

"The solitary man," presumably, would not think of number as an accurate measure, since he would have nothing to measure it against. Molloy, in trying to apportion his sucking-stones equally around his pockets, so that each of the sixteen gets sucked in turn, faces several "defeats": "For I was beginning to lose all sense of measure, after all this wrestling or wrangling" (*Molloy*, 71). Matthew Feldman has written compellingly about the ways in which, for Beckett, "a mathematical appropriation is not heretical, but heuristically useful," but only so once it embraces a non-Euclidean sense of number and geometry.[22] But Berkeley had embraced "[t]he surds, doubling the cube &c." (*Commonplace Book*, 36) previously—indeed, to do so is the necessary beginning of the *New Theory* which his philosophy presents:

> 580. They talk of determining all the points of a curve by an equation. Wt mean they by this? Wt would they signify by the word points? Do they stick to the definition of Euclid? (69)

Berkeley's use of the third person plural pronoun at such moments is very telling. It preserves "thoughts" from becoming objects of derision. But it presents the "they" as the objects of all that the *New Theory* needs to be written against: "There is nevertheless a use of computation by them to determine the apparent magnitude of things" (*Vision*, 50). *Apparent*: "they" do not really understand computation, which can never be "very precise and exact since the judgments we make of the magnitude of external things do often depend upon several circumstances" (50). Beckett's late envisagings of geometrical worlds devoid of "circumstances" ("Imagination Dead Imag-

---

[22] Matthew Feldman, *Beckett's Books: A Cultural History of Samuel Beckett's "Interwar Notes"* (London: Continuum, 2006), 17.

ine," *The Lost Ones*) end by acknowledging the irredeemable nature of their content. Like Berkeley, Beckett's writing, at its various outsets, is more dependent upon these "several circumstances," than upon what "they" want to make of them. Near the start of *Molloy*, for instance:

> What I'd like now is to speak of the things that are left, say my goodbyes, finish dying. They won't want that. Yes, there is more than one, apparently .... I've forgotten how to spell too, and half the words. That doesn't matter apparently. (*Molloy*, 3)

Berkeley's *An Essay towards a New Theory of Vision* predicts his mature philosophy, in that it proves that the "apparent" computations, principally of the distance of objects and their "magnitude," are dependent upon an individual's experience, and not upon some measurement founded upon "lines and angles":

> 24. What seems to have misled the writers of optics in this matter is that they imagine men judge of distance as they do of a conclusion in mathematics, betwixt which and the premises it is indeed absolutely requisite there be an apparent necessary connexion: but it is far otherwise in the sudden judgments men make of distance. We are not to think that brutes and children, or even grown reasonable men, whenever they perceive an object to approach, or depart from them, do it by virtue of geometry and demonstration. (*Vision*, 18–19)

As ever, the failure of mathematical explication of what is before the eyes (of everyone), allows Berkeley to take his epistemological point further. The "confusion" brought to vision by distance, a confusion only overcome by use (Malone moving his objects to and from him), demonstrates the variability of experience with relation to the world:

> Again, suppose I perceive by sight the faint and obscure idea of something which I doubt whether it be a man, or a tree, or a tower, but judge it to be at the distance of about a mile. It is plain I cannot mean that what I see is a mile off or that it is the image or likeness of anything which is a mile off, since that every step I take towards it the appearance alters, and from being obscure, small, and faint, grows clear, large, and vigorous. And when I come to the mile's end, that which I saw first is quite lost, neither do I find anything in the likeness of it. (*Vision*, 32)

Given the perspective of distance, all apprehension risks misapprehension, or at least risks imaginative embellishment. Such is the epistemology established at the outset of Beckett's *Trilogy,* as the speaker casts his eye across the landscape:

> So I saw A and C going slowly towards each other, unconscious of what they were doing. It was on a road remarkably bare, I mean without hedges or ditches or any kind of edge, in the country, for cows were chewing in enormous fields, lying and standing, in the evening silence. Perhaps I'm inventing a little, perhaps embellishing, but on the whole that's the way it was. (*Molloy*, 4)

What Berkeley calls in section 15 of his *Essay* the inexplicable "phenomena of *distance*" opens for Beckett the fictive prospect ("without an edge"). The speaker, presumably on a bluff or incline, posthumously writes out (if that is what he is doing) what it was "I saw" at a distance. If what he had seen was more proximate it might be more irrefutable; distance, in space or time, ensures that he alone remains "conscious" "of what they were doing," but in turn becomes emblematic of all processes of experience and comprehension across the novels.

"Consciousness," and its opposite, seem to be one key facet of Berkeley's epistemology, and thence his aesthetics, which Beckett to an extent shares with him. A and C are "unconscious" that they are approaching each other only from the speaker's superior perspective. As section III of the *Principles*, cited above, makes clear, perception only establishes the relative "existence of *un*thinking things" (my emphasis). But while section III of the *Principles* seems, at least syntactically, to grant that matter, objects might exist independently of a perceiving mind; yet section XC would seem to deny this to be so:

> Sensible objects may likewise be said to be without the mind, in another sense, namely *when they exist in some other mind*. Thus when I shut my eyes, the things I saw may still exist, but it must be in another mind. (*Vision*, 158)

The "metaphysical leap" again, or, in Beckett, the frequent "mark" of the leap into the consciousness of the drama, as when Clov turns his telescope upon the audience in *Endgame*. But about the relation between the "perceiving mind" and the "other" perceiving mind, Berkeley is necessarily silent, given his version of the solving "solitariness" of the first mind, its necessary "distance" from what it might seek to connect with ("that's nothing to me").[23] The extremity of this position seems to have been one that Berkeley could not always live with. This, I take it, is the strange motivation behind the seemingly meaningless semi-concession made by Philonous to Hylas in the final pages of Berkeley's otherwise fluent and consistent *Three Dialogues*:

> HYLAS: ... To say, there is no *matter* in the world, is still shocking to me. Whereas to say, there is no *matter*, if by that term be meant an unthinking substance existing without the mind; but if by matter is meant some sensible thing, whose existence consists in being perceived, then there is *matter*: this distinction gives it quite another turn ... (*Vision*, 301)

Philonous is not antipathetic, surprisingly, but links the issue to a growing feeling that Berkeley later presents in the final pages of *Three Dialogues*, that language is decaying into incoherence. "Matter," as a term in philosophical discourse generally, Philonous claims amazingly, has become dangerous: "there is not perhaps any one that hath more favoured and strengthened the depraved bent of mind toward *atheism*, than the use of that general confused term" (302).

---

[23] Beckett, *Endgame*, 20. Aphorism 902 of the *Commonplace Book* quotes a scholar called Clov on the predictabilities of human behavior relative to social status.

"Confused," but prevalent in his own discourse across the dialogues, and in Berkeley's philosophy throughout; the ending of the *Three Dialogues* is obviously, and self-destructively, ironic. Philonous lapses further into incoherence, seeking a fine and unconvincing distinction between "vulgar" and "philosophical" uses of the term "matter." Hylas seems happy, in contrast, with his concession that "matter" might be "a collection of sensible qualities subsisting only in the mind." For Berkeley, as for Beckett, the establishment of "company" between "thinking things" (only humans?), or of true relation between humans and the "sensible" external world ("matter"), would remove the "necessity" of an all-containing, all-seeing, and all-foreseeing God—a thought shied away from by Berkeley, and never unambiguously endorsed in the dramatic contexts created by Beckett either.

Beckett's *Three Dialogues With Georges Duthuit* stand in ironic relation to their titular and generic counterpart, Berkeley's *Three Dialogues Between Hylas and Philonous*: ironic firstly in their opacity, compared to the original's eloquence, even when increasingly "confused" in their last pages. Also, ironic in that, rather than "witnessing" a discourse, as in Berkeley, the figure B in Beckett's version bears some more or less distant relation to a person discoursing along to some other more or less identifiable other ("with"). But Beckett's version is instructive, in that it recognizes that the "difficulty" which Berkeley fails to negotiate in these matters is at least partly one of aesthetics, rather than of "epistemology." Beckett's *Three Dialogues* predicts to that extent the evolution of the *Trilogy*. Taken with the 1948 essay "Peintres de l'Empêchement," *Three Dialogues*' sense of the "obstacle" that the external object of painting presents to painting itself—the challenge to its history, and to the process of seeing—launches the concept of unknowability characteristic of Beckett's later work. Mr. Knott in *Watt* (1944) needs his servants, because their seeing him confirms that he has existence; the speaker at the opening of *Molloy* "knows" A and C to the extent that he chooses to, and is no longer concerned, amid what Alan Ackerman has called the "layering of contradictions" in Beckett's later aesthetic, to validate their reality.[24]

Berkeley's Philonous mounts a similar understanding that there is an unaccountable distinction between the "perceiving subject" and the things perceived, one which the "I" will never succeed in articulating:

> I know what I mean by the terms *I* and *myself*; and I know this immediately, or intuitively, though I do not perceive it as I perceive a triangle, a colour, or a sound. The mind, spirit, or soul, is that indivisible unextended thing, which thinks, acts, and perceives. I say *indivisible*, because unextended; and *unextended*, because extended, figured, moveable things, are ideas ...
> (*Vision*, 267)

"Les Peintres" offers a parallel, if inverse, radical "resolution" to the intractable difficulty, on the one hand envisaging "abandoning [the object as a thing of] weight, density, solidity," and, on the other, "by admitting that the object is...locked up and buried always in itself, without traces."[25] But this does not mean that Beckett is the more sanguine either, about the articulation of what he calls, in conversation with Lawrence E. Harvey, the "perceiving subject." B's "inability," at the end of the final dialogue, to "submit" or "admit" the notion that what is needed is a "new occasion," a "new term of relation" through a "fidelity to failure," marks his continued alertness to his countryman Berkeley's frustrated sense that such issues remain indeterminate, that they must continually be considered again (*Disjecta*, 145).

Berkeley's seeming "difficulties," "peril" in establishing a relation between "mind" and "matter," "perception" and "the real," dramatize for Beckett the necessity to present art as the site for a continuing and continuously changing negotiation between the two. Use-

---

[24] Alan Ackerman, "'Spectres du Noir': The Being of Painting and the Flatness of *Film*," *Contemporary Literature*, Vol. 44, No. 3 (Autumn 2003), 416.

[25] *Disjecta*, 136. I quote Ackerman's translation (made to different ends), from page 417 of his article cited above.

fully for Beckett, Berkeley presents an oppositional aesthetics which situates such negotiation itself as the subject and object of art, and one which renders distance and failure as the ironically positive outcome of that experience.

Beckett's "Guignol" Worlds: Arnold Geulincx and Heinrich von Kleist

David Tucker (University of Sussex, UK)

Geulincx and the "guignol world"

In December 1935, Beckett returned to his family home in the south Dublin suburb of Foxrock for Christmas. He arrived from London, where he had been living and struggling with the composition of his first published novel, *Murphy*. His correspondence with Thomas MacGreevy gives some insightful clues to that novel's fitful progress. *Murphy* had been started months earlier, around the middle of August 1935.[1] By 22 September Beckett had written about 9,000 words. This rose to 20,000 over the following couple of weeks.[2] Beckett described how the labor of *Murphy*'s composition had "little excitement attached to it" and, despite working hard at it, the book was proceeding "very slowly" (*Letters*, 283). Upon his arrival back in Ireland, things did not improve immediately for Beckett. He became quite ill, and was forced to spend a week in bed with a bout of pleurisy.

In January 1936, however, while still recovering from illness, work on *Murphy* was to be reinvigorated by a determined period of autodidactic research. Venturing within what he called "the abhorred gates"[3] of Trinity College, Dublin (hereafter TCD) library for the first

---

[1] See John Pilling, *A Samuel Beckett Chronology* (Houndmills: Palgrave Macmillan, 2006), 55.

[2] See Samuel Beckett to MacGreevy, 22 September 1935, in Samuel Beckett, *The Letters of Samuel Beckett, Volume 1: 1929–1940*, edited by Martha Fehsenfeld and Lois More Overbeck (Cambridge: Cambridge University Press, 2009), 277; and Beckett to MacGreevy, 8 October 1935 (283).

[3] Beckett to MacGreevy, 9 January 1936. In Matthijs Engelberts, Everett Frost and Jane Maxwell, eds., *Notes diverse holo—Catalogues of Beckett's Reading Notes and other Manuscripts at Trinity College Dublin, with Supporting*

time since resigning from a teaching post at the university four years earlier, Beckett embarked on a three-month period of highly organized and focused research into the obscure seventeenth-century philosopher of what history has dubbed "Occasionalism," Arnold Geulincx. Beckett revisited the library at TCD numerous times between January and April 1936 to transcribe over fifty pages of notes in the original Latin from three of Geulincx's major works found in the collected three-volume edition *Arnoldi Geulincx: Anverpiensis Opera Philosophica*, edited by Jan Pieter Nicolaas Land, published between 1891 and 1893.

Beckett was fascinated by Geulincx's obscure and idiosyncratic philosophy. Indeed, he even speculated in correspondence with MacGreevy that it was precisely the fact that "the text is so hard to come by" (*Letters*, 318) that drew him to the philosopher's Latin volumes in TCD, after discovering Ireland's National Library did not hold copies. On the other hand, in the same letter Beckett also acknowledged what he called his "instinct" for Geulincx's work, a less rationalized intimation of affinity, or an exploratory need to know. Geulincx's singular project of completing the Cartesian program in an epistemologically grounded, rationalist, Christian-mystical ethics was not simply a blind spot in Beckett's private records of the history of Western philosophy, though his interest in the topic had been piqued a few years earlier by reading Wilhelm Windelband's *A History of Philosophy*. Geulincx's melding together of diverse ideas into something wholly new, a system that was, despite its variety, thoroughly cohered by a foregrounding of ignorance and impotence—the thoroughgoing incapacity of humanity to do anything in the world—certainly strikes a chord with what we know in hindsight of Beckett's aesthetic development over the decades after 1936. And while Beckett's commitment to this research was not so disciplined as to reach the end of Geulincx's major *Ethica*, his handwritten and then typed transcriptions (and re-transcriptions) from this work as well as from

Metaphysica Vera testify to a deep immersion in this philosopher's thought, as well as to the more prosaic desire to escape the sometimes claustrophobic family house.

Picking up the word *occasion* that was left underdeveloped by Descartes' discussions of mind-body interaction, Geulincx argued that the only way anyone can be said to do anything at all, the only way that anything can be said to have *occasion* for occurring, is due to the agency of God. My mind, like Murphy's mind when his body is hushed into stillness in his chair, is cut off from the physical world unless and until God deigns to forge connections between them. This God does, fortunately, and continually, evidenced by the fact that things in the physical world do indeed move. Yet Geulincx argues that I cannot be the cause of any action or thought because I cannot articulate (and so, his rationalist epistemology goes, I cannot be said to know) clearly and with reason *how* such a thing happens. It is this interest in epistemology that primarily distinguishes Geulincx's Occasionalism from that of his contemporaries Nicholas Malebranche (1638–1715), Louis de la Forge (1632–1666), and Géraud de Cordemoy (1614–1684). In defining what might qualify as knowledge stated of an event, such that knowledge passes his stringent epistemic tests, Geulincx argues that even an anatomist (in a paradigm of scientific knowledge) cannot properly say how their arm is moved. There is, according to Geulincx, something missing from a purely physical account of such movement, of blood flow and what he calls the movement of "animal spirits." Anatomy does not reach, cannot speak of, the ineffable how of causation that is missing from such an account. Geulincx describes such scientific knowledge as merely *a posteriori*, according to which it is "no more than a consciousness and perception of *the fact that* motion is taking place."[4] It is not a substantive explanation of *how* that motion takes place.

---

[4] Arnold Geulincx, *Ethics: with Samuel Beckett's Notes*, edited by Han van Ruler and Anthony Uhlmann, translated by Martin Wilson (Leiden: Brill, 2006), 228 (emphasis added).

This ineffable *how* is hugely important for Geulincx, for it is with his idea of the ineffable that Geulincx distils and fuses his contrasting impetuses as a rationalist-Christian-mystic. Something is "ineffable" for Geulincx because it cannot be articulated with rational discourse:

Something is said to be *ineffable* not because we cannot speak or think of it (for this would be *nothing, nothing* and *unthinkable* being the same), but because we cannot think about or encompass with our reason how it is done.

> As Geulincx writes, "an ineffable something is always missing" (*Ethics*, 334); there always remains a residue of experience not exhausted by knowledge of that experience. Only God, as Arsene in *Watt* might say of "what has so happily been called the unutterable or ineffable,"[5] can properly know such ineffable forces. For limited, non-knowing humanity, Geulincx would concur with the servant's appraisal that "any attempt to utter or eff it is doomed to fail, doomed, doomed to fail" (*Watt*, 61).

Beckett's period of 1936 research into Geulincx's philosophy has been known of for many years, and has been acknowledged a number of times. The research's temporal contiguity with the composition of the final stages of *Murphy*, and the many references to Geulincx in the book, have concomitantly led critics to discuss that novel as, to cite Ruby Cohn's characterization from 1960, by far "the most Geulincxian of the works."[6] Cohn was discussing an article by Samuel Mintz that had appeared in a special issue of *Transition* (1959).[7] In that first article on Beckett's critical and creative relationship with Geulincx, Mintz cites, as he was obliged to do and as others must also do when discussing the "Geulincxian" aspects of *Murphy*, the moment at which the novel's narrator climactically describes their pro-

---

[5] Samuel Beckett, *Watt*, edited by C.J. Ackerley (London: Faber and Faber, 2009), 61.
[6] Ruby Cohn, "A Note on Beckett, Dante, and Geulincx," *Comparative Literature*, vol. 12, no. 1 (Winter 1960): 93–94.
[7] See Samuel Mintz, "Beckett's Murphy: A Cartesian Novel," *Perspective*, vol. 11 (Autumn 1959): 156–165.

tagonist's selfhood. Getting to what is, for Murphy, the crux of the matter (that matter being, narcissistically, the very nature of Murphy himself) becomes, in turn, a matter of philosophy. Specifically, for Murphy this is a matter that could and should be placed in the terms in which Geulincx summarizes his ethical philosophy, in the axiom *ubi nihil vales, ibi nihil velis*, translated in the 2006 publication of *Ethica* as "*wherein you have no power, therein you should not will*" (*Ethics*, 337) (though critics have previously translated this as "where you are worth nothing, there you should want nothing,"[8] following Beckett's own translation of the axiom in *Murphy*). The Geulingian nature of Murphy's self is the paradigm according to which, at a crucial moment, Murphy commits himself to the "little world" of his interiority:

> His vote was cast. 'I am not of the big world, I am of the little world' was an old refrain with Murphy, and a conviction, two convictions, the negative first. How should he tolerate, let alone cultivate, the occasions of fiasco, having once beheld the beatific idols of his cave? In the beautiful Belgo-Latin of Arnold Geulincx: *Ubi nihil vales, ibi nihil velis.*[9]

In his ethical conviction Murphy also commits himself to the asylum, and so to the ignominious fate that imprisonment as a consequence of this commitment eventually brings. Murphy is responsible for "two convictions" as two commitments—firstly his ethical belief, but secondly his (self-)imprisonment, his being unable to escape his death in an asylum along with the rest of the *committed*.

There are further reasons for critics to explore *Murphy*'s Geulingian themes and specific allusions. In 1967 Beckett wrote to Sighle Kennedy in response to questions the latter had sent about how "the critical statements in your essay '*Dante...Bruno.Vico..Joyce*'" might

---

[8] C.J. Ackerley, *Demented Particulars: The Annotated Murphy* (Tallahassee, FL: Journal of Beckett Studies Books, 2008), 157.

[9] Samuel Beckett, *Murphy*, edited by J.C.C. Mays (London: Faber and Faber, 2009), 112.

"serve as a valid yardstick for measurement of your later work."[10] Beckett wrote, in an oft-cited letter:

> I simply do not feel the presence in my writings as a whole of the Proust & Joyce situations you evoke. If I were in the unenviable position of having to study my work my points of departure would be the "Naught is more real..." and the "Ubi nihil vales..." both already in *Murphy* and neither very rational.[11]

Whenever Beckett mentions his work in correspondence in the context of his fascination with Geulincx, it is always *Murphy* that must somehow bear the weight of the obscure reference. This widely cited letter to Kennedy (which is reprinted in *Disjecta*)[12] broadly repeats the kinds of thoughts Beckett had expressed a number of times to other correspondents while he was researching Geulincx thirty years earlier.

However, further correspondence—parts of which remain unpublished—complicates what might otherwise appear to be a fairly straightforward lineage of commentary by Beckett on his interest in Geulincx. In late 1956 Beckett wrote to the writer and lifelong friend of T.S. Eliot, Mary Hutchinson,[13] in a very similar way to how he would write to Kennedy some eleven years later:

---

[10] Kennedy to Beckett, 7 May 1967, in Sighle Kennedy, *Murphy's Bed: A Study of Real Sources and Sur-Real Associations in Samuel Beckett's First Novel* (Lewisburg: Bucknell University Press, 1971), 302.
[11] Beckett to Kennedy, 14 June 1967. In Kennedy, *Murphy's Bed*, 300.
[12] Samuel Beckett, *Disjecta: Miscellaneous Writings and a Dramatic Fragment*, edited by Ruby Cohn (London: Calder, 1983), 113.
[13] Hutchinson, a member of the Bloomsbury group, published a book of short stories in 1927 entitled *Fugitive Pieces*. See Pilling, *Chronology*, 235.

> I feel more and more something that is almost if not quite a loathing for almost everything I have written and simply cannot bear to go back over it and into it. If there is a queer real there somewhere it is the Abderites, mentioned in Murphy, complicated by—ibidem—the Geulincx 'ubi nihil vales etc.' I suppose these are its foci and where a commentary might take its rise. But I really do not know myself—and don't want to know—par quel bout le prendre [by whatever end it is grabbed], and can't help anyone.[14]

Beckett and Hutchinson then corresponded further on the subject of Geulincx, and on 28 November Beckett referred to his difficulties of twenty years earlier in locating editions of Geulincx's works. He also described Geulincx's ontological foregrounding of incapacity and dependence upon God as a world of puppetry, a world in which God is the all-powerful puppet-master and people are His puppets, entirely reliant on God for their capacities of movement:

> Geulincx hard to come by. I read him in TCD library, the National Library didn't boast the Ethics. Frightful kitchen Latin but fascinating guignol world.[15]

Beckett's assessment in this letter of Geulincx's language complicates the earlier admiration voiced in *Murphy* for the "beautiful Belgo-Latin." Also very intriguing is Beckett's description of Geulincx's world as "guignol," a world of puppetry. Guignol himself was a French forerunner of the English puppet Punch, and colloquial French use of his name is as an insult, despite the fact that Guignol himself is witty and tends to triumph over adverse circumstances. The puppet was designed as a peasant figure intended to represent provincial men from the Dauphiné region by the puppet-master Laurent Mourguet (1769–1844). As will be argued below, however, there is more to Beckett's reference than just this character.

---

[14] Beckett to Hutchinson, 7 November 1956. Mary Hutchinson Papers, Series II, Subseries B, box 2, folder 4, Harry Ransom Humanities Research Center (HRHRC).

[15] Beckett to Hutchinson, 28 November 1956. Mary Hutchinson Papers, Series II, Subseries B, box 2, folder 4, HRHRC.

Tropes of puppetry appear throughout Beckett's *oeuvre* from his earliest works written before the 1936 Geulincx research. In "Love and Lethe," for example, the courting couple are likened to puppets not fully in control of their actions, who appear to the narrator, and therefore also to the reader, as not especially authentic:

> Like fantoccini controlled by a single wire they flung themselves down on the western slope of heath. From now on till the end there is something very secco and Punch and Judy about their proceedings [...][16]

This critique of Belacqua and his lover Ruby Tough is, perhaps, just as much a self-deprecating comment on the abilities of the narrator as a personal judgment about the characters' "character."

The narrator of *Murphy* insists along similar lines that their star protagonist is distinguished from the other characters in the novel precisely in being the only one properly free from constraint:

> All the puppets in this book whinge sooner or later, except Murphy, who is not a puppet. (*Murphy*, 78)

Yet Murphy's self-determination, manifested in his rejection of Suk's horoscope, and his refusal to search out a job, for example, or again, refusing to explain himself to curious onlookers such as Ticklepenny, comes with its own problems that undermine the distinction conferred by the narrator. In July 1936, shortly after finishing writing the novel, Beckett described Murphy's apartness to MacGreevy; this time he admitted its flaw:

> There seemed to me always the risk of taking him too seriously and separating him too sharply from the others. As it is I do not think the mistake (Aliosha mistake) has been altogether avoided.[17]

---

[16] Samuel Beckett, *More Pricks than Kicks*, edited by Cassandra Nelson (London: Faber and Faber, 2010), 87 ("fantoccini"—"puppet" or "doll;" "secco"—"dry").

[17] Beckett to MacGreevy, 7 July 1936 (*Letters*, 350). Beckett's reference to Aliosha is to one of the brothers in Dostoevsky's *The Brothers Karamazov*.

Murphy's freedom, the thing that Murphy takes most seriously, separates him from the other puppets of the novel a little too baldly; he thereby becomes a different kind of puppet.

Similarly, the narrator of *The Unnamable* describes himself as being "in my Punch and Judy box,"[18] and promises to finish telling their stories once "a few puppets" contrived for "company" (2, 1) have been scattered. When using the tropes of puppetry, then, Beckett is most frequently concerned with how puppets and puppetry might function as framing imagery for a fictional character—for a writer's, or narrator's "vice-exister" (26) as *The Unnamable* dubs it—and for that character's dependence on the controlling, behind-the-scenes puppet-master that is the author.

Moreover, such puppetry of Beckett's early and middle periods, specifically the puppetry of a "guignol world" that owes a debt to Beckett's 1936 fascination with Geulincx, finds a reinvigorated and particularly focused manifestation in certain of Beckett's late works. Indeed, there are specific and identifiable reasons for Beckett's early concerns being reinvigorated. In introducing these arguments, focus will shift some twenty years after Beckett's early research, to the short mime *Act Without Words 1*, before going on to look at the even later prose text "Still."

Act Without Words I

Beckett appears to have also had such guignol worlds—worlds in which humanity depends upon an anonymous and invisible puppet master—very much in his mind in 1956. The 28 November letter to Hutchinson in which he described Geulincx's "fascinating guignol world" was written around the time Beckett was working on the play he nicknamed, in a letter to Alan Schneider on 15 October 1956, "the

---

[18] Samuel Beckett, *The Unnamable*, edited by Steven Connor (London: Faber and Faber, 2010), 53.

desert mime."[19] This short mime, *Act Without Words I*, presents a man taunted in a desert, a man whom Beckett later described as "human meat—or bones."[20] The nameless man is pushed and pulled around by an offstage, unseen authority, sometimes even with the explicit use of ropes, indicating the figure's status as a mere puppet for forms of manipulation and torture. A number of critics including Ackerley, Matthew Feldman and Shane Weller, argue that at least in part (to quote Feldman), "Beckett's source for *Act Without Words I* is [...] Köhler via Woodworth."[21] This reading refers back to Beckett's psychology notes of 1935, where he transcribed a passage from Robert Woodworth's *Contemporary Schools of Psychology* that describes Wolfgang Köhler's experiments recorded in *The Mentality of Apes*. Beckett noted that he should read Köhler's book (though there are no extant records that he did in fact go on to do so), and recorded Woodworth's summary of Köhler's experiments conducted in Tenerife of 1913–1917, many of which involved chimpanzees and monkeys trying to reach food baskets and single food items suspended from above by climbing trees or standing on boxes, sometimes boxes stacked (usually precariously) one upon the other. The imagery evoked, diagrammed and even reproduced in nine photographs by Köhler in *The Mentality of Apes* is certainly suggestive of "the action and setting,"[22] as Ackerley describes them, of *Act Without Words I*. The heated confines of a pen in Tenerife, for example, might go some way to accounting for why Beckett chose a "desert" as the uncharacteristic setting for the mime.

---

[19] Beckett to Alan Schneider, 15 October 1956, cited in Maurice Harmon, ed., *No Author Better Served: The Correspondence of Samuel Beckett and Alan Schneider* (Cambridge, MA.: Harvard University Press, 1998), 12.

[20] Quoted in S.E. Gontarski, "'Birth Astride of a Grave': Samuel Beckett's *Act Without Words I*," in S.E. Gontarski, ed., *The Beckett Studies Reader* (Gainsville, FL: University of Florida Press, 1993), 31.

[21] Matthew Feldman, *Beckett's Books: A Cultural History of Samuel Beckett's "Interwar Notes"* (London: Continuum, 2006), 106.

[22] C.J. Ackerley, *Demented Particulars: The Annotated Murphy*, second edition (Tallahassee, FL: Journal of Beckett Studies Books, 2004), 37.

Weller argues on this topic, referring specifically to a female chimpanzee observed by Köhler who would wrap her own arms around herself when she wanted to be held:

> the movement in his [Beckett's] later dramatic works towards a purely bodily language is arguably a movement towards the language of an animal, not as what the Oxford English Dictionary terms a being "endowed with life, sensation, and voluntary motion," but as a suffering being, defined by lack not in Descartes's, Kant's, or Heidegger's sense, but because this being 'experiences' lack and 'expresses' that lack by making of her own body both a stage and a substitute.[23]

Weller's incorporation of Beckett's much earlier reading about Köhler under a broader banner of "suffering" reconciles the very differently shaped ideas with which Beckett appears to have himself been experimentally building *Act Without Words I*. That is to say, if Köhler is important to Beckett as some kind of "source" for this mime, then *why* this might be so is as important a question as the comparative *how*.[24] As will be argued, multifaceted dynamics of suffering operate within both *Act Without Words 1* and "Still," understandings of which can be deepened if we move beyond Köhler and the apes, and into the more abstract territory of puppetry.[25]

---

[23] Shane Weller, "Not Rightly Human: Beckett and Animality," in Minako Okamuro, Naoya Mori and Bruno Clément, eds., *Borderless Beckett/Beckett sans frontières: Tokyo 2006, Samuel Beckett Today/Aujourd'hui* (Amsterdam & New York: Rodopi, 2008), 218.

[24] The congruity between the imagery in Köhler's study and *Act Without Words I* is both striking and surprising; it is highly unusual that Beckett would take such imagery as so straightforward and thoroughgoing a "source" for an entire work, albeit a short work, as is maintained by Feldman and Ackerley, particularly when there is a gap of some twenty years between his reading Woodworth and writing *Act Without Words I*. The unknown quantity in such a direct extrapolation from Köhler to this mime is this intervening twenty years, and whether or not Beckett ever made good on his note to himself to read *The Mentality of Apes* in the original. The book was not in Beckett's Paris library, though that proves little.

[25] *Act Without Words I* has indeed been produced as a mime using puppets. In 1964 Bruno and Guido Bettiol made a ten-minute film of the mime using

The man enters the stage of *Act Without Words I* "flung backwards"; he is whistled back offstage and is flung back on again twice before he "hesitates, thinks better of it, halts, turns aside, reflects."[26] The whistle continues to direct his action, calling his attention to objects or locations on stage. It makes him aware of the palm tree, carafe of relieving water, the scissors with which he attempts to cut the rope and ponders how they might also sever his neck, and the cubes with which he builds. But it is perhaps the ropes of the play that most forcefully illustrate him as puppet. The text does not specify how any of the objects should be lowered, only stating a rope when one is dropped for the man to climb up (the "umbilical rope"[27] as Gontarski describes it in an Existentialist reading), which he then severs with the scissors. Yet the practicalities of performance dictate that objects would be lowered either by rope or some other kind of thread, amenable to being hoisted slower or more quickly as the text specifies. Such ties are akin to those of a puppet, and as the man reaches up to the water, bundles cubes on each other and falls off them trying to reach skywards like Köhler's apes, his movements appear as those of a marionette. Though, importantly, a marionette separated from his puppeteer. As the water is lowered so the man raises his hands, and as the cubes are deposited so he goes to them. He is brought *"hither"* to act *"here"* just as for Geulincx God brings humanity into the world to act here, connected invisibly and conducted entirely at the mercy of this unknowable, unspeakable, "ineffable" authority.

Yet there is self-consciousness to this puppet, an awareness of his impotence. The puppet-like man is continually preoccupied with his own hands; he looks at them at the beginning of the play, cuts his fingernails part way through the play, and in his final gesture prior to

---

puppets, and in 1983 Margaret Jordan filmed a seventeen-minute animated version (source: British Film Institute).

[26] Samuel Beckett, *Krapp's Last Tape and Other Shorter Plays*, preface by S.E. Gontarski (London: Faber and Faber, 2009), 41.

[27] S.E. Gontarski, "'Birth Astride a Grave': Samuel Beckett's Act Without Words I," 32.

the curtain, "[h]e looks at his hands" (44) again. This is a man decidedly in a world where his own instruments of capacity are no use, "despite a prehensile thumb."[28] They cannot prevent his being tortured, however much he might rebel, and as the play progresses his frustration turns to disillusion. As the man stares at his own impotent hands while the curtain falls the effect is one of witnessing his implicitly, silently, in mime, asking similar questions to those asked by Geulincx of his "guignol world":

> Why do so many and such great calamities conspire against me? Have I offended God in some way? [...] Thrust into a body as if into a prison, am I paying the penalties that I have deserved, and among others this grave one, that I am oblivious of the offence that I am expiating? (*Ethics*, 351)

In order to see more clearly how *Act Without Words I* functions within Beckett's changeable dynamics of suffering as an instance of tortured puppetry, however, the arguments will benefit by contrasting it with the later, short prose piece "Still."

"Still"

Written between 17 June and the end of July 1972,[29] "Still" has a multivalent relationship to what, in 1947 and 1948, Beckett referred to as his "series" of works.[30] Standing apart as an individual piece, the only one of the *Foirades/Fizzles* initially written in English (before Beckett's self-translation, something he undertook with most of

---

[28] C.J. Ackerley and S.E. Gontarski, *The Grove Companion to Samuel Beckett*, 380.

[29] See Mary Bryden, Julian Garforth and Peter Mills, eds., *Beckett at Reading: Catalogue of the Beckett Manuscript Collection at The University of Reading* (Reading: Whiteknights Press and the Beckett International Foundation, 1998), 172.

[30] See C.J. Ackerley, *Obscure Locks, Simple Keys: The Annotated Watt* (Tallahassee, FL: Journal of Beckett Studies Books, 2005), 12, and Beckett to George Reavey, 8 July 1948, HRHRC.

his published texts), "Still" constituted some of the final work in that series. It was also the first text of the tripartite collection that includes "Sounds" (1972–1973) and "Still 3" (1973). Both these later pieces received their first publication alongside an essay by John Pilling in *Essays in Criticism* (1978) in which Pilling praises "Still" as an achievement of Beckett's "syntax of weakness," a phrase Beckett used in correspondence with Barbara Bray in 1959 and again in an interview with Lawrence Harvey in 1962.[31] "Still" also conveys a tripartite series that is internal to the text—before, during, and after a specific event; its first and third sections are comprised predominantly of strong declarative sentences describing the scene, one of stilled energy that is unsettled, in the piece's middle section, by the physical movement of the narrated protagonist's hand and head.

Even in this tripartite structure, "Still" retains traces of Beckett's fascination with Geulincx. Back in 1936, Beckett had transcribed a passage from Geulincx's *Ethics* that summarizes the importance of a tripartite structure for Geulincx; interestingly, it is a passage that in its English translation retains Beckett-like brevity:

> Totus fum (totus huc veniendo, totus hic agendo, totus hinc abeundo).[32]
> I have my whole being (in coming hither, acting here, departing hence). (*Ethics*, 337)

According to Geulincx, I live, or rather transit, my life entirely in relation to the fixed presence of God. I orbit God's stable pres-

---

[31] Beckett used the term in communication with Bray to describe his work in the second notebook in which he was composing the beginning of *Pim*, as *Comment c'est* was then called. On 11 March 1959 Beckett wrote, "I'm struggling along with the new moan, trying to find the rhythm and syntax of extreme weakness, penury perhaps I should say" (TCD MS 10948/1/22). I am grateful to Mark Nixon for his help with these quotations from TCD MS 10948/1. See also Lawrence E. Harvey, *Samuel Beckett: Poet and Critic* (Princeton, NJ: Princeton University Press, 1970), 249.

[32] Arnold Geulincx, *Arnoldi Geulincx Opera Philosophica, Volumes I-III*, edited by Jan Pieter Nicolaas Land (Hagae Comitum: Apud Nijhoff, 1891–1893), vol. 3, 37. Cf. TCD MS 10971/6/25.

ence—perhaps in a similar manner to that in which "Malone passes" the narrator of *The Unnamable* in their nether-world, along with what resembles "the pseudocouple Mercier-Camier" (4, 7), all of whom wheel round the apparently stilled narrator. Such a tripartite coming, being, and going had also served to structure the narrative of works prior to "Still." Parts of the six notebooks in which *Watt* was composed, for instance, set out from Beckett's concern with precisely these terms. As Cohn has noted, the character Watt emerges from the chrysalis of a first-person plural narrator through a conceptual apparatus of coming, being, and going:

> It is in A3, penned in several places while Beckett eluded the Nazis, that the character Watt moves to the forefront. On the very first page Beckett lists: "1. The Coming; 2. Downstairs; 3. Upstairs. [These are grouped as "The Being."] 4. The Going."[33]

Aspects of this tripartite structure are then retained and echoed, in refined form, in the finished novel of 1953:

> Mr Knott was harbour, Mr Knott was haven, calmly entered, freely ridden, gladly left. (*Watt*, 115)

It is a pattern that echoes Beckett's transcriptions of Geulincx's description of ethical life and humanity's corresponding obligations, according to which "every Obligation of man is concerned with either coming hither, being here, or departing hence; in short, with *hither*, *here*, or *hence*" (*Ethics*, 350).

Yet "Still" reflects a Geulingian impetus in much more than its tripartite structure of the hand and head coming "*hither*" towards each other, being "*here*" if only for a moment with each other, before departing "*hence*" from each other. In *The Grove Companion to Samuel Beckett*, C.J. Ackerley and S.E. Gontarski suggest that the nature of the middle section's movement itself, the protagonist's arm rising up to meet his head and his head lowering down to meet his arm, the ac-

---

[33] Ruby Cohn, *A Beckett Canon* (Ann Arbor: University of Michigan Press, 2001), 110. "A3" is the third notebook of six, according to Cohn's own system.

tion around which the work centers and which disturbs the surface of the first part's declarative stasis, "constitutes a return to the concerns of Geulincx and the Occasionalists."[34] These Occasionalist "concerns" to which Ackerley and Gontarski point are primarily metaphysical in nature. Paralleling Geulincx's ethical axiom of *ubi nihil vales, ibi nihil velis* is a metaphysical axiom that appears in Beckett's notes from both *Metaphysica Vera* and *Ethica*:

> Quod nescis quomodo fiat, id non facis.[35]
> What you do not know how to do, is not your action.[36]

This axiom summarizes the unusual epistemological criterion of Geulincx's Occasionalism, described above, which concludes that no one can be said to actually do anything at all, even something as simple as lifting an arm, because they do not how they could possibly do it.

"Still" describes physical movement as an occurrence that is separate from the protagonist thinking about this movement, let alone willing that movement. As the narrative pace is quickened in the transition from the first to the second section of the text, the nameless man's body seemingly moves of its own, or of someone else's, accord; "this movement impossible to follow let alone describe":

---

[34] C.J. Ackerley and S.E. Gontarski, *The Grove Companion to Samuel Beckett*, 543.

[35] Geulincx, *Opera*, vol. 2, 150 & vol. 3, 207. Cf. TCD MS 10971/6/2v (*Metaphysica Vera*), TCD MS 10971/6/14v and TCD MS 10971/6/35 (*Ethica*).

[36] Arnold Geulincx, *Metaphysics*, translated by Martin Wilson (Wisbech: Christoffel Press, 1999), 35.

> The right hand slowly opening leaves the armrest taking with it the whole forearm complete with elbow and slowly rises opening further as it goes and turning a little deasil till midway to the head it hesitates and hangs half open trembling in mid air. Hangs there as if half inclined to return that is sink back slowly closing as it goes and turning the other way till as and where it began clenched lightly on end of rest.[37]

The man's right hand here takes "with it" the entire forearm. This right hand has the ability to hesitate, and it can seemingly choose to hang there, deciding on its own to return to the armrest. It is a steady and graceful movement that disturbs the declarative stasis of the first part of "Still," and in this steadiness the movement contrasts with the body's un-still-able "trembling all over" (155) of the first part, thereby constituting an opposition of stasis to movement, as well as one of movement to stasis. The arm's graceful movement is described not wholly unlike a budding plant, its "opening leaves" referring not only to the arm's leaving behind the armrest, but like "slowly opening" and "opening further" also do, revealing a pastoral impetus in the movement that echoes both Arsene's contrarian diagnosis in *Watt*—that any budding will inevitably wither—as well as nature's sun and valley seen through the windows by the protagonist in "Still"'s first part. The scene also carries an echo of a Celtic past in "deasil," a Scottish (perhaps surprisingly not Irish) Celtic word which the OED defines as meaning "[r]ighthandwise, towards the right; motion with continuous turning to the right." The word connotes of magic, and of rituals involving people moving clockwise round a sacred stone or a significant building.

The movement of this hand, then, read by Ackerley and Gontarski as a "return to the concerns of Geulincx and the Occasionalists," can indeed appear to illustrate Occasionalist incapacity. The narrator does not substitute for God, "the Bastard, he [who] doesn't exist,"[38] a

---

[37] Samuel Beckett, *Texts for Nothing and Other Shorter Prose, 1950–1976*, edited by Mark Nixon (London: Faber and Faber, 2010), 156.

[38] "[T]he bastard, he doesn't exist" paraphrases a quotation from Hamm in *Endgame*, but Beckett reportedly also replied to a question from Edna

farcical astrological backdrop such as Suk's Horoscope in *Murphy*. But with the Celtic interjection (of a word that also appears repeatedly in 1964's "All Strange Away") nevertheless brings a hint of otherworldly magic, ritual and witchery to this familiar movement, yet one that in "Still" is made strange.

The fact that Beckett focuses specifically on the movement of a hand, as Geulincx does in *Ethics*, adds further weight to the suggestion that such movement draws upon Beckett's Geulingian interests. His emphasis, in the 1936 transcriptions from Geulincx, on the movement of a hand, arm or body follows examples given in *Ethica*. Transcriptions from *Metaphysica Vera*, for example, contain the following on the movement of a hand:

> Manus nostra non movetur ad imperium voluntatis, sed ad concensum.[39]
> But my hand is moved not at the command of my will, but by consent to it. (42)

For Geulincx, as we have seen, movement in the physical world is entirely dependent upon God's willing the action, a God who "in an ineffable manner conjoins certain motions" (*Ethics*, 231) with an individual's will. A human body, according to Geulincx, has no more capacity for being independently influenced than any other material in the external world. Movement only takes place by a miracle of divine coordination. Thus, one is conjoined to all only when God wills it.

Intriguingly, however, there is a gulf of difference between the guignol worlds of *Act Without Words I* and "Still." The slapstick music-hall knockabout of *Act Without Words I*—which takes place under the bright light of a blazing sun, using comic props, with the man's

---

O'Brien (who was writing an article for the *Sunday Times Magazine* in 1986) with the same sentence: "'God—do you have any thoughts you would like to air, about God?' 'No ... no ... none ... Wait, [vigorously] I do—the bastard, he doesn't exist'" (Edna O'Brien, "Samuel Beckett at 80," *The Sunday Times Magazine* [6 April 1986], 53).

[39] Geulincx, *Opera*, vol. 2, 270. Cf. TCD MS 10971/6/3v.

action directed by sudden and surprising whistles—makes way for an interior that resembles Beckett's own house at Cooldrinagh, perhaps even Molloy's destination—his mother's room. The puppet-like movements themselves also change; there is slow and steady movement in place of what was rapid and jerky. Pilling notes how the stasis of "Still" enacts Beckett's simultaneous achievement and reconciliation with earlier authorial aspirations:

> Nothing better illustrates how far Beckett has travelled in forty years of writing than the way he has 'enlivened the last phase of his solipsism' not, as his 'sometime friend' Belacqua did (in *More Pricks than Kicks*, 1934), 'with the belief that the best thing he had to do was to move constantly from place to place', but rather with the belief that the best thing he can do is to keep still.[40]

How might such a transition in Beckett's guignol worlds, from movement to stasis, be thought of? What can be said about the nature of Beckett's "return to the concerns of" an apparent Occasionalist philosophy in his late work, beyond its echoes of earlier Geulingian themes and allusions? An answer to these questions reveals an important instance of Beckett's ability to combine different philosophical analects into a new, entirely coherent aesthetic idiom. It is a process that itself recalls Geulincx's multifaceted approach to philosophy. As the narrator of 1954/5's *From an Abandoned Work* put it, "[s]o in some way even olden things each time are first things, no two breaths the same, all a going over and over and all once and never more" (*Texts*, 63). As this suggests, in "Still" Beckett combines an "olden" thing with a new "first" thing, in order to make something that is at once "a going over and over" old "concerns" and that is also "once and never more." It was, it appears, Beckett's reading Heinrich von Kleist at this time which prompted a "return" to the concerns of Occasionalism as a concern with puppetry. At least in part, it is Kleist who accounts for the huge differences between the guignol worlds of earlier work such as *Act Without Words 1* and that of "Still."

---

[40] John Pilling, "The Significance of Beckett's *Still*," in *Essays in Criticism*, XXVIII, no. 2, 1978, 143.

Kleist

Beckett's interest in Kleist's famous essay on puppetry and grace was first brought to light in Knowlson and Pilling's groundbreaking 1979 collaboration, prior to Knowlson sharpening the matter further in his biography of 1996.[41] When Beckett's interest was first reported in 1979 it was with an important caveat:

> If, on the little evidence available, there is no justification for speaking of actual influence, there is much common ground to be explored between Kleist's essay and Beckett's own ways of thinking about art, the theatre and life. (*Frescoes*, 277)

More than thirty years on there now appears to be a little more evidence for something resembling a complex kind of "influence." Beckett's interest in puppetry, an interest that betrayed a pivotal debt to Geulincx, was revived and intensified following what appears to be a discovery made by Beckett datable to late 1969, and that resulted from Beckett's friendship with Barbara Bray. It is clear from their correspondence that Bray frequently sent Beckett works to read, and this is what appears to have happened with Kleist. In a letter from Beckett to Bray, dated 2 September 1969 (around thirteen years into their voluminous correspondence), Beckett mentioned what he called "grace in the Kleistian sense,"[42] and a month later he wrote: "Got the Kleist Marionetten theater ([?]) and other essays."[43] On 13 October of the same year, Beckett told Bray that he had "read Kleist's marvellous essay on Marionetten theatre with unforgettable anecdote of duel with bear."[44] There is also circumstantial evidence that points to these dates as Beckett's major period of thinking about Kleist. For instance,

---

[41] See James Knowlson and John Pilling, *Frescoes of the Skull: The Later Prose and Drama of Samuel Beckett* (London: John Calder, 1979), 275–285; and James Knowlson, *Damned to Fame: The Life of Samuel Beckett* (London: Bloomsbury, 1996), 569, 584, 632–633.
[42] Beckett to Bray, 2 September 1969, TCD MS 10948/1/432.
[43] Beckett to Bray, 3 October 1969, TCD MS 10948/1/440.
[44] Beckett to Bray, 13 October 1969, TCD MS 10948/1/443.

Knowlson reveals that in late 1969 Beckett went looking for Kleist's memorial at Wannsee (which he did not find), and not long after the correspondence with Bray in Autumn 1969, Beckett further mentioned Kleist on a number of occasions. During rehearsals for *Happy Days* in 1971, at the Schiller-Theater, Beckett was apparently trying to imbue Winnie with an air of what he had earlier termed "grace in the Kleistian sense":

> He was anxious to ensure that all of Winnie's movements should be as crisp, precise and economical as possible. He argued that precision and economy would produce the maximum of grace, quoting Kleist's essay on the Marionetten theatre to reinforce his argument. (*Damned to Fame*, 584)

In 1976 Beckett again referred Knowlson and Ronald Pickup to Kleist. According to Knowlson, Beckett cited the essay on this occasion to "illustrate what he said about the relations between economy and the grace and harmony that he wanted to see in the movements of the protagonist of *Ghost Trio*" (632).

Kleist's *Über das Marionettentheater* (1810) describes the marionettes of puppet-theatre as embodying a state of grace unattainable in a human world of self-consciousness. In a fictional dialogue between two men in a public park, narrated in the past tense by one of the interlocutors, Kleist uses a number of examples to argue that self-consciousness destroys the possibility of what he calls "grace." In one of these examples a "young acquaintance of mine had lost his innocence before my very eyes."[45] An attractive youth of about fifteen, who had started to show "faintly the first traces of vanity, a product of the favour shown him by women," noticed that he resembled a well-known *Spinario* statue in one particular movement he made while putting his foot on a stool. The youth's interlocutor had apparently just been noting to himself this same resemblance, and the coincidence flattered the youth's burgeoning vanity. Yet as he tried to

---

[45] Heinrich von Kleist, "On the Marionette Theatre," translated by Idris Parry (*The Times Literary Supplement*, 20 October 1978), 1211.

replicate the movement in the mirror in which he had originally noticed the resemblance, to witness it again, the movements that had once manifested his spontaneous grace became grotesquely comic; his consciousness of the movement prevented him from actually performing that movement again, even as his awareness of it taunted him with its proximity. Over the following year the boy's attractiveness entirely vanished.

A similar story involved the "fencing bear." Kleist tells of a bear (a paradigm naturally lacking human self-consciousness) that could fence better than any human because it would never be fooled by its opponent's feints, responding only to genuine thrusts, which it could successfully parry. The encounter is visceral and salutary for the bear's human combatant:

> No human fencer could equal his perception in this respect. He stood upright, his paw raised ready for battle, his eye fixed on mine as if he could read my soul there, and when my thrusts were not meant seriously he did not move. ("Marionette," 1212)

According to Kleist, marionettes embody the state of grace that was in the boy before his narcissistic fall, and in the fighting bear that responds only to what is authentically intended; the selfless puppet affirms and enables the state of grace that humanity's self-consciousness prevents.

For Beckett, this conclusion is comparable to and compatible with Geulincx's "guignol world," a world in which all is puppetry because all is dependent on God. Yet it is also different from Geulincx's thoughts along these lines, and Geulincx and Kleist taken together form something entirely new—something that might be productively termed a philosophical poetics of suffering. According to Geulincx, humanity lacks knowledge of how it is connected to the world around it, yet there is a connection, and it is the work of humanity's "Pater ineffabilis"[46] ["ineffable Father" (*Metaphysics*, 97)]. God (as Beckett

---

[46] Geulincx, *Opera*, vol. 2, 188. Cf. TCD MS 10971/6/5r.

noted from Geulincx's *Metaphysics*) is "[t]he Author of this union"[47] between humanity and the world, and "neither we, nor our bodies, nor anything else, can move something without the cooperation of Him who is the author of motion."[48] Any motion that we experience is only thanks to God's use of it "as an instrument to engender various thoughts in our mind."[49] These "thoughts in our mind" are what distinguish Geulincx's puppetry from that of Kleist. Both Kleist's and Geulincx's puppets are dependent on an external authority for anything to happen. But with an awareness of being tied, Geulincx's puppets are subjected to further suffering—to perceiving their own enslavement. No Kleistian puppet has to suffer this further ignominy. For Kleist, no puppet is capable of attaining this awareness of its own state; it is precisely a lack of such self-awareness that brings about the "grace" of Kleist's puppets as one of blissful ignorance. A Geulingian "guignol world," then, is arguably a much crueler place than that of the Kleistian puppet-world.

Perhaps something like this distinction accounts for Beckett's description of Geulincx's world as "guignol," a world that is not just playfully puppet-like, but cruel and autocratic. Indeed, when he named Geulincx's world as "guignol," Beckett may have had in mind the Parisian *Théâtre du Grand-Guignol*, a theater once famous for its gothic depictions of murder, rape and suicide, its name for a time even becoming shorthand for confrontational, violent performances.[50]

---

[47] Geulincx, *Metaphysics*, 94. Cf. TCD MS 10971/6/5r.
[48] Geulincx, *Metaphysics*, 100. Cf. TCD MS 10971/6/5r.
[49] Geulincx, *Metaphysics*, 105. Cf. TCD MS 10971/6/5v.
[50] *Théâtre du Grand Guignol* was founded in 1897, and had its heyday (under various directors) in the first three decades of the twentieth century prior to its being taken over in 1930 by Jack Jouvin. After the Second World War the theater declined until eventually it closed in 1962. "Nous n'aurions pas pu concurrencer Buchenwald" [We could not compete with Buchenwald] was the assessment of Charles Nonon, the theater's final director, on why the postwar audience had less appetite for fictional visceral horror (quoted in Agnès Pierron, *Le Grand Guignol: le théâtre des peurs de la Belle Époque* [Paris: R. Laffont, 1995], xxxiv). There were, however, also accusations of wartime collaboration levelled at the theater. For a history of *Le Grand*

This conception of the more blatant savagery in puppetry was figured in the slapstick existentialist taunting of *Act Without Words 1* in 1956. Köhler's experiments, indeed, were designed precisely in order to discern whether or not the animals possessed anything approaching a careful definition of "intelligence." Bringing Kleist into contact with this imagining of puppetry would allow Beckett to present a new, unique world of both grace and horror. "Still" presents just such a hybridized "guignol world." The estranged action in the short, tense piece is not only that of returning, echoing Occasionalist disconnection and the horror it engenders. It is also a graceful action, a movement of steady, Kleistian puppet-like unselfconsciousness.

The nameless man of "Still" is one of Beckett's exhausted protagonists. He is almost totally collapsed, and not a little "[c]orpsed,"[51] as Clov describes the world outside the window in *Endgame*. His "side by side" legs are "*broken* right angles" seen in a "*failing* light." His "trunk likewise *dead* plumb" (emphases added), his arms, like his legs, are "broken right angles at the elbows" (155). From this crumpled and half-alive trembling pile a movement arises that is not fully resistance, yet neither is it fully resignation. As one part of his body comes together with another part, the extremities with the shell of interiority, the fingers with the head, a circuit is made that visualizes a kind of gentle, graceful climax of Beckett's late-period works. It is a climax constructed in realist, visualizing prose: an image that resembles the pose of Rodin's monument to poetic and philosophical reflection, the sculpture "The Thinker," and that locates this part of Beckett's late period as a period of imagistic philosophical poetics.[52] Beckett does not, however, rest with this stillness for long. The in-

---

Guignol, see Richard J. Hand and Michael Wilson, *The Grand-Guignol: The French Theatre of Horror* (Exeter: Exeter University Press), 2002.

[51] Samuel Beckett, *Endgame*, preface by Rónán McDonald (London: Faber and Faber, 2009), 20.

[52] Interestingly, "The Thinker" was originally intended by Rodin to represent Dante contemplating his epic poem while sitting beside the gate to Hell. Rodin's pose, then, of "broken right angles," the head in the hands, is an image of poetic as well as of philosophical thinking.

tensely visual "Still" makes a sudden change in its final sentence, moving to a "*hence*" that veers entirely away from consolations and possibilities of the visual: "Leave it so all quite still or try listening to the sounds all quite still head in hand listening for a sound" (156). The achievements of philosophical, imagistic pause somewhere between resistance and resignation to the sufferings of a "guignol world" in the minimalist prose of "Still" are, as Krapp realizes of his life's highlights, only momentary and transient. Just as for Geulincx life is a fleeting orbit around a still point, for Beckett in 1972 a finely calibrated stasis cannot be still for long before it must become something else.

Beckett's Critique of Kant

P.J. Murphy (Thompson Rivers University, Canada)

To begin *in medias res*, in the thick of things: in his 5 January 1938 letter to Thomas MacGreevy, Beckett details a host of social activities, particularly with Joyce and his family, which were part and parcel of his busy life in Paris as he was waiting for the publication of *Murphy*. In one of his concluding remarks—most definitely not a throwaway—Beckett reports that "the entire works of Kant arrived from Munich," consisting of "two immense parcels" that, in an almost vaudevillian depiction, he "could hardly carry from customs to taxi."[1] These were the eleven volumes of the Berlin Academy (1912–1923), edited by Ernst Cassirer et al. Taking possession of the complete works is the culmination of a series of engagements with Kant throughout the key decade of the 1930s, beginning with the last sentence of Jean du Chas' mock lecture "Le Concentrisme" (1930), which counsels against "concretizing Kant's Thing-in-itself," and the Kantian marginalia in his own set of Proust's *Recherche*; to the entries from Jules de Gaultier's *De Kant à Nietzsche* in the *"Dream" Notebook*; to the "Philosophy Notes," 1932–1933, derived from Wilhelm Windelband's *A History of Philosophy*, in which fully a quarter of just under a hundred sides is dedicated to Kant; to the important entries in the *"Whoroscope" Notebook*.[2] As I have argued elsewhere, Kant is the seminal modern philosopher who has exercised a decisive

---

[1] Samuel Beckett, *The Letters of Samuel Beckett*, Volume 1: 1929–1940, edited by Martha Dow Fehsenfeld and Lois More Overbeck (Cambridge: Cambridge University Press, 2009), 581.

[2] Samuel Beckett, "Le Concentrisme," in *Disjecta: Miscellaneous Writings and a Dramatic Fragment*, edited by Ruby Cohn (New York: Grove Press, 1984), 35; John Pilling, "Beckett's Proust," *Journal of Beckett Studies*, I, 1976, 14; John Pilling, *Beckett's "Dream" Notebook* (Reading: Beckett International Foundation, 1999), 164–166; Matthew Feldman and Ulrika Maude, eds., *Beckett and Phenomenology* (London: Continuum, 2009), 24.

vision-shaping influence on Beckett.[3] In working out his own highly original responses to a number of critical philosophical questions, Beckett found Kant to be an indispensable figure who supplied him with a philosophical grammar for realigning the proliferation of negatives encountered at the boundary lines of word and world.

Beckett read Kant in two distinct ways: the first might be termed "post-Kantian" insofar as it pursues a historico-contextualist approach that goes against Kant's own fundamental principle of philosophy as a supratemporal activity, essentially self-contained or "transcendental." Indeed, the major steps forward in German Idealism after Kant, beginning with Fichte, entailed a focus upon a finite human subject in a specific social context. This point was made in melodramatic fashion the very day after Beckett received Kant's works: on the night of the sixth of January, Beckett was stabbed by a pimp in a street altercation and rushed to hospital with a life-threatening injury. As Beckett wryly remarked, "It was a new kind of 12th Night certainly" (*Letters*, 585).

In a letter to Arland Ussher several months later, Beckett ends with "I read nothing and write nothing, unless it is Kant (de nobis ipsis silemus) and French anacreontics" (*Letters*, 622) (the latter supposedly supplying relief from the former). John Pilling has pointed out that Beckett went to the trouble of typing up his own index of Kant's works (thereby enhancing the value of his not insignificant investment) and that Beckett started his reading with the final volume, Ernst Cassirer's study of Kant's "Life and Teaching," "using this as

---

[3] The Beckett-Kant relationship is indeed at the heart of my reading of Beckett: see especially "Beckett and the Philosophers," *The Cambridge Companion to Beckett*, ed. John Pilling (Cambridge: Cambridge University Press, 1994), 229–237; the chapter on *Watt* in *Beckett's Dedalus* (Toronto: University of Toronto Press, 2009), 127–140 (note also the Kantian structure of the argument: the introduction, "Prolegomenon to Any Future Beckett Criticism," and the conclusion, "Critical Beckett"). Furthermore, my study of Beckett criticism with Werner Huber, Rolf Breuer, and Konrad Schoell was entitled *Critique of Beckett Criticism: A Guide to Research in English, French, and German* (Columbia, SC: Camden House, 1994).

the base from which to explore the *Critique of Judgment* and the *Critique of Pure Reason*."[4] Furthermore, Pilling draws attention to the first direct literary application of this reading: in the poem "ainsi a-t-on beau," the line "sur Lisbonne fumante Kant froidement penché" is taken directly from Cassirer's biographical volume. The flux of vast historical periods depicted in the poem destroys in Lawrence Harvey's judgment the "unfeeling and futile manipulations of icy reason,"[5] with its pretensions to the immobility of fixed categories of cognition.

When Beckett wrote to Germany to order Kant's works, he asked the bookseller for an "antediluvian"[6] edition, a suggestive descriptor for a number of reasons. First of all, it conjures up a sense of Beckett's own ironic self-reflection about why an avant-garde artist in 1930s Paris should be so interested in immersing himself in a 150-year-old philosophical and aesthetic credo. The "Black Letter" typography aside[7] (which would certainly render its appearance antiquarian), more telling is the enveloping historical topography. Beckett's six-month German *Wanderjahre* from which he returned in April of 1937 gave him first-hand contact with the realities of National Socialism and in this historical context the particular edition of Kant Beckett ordered would have indeed preceded the flood of fascism, most pointedly in that it was edited by Ernst Cassirer, a Jewish Kantian scholar, who had resigned his post as Rector of Hamburg University when the Nazis came to power in 1933.

The second way in which Beckett read Kant might be termed "neo-Kantian" in that it is predicated upon a careful study of Kantian principles and proceeds toward a series of innovative and imaginative

---

[4] John Pilling, "Beckett and Mauthner Revisited," in *Beckett After Beckett*, ed. S.E. Gontarski and Anthony Uhlmann (Gainesville, FL: University Press of Florida, 2006), 163.

[5] Lawrence E. Harvey, *Samuel Beckett: Poet and Critic* (Princeton, NJ: Princeton University Press, 1970), 209.

[6] Brian Coffey, "Memory Murphy's Maker: Some Notes on Samuel Beckett," *Threshold*, 17 (1963), 33–34.

[7] Pilling, "Beckett and Mauthner Revisited," 166.

speculations of Beckett's own devising. Particularly revealing are two seminal entries in the *"Whoroscope" Notebook*. The first dramatizes Beckett's appreciation of Kant's master stratagem in his "Copernican Revolution," namely the overturning of the very means by which our understanding of the world develops: "Kant's proof that the conditions of the possibility of experience are also the conditions of the possibility of the objects of experience!!!"[8] The other major Kantian citation, transcribed from Jules de Gaultier's *De Kant à Nietzsche*, supplies a veritable gloss on the first, underlining the three major points inherent in Kant's "Copernican Revolution" and supplying further justification for Beckett's use of the notation for a masterful move in a chess game:

> It is the great achievement of Kant, accomplished in the fifty pages of the *Transcendental Esthetic*, to have shown space and time are in no way on the one hand, a substantial reality nor, on the other, properties of the object; but on the contrary, belong to the subject of knowledge and are the categories of sensibility of such a subject. (Pilling, "(W)horoscope," 18)

Or in the more succinct form which Beckett encountered in Windelband: "Kant discovered that the objects of thought are none other than the products of thought itself."[9]

So much for Beckett's "notesnatching" of Kantian materials: things get immeasurably more complex—not to say much more interesting—in the application of these ideas in his own writing. That Kant plays a seminal as well as a problematic role in Beckett's thinking is implicit throughout his passionately engaged assessment in 1967 of the philosophical tradition and how he sought instead to create worlds of his own by "pure force of the imagination":

---

[8] John Pilling, "From a (W)horoscope to *Murphy*," in John Pilling and Mary Bryden, eds., *The Ideal Core of the Onion: Reading Beckett Archives* (Reading: Beckett International Foundation, 1992), 16.

[9] Wilhelm Windelband, *A History of Philosophy*, translated by J.H. Tufts (New York: The MacMillan Company, 1956), 543.

The crisis started with the end of the seventeenth century, after Galileo. The eighteenth century has been called the century of reason, *le siècle de la raison*. I've never understood that: they're all mad, *ils sont tous fous, ils déraissonent*! They give reason a responsibility which it simply can't bear, it's too weak. The Encyclopedists wanted to know everything ... But that direct relation between the self and—as the Italians say—*lo scibile*, the knowable, was already broken.[10]

For Beckett, Kant was first and foremost the modern philosopher who recognized that this "direct relation" was ruptured, Kant had rejected the basic Greek theory of knowledge which had held sway to his time that "objects" were given independently of thought. That the subject is incapable of knowing the essence of the object (its noumenon) is a guiding axiom of Beckett's early aesthetic speculations in *Watt* and is also evident throughout his art criticism on the Van Veldes in the 1940s.[11] Beckett's vehement denunciation of the pretensions of the age of reason is prefaced by an implied acknowledgment of the limitations of the Kantian approach: to create new worlds through "pure force of the imagination" dialogically engages Kant's *Critique of Pure Reason* and the failure therein to recognize fully the transformative powers of the imagination. Beckett's critique of Kant incorporates an in-depth awareness of both the strengths and weaknesses in his thought and this critical evaluation leads towards Beckett's own original aesthetic speculations, and this is nowhere more decisively the case than in Beckett's "war novel" *Watt*, which was begun in 1941 and not completed until 1945.

Critics have found it very difficult to determine the same philosophic consistency in *Watt* as there was in *Murphy*'s combination of Democritean, Geulincxian, and Spinozan elements.[12] John Fletcher, for example, concludes that it would be safer to attribute the various philosophical conundrums foregrounded in *Watt* "to a general influ-

---

[10] Interview with Michael Haerdter, cited in Dougald McMillan and Martha Fehsenfeld, *Beckett in the Theatre* (New York: Riverrun Press, 1988), 231.
[11] Lawrence Harvey, *Samuel Beckett: Poet and Critic*, 209–210.
[12] See my discussion of *Murphy* in "Beckett and the Philosophers," 224–229.

ence emanating from the sceptical tradition of empiricism."[13] Indeed, such perplexities are strikingly similar to those confronted by Kant when he was roused from his "dogmatic slumber"[14] by David Hume's skeptical arguments that knowledge of necessity is not given in perception, and that this is crucial when considering the question of causality. A case in point is Watt's troubled deliberations in the house of Mr. Knott about the bell that sounded in the night in Erskine's room: when Watt the amateur detective tries to solve this "locked room" mystery, he discovers to his utter dismay that "[t]here was a bell in Erskine's room, but it was broken."[15] Kant mounts his defense of "pure reason" against Hume's arguments by positing a fundamental distinction between mere appearances and "things-in-themselves." That is, we have no direct knowledge of the world, only representations. But the central problem is that the so-called eponymous subject Watt is a gormless milquetoast who wants above all to continue endorsing the everyday reality he has been schooled to accept. As Vivian Mercier astutely remarked, "the point to remember about poor Watt is that, far from being an aggressive Pyrrhonist, he is not even a conscious sceptic."[16] Nevertheless, Beckett has transported his hapless fictional probe to the domain of Mr. Knott where a series of Humean impasses pertaining to causality and predictability are countered with a number of strategic maneuvers of a distinctly Kantian variety.[17] In short, *Watt* is a Kantian novel: its conception, characteriza-

---

[13] John Fletcher, "Samuel Beckett and the Philosophers," *Comparative Literature*, 17 (1965), 55.
[14] Immanuel Kant, *Prolegomena to Any Future Metaphysics* (New York: The Bobbs-Merrill Company, 1950), x1.
[15] Samuel Beckett, *Watt*, edited by C.J. Ackerley (London: Faber and Faber, 2009), 109.
[16] Vivian Mercier, *Beckett/Beckett* (New York: Oxford University Press, 1977), 167.
[17] References to Hume in discussions of Beckett are surprisingly rare. An exception is Sidney Feshbach's "On Names in James Aloysius Augustine Joyce and Samuel Barclay Beckett," *Massachusetts Review*, Winter 93/94, Vol. 34 (1953), 593–616, which refers to *Watt* as "Beckett's Humean novel" (601). There is, however, no linkage with Kant in Feshbach's argument.

tion, a number of crucial scenes, and its tantalizing last words, "no symbols where none intended," cannot be fully appreciated without recognizing how Beckett adapted Kant in this work.

The Kantian negatives concerning what man could and could not know are dramatized in the journey of Watt to take up a position as a servant at Mr. Knott's establishment. Kant/Knott is itself a double negative whereby Beckett punningly sorts "can't" from "cant," the knowable from the unknowable. For example, after discovering, at the veritable center of the novel the broken bell in Erskine's room, Watt is fixated by "[t]he only other object of note" present there, a picture which greatly upsets him since it suggests disorientating thoughts about "a circle and a centre not its centre in search of a centre and its circle respectively, in boundless space, in endless time" (*Watt*, 109, 110). Watt's private viewing is structured around the Kantian distinction between the beautiful and the sublime in the *Critique of Judgment* where Kant maintains that the beautiful in nature concerns the form of the object, which consists in its being bound, whereas the sublime can be located in a formless object: "Insofar as *unboundedness* is presented, either in the object or because the object prompts us to present it, while we add to this unboundedness the thought of the totality." The sublime is a pleasure that arises only "indirectly": "it is produced by the feeling of a momentary inhibition of vital forces followed immediately by an outpouring of them that is all the stronger."[18] Before such a spectacle Watt can only stand and weep.

From the sublime to the ridiculous: even the most humdrum of daily objects, such as Mr. Knott's pots, were not for Watt any longer amenable to being neatly identified. They were no longer quite themselves and there is, of course, no access to the noumenal "pot-in-itself" which might in Kantian terms be "thinkable," but perforce remains "unknowable." The liminal nature of so-called commonplace realities is such that Watt is compelled to adopt in self-defense a

---

[18] Immanuel Kant, *Critique of Judgment*, translated and with an introduction by Werner S. Pluhar (Indianapolis: Hackett, 1987), 74.

Kantian manipulation of a priori categories in order to "extract" semblances of meaningful patterns, as exemplified in the episode with the Galls. There are other instances of "great formal brilliance" but alas of "indeterminable purport" (*Watt*, 61) as Watt tries to carry out what might ironically be dubbed his "Transcendental Deduction."

Sam, the narrator of Watt's tale, characterizes his subject's behavior as raising a number of "delicate questions," namely, what was the point of "this pursuit of meaning, in this indifference to meaning" (62)? The point is moot, but the long-term consequence is certainly of determinable purport: after Watt leaves Mr. Knott's employ, he can no longer fit into conventional society and ends up in an asylum where he meets the narrator-to-be of his story. Watt suffers from a series of progressively more severe aphasic disturbances and this is further confounded by the painfully obvious inadequacies of Sam as a recorder of Watt's quixotic "pursuit of meaning." For, while Sam admits his physical senses are failing, he steadfastly maintains that his "purely mental faculties" were "if possible more vigorous than ever" (*Watt*, 169); but the five blanks allotted to these faculties contain only question marks! As Beckett declared with reference to the *philosophes*, who—like Sam—wanted to know everything, "*ils sont tous fous, ils déraisonnent!*"

Comparing the two endings of *Watt* brings to the forefront the question of meaning in terms of symbolic presentation and indeed the very status of the "symbol" itself as highlighted in the last entry of the "Addenda," the second ending: "no symbols where none intended" (223). Here Beckett has extended his reading of Kant to include a critique of modernist aesthetics as represented primarily by Joyce whose views are reincarnated in the figure of Arsene, whose vision of transcendence gained and lost is at the heart of the first section of the novel.[19] An "antediluvian" Kant is thus brought into play at the cutting edge of Beckett's avant-garde aesthetic speculations. In the novel's first ending, the locals offer their dogmatic views on man, nature,

---

[19] For a more detailed argument in support of the Joyce-Arsene analogy see my *Beckett's Dedalus*, 130–141.

and God as they watch Watt depart Mr. Knott's. Speaking "practically," Kant emphasized that the elevated thoughts which nature affords us do have application in the everyday world and the locals certainly have no doubts about the Kantian equation of beauty, nature's symbols, and God's sanction:

> The trembling sea could not but be admired. The leaves quivered, or gave the impression of doing so, and the grasses also, beneath the drops, or beads, of gaily expiring dew [... Mr. Gorman] raised high his hands and spread them out, in a gesture of worship. (213)

But they cannot make any sense of Watt, who does not fit into their scheme of things. The conventional symbolism of Mr. Gorman and his ilk is obviously not "intended" as any resolution to Watt's dilemmas. Watt saw his picture, and it was not pretty or charming, nor could its "unboundedness" be so neatly domesticated. In the midst of such ineffable mysteries, Watt has lost his own sense of "whatness" amongst the proliferation of unnamable entities.

Kant and Beckett might seem strange bedfellows, but the ménage à trois with Joyce (Arsene) is when things get really interesting and the stratagems whereby this conjunction is effected in *Watt* are worthy of their own "!!!" notation. Throughout *Beckett's Dedalus*, I argued in detail that Beckett could not for critical reasons accept either the Proustian "miracle" of involuntary memory or Joyce's epiphany in which, in his estimation, the boundary lines between the phenomenal and the noumenal have unjustifiably been breached. In Arsene's vision of transcendence, Beckett employs a Kantian allusion to set things in a critical perspective. Arsene recalls how he was one with nature and yet somehow also beyond it: "I was the sun ..." (34) and "my personal system was so distended at the period of which I speak that the distinction between what was inside it and what was outside it was not at all easy to draw" (35), summing up with, "I perceived it with a perception so sensuous that in comparison the impressions of a man buried alive in Lisbon on Lisbon's great day seem a frigid and artificial construction of the understanding" (35). This echoing of the line of Beckett's poem "ainsi a-t-on beau" cited earlier is not, however, simply an ironic reference to Kant's philosophical sangfroid; in this context, the allusion also helps to put into critical perspective Arsene's vision, which cannot sustain itself and falls back into the world in which Kantian distinctions and boundaries between the noumenal and the phenomenal do indeed unfortunately apply.

Arsene's "short statement" (31) of some twenty-five pages is divided into two very long paragraphs: the first deals with his visionary experience and the loss thereof; the second consists of his efforts to make some sense of his stay at Mr. Knott's and to pass it on to his successor: "I have information of a practical nature to impart" (36–37). This consists of his view that his visionary experience "was not an illusion, as long as it lasted, that presence of what did not exist" (37), as well as the vital question of whether what has happened to Arsene will necessarily also happen to Watt. Here Beckett invokes the concept of the "categorical imperative" in order to question the equating of individual acts with universal laws. The point is reinforced by the anecdote of Mr. Ash's meeting with Arsene on Westminster Bridge, which begins his second paragraph and which in Beckett's mind is specifically associated with Kant. In the *"Whoroscope" Notebook* one of Beckett's notes on Kant conjures up the mise-en-scène of the Mr. Ash story: "Kant's exact description of Westminster Bridge (having never set foot outside Prussia)."[20] Kant was famous for his precise and exacting schedule: the inhabitants of Königsberg could set their watches by his daily constitutional on the "Philosopher's Walk." There is hence a telling contrast between Kant's neatly ordered world and the maddening disparity between Mr. Ash's own calculation of what time it is and the authorized version supplied by Big Ben. Enlightenment master narratives are conspicuous only by their absence.

Beckett also draws on Kant's well-known dictum in the *Critique of Judgment* that "Beauty is an object's form of purposiveness in so far as it is perceived in the object *without the precondition of a*

---

[20] Cited in John Pilling, "From a (W)horoscope to *Murphy*," 15.

purpose"[21] in order to put into critical perspective Arsene's vision of man's existential realities and how these could not be accommodated by the would-be epiphanies of modernist aesthetics: "And what is this coming that was not our coming and this being that is not our being and this going that will not be our going but the coming and being and going in purposelessness?" (48-49). Nevertheless, the issues of "aesthetic judgement" (141) and the role of the imagination are pointed to in *Watt* as a way and means of escaping from madness and demented logic. An artist figure needs to emerge whose vision can incorporate "somethings" and "nothings" without becoming entangled with symbols (intended or not), a figure who can create viable "as if"[22] propositions or fictions that will allow for the formulation of his own predicaments.

Beckett's great postwar *Trilogy* harbors some suggestive analogies with Kant's *Critiques* in terms of differentiating the claims of reason and the imagination. The opening sequence of *Molloy* depicts the narrator watching two characters (A and B in the original French, A and C in the English translation), who briefly meet and then separate, one going back to the town, the other "on by ways he seemed hardly to know."[23] This parable foreshadows the parting of the ways of the troubadour-vagabond Molloy and the petty bourgeois tyrant Moran, even though over the course of the two parts of the novel they are drawn closer together, without, however, ever becoming one. A and B might—amongst a number of other possibilities—bring to mind Kant's A and B versions of the *Critique of Pure Reason* (in which the 1787 revision of the original 1781 edition downgrades the

---

[21] Kant, *Critique of Judgment*, 74.
[22] The "as if" of nature's purposiveness is a key concept in Part II of the *Critique of Judgment*, "Critique of Teleological Judgment." The Kant scholar Hans Vaihinger developed systematically the "fictional" dimensions of "as if" and such "fictionism" is also very evident in Jules de Gaultier's *From Kant to Nietzsche*, translated by G.M. Spring (Freeport, NY: Books for Libraries Press, 1961), with which Beckett was familiar.
[23] Samuel Beckett, *Molloy*, edited by Shane Weller (London: Faber and Faber, 2009), 5.

faculty of the imagination vis-à-vis the more ordered categories of the understanding). To blur such parallels might be one of the reasons Beckett changed the designations in the English translation. Among other possibilities, A and C could be taken as a shorthand version of the Author-Character functions which are a driving force throughout the *Trilogy*. Malone in the next novel is totally uninterested in any type of "categorical imperative" of general significance; his application of "practical reason" is completely for his own ends as he tries to transcend his mortal situation by making his own death coincide with that of his fictional creations.

The most telling comparisons are between the final works of each trilogy: *The Unnamable* might be termed Beckett's "Critique of Pure Imagination," in contrast to Kant's *Critique of Judgment* which sets the schematic ways of making a concept "sensible" or known above those of the symbolic: "Schemata contain direct, symbols indirect, exhibitions of the concept."[24] "No symbols where none intended," to be sure. The "preamble"[25] of *The Unnamable* (perhaps more accurately its "prolegomenon" given its critical-discursive elements) is concerned primarily with setting up its own version of Kant's "Copernican Revolution" in regard to Author-Character roles and functions. The Unnamable asserts that he is at the center and does not move, whereas Malone—now fully revealed as a fictional construct—orbits him, "he wheels, I feel it, and about me, like a planet around its sun" (5). But as this novel spirals away from any would-be authorial control, it is excruciatingly obvious that there is no way to speak in a "transcendental" manner about an originating self since the very nature of language itself in its imaginative capacities ineluctably generates a host of fictional projections which need somehow to be accommodated. As commentators as diverse as Schopenhauer,

---

[24] Kant, *Critique of Judgment*, 227.
[25] Samuel Beckett, *The Unnamable*, edited by Steven Connor (London: Faber and Faber, 2010), 13.

Mauthner and Cassirer have emphasized,[26] Kant's system lacks, above all, a critique of language and its operations. Hence the ironic implications of the Unnamable's declaration that Kant's Baconian motto for the second (B) edition of the *Critique of Pure Reason*, *De nobis ipsis silemus* ("As concerns ourselves we remain silent"), "should have been my motto" (42): all the Unnamable does is to try to talk about himself, while miserably failing to do so since the stories of his fictional creations endlessly intertwine with those he would keep "pure" for himself. This would-be "Copernican Revolution" has failed categorically in that a "pure imagination" cannot exist solely in its own right in a priori fashion but must create a world of its own in which the question of language is bound to be absolutely critical. The Unnamable's last words—truly his "motto"—"I can't go on, I will go on," carry an acknowledgment of the limitations of the Kantian enterprise. As this suggests, and as he pointed out late in life, Beckett remained a self-declared "non-can-er"[27] when it comes to the systematic application of philosophical reason.

How It Is (1964) represents the decisive breakthrough in the post-*Trilogy* period whereby Beckett moves towards a re-engagement with the world, with the depiction of a subject in time. The status of Kantian ideas in this novel is profoundly ambiguous in that even as certain ideas are subjected to a scathing critique, other aspects of a thoroughgoing critical stance toward certain dogmatic cultural fictions are still of vital importance. It would be easy—all too easy—to apply the Horkheimer-Adorno thesis of *Dialectic of Enlightenment* to *How It Is*, namely, how an unthinking endorsement of instrumental reason leads from the Jacobin Terror to Auschwitz-Birkenau, thereby

---

[26] For a more thorough discussion of Kant's relationship with other philosophers who have played an important role in the discussion of Beckett's works see Matthew Feldman's stimulating discussion in the first chapter of *Beckett and Phenomenology*.

[27] The phrase Beckett used in his "interview" with Israel Shenker, "Moody Man of Letters", *New York Times*, 6 May 1956, sec. 2, x, 1.

rendering Kant and Sade "bedfellows" of sorts.[28] In *How It Is* Beckett has flattened out the great chain of being of Western philosophy, with its hierarchical divisions, and presents instead a great chain of torturers and victims crawling their way through an excremental underground (a sort of metaphysical *nostalgie de la boue*), replete with the grotesque paraphernalia of sacks of tinned fish and armed with tin-openers which can also be used to jab one's partner up the rectum in the highly regulated system of designated "couplings." So much for love and joy in the great chain of being. As the narrating voice maintains, "we have our being in justice,"[29] and this is characterized by a whole series of mathematical calculations whereby each member of the great chain is guaranteed his due and, turn and turn about, gets to be torturer and victim. In his preliminary comment on the *philosophes* cited earlier, Beckett argues that "the crisis started with the end of the seventeenth century, after Galileo," and *How It Is* shows how a scientific world-view with its mathematization of reality can construct such a demented parody of a rational world.

And, naturally enough, this type of reason needs a God to justify and make sense of the whole proceedings. At the end of part I, the narrating voice refers to "a celestial tin miraculous sardines sent down by God" (40). Here Beckett would seem to be alluding to the most famous sardine can in world literature, the one which contains a ticking time-bomb and winds its way throughout Andrey Biely's *St. Petersburg*.[30] At the novel's climax, the bomb goes off in the study of

---

[28] For example: Jean-Michel Rabaté, "'Formal Brilliance and Indeterminate Purport': The Poetry of Beckett's Philosophemes," *Fulcrum*, Number 6, 2007, 530–550; David Cunningham, "'We have our being in justice': Formalism, Abstraction and Beckett's 'Ethics,'" in Russell Smith, ed., *Beckett and Ethics* (London: Continuum, 2008), 21–37.

[29] Samuel Beckett, *How It Is*, edited by Édouard Magessa O'Reilly (London: Faber and Faber, 2009), 108.

[30] The sequence begins with "There was a handsome bust—of Kant, needless to say", and ends with "As for Kant? Kant was forgotten" , after the bomb has gone off; Andrey Biely, *St. Petersburg*, translated by John Cournos, "Foreword" by George Reavey (New York: Grove Press, 1959), 28, 309. In a letter to George Reavey (22 February 1937), Beckett mentions that he heard "an in-

a high Tsarist official in which a bust of Kant has been prominently on display as a means of symbolically representing a host of contestatory views on reason and revolution. Beckett's "characters" Bem and Bom, whose names are borrowed from a duo of Stalinist clowns, provide an implicit historical critique of the totalitarian theocracy across *How It Is*. The reactionary conservatism of Biely's ending is diametrically opposed to Beckett's in which an act of justifiable literary terrorism blows up the whole absurdly contrived chain of being and all the rituals which accompany it, culminating with a God-figure. The radical solution the narrating voice opts for is to "eliminate" all such fabrications, "rendering me in the same breath sole responsible for this unqualifiable murmur" (126). Beckett, in my judgment, is one of Horkheimer's "dark writers"[31] whose explorations outside of more conventional definitions of "reason" salvage the very possibility of the Enlightenment's more positive achievements. Odd as it might at first sound, the ending of *How It Is* can be legitimately identified with the guiding principle of Kant's justly famous essay, "What is Enlightenment?" (1794): "Nonage is inability to use one's own understanding without another's guidance."[32] The courage to subject everything to a thorough critical enquiry is—all Beckett's disclaimers aside—heroic.

Beckett is the most philosophical of writers precisely because he is the most literary; the opening sentences of "Assumption" (1929) raise the vital questions of who is speaking, with what authority, and how the words of literature have (or do not have) reference to the world outside the text-in-itself: "He could have shouted and could not. The buffoon in the loft swung steadily on his stick and the organ-

---

teresting" lecture (on February 18) on Biely by Prof. Fedur Stepun (*Letters*, 455).

[31] Max Horkheimer and Theodor W. Adorno, *Dialectic of Enlightenment*, translated by John Cumming (New York: Continuum, 1989), 116.

[32] Immanuel Kant, "What is Enlightenment?" in Peter Gay, ed., *The Enlightenment: A Comprehensive Anthology* (New York: Simon and Shuster, 1973), 383.

ist sat dreaming with his hands in his pockets."[33] The Kant-Beckett relationship is not all that surprising since, as Tom Rockmore has recently underlined, Kant "provides the problems, vocabulary, and the main insights that continue to shape the debates over the problem of knowledge."[34] Beckett may have stopped reading the philosophers when he realized, around the time of writing *Molloy*, that he had to confront his own "darkness" and acknowledge his own lack of knowledge about it. Nevertheless, he continued to think his way through the aesthetic issues that Kant's works led him to in *Watt*, toward what might be termed his own "endarkenment." As Rockmore further contends, many of the principal thinkers of the twentieth century are "in dialogue with each other on the basis of a shared Kantian tradition" (Rockmore, 19), albeit one which they approach in quite distinct ways. This is certainly the case, for example, with Husserl and Mauthner whose works have been brought to bear in Beckett studies, and also especially relevant with reference to Heidegger, whose assessment of Kant's failure to validate the powers of the imagination in ontological investigations is remarkably similar to Beckett's comments on the world-making "pure force of the imagination."[35] Moreover, Kant's failure to embrace the so-called "lower" faculty of the imagination "might on the empirical level have to do with a failure of nerve when it came to a reckoning with the body, its feelings, and desires."[36] Kant's last word, "*Sufficit*" ("It is enough"),[37] makes for a revealing comparison with Beckett's last words in one of

---

[33] Samuel Beckett, *The Complete Short Prose 1929–1989*, edited by S.E. Gontarski (New York Grove Press, 1995), 3.
[34] Tom Rockmore, *In Kant's Wake: Philosophy in the Twentieth Century* (Oxford: Blackwell Publishing, 2006), 7.
[35] See my comments on Beckett and Heidegger in "Beckett and the Philosophers," 236.
[36] Jane Kneller, "The Failure of Kant's Imagination," in *What is Enlightenment?: Eighteenth-Century Answers and Twentieth-Century Questions*, ed. James Schmidt (Berkeley: University of California Press, 1996), 466.
[37] Simon Critchley, *The Book of Dead Philosophers* (London: Granta, 2009), 187.

his most moving later ontological fables about a love lost and recalled through the powers of the imagination: "Enough my old breasts feel his old hand."[38]

In 1956, on December 23 to be exact, Beckett presented his artist friend Avigdor Arikha with his complete set of Kant's works.[39] Suffice it to say, this is fitting in that Beckett's "For Avigdor Arikha," written for a 1966 exhibition, has a strongly "Kantian" ethos:

> Siege laid again to the impregnable without. Eye and hand fevering after the unself. By the hand it unceasingly changes the eye unceasingly changed. Back and forth the gaze beating against the unseeable and unmakable. Truce for a space and the marks of what it is to be and be in face of. These deep marks to show (*Disjecta*, 152).

This "lyric of criticism," in Ruby Cohn's words (*Disjecta*, 178), is typical of many of the later texts in that it turns away from the within to the greater problem of devising means of accommodation with the outside world. The subject is located in a "thereness" that brings him face to face with the world. For, though man cannot overstep the boundaries of his situation in time, he can create marks which are characterized as possessing depth. Beckett's works are not, "perhaps uniquely, resistant to philosophical interpretation"[40] as Simon Critchley has suggested. Beckett's relationship with Kant is complex and multidimensional: critical commentary cannot turn away from the dialogical aspects of this exchange and how Beckett's thought and the shape of his ideas were thereby transformed. Moreover, a critical evaluation of the Kant-Beckett relationship leads toward a reappraisal of the more affirmative dimensions of Beckett's art, especially in the post-*Trilogy* period. It is perhaps time for a "Copernican Revolution"

---

[38] Samuel Beckett, "Enough," in *Texts for Nothing and Other Shorter Prose, 1950–1976*, edited by Mark Nixon (London: Faber and Faber, 2010), 98.
[39] Pilling, "Beckett and Mauthner Revisited," 163.
[40] Simon Critchley, *Very Little ... Almost Nothing: Death, Philosophy, Literature* (London: Routledge, 2004), 165. This view is, for example, endorsed by Bjorn K. Myska in *The Sublime in Kant and Beckett* (Berlin: Walter de Gruyter, 2002, 13). Myska's argument focuses on *Molloy* and how it generates complex reactions which could be likened to the encounter with the sublime.

in Beckett studies, one whereby we can move beyond the ideology of negativity that has restricted our ability to appreciate some of the more reconstructive aspects of Beckett's remarkable oeuvre.

Dedication

This essay is dedicated to Patricia Merivale who first introduced me to Beckett's work and to Ian Ross with whom I started to work out the Kantian dimensions of *Watt*—all those years ago at the University of British Columbia.

"Eff it": Beckett and Linguistic Skepticism

Dirk Van Hulle (University of Antwerp, Belgium)

Samuel Beckett's complex attitude toward language is often linked to his reading of Fritz Mauthner's *Beiträge zu einer Kritik der Sprache* [*Contributions to a Critique of Language*] and its possible impact on his writings. David Hesla's note at the end of *The Shape of Chaos*—"One of the howlers in this study may well be the omission of Fritz Mauthner"[1]—indicates an awareness in the early 1970s of the potential importance of Mauthner's *Beiträge* for Beckett's work. In the meantime, several attempts have been made to assess and reassess Beckett's relation to Mauthner's work on the basis of his typed notes preserved at Trinity College Dublin (TCD MS 10971/5), the excerpts in his so-called "Whoroscope" Notebook at the University of Reading (UoR MS 3000), and James Joyce's notes on Mauthner (in *Finnegans Wake* notebooks VI.B.41 and VI.B.46), made in 1938 when Beckett was helping Joyce.[2] In the last two decades of Samuel Beckett's life,

---

[1] David H. Hesla, *The Shape of Chaos: An Interpretation of the Art of Samuel Beckett* (Minneapolis: University of Minnesota Press, 1971), 234 n. 18.

[2] Linda Ben-Zvi, "Samuel Beckett, Fritz Mauthner, and the Limits of Language," *PMLA* 95 (1980): 183–200; and "Fritz Mauthner for *Company*," *Journal of Beckett Studies* 9 (1984): 65–88. Richard Ellmann, *James Joyce*, revised edition (Oxford: Oxford University Press, 1983). Matthew Feldman, *Beckett's Books: A Cultural History of Samuel Beckett's "Interwar Notes"* (New York and London: Continuum, 2006); and "Beckett and Popper, or, 'What Stink of Artifice': Some Notes on Methodology, Falsifiability, and Criticism in Beckett Studies," *Samuel Beckett Today/Aujourd'hui* 16 (2006): 373–391. Julian Garforth, "Samuel Beckett, Fritz Mauthner, and the *Whoroscope* Notebook: Beckett's Beiträge zu einer Kritik der Sprache," in Dirk Van Hulle, ed., *Beckett the European* (Tallahassee, FL: Journal of Beckett Studies Books, 2005), 49–68. Edith Kern, *Existential Thought and Fictional Technique: Kierkegaard, Sartre, Beckett* (New Haven and London: Yale University Press, 1970). Geert Lernout, "James Joyce and Fritz Mauthner and Samuel Beckett," in Friedhelm Rathjen, ed., *In Principle, Beckett Is Joyce* (Edinburgh: Split Pea Press, 1994), 21–27. John Pilling,

critics such as John Pilling and Linda Ben-Zvi emphasized the considerable (though by no means exclusive or overriding) impact of Mauthner's writings, which was noticeable throughout Beckett's *oeuvre*: "For over fifty years—from the composition of *Dream of Fair to Middling Women* in 1932 to the 1979 completion of *Company*—two Mauthner themes appear and reappear in Beckett's works: the impossibility of verification and the impossibility of proving this impossibility" (Ben-Zvi, "Mauthner for *Company*," 70). In 1976, John Pilling argued that "Mauthner in fact provided Beckett with the necessary ammunition to destroy all systems of thought whatever, even 'irrationalism'" (*Samuel Beckett*, 128). Thirty years later, in his impressive analysis of the chronology of Beckett's notes on Mauthner, Pilling toned down his initial enthusiasm by suggesting that "perhaps [...] it may not matter very much that Beckett encountered Mauthner at all" (*Chronology*, 165).

In order to interpret these changing views in Beckett studies, this essay will examine Beckett's works in the context of linguistic skepticism in general, comprising (a) Austrian and German "Sprachskepsis," with a focus on Hugo von Hofmannsthal's letter, "Ein Brief," written by the fictitious Lord Chandos to Francis Bacon; (b) Bacon's "idols" and empiricism as applied by Mauthner; (c) the

---

Samuel Beckett (London: Routledge and Kegan Paul, 1976); "From a (W)horoscope to *Murphy*," in John Pilling and Mary Bryden, eds., *The Ideal Core of the Onion* (Reading: Beckett International Foundation, 1992), 1–20; "Dates and Difficulties in Beckett's *Whoroscope* Notebook," in Dirk Van Hulle, ed., *Beckett the European*, 39–48; Beckett and Mauthner Revisited," in S.E. Gontarski and Anthony Uhlmann, eds., *Beckett After Beckett* (Gainesville: University Press of Florida, 2006), 158–166; and *A Samuel Beckett Chronology* (Houndmills, Basingstoke: Palgrave Macmillan, 2006). Jenny Skerl, "Fritz Mauthner's 'Critique of Language' in Samuel Beckett's *Watt*," *Contemporary Literature* 15/4 (1974): 474–487; and "Beckett and Mauthner's Influence: To the Editor," *PMLA* 95.5 (Oct. 1980): 877–878. Dirk Van Hulle, "Beckett—Mauthner—Zimmer—Joyce," *Joyce Studies Annual* 10 (1999): 143–183; and "'Out of Metaphor': Mauthner, Richards, and the Development of Wakese," in Dirk Van Hulle, ed., *James Joyce: The Study of Languages* (Brussels: Peter Lang, 2002).

cognitive functions of writing, as explored in *Pochade radiophonique / Rough for Radio II*, which contains the only explicit reference to Mauthner in Beckett's published works. This is undertaken in order (d) to revisit the debates on Mauthner in Beckett studies and (e) to reconsider the notions of epistemology and empiricism in criticism on Beckett's works.

A. Austrian and German "Sprachskepsis"

When, in a letter of 21 September 1937, Samuel Beckett told Thomas MacGreevy that Schopenhauer "was one of the ones that mattered most" to him, he added that "his generalisation shows fewer cracks than most generalisations."[3] Most probably Beckett was referring to what the editor Julius Frauenstädt called Schopenhauer's generalization of the Will, which according to Beckett was more valuable than the generalizations Schopenhauer himself fulminated against. These generalizations were universals. Schopenhauer had claimed that, ever since the time of the scholastics (and actually even since Plato and Aristotle), philosophy had been a sustained abuse of general concepts and abstractions, by means of which one separated what was inseparable and united what was incompatible.[4]

---

[3] Samuel Beckett, *The Letters of Samuel Beckett, Vol. 1: 1929–1940*, edited by Martha Dow Fehsenfeld and Lois More Overbeck (Cambridge: Cambridge University Press, 2009), 550.

[4] "Aber freilich, das ist eben sein Kunststück, daß er durch solche Begriffe, in denen, vermöge der Abstraktion, als getrennt gedacht wird, was unzertrennlich, und als vereint, was unvereinbar ist, weit über die Anschauung, die ihnen den Ursprung gab, und damit über die Grenzen ihrer Anwendbarkeit hinausgeht zu einer ganz anderen Welt, als die ist, welche den Baustoff hergab, aber eben deshalb zu einer Welt von Hirngespinsten"; Arthur Schopenhauer, *Die Welt als Wille und Vorstellung* (Zürcher Ausgabe: Werke in zehn Bänden, Band III. Zürich: Diogenes, 1977), II, 101. ["But, of course, this is just his trick. Through such concepts, in which, by virtue of abstraction, what is inseparable is thought as separated, and what cannot be united as united, he goes far beyond the perception that was their origin, and thus beyond the limits of their applicability, to an entirely different world

Building on Schopenhauer, Friedrich Nietzsche came to several—often divergent—philosophical conclusions, but with regard to language he similarly stated in his essay "Über Wahrheit und Lüge im aussermoralischen Sinn" ["On Truth and Lies in a Nonmoral Sense"] that every concept is created by treating different phenomena as if they were the same.

> What then is truth? A movable host of metaphors, metonymies, and anthropomorphisms: in short, a sum of human relations which have been poetically and rhetorically intensified, transferred, and embellished, and which, after long usage, seem to a people to be fixed, canonical, and binding. Truths are illusions which we have forgotten are illusions—they are metaphors that have become worn out and have been drained of sensuous force, coins which have lost their embossing and are now considered as metal and no longer as coins.[5]

In this essay (written in 1873, but not published until 1896 in *Nietzsches Werke*, vol. X "Schriften und Entwürfe 1872 bis 1876," ed. Fritz Koegel, 161–179), Nietzsche defines a word as nothing but an auditory copy of a nerve stimulus (312). This nerve stimulus is transferred into an image; the image, in turn, is imitated in a sound (312). Nietzsche first presents this process as a succession of metaphors and subsequently gives this insight a crucial epistemological turn:

> It is this way with all of us concerning language; we believe that we know something about the things themselves when we speak of trees, colors, snow, and flowers; and yet we possess nothing but metaphors for things—metaphors which correspond in no way to the original entities. (312–313)

---

from the one that supplied the building material, and on this very account to a world of chimeras and phantasms"; Schopenhauer, *The World as Will and Representation*, vol. 2, translated by E.F.J. Payne (New York: Dover, 1969), 84.]

[5] Friedrich Nietzsche, "Über Wahrheit und Lüge im Aussermoralischen Sinn," in *Werke in drei Bänden* III, edited by Karl Schlechta (Darmstadt: Wissenschaftliche Buchgesellschaft, 1997), 314.English translation available online: http://faculty.uml.edu/enelson/truth&lies.htm

The role of the nerve stimuli, to which Nietzsche had drawn attention, was to become a crucial element in Fritz Mauthner's critique of language. Arguably the most important and innovative concept he coined in his *Beiträge* is that of "Zufallssinne," i.e. the contingency of our senses. Mauthner has recourse to Charles Darwin's theories to argue that the evolution of our senses is just the work of chance, which implies that the "laws" of nature have the status of a law only because human beings' senses have developed in more or less the same way.

The contingent development of the sense organs implies an equally contingent history of the world, or "Zufallsgeschichte."[6] This history does not lead to an ultimate goal. Instead, Mauthner's critique is explicitly dysteleological: the evolutionary history of human reason will not eventually lead to knowledge of the world (I, 690). Mauthner often refers to Darwin's notion of contingency, but he takes pains to point out that so-called "Darwinians" or "Social Darwinists" such as Herbert Spencer and Ernst Haeckel have abused the term "evolution" to reinstate the type of teleological explanation Darwin himself had rejected.[7] The word "evolution" therefore can only be salvaged if it is completely freed from these self-proclaimed Darwinians' notion of "Zweck" [purpose] and the connotations of "development" and "progress" (III, 586).

Mauthner's admiration for Darwin shows even in his writing style. The summary of Chapter IV ("Natural Selection") of *On the Origin of Species* is famously presented as a form of conditional reasoning:

---

[6] Fritz Mauthner, *Beiträge zu einer Kritik der Sprache*, 3 vols, 3rd revised edition (Leipzig: Felix Meiner, 1923), I, 689.

[7] See Elizabeth Bredeck, *Metaphors of Knowledge: Language and Thought in Mauthner's Critique* (Detroit: Wayne State University Press, 1992), 42.

> *Summary of Chapter.* **–If** during the long course of ages and under varying conditions of life, organic beings vary at all in the several parts of their organisation, and I think this cannot be disputed; **if** there be, owing to the high geometrical powers of increase of each species, at some age, season, or year, a severe struggle for life, and this certainly cannot be disputed; **then** [...] I think it would be a most extraordinary fact if no variation ever had occurred useful to each being's own welfare, in the same way as so many variations have occurred useful to man.[8]

In a passage in the second volume of the *Beiträge* Mauthner employs a similar rhetorical structure to summarize his accounting of the origin and history of human reasoning—with one difference, namely that the German word "wenn" can mean both "if" and "when," and this makes the construction less conditional:

> **When** we thus through one of the simplest sensations, namely perception of the colour blue, realised that human reason could come to take note of this perception by chance, **when** we feel with terrible resignation, that reason is therefore not a superhuman gift bestowed on humanity, that it is not an unchanging and eternal deity, that reason evolved in humanity and evolved into what it is, but that it also, however, could have evolved differently; **when** we recognise with a twitch as that of a wriggling worm that we are, not only in every step in our miserable existence, but also in what we hold to be the eternal and unalterably fixed fundamental laws of our intellectual being, merely a game played by the coincidence that is the world; **when** we recognise that our reason (which, after all, is language) can only be a coincidental reason, because it rests on coincidental senses, **then** we will only smile when we consider the argumentative passion with which anthropologists have laboured over questions of custom, belief and other collective psychological 'facts'.[9]

Beckett excerpted this passage in the "Whoroscope" Notebook (UoR MS 3000, 55r-56v) in which he also made several notes on

---

[8] Charles Darwin, *On the Origin of Species by Means of Natural Selection, or the Preservation of Favoured Races in the Struggle for Life* (London: John Murray, 1859), 126–127. Online version: http://darwin-online.org.uk

[9] II, 689–90; translation in Feldman, *Beckett's Books*, 130; emphasis added.

Darwin. The physical proximity of the notes on these two thinkers in the "Whoroscope" Notebook may be a coincidence, but there is also an intrinsic proximity in their respective views. Darwin's notion of contingency had made him more aware of (the dangers posed by) anthropocentrism. Once one accepts that a species can transmute into another one, the entire anthropocentric worldview collapses, as he noted in his notebooks.[10] Moreover, Darwin notes: "It is absurd to talk of one animal being higher than another.—We consider those, when the intellectual faculties [/] cerebral structure most developed, as highest.—A bee doubtless would when the instincts were" (189; notebook B.74). To a large extent, Mauthner's critique starts from an equally alert awareness of anthropomorphic tendencies, which Nietzsche had pointed out in his essay quoted above, and which the narrator in Beckett's *Watt* rejects as "an anthropomorphic insolence"[11]— a comment following the epistemological question posed with regard to Mr Knott: "Does he seek to know again, what is cold, what is heat?" (175).[12] The link with epistemology is equally direct in Mauthner's *Beiträge*: because of our "Zufallssinne" our power of reason is also contingent, a "Zufallsvernunft" (II, 689).

The first edition of the *Beiträge zu einer Kritik der Sprache* was published in 1901 (volumes I, "Sprache und Psychologie," and II, "Zur Sprachwissenschaft") and 1902 (volume III, "Zur Grammatik und Logik"). In 1902, another landmark in terms of linguistic skepticism was published in the 18–19 October issue of the Berlin newspaper *Der Tag*: Hugo von Hofmannsthal's "Ein Brief"—a fictitious letter allegedly written in 1603 by Philip, Lord Chandos, younger son of

---

[10] P.H. Barrett, P.J. Gautrey, S. Herbert, D. Kohn, S. Smith, eds., *Charles Darwin's Notebooks, 1836–1844: Geology, transmutation of species, metaphysical enquiries* (Cambridge: Cambridge University Press, 1987), 263; notebook C.76–77. Online version: http://darwin-online.org.uk

[11] Samuel Beckett, *Watt*, edited by C.J. Ackerley (London: Faber and Faber, 2009), 175.

[12] In 1980, Jennie Skerl already pointed out the many affinities between Mauthner's *Beiträge* and Beckett's *Watt*, which he started writing only a few years after reading Mauthner in 1938.

the Earl of Bath. The letter is preceded by a short, one-sentence introduction, explaining that Lord Chandos addressed this letter to Francis Bacon to apologize for his complete abandonment of creative activity, which Bacon had interpreted as a sign of mental stagnation. What happens in his mind, however, is anything but stagnant. Chandos struggles but hardly manages to explain the hubbub in his head. He sums up his condition by indicating that he has lost the ability to think or speak of anything coherently. This lost ability manifests itself particularly in abstract terms, which crumble in his mouth like moldy fungi ["modrige Pilze"].

The philosophical concerns voiced by Mauthner in 1901–1902 were given literary shape in this letter, which became the precursor of other expressions of linguistic skepticism in Austrian literature, from Robert Musil's *Die Verwirrungen des Zöglings Törless* (1906) to the later experimental writings of Friederike Mayröcker and Elfriede Jelinek.[13] The linguistic concerns voiced in Hofmannsthal's letter also reverberate in his own works, with which Samuel Beckett was not unfamiliar. On 21 November 1936, Claudia Asher presented him with Hofmannsthal's *Der Tor und der Tod* (1894; first book publication 1900) and Beckett's personal library in his apartment in Paris contains a copy (one of only twenty copies in a manual impression) of "Das dichterische Element in unserer Zeit"—an excerpt from a lecture Hofmannsthal gave in Vienna in 1907, composed in Claudius-Fraktur by Axel Kaun at the printing office Haag-Drugulin (Leipzig) in the autumn of 1937.[14] The lecture contains a few remarks on the

---

[13] Walter Eschenbacher, *Fritz Mauthner und die deutsche Literatur um 1900: Eine Untersuchung zur Sprachkrise der Jahrhundertwende* (Bern and Frankfurt am Main: Peter Lang, 1977).

[14] The opening sentence of the 1907 lecture "Der Dichter und diese Zeit" mentions both the notions of the "poetical element" and "our time" explicitly: "Man hat Ihnen angekündigt, daß ich zu Ihnen über den Dichter und diese Zeit sprechen will, über das Dasein des Dichters oder des dichterischen Elementes in dieser unserer Zeit, und manche Ankündigungen, höre ich, formulieren das Thema noch ernsthafter, indem sie von dem Problem des dichterischen Daseins in der Gegenwart sprechen"; Hugo von Hofmannsthal,

direct link between thought and language[15] that are fully in line with Mauthner's *Beiträge zu einer Kritik der Sprache* and with "Ein Brief"—Hofmannsthal's own fictitious letter, which also relates to Anglophone cultural history, as it is addressed to Francis Bacon.

B. Bacon's Idols and Empiricism

Francis Bacon is known as the father of empiricism, which was Fritz Mauthner's methodological starting point. The guiding principle of empiricism—*nihil in intellectu nisi prius in sensu*—occurs frequently in the *Beiträge*, especially in the first volume (I, 273, 324–325, 332–333). Toward the end of the last volume, Mauthner mentions the famous phrase again: "Nothing is knowledge in human thought that was not first in the senses. And nothing enters into the senses that is unable to assume—contingently—the form of these senses" (III, 639). Beckett was quite familiar with this phrase. He had already employed it in his 1929 essay on Joyce and jotted it down again in his "Whoroscope" Notebook among his notes on Sartre's *L'Imagination* (UoR MS 3000, 62r).

As Elizabeth Bredeck notes, Mauthner's interpretation of this empiricist dictum differs from previous interpretations in that (1) he rejects the notion of a clear boundary between physical and mental aspects of knowledge, suggesting instead a continuum; and (2) he undermines the notion of an epistemological foundation by asserting that our existing sense organs have not remained the same over time but continue to evolve, meaning that other sense organs are conceivable (Bredeck, 37–39). The parrot in *Malone meurt* ironically con-

---

Gesammelte Werke in zehn Einzelbänden. Reden und Aufsätze 1–3. Vol. 1, Frankfurt am Main: Fischer, 1979, 54–81; 54.

[15] "Alles, was in einer Sprache geschrieben wird, und, wagen wir das Wort, alles, was in ihr gedacht wird, deszendiert von den Produkten der wenigen, die jemals mit dieser Sprache schöpferisch geschaltet haben" (63).

cludes in Latin: "[n]ihil in intellectu,"[16] thus commenting not only on the empirical principle, but also on the issue of multilingualism, mentioned toward the end of Lord Chandos' letter: for unlike Belacqua, who announces in *Dream of Fair to Middling Women* that he was going to write a book, Lord Chandos tells Bacon that he will *not* write a book, neither in English nor in Latin, because the language in which he might be able to write and think is neither Latin nor English.

Another reason why Bacon is an appropriate addressee of the Chandos letter is the former's theory of idols, developed in *Novum Organum* [*The New Organon* (1620)]. Bacon discerns four types: "Idols of the Tribe" [*idola tribus*], which are common to the human species; "Idols of the Den" [*idola specus*], which are peculiar to an individual; "Idols of the Marketplace" [*idola fori*], originating in the misuse of language; and "Idols of the Theater" [*idola theatri*], which result from an abuse of authority. In aphorism 43 of Book One, Bacon explains how the idols "formed by the intercourse and association of men with each other" can become an obstacle for reasoning, since "the ill and unfit choice of words wonderfully obstructs the understanding." As a result, "words plainly force and overrule the understanding, and throw all into confusion, and lead men away into numberless empty controversies and idle fancies."[17] In aphorisms 59 and 60, Bacon stresses that the Idols of the Marketplace are the most troublesome of all:

---

[16] Samuel Beckett, *Malone Dies*, edited by Peter Boxall (London: Faber and Faber, 2010), 44.

[17] Francis Bacon, *Novum Organum* [1620], translated by James Spedding, Robert Leslie Ellis, and Douglas Denon Heath, in Francis Bacon, *The Works*, Vol. VIII (Boston: Taggard and Thompson, 1863), I, 4. Avalaible online at www.constitution.org/ bacon/nov_org.htm.

> For men believe that their reason governs words; but it is also true that words react on the understanding; and this it is that has rendered philosophy and the sciences sophistical and inactive. Now words, being commonly framed and applied according to the capacity of the vulgar, follow those lines of division which are most obvious to the vulgar understanding. And whenever an understanding of greater acuteness or a more diligent observation would alter those lines to suit the true divisions of nature, words stand in the way and resist the change. (I, 59)

Bacon's idea that language can actually be an "obstacle"[18] to understanding still reverberated in the nineteenth century. As Mauthner observed, the point of most nineteenth-century linguistic skeptics was that we can only think what language allows us to think.[19] If there is any truth to the thesis that language governs cognition by determining the distinctions and categories we make, an important part in this process is played by metaphors. Mauthner interpreted this phenomenon as a confirmation of his epistemological skepticism, based on the limits imposed upon our cognition by language. But this is also a matter of perspective. If language really has such a significant impact on our thought processes, it might also be possible to use language (for instance by means of multilingualism, or by introducing neologisms and portmanteau words as in Joyce's *Finnegans Wake*) in order to broaden our cognitive faculties.

---

[18] Mauthner articulates the idea of language as an obstacle to human communication and employs the image of an ocean to express this double aspect of language—suggesting a thin line between poetry and seasickness: "Wie der Ozean zwischen den Kontinenten, so bewegt sich die Sprache zwischen den einzelnen Menschen. Der Ozean verbindet die Länder, so sagt man, weil ab und zu ein Schiff herüber- und hinüberfährt und landet, wenn es nicht vorher versunken ist. Das Wasser trennt, und nur die Flutwelle, die von fremden Gewalten emporgehoben wird, schlägt bald da, bald dort an das fremde Gestade und wirft Tang und Kies heraus. Nur das Gemeine trägt so die Sprache von einem zum anderen. Mitten inne, wenn es rauscht und stürmt und hohler Gischt zum Himmel spritzt, wohnen fern von allen Menschenländern Poesie und Seekrankheit dicht beisammen" (I, 40).

[19] "Wir können nur denken, was die Sprache uns gestattet, was die Sprache und ihr individueller Gebrauch uns denken lässt" (II, 533).

C. Cognitive Functions of Writing

Samuel Beckett was intrigued by these cognitive faculties and seems to have been particularly interested in the mental processes involved in the act of creative writing. His works, especially his radio plays, often thematize these metacognitive reflections, and it is probably not a coincidence that the only explicit reference to Mauthner in his published works occurs in one of these very radio plays. Unlike his empiricist predecessors, Mauthner suggested a gradual continuum between physical and mental aspects of knowledge instead of a clear boundary. This also implies a gradual transition from what is supposed to be "unconscious" to what is called "consciousness." The adaptation of the sense organs to the outside world—and according to Mauthner, to some extent, the adaptation of the outside world to our sense organs as well—bears a strong resemblance to the instinctive activity of breathing (I, 189), an activity that continues even while we sleep. This analogy between sleeping/waking and unconscious/conscious mental activity had a long tradition, which Beckett may have first encountered in Windelband as ascribed to Leibniz. In the transition from sleeping (unconscious) thoughts to wide-awake (conscious) ratiocination, the act of writing has been presented as an effective catalyst. For instance, the German experimental physicist and writer Georg Christoph Lichtenberg noted in his so-called "Sudelbücher" that the act of writing often wakes up or stirs something inside us which, until then, we had not clearly recognized.[20]

With his metaphor of a sleeping system inside every human being—which can be woken by means of writing—Lichtenberg ex-

---

[20] "Zu Aufweckung des in jedem Menschen schlafenden Systems ist das schreiben vortrefflich, und jeder der je geschrieben hat, wird gefunden haben, dass schreiben immer etwas erweckt, was man vorher nicht deutlich erkannte, ob es gleich in uns lag" ["Writing is excellent for waking up the sleeping system in every person, and anyone who has ever written will have found that writing always awakens something that one did not clearly recognize before, even though it lay within us just the same"] (cited in Hanspeter Ortner, *Schreibe und Denken* [Tübingen: Niemeyer, 2000], 74).

pressed a view that was predominant over the last few centuries. Until recently, neuroscientists assumed that neural activity when at rest could be compared to a somnolent state. However, recent developments in cognitive neuroscience and neuro-imaging have revealed that even when a human being is doing nothing at all, a huge amount of meaningful activity is going "on" in the brain. These "stirrings still," in Beckettian terms, are called the brain's default mode; they take place in a network of brain regions that are at work even when a person is not focused upon the outside world.[21]

For a long time, notably since Descartes' idea of the pineal gland as the physical place where the mind interacts with the body, the *communis opinio* was that consciousness took place in a privileged spot in the brain. In contrast to this Cartesian dichotomy between what is pre-conscious and what is conscious, Daniel C. Dennett suggested that there is no such place that suggests a sharp boundary; there are only various sensory inputs and various interpretations of these inputs. The succession of interpretations is comparable to the multiple drafts of a narrative. According to this "multiple drafts model," conscious experience is a process; it occurs over time, and there is no clear boundary or exact moment when a conscious experience is precisely separated from all other mental processing. Moreover, "no

---

[21] "The concept of a default mode of brain function arose out of a focused need to explain the appearance of activity decreases in functional neuroimaging data when the control state was passive visual fixation or eyes closed resting. The problem was particularly compelling because these activity decreases were remarkably consistent across a wide variety of task conditions. Using PET, we determined that these activity decreases did not arise from activations in the resting state. Hence, their presence implied the existence of a default mode. While the unique constellation of brain areas provoking this analysis has come to be known as the default system, all areas of the brain have a high level of organized default functional activity"; see Marcus E. Raichle, Abraham Z. Snyder, "A default mode of brain function: a brief history of an evolving idea," *Neuroimage* 37.4 (2007): 1083–90.

central experiencer confers a durable stamp of approval on any particular draft."[22]

In Beckett's radio play featuring Mauthner's name, this process becomes thematic and each of the four characters (Dick, Fox, Stenographer, Animator) can be interpreted as a cognitive function or "rôle"[23] in the creative process. The fictionalized creative process employed in *Rough for Radio II* is preceded by a "report on yesterday's results" (which includes the oft-cited reference to Mauthner) and by a rereading of "yesterday's close" (61). Whether Dick is seen as the Schopenhauerian "Will" or the young Beckett's "itch to make,"[24] he is only one part of the mental "stirrings" that constitute the act(s) of composition. Fox is not necessarily asleep; he is said to have "gone off" (66); and while he is "off" the words he has uttered are amended by Stenographer at the Animator's instigation (68–69). As Beckett indicates, the agency of textual change is much more complicated than what used to be referred to as a singular "authorial intention." Animator may be extremely authoritarian, but he does not know exactly what he is after: "Of course we do not know, any more than you, what exactly it is we are after, what sign or set of words. But since you have failed so far to let it escape you, it is not by harking on the same old themes that you are likely to succeed, that would astonish me" (66). Mauthner is referred to in the radio play as the author who had shown that the least word dropped in solitude "*may be it.*"[25] By underlining these three words, Stenographer creates the false impression of accuracy and precision, whereas the stressed suggestion of finding "*it*" only emphasizes the extreme vagueness of the "exhor-

---

[22] Daniel C. Dennett and Marcel Kinsbourne, "Response to Glicksohn and Salter," *Behavioral and Brain Sciences* 18.4 (1995): 810–11.

[23] Samuel Beckett, *All That Fall and Other Plays for Radio and Screen*, preface and notes by Everett Frost (London: Faber and Faber, 2009), 67.

[24] Deirdre Bair, *Samuel Beckett: A Biography* (New York and London: Harcourt Brace Jovanovich, 1978), 90.

[25] "The least word let fall in solitude and thereby in danger, as Mauthner has shown, of being no longer needed, *may be it*—three words underlined" (60; emphasis in original).

tations" (60). Yet despite Mauthner being presented in *Rough for Theatre II* as a connoisseur in the matter, he did not know exactly what he was after either. He *did* know, however, that it was not the word "silence," and suggested the "not-word" ("Nichtwort") instead, because "silence is still a word" (I, 83).

D. Dupe of Expression

"Whereof one cannot speak, thereof one must be silent," was Ludwig Wittgenstein's final word in his *Tractatus Logico-Philosophicus*, after having indicated in paragraph 6.45: "The feeling that the world is a limited whole is the mystical feeling."[26] In many ways Mauthner's *Beiträge* has more affinities with the later Wittgenstein of the *Philosophical Investigations* than with this earlier Wittgenstein.[27] The Wittgenstein of the *Tractatus* claimed: "The name means the object. The object is its meaning" ["Der Name bedeutet den Gegenstand. Der Gegenstand ist seine Bedeutung" (3.203)]; whereas the Wittgenstein of the *Philosophical Investigations* defined the notion of "meaning" quite differently: "For a *large* class of cases—though not for all—in which we employ the word 'meaning' it can be defined thus: the meaning of a word is its use in the language" ["Die Bedeutung eines Wortes ist sein Gebrauch in der Sprache" (*Philosophische Untersuchungen* §43)]. The latter definition is close to Mauthner's idea that language is among or between people ["zwischen den Menschen" (I, 19)]. Language is not an object or a tool; it merely is its use: "Die Sprache ist aber kein Gegenstand des Gebrauchs [...], sie ist gar nichts anderes als ihr Gebrauch. Sprache ist

---

[26] Ludwig Wittgenstein, *Tractatus Logico-philosophicus; Tagebücher 1914–1916; Philosophische Untersuchungen*, Werkausgabe Band 1 (Frankfurt am Main: Suhrkamp, 2006), 6.25, translated by C.K. Ogden, 1922. Hypertext edition by Jonathan Laventhol at www.kfs.org/~jonathan/witt/tlph.html.

[27] Feldman, *Beckett's Books*, 123; Joachim Kühn, *Gescheiterte Sprachkritik: Fritz Mauthners Leben und Werk* (Berlin: de Gruyter, 1975); Gershon Weiler, *Mauthner's "Critique of Language"* (Cambridge: Cambridge University Press, 1970).

Sprachgebrauch" [Language is not a utensil (...), it is nothing but its use. Language is language usage; I, 24]. Wittgenstein's language games may also be seen to be prefigured in Mauthner's *Beiträge*, when he compares language to a party game ["Gesellschaftsspiel der Sprache"]: "Die Sprache ist nur ein Scheinwert wie eine Spielregel, die auch umso zwingender wird, je mehr Mitspieler sich ihr unterwerfen" [Language is only a pseudovalue, like the rule of a game, which also becomes more compelling as more people subject themselves to it; I, 25]. As Beckett told John Fletcher in 1961, he only started reading Wittgenstein "within the last two years."[28] The books by and about Wittgenstein in Beckett's personal library indicate that he must have been aware of Wittgenstein's notion of language games, but also of the earlier notion of the mystical, as expressed in entry 6.44 of the *Tractatus*: "'Nicht *wie* die Welt ist, ist das Mystische, sondern *dass* sie ist" ["Not *how* the world is, is the mystical, but *that* it is"].

Mauthner had tried to "suppress" any tendency toward the mystical, no matter how much he liked some of the leading European mystics and their stammering eloquence (III, 617). He was well aware of the fundamental paradox underpinning his magnum opus— that he needed to make such an extensive appeal to language (more than two thousand pages) in order to critique it (I, 1). But, in and of itself, this sheer quantitative aspect of his work is already an indication of his philosophical stance: whereas a mystic is ultimately reduced to silence, Mauthner's critique comes closer to a pragmatist's approach, suggesting that the conversation needs to go on and disapproving of the way mystics posit some single correct view, which they feel can never be attained. Elizabeth Bredeck refers to Nelson Goodman's alternative, which is not "a shush, but a chatter" (Bredeck, 50).[29]

---

[28] John Fletcher, *The Novels of Samuel Beckett* (New York: Barnes & Noble, 1964), 87–88.
[29] Nelson Goodman, *Problems and Projects* (Indianapolis: Bobbs-Merrill, 1972), 31.

"I chatter too much", says the Animator in *Rough for Radio II* (67), to which Stenographer replies: "Come, come, sir, don't say that, it is part of your rôle, as animator" (67). In the same capacity, the Unnamable describes his "rôle" as follows: "I have to speak, whatever that means. Having nothing to say, no words but the words of others, I have to speak. No one compels me to."[30] In other words, the Unnamable is his own Animator. Unlike the young Beckett (the Beckett who wrote the German letter to Axel Kaun in July 1937), the Unnamable does not expect to find anything behind the veil: "there is nothing, nothing to discover, nothing to recover" (25). And yet he has to speak, because otherwise he will be the dupe of his expression: "Not to have been a dupe, that will have been my best possession, my best deed, to have been a dupe, wishing I wasn't, thinking I wasn't, knowing I was, not being a dupe of not being a dupe" (25).

This notion of being a "dupe" has a prehistory: in 1926 Francis Ponge had published his *Douze petits écrits*, which opens with a short apology and ends with the explanation that "la parole me garde mieux que le silence. Ma tête de mort paraîtra dupe de son expression. Cela n'arrivait pas à Yorick quand il parlait"[31] ["speech guards me better than silence. My skull will turn out to be the dupe of its expression. This did not happen to Yorick when he was talking"]. Yorick's skull was the dupe of his own expression—the skull's unintentional grin. This was not the case as long as the fellow of infinite jest could talk. His skull's "expression" is merely a fossilized silence. To speak is the only way not to become the dupe of this unwitting expression.

E. Epistemology and Empiricism Revisited

Beckett scholars have been studying the relationship between Beckett and Mauthner for several decades. Mauthner's "influence" was the topic of critical exchanges in the "Forum" of the *PMLA* in the

---

[30] Samuel Beckett, *The Unnamable*, edited by Steven Connor (London: Faber and Faber, 2010), 25.

[31] Francis Ponge, *Oeuvres Complètes* (Paris: Gallimard Pléiade, 1999), I, 3.

1980s. In October 1980, Jennie Skerl (author of "Fritz Mauthner's 'Critique of Language' in Samuel Beckett's *Watt*") wrote a letter to the editor of *PMLA*, reacting to Linda Ben-Zvi's article "Samuel Beckett, Fritz Mauthner, and the Limits of Language," in which Ben-Zvi—according to Skerl—"fails to point out that Beckett first becomes a 'Mauthnerian' artist in *Watt*" ("To the Editor," 877). In her reply, Linda Ben-Zvi objected to the term "Mauthnerian," "implying as it does a derivative position to Beckett and a definite oversimplification of Mauthner." According to Ben-Zvi, Beckett himself warned against this kind of "pigeonholing" and "Skerl falls into just such a critical trap" ("Ben-Zvi Replies," 879).

A quarter of a century later, research on Mauthner stood at the center of another methodological debate in Beckett studies. Having recourse to Karl Popper, Matthew Feldman argued for a form of "empirical scholarship" based on the criteria of "falsifiability" and "empirical corroboration" ("Beckett and Popper," 376ff.). A polemic with Garin Dowd ensued,[32] in which the latter expressed concern regarding the potentially narrowing effect of a rigidly applied empirical methodology. The debate has been invigorating and thought-provoking. In particular, it has increased critical awareness of both the advantages and disadvantages of empiricism in literary studies. Material documents can be very useful for literary interpretation, but the empirical data they contain often require interpretation in their own right. For instance, a recent examination of the books in Beckett's personal library from his apartment in Paris has revealed that it not only contains a copy of the three-volume *Beiträge zu einer Kritik der Sprache*, but that hundreds of pages feature pencil lines in the margins: 340 marked pages in volume I; 217 pages in volume II; 164 pages in volume III. These data are certain to be of interest to Beckett studies, but questions remain. The mere fact that these volumes are among the books in Beckett's personal library does not necessarily imply that the remarkably straight pencil marks they contain indicate Beckett's interest in these passages. There is no explicit indication or

---

[32] See *Samuel Beckett Today / Aujourd'hui* 20 (2008), 375–399.

conclusive evidence to corroborate the conjecture that the markings were made by Beckett. Unless more evidence is found, one cannot exclude the possibility that the marks were made by someone else. A comparison of the marked passages with the typed Mauthner notes in Trinity College, Dublin and the excerpts in the "Whoroscope Notebook" (UoR MS 3000) reveals that half of the excerpts correspond to twelve marked pages; the other half corresponds to eleven unmarked pages. If the twelve marked pages reinforce the likelihood that Beckett was the author of the marginal lines, the eleven unmarked pages diminish this plausibility with almost equal (quantitative) force. Even though the data are quite abundant, the archival record still shows lacunae.

Obviously these lacunae are not a reason to shun an empirical approach, for any trace of the writing may be of potential use to corroborate interpretations of Beckett's works. But (especially in the context of the contingency of our sense organs; Mauthner's "Zufallssinne"; and his philosophical approach to empiricism as one of several divergent views on epistemology) the uncertainties and gaps in the archival record call for a careful approach to the interpretation of writing traces and for the discreet use of critical rhetoric, mindful of Francis Bacon's idols and Fritz Mauthner's critique of language. Within Beckett studies, the author's interest in Mauthner's theory of language and epistemology continues to be a benchmark test case in a constant effort to assess our knowledge/ignorance of Beckett's writings, and to keep the methodological conversation open. The last word about Mauthner and Beckett will possibly never be spoken, but the research is as gripping as Beckett's sustained search for what he called the "ineffable departure," concluding that there was "Nothing left but try –"

F. "eff it."[33]

---

[33] Cited in James Knowlson, *Damned to Fame: The Life of Samuel Beckett* (London: Bloomsbury, 1996), 697.

Beckett, Samuel Johnson, and the "Vacuity of Life"

Emilie Morin (University of York, UK)

"They [the critics] can put me wherever they want, but it's Johnson, always Johnson, who is with me. And if I follow any tradition, it is his."[1] As Ruby Cohn and Stephen Dilks have noted, this statement, recorded by Deirdre Bair, sounds quite unlike something that Beckett might have proffered; it does, nonetheless, convey Beckett's lifelong interest in both Dr. Johnson and an English Age of Enlightenment.[2] Indeed, Beckett regularly revisited writings by and about Johnson until his death, and Johnson's shadow continues to hang over Beckett's *oeuvre* and Beckett scholarship.[3]

Initially, Beckett's enthusiasm expressed itself in the form of an attempt to adapt Johnson's life for the stage during the 1930s, leading to the dramatic fragment *Human Wishes*. Little is known with certainty about the difficulties that Beckett faced in relation to the play's contents; however, the material remnants of the project, three copybooks of extensive preparatory notes, suggest that reading Dr. Johnson provided Beckett with new insights into the relationship between literature, philosophy, and history. The sources featuring in his notes

---

[1] Beckett [1972], cited in Deirdre Bair, *Samuel Beckett: A Biography* (London: Vintage, 1990), 272.

[2] Ruby Cohn, *Just Play: Beckett's Theater* (Princeton, NJ: Princeton University Press, 1980), 284 n. 1; Stephen Dilks, "Samuel Beckett's Samuel Johnson," *The Modern Language Review* 98, no. 2 (2003): 285.

[3] Lionel Kelly, "Beckett's Human Wishes," in John Pilling and Mary Bryden, eds., *The Ideal Core of the Onion* (Reading: Beckett International Foundation, 1992), 21–44; See Frederik N. Smith, *Beckett's Eighteenth Century* (Basingstoke: Palgrave Macmillan, 2002), 165–167, 110–131; C.J. Ackerley, "'Human Wishes': Samuel Beckett and Johnson," *The Johnson Society of Australia Papers* 9 (2005): 11–28; Helen Deutsch, *Loving Dr. Johnson* (Chicago: University of Chicago Press, 2005), 225–239.

are varied, and include James Boswell's *Life of Johnson*; Johnson's *Annals* and *Prayers and Meditations*; Hester Thrale's *Anecdotes of the Late Samuel Johnson*; John Hawkins' *The Life of Samuel Johnson, LL.D.*; Leslie Stephen's *Samuel Johnson*; Thomas Seccombe's "Essay Introductory" to A. M. Broadley's *Doctor Johnson and Mrs Thrale*; *The Dictionary of National Biography*; C.E. Vulliamy's *Mrs Thrale of Streatham*; A. Hayward's *Autobiography Letters and Literary Remains of Mrs Piozzi*.[4] The *"Whoroscope" Notebook*, which accompanied Beckett during the same decade, also features quotations from Johnson's *Life of Ascham*, *Life of Dryden*, *Rasselas*, Boswell's biography of Johnson and *The Journal of a Tour to the Hebrides* (Smith, 111). Beckett began to think about the project in 1936, while in Nazi Germany, carried out the background research at the National Library of Ireland upon his return to Dublin, and then abandoned his notes, eventually returning to them in occupied France in 1940.[5] The twice-abandoned project was, then, concurrent with Beckett's experience of the rise of totalitarianism in Europe.

The Dr. Johnson emerging from these protracted circumstances defies the historical record and the rules of biography: indeed, to open the notebooks is to find oneself confronted with manic datekeeping—births, deaths, failures, successes, and mundane events; as such, the notebooks literalize Johnson's no less than Beckett's dislike for attempted systematizations of existence.[6] Beckett's focus alters over time: the first notebook gives precedence to Johnson the moral-

---

[4] Smith, 112; Ackerley, 12. Quotations from and comments about Johnson also appear in the later "Sottisier" Notebook and in Beckett's later correspondence, particularly with Barbara Bray.

[5] See John Pilling, *Samuel Beckett: A Chronology* (Basingstoke: Palgrave Macmillan, 2006), 67, 69, 80–81; Samuel Beckett, *The Letters of Samuel Beckett, Volume 1: 1929–1940*, edited by Martha Dow Fehsenfeld and Lois More Overbeck (Cambridge: Cambridge University Press, 2009), 680.

[6] I am here referring to Beckett's praise of historical chaos in the *German Diaries*, Notebook 4 (15 January 1937), as cited in James Knowlson, *Damned to Fame: The Life of Samuel Beckett* (London: Bloomsbury, 1996), 244.

ist, devoured by love for Mrs. Thrale; the second pays particular attention to Johnson's medical symptoms and melancholy; and the third reiterates some of the contents of its predecessors, while revealing the difficulties in transforming Johnson's everyday life into naturalistic drama. Here, Beckett emphasizes Johnson's resignation at the approach of death and lack of control over a "seraglio" torn by internal conflicts and a body afflicted by a series of ailments.[7] The first notebook, which attempts to provide a rational explanation for Johnson's devotion for Mrs. Thrale and the sudden interruption of their friendship, certainly prefigures this transformation of Johnson into a tragic puppet. But the third notebook adds a poignant note to its predecessor: Johnson's acknowledged eccentricities (such as providing a diet of oysters for Hodge, his cat) are presented as marks of powerlessness rather than imagination, as necessary consequences of the elderly man's efforts to preserve a semblance of domestic peace in a home ruled by petty hatreds.[8]

In these numerous anecdotes one can trace an attentiveness to Johnson's "impotence"—a recurrent term in Beckett's comments, whose meaning is aligned with the definition given in Johnson's *Dictionary*, itself based on the Latin *impotentia*: want of power, incapacity, feebleness.[9] As such, Beckett displays scant interest in the consecrated view of Johnson as an authoritarian Tory moralist with a staunch distrust of abstraction; his notebooks likewise allocate little space to the moral and political writer occupying the center of literary London. Instead, he remains alert to Johnson's isolation; he notes that, in 1765 (the year of his meeting the Thrales, of his being awarded an honorary Doctorate from Trinity College Dublin, and of his edition of Shakespeare's plays), Johnson was a relatively unknown, soli-

---

[7] See *Human Wishes*, UoR MS 3461/3, f. 4, 5, 6, 41, 42.
[8] See *Human Wishes*, UoR MS 3461/3, f. 5.
[9] Johnson's definition of impotence does not appear in all revised editions of the *Dictionary*. It does feature, for instance, in the 1766 third corrected edition. See Samuel Johnson, *A Dictionary of the English Language*, 3rd ed. (London: W. Strahan, 1766), n.p.

tary, and much-avoided figure.[10] Beckett's attention to these aspects of Johnson's career suggests that the latter's struggles with complex structures of publishing and patronage struck a chord with him, at a time when he himself was faced with insurmountable difficulties when it came to being published and read. His jottings portray Johnson's aspiration to moral integrity as engendered by psychological instability ("His morality the typical bulwark of neurosis," he emphasizes in notes from Vulliamy's book, for instance), and present his generosity towards the poor and needy as a consequence of self-doubt.[11] Johnson's anguish is designated as the trigger for daily confrontations with human misery, and much attention is paid to Johnson's conversations with prostitutes during his evening jaunts through the streets of London as well as to his affection for the destitute Polly Carmichael, herself a former prostitute, and Frank Barber, a freed slave.[12]

The long-term effects upon Beckett's *oeuvre* of his exposure to the follies, doubts, and anxieties of Johnson and his contemporaries have now been amply documented.[13] As for the short-term effects, these include an amusing proximity between Beckett's handwriting in the *Human Wishes* notebooks and the adornments and elongated ∫ of eighteenth-century writing and printing conventions, granting assuredness and authority to Beckett's notes and reflecting his close involvement with his subject. Even before Beckett began his research, Johnson's ornate signature began to capture his imagination: his

---

[10] *Human Wishes*, UoR MS 3461/1, f. 41. See also Colwyn Edward Vulliamy, *Mrs. Thrale of Streatham* (London: Jonathan Cape, 1936), 58.
[11] Vulliamy, 103. See also *Human Wishes*, UoR MS 3461/1, f. 48.
[12] *Human Wishes*, UoR MS 3461/2, f. 29–36, 44–45; Leslie Stephen, *Samuel Johnson* (London: Macmillan, 1925), 145–148.
[13] In particular, Erik Tonning has perceptively argued that *Malone Dies* exists in close proximity to Johnson's perception of the "vacuity of life," since the novel portrays "a hell which consists precisely in an unending, self-reflexive 'apprehension of annihilation.'" Erik Tonning, "Beckett's Unholy Dying: From *Malone Dies* to *The Unnamable*," in Steven Barfield, Matthew Feldman and Philip Tew, eds., *Beckett and Death* (London: Continuum, 2009), 108.

translation of Johnson's infamous letter to Lord Chesterfield into German in another notebook in August 1936 even includes a faithful imitation of Johnson's autograph (Sam: Johnson). That year, in a fashion that recalls Boswell's transcription of Johnson's signature, Beckett began to sign his letters to the publishing house Chatto & Windus "Sam. Beckett."[14]

The cacophony of anecdotes and aphorisms emerging from the *Human Wishes* notebooks does not square with the singular Johnsonian tradition evoked in Deirdre Bair's biography; as Frederik Smith has pointed out, casting the net far and wide in his search for insights into Johnson's life led Beckett into an entanglement familiar to Johnson scholars, between an author belonging to the learned tradition, and a personality issued from the popular tradition (Smith, 129–130). Beckett's notes leave such a dialectic unresolved, portraying Johnson's thought as operating across literature, linguistics, theology, and philosophy. In this respect, although Johnson is not often categorized as a philosopher in the strict sense of the term, there is a strong case to be made for thinking about Beckett's understanding of European intellectual history as informed by Johnson's ongoing reflection upon the limits of philosophical thought. His regard for Johnson's philosophical stature is revealed in the peculiar triangulation that unfolds between editions of *En attendant Godot* and *Waiting for Godot*: in the variants between the French and English versions of Lucky's fragmented monologue, Johnson stands as a counterpart to Voltaire and Bishop Berkeley.[15] In this instance, Beckett's decision to pit Johnson against his two main philosophical antagonists reveals much about his perception of Johnson's orientation, and conveys his respect for Johnson's ability to voice a non-systematic philosophy of experience, able

---

[14] See "German Notes and Translations," UoR MS 5003, f. 49; Beckett to Ian Parsons, *Letters*, 349, 357.

[15] Vivien Mercier, "The Uneventful Event," in *Critical Essays on Samuel Beckett, Critical Thought Series, 4*, ed. Lance St. John Butler (Aldershot: Scolar Press, 1993), 29.

to provide precious insights into human irrationality and social inequality.

Beckett was only too aware of the gulf which separated these diverse thinkers; nevertheless, like Fritz Mauthner, whom Beckett also read during the late 1930s, Johnson provided the salutary example of a maverick intellectual engaged in the thankless task of proving that the boundaries of philosophy are more constricting than can possibly be fathomed. In this respect, Beckett's perception of Johnson is in keeping with that of Boswell: the idea of Johnson as an anticanonical philosopher is certainly prominent in his *Life of Johnson*, in which the transformation of Johnson into a philosopher blessed with great intellectual prowess, rather than a mere facility for producing witticisms, occurs via his refutation of Berkeley's "ingenious sophistry."[16] Johnson's capacity for philosophical thought is here presented as corollary to his acquaintance with developments in science, more precisely Newtonian physics: to Boswell's observation that "though we are satisfied [Berkeley's] doctrine is not true, it is impossible to refute it," Johnson answered, "striking his foot with mighty force against a large stone, till he rebounded from it, 'I refute it *thus*.'"[17] A decade before Beckett started work on *Human Wishes*, this episode was brought to the attention of *Dublin Magazine* readers; Joseph Maunsell Hone converted Boswell's account of Johnson's belief in scientific empiricism into an expression of ignorance, in order to posit Berkeley's idealism as existing beyond the possibility of refutation.[18]

Johnson's endeavor to acknowledge the complexities of the intellect finds outlets in many other areas of greater interest to Beckett. In particular, the notebooks betray his curiosity regarding Johnson's search for remedies to metaphysical anguish and his falling prey to

---

[16] James Boswell, *Life of Johnson* (London: Oxford University Press, 1953), 333.

[17] Ibid., 333. See also Charles Hinnant's essay "Johnson and Newton: Dismantling the Plenum," in *Samuel Johnson: An Analysis* (Basingstoke: Macmillan, 1988), 1–10.

[18] Joseph Hone, "Bishop Berkeley in Ireland," *Dublin Magazine* 1, no. 1 (1926): 16.

the torment caused by that which Beckett, writing to Hone in July 1937, evoked as "the notion of *positive* annihilation" (*Letters*, 509). To the Johnsonian mind, beset by melancholy and fear at the termination of life, confrontations with philosophy bring more indignation at the limitations of human intelligence than consolation—as revealed in Johnson's dismissal of Hume's resignation before the finality of death, to which (as Beckett notes) he responded by affirming his preference for eternal torment over annihilation.[19] These preoccupations filter through Johnson's "The Vanity of Human Wishes," which tells of the blurred boundaries between reason and unreason, and of the mind's restless search for remedies to vacuity, echoing a section in Boswell's biography which Beckett copied (in truncated form): "That man is never happy for the present is so true, that all his relief from unhappiness is only forgetting himself for a little while. Life is a progress from want to want, not from enjoyment to enjoyment."[20]

Johnson's *Dictionary* further illustrates his antagonistic relationship to idealism; it presents philosophy as branching out of empirical practice, theology, and science, rather than the possibility of transcendence. Philosophy is defined as "[k]nowledge, natural or moral," "[h]ypothesis or system upon which natural effects are explained"; hence, as a knowledge that remains contained within the limitations that arise in its being put to use.[21] The idea of philosophy as an institutionalized discipline is met with tongue firmly in cheek: the *Dictionary* associates "a professor of philosophy" with "a sophist" (686). Indeed, the philosopher, "a man deep in knowledge, either moral or natural," is too far removed from the observation of worldly experience to gain an understanding of it (324). By contrast, the realm of morals, which, for Johnson, precedes the establishment of any philosophical system, knows no boundaries in its application since it

---

[19] Boswell, 839. See also *Human Wishes*, UoR MS 3461/1, f. 32. Johnson's letter to Dr. Taylor is quoted in UoR MS 3461/2, f. 101.
[20] Boswell, 754. See also *Human Wishes*, UoR MS 3461/1, f. 32. Beckett omits Johnson's final clause on "enjoyment."
[21] Samuel Johnson, *A Dictionary of the English Language*, vol. 2, 8th ed. (Dublin: R. Marchbank, 1798), 324.

exists first and foremost as social practice; "moral" is defined as "relating to the practice of men towards each other; as it may be virtuous or criminal; good or bad" (161). Reporting an exchange between Johnson and his friend Oliver Edwards, Boswell suggests that it was not Johnson's nuanced understanding of morals, but his pessimism which dominated his contemporaries' perception of his intellectual contribution: "You are a philosopher, Dr. Johnson. I have tried too in my time to be a philosopher; but, I don't know how, cheerfulness was always breaking in" (Boswell, 957).

In Beckett's notes for *Human Wishes*, an empiricist Johnson, torn by a metaphysical despair which morals cannot soothe, provides the stuff of drama. Writing to MacGreevy in 1937, Beckett described Johnson's dogmatism as "the facade of consternation" in an age "full of ahuris" [bewildered people], concluding: "there can hardly have been many so completely at sea in their solitude as he was or so horrifiedly aware of it" (*Letters*, 529). The *Human Wishes* notebooks evidence Beckett's marked interest in the stuff of unreason; seen through various biographical lenses, Johnson paves the way toward a particular kind of pessimistic humanism, one that posits the possibility of betterment through learning as a process necessarily overshadowed by the mind's irrationality. Johnson's "unsystematic and antisystematic" approach to the workings of the intellect is subjected to frequent scrutiny; Beckett's notes include a passage dutifully copied from *Rasselas*, in which the philosopher Imlac highlights the unavoidable preeminence of the irrational over the rational: "All power of fancy over reason is a degree of insanity."[22] Beckett was equally sensitive to Johnson's own attempts to handle the mind's instability; his notebooks carefully record Johnson's curious devices for keeping his chronic melancholy in check, from the practice of arithmetic to

---

[22] Samuel Johnson, *Rasselas and Other Tales*, edited by Gwin J. Kolb (New Haven: Yale University Press, 1990), 150; *Human Wishes*, UoR MS 3461/2, f. 95. I am here borrowing Fred Parker's phrase; see Fred Parker, "'We Are Perpetually Moralists': Johnson and Moral Philosophy," in Greg Clingham and Philip Smallwood, eds., *Johnson After 300 Years* (Cambridge: Cambridge University Press, 2009), 15.

the reading of Robert Burton's *Anatomy of Melancholy* (a book that Beckett also admired).[23] As such, Beckett's notes confirm the value of this state of mind which, for Johnson, is germane to creativity and spiritual insight, once marshaled in the right direction by the imagination; the *Dictionary* illustrates such ambivalence, defining melancholy as a "disease," a "kind of madness," and a "pensive" temper, harboring the promise of intellectual revelation.[24] Johnson's "The Vanity of Human Wishes," taking its cue from the Biblical Book of Ecclesiastes, stands as a poetic counterpart to these definitions, as it envisions the tragic consequences of a civilization of conquest that no longer abides by spiritual and moral values. The scriptures, rather than philosophical reflection, are here given precedence as documentation of humankind's vain search for happiness. Likewise, Boswell reports Johnson's jibe at Platonist attempts to speak of happiness on earth and beyond it: "What philosophy suggests to us on this topic is probable: what scripture tells us is certain. Dr. Henry More has carried it as far as philosophy can. You may buy both his theological and philosophical works in two volumes folio, for about eight shillings" (Boswell, 471).

Although Beckett presented Johnson's life as a treasure trove for playwriting and screenwriting in his correspondence, his notebooks read less as an attempt to gather suitable material for writing about Johnson than as a research journal tracing his own intellectual and philosophical maturation (see *Letters*, 397). Both Boswell's and Hawkins' biographies display discernible limits, and Beckett was quick to note their flaws of methodology and perspective.[25] As he began to discern discrepancies between sources, he also commented upon their irrelevance or inaccuracy. Responding to the evocation of Johnson's delight at "seeing his name in a new character flaming

---

[23] *Human Wishes*, UoR MS 3461/1, f. 71; UoR MS 3461/2, f. 61, 26.
[24] Johnson, *Dictionary*, vol. 2, 122; see also Thomas Kass, "Morbid Melancholy, the Imagination, and Samuel Johnson's Sermons," *Logos: A Journal of Catholic Thought and Culture* 8.4 (2005): 47–63.
[25] *Human Wishes*, UoR 2461/2, f. 78, 51.

away at the bottom of bonds and leases" in Hayward's *Autobiography, Letters and Literary Remains of Mrs Piozzi*, he writes in the margin: "as symptomatic of impotence as his love of driving rapidly in a post chaise."[26] And to Hawkins' account of Levett's taciturn nature and lack of formal education, Beckett replies: "Balls. He was a symptom of J.'s anxiety."[27] In their turn, other readings and preoccupations impacted upon Beckett's perception of Johnson; the simultaneous desire for and desperate fear of isolation, which Beckett diagnoses as expressions of "impotence" and "anxiety," recall Jules Renard, whose *Journal* Beckett was re-reading at the time of the second *Human Wishes* notebook. In dramatic terms, it is clear that Beckett was initially more interested in Johnson's emotional poverty than in his non-systematic philosophy of existence. In a letter to Mary Manning Howe, he wrote of his fascination for Johnson's peculiar living arrangement at the Thrales' residence at Streatham, arguing that Johnson's platonic love for Mrs. Thrale provided both the justification for, and the means of, maintaining a degree of emotional apathy; as such, for Beckett, the death of Mr. Thrale posed serious challenges to Johnson's psyche, since it called for the invention of new pretexts in order to rationalize his own emotional impotence (*Letters*, 396–397). Johnson's love for Mrs. Thrale, he concluded in a later missive to Thomas MacGreevy, was yet another expression of his bottomless fear of death, conveyed in Johnson's declaration to his friend Charles Taylor that he would prefer an eternity of torment over annihilation (*Letters*, 529).

The stage proved to be an unsuitable receptacle for Johnson's unrivalled dramatic potential, perhaps because drawing-room naturalism could not domesticate the monstrous specter which arises from Beckett's notebooks—monstrous by virtue of the Doctor's appetite for coarse foods, opium, alcohol, wit, and company, and by virtue of his terror of death and ability to evade biographical scrutiny. Initially, Beckett included Johnson in the list of characters and imagined an

---

[26] Boswell, 845; *Human Wishes*, UoR MS 3461/1, f. 91.
[27] *Human Wishes*, UoR MS 3461/2, f. 44; see also Kelly, 34.

ending that rested upon a vision of Johnson panting in silence and threatening forever to remain.[28] This ending failed to materialize: Johnson does not appear in the *Human Wishes* fragment but is *spoken* into life by his "seraglio," whose conversations find many direct referents in the sources consulted by Beckett.[29] If Johnson failed to find embodiment outside of Beckett's imagination at this particular moment in time, he certainly continued to haunt Beckett's drama; indeed, many of Beckett's characters possess Johnson's mannerisms, gesticulations and ailments—allusions which the reader of Beckett's notebooks can easily trace back to biographies of Johnson.[30] This Johnsonian repertoire finds an afterlife in, for example, *Krapp's Last Tape*, which echoes Johnson's love for the tavern and the word "scoundrel," and in *That Time*, in which Johnson's "ghastly smile" finds equally powerful resonance.[31] Still another example might be found in *Breath*, which, as it repudiates the possibility of embodiment, evokes the ending initially planned for *Human Wishes* by reducing the scope of human existence to a brief occurrence of exhausted panting, in a literal illustration of Johnson's fear of annihilation.

* * *

A consideration of Beckett's motives for thinking so intensively about Samuel Johnson in relation to the immediate context of his re-

---

[28] *Human Wishes*, UoR MS 3458, f. 1; UoR MS 3461/3, f. 26. Helen Deutsch shows that Johnson's body was "an object of spectacular importance" in eighteenth-century literature and science; see Deutsch, 28–29. Johnson's characterization of asthma specialist John Floyer as having "panted on to 90" in Boswell's biography struck Beckett, and he copied Johnson's phrase on two occasions; *Human Wishes*, UoR MS 3461/2, f. 22; 3461/3, f. 26. See also Boswell, 1271.

[29] Stephen, 147. See also *Human Wishes*, UoR MS 3461/3, f. 42.

[30] C.J. Ackerley, Helen Deutsch, Stephen Dilks, Lionel Kelly, and Frederik Smith have commented upon these allusions.

[31] Boswell, 718; George Birkbeck Hill, ed., *The Journal of a Tour to the Hebrides*, in James Boswell, *Boswell's Life of Johnson*, vol. 5 (Oxford: Clarendon Press, 1887), 48 n. 1; *Human Wishes*, UoR MS 3461/1, f. 16, f. 17; UoR MS 3461/3, f. 42.

search illuminates the circumstantial nature of *Human Wishes* and its abridged life-span. Indeed, the project entertains an ambivalent relationship to the re-imagining of eighteenth-century Anglo-Ireland emanating from the Protestant intelligentsia in 1920s and 1930s Dublin; against this background, the difficulties faced by Beckett are placed in stark relief, not least because certain aspects of the Irish Enlightenment created by his contemporaries were concurrent with staunch displays of sympathy for Italian fascism: indeed, as W.J. McCormack has argued, the large-scale reappraisal of Ireland's colonial history under way during the 1930s was enlisted in the service of a far-right politics which appeared at its most salient in revisionist accounts of Bishop Berkeley's idealism.[32] Beckett, after abandoning plans to write a poem about Swift's relationship with Stella, kept his thoughts fixed upon Dr. Johnson precisely as his contemporaries reassessed the Irish origins of Bishop Berkeley, Jonathan Swift, Oliver Goldsmith, and Edmund Burke—a gallery against which Johnson was presented as a mere lexicographer and as a second-rate intellect unable to comprehend the sophistication of Berkeley's thought.[33]

The *Dublin Magazine* remained an important channel for this reflection during the interwar years, mostly through the agency of Joseph Hone, whose journalistic career was then marked by his sympathy for Mussolini and Charles Maurras' *Action Française*.[34] In addition, throughout the 1930s, a flurry of projects and publications reestablished the centrality of the eighteenth century to Irish culture: A.A. Luce, Beckett's tutor at Trinity College Dublin, published a

---

[32] See W.J. McCormack, *"We Irish" in Europe: Yeats, Berkeley, and Joseph Hone* (Dublin: UCD Press, 2010). Michael McAteer suggests that greater caution is necessary in attempting to categorize Yeats' late politics; see Michael McAteer, *Yeats and European Drama* (Cambridge: Cambridge University Press, 2010), 156–157, 183, 196.

[33] Beckett pondered on the poem after spending an evening with Hone and hearing about his book on Swift; see Beckett to MacGreeevy, 5 January 1933 (*Letters*, 149–150).

[34] See the issues of January-March 1926; April-June 1930; October-December 1935; January-March 1936; April-June 1937; McCormack, 10, 75, 95.

study of Berkeley and Malebranche; Hone, with whom Beckett was acquainted, published biographies of Berkeley and Swift with Mario Manlio Rossi; Oliver St John Gogarty and James Starkey (the given name of Seumas O'Sullivan, the editor of the *Dublin Magazine*) collaborated on a biography of Oliver Goldsmith; and W.B. Yeats celebrated the eighteenth-century Ascendancy in both *The Winding Stair and Other Poems* and *The Words upon the Window-pane*.[35] Yeats' keenness to emphasize the contribution of Irish Protestants to an enlightened past was already evident in a 1925 Senate address in which he proclaimed the cultural supremacy of the Anglo-Irish Ascendancy, which, he argued, had created "the best of [Ireland's] political intelligence."[36] Going further still, in a 1931 introductory essay to *The Words upon the Window-pane*, Yeats pondered the imaginative benefits of returning to the political philosophy of either Swift or Giambattista Vico as alternatives to base materialism: "What shall occupy our imagination? We must, I think, decide among these three ideas of national life: that of Swift, that of a great Italian of his day; that of modern England. [...] I seek an image of the modern mind's discovery of itself, of its own permanent form, in that one Irish century escaped from darkness and confusion."[37]

Thus, while a fraction of the Dublin bourgeoisie followed Yeats' lead and rewrote the history of the Anglo-Irish Ascendancy in an attempt to curb the erosion of its political authority, Beckett focused upon the same period of English literary history in order to think about unreason, vacuity, and melancholy. Aware of Johnson's strong stance against the Crown's economic and cultural policies in Ireland, he particularly resented "foul" readings of Johnson such as that published by Llewelyn Powys in the *Dublin Magazine* who, in Beckett's view, assimilated the writer to "a John Bull, the orthodox

---

[35] Concerning Gogarty and O'Sullivan's unpublished biography of Goldsmith, see Beckett to MacGreevy, 4 August 1938 (*Letters*, 637, 639 n. 7).
[36] W.B. Yeats, *The Senate Speeches of W.B. Yeats*, edited by Donald R. Pearce (Bloomington: Indiana University Press, 1960), 99.
[37] W.B. Yeats, *Explorations* (London: Macmillan, 1962), 343, 345.

balls in fact" (*Letters*, 488; this appears to be a fair criticism of the article). His own recreation of the Johnsonian imaginary provides a response to the dilemma presented by Yeats, posing as a philosopher of political degeneracy and renewal, and to Yeats' and Hone's affiliations with, and admiration for, European fascism: to their transformations of Swift and Berkeley into the founders of the national intellect, Beckett opposes a democratic and humanist Dr. Johnson, whom he depicts in his notebooks as a motor force in the age of Swift, Goldsmith, Berkeley, and Burke.

In this respect, Deirdre Bair's disputed interpretation of the genesis of Beckett's fragment is relevant; indeed, she suggests that the aborted conception of *Human Wishes* was linked to problems of form and coherence raised by Beckett's plan to make Johnson's life amenable to the Dublin stage—problems which Yeats had successfully addressed in his tribute to Swift, *The Words upon the Window-pane*. For Beckett's part, Johnson was to speak the words recorded in Boswell's biography, while his "seraglio" would speak Hiberno-English (Bair, 271). In keeping with this planned mixture of idioms, the first scenes of *Human Wishes* contain mofdest and stylized resonances which recall the Anglo-Irish peasant speech developed by John Millington Synge and Lady Augusta Gregory, as revealed in lines such as "[g]ive it to me here in my hand" and "[i]s it possible she reads and does not know what she reads."[38] Such an integration of Irish echoes into an idiosyncratic brand of eighteenth-century English was also a subversion of the Revivalist belief that Hiberno-English had preserved an Elizabethan quality long excised from the English spoken in England—that which Yeats described as a "distant excellence" (*Explorations*, 294).

Beckett's Dr. Johnson is certainly no beacon of English imperialism, for his notes register Johnson's inadequacy as a proponent of standardized English and his strong Staffordshire accent.[39] This Dr.

---

[38] Beckett, *Disjecta: Miscellaneous Writings and a Dramatic Fragment*, edited by Ruby Cohn (London: Calder, 1983), 157, 166.
[39] *Human Wishes*, UoR MS 3461/1, f. 16; UoR MS 3461/3, f. 42; Boswell, 707.

Johnson is also an apt critic of the excesses of English society and displays something of the Wildean in his ability to manufacture witticisms without cease and his insistence upon good conversation being conducted effortlessly.[40] More importantly, Beckett's notes from Boswell's biography reveal that he paid close attention to Johnson's ruthless opposition to Hanoverian policies in Ireland, as reported by Boswell; indeed, this facet of Johnson's politics features as a preface to the bulk of Beckett's notes.[41] Johnson's ethic of self-questioning and pessimistic empiricism provide an ideal vehicle for political protest, and Beckett's notes highlight Johnson's indignation towards the inequities bred by Protestant landlordism and his sympathy for Catholic emancipation. In his jottings, Beckett substitutes "British Government" for "English Government"; this telling lapsus tailors Johnson's political argument to a more recent past and grants new weight to it:

> Apropos of barbarous debilitating policy of British Government in Ireland: "Let the authority of the British Government perish rather than be maintained by iniquity. Better wd. it be to restrain the turbulence of the natives by the authority of the sword, & to make them amenable to law & justice in an effectual & vigorous police, than to grind them to powder by all manner of disabilities & incapacities. Better to hang or drown people at once than by an unrelenting persecution, to beggar and starve them."[42]

In this instance, Johnson's integration of the political into the economic may have held a particular appeal for Beckett, whose "Censorship in the Saorstat" pursues a similar line in relation to Irish censorship laws. But Beckett's interest in Johnson's "pro-Irish" sensibilities extends beyond the political and shapes his view of Johnson's literary environment, which he portrays as peopled by Irish writers such

---

[40] *Human Wishes*, UoR MS 3461/1, f. 74; Hester Lynch Piozzi, *Anecdotes of the Late Samuel Johnson, LL.D.*, edited by S.C. Roberts (Cambridge: Cambridge University Press, 1925), 120.
[41] *Human Wishes*, UoR MS 3461/1, f. 2.
[42] *Human Wishes*, UoR MS 3461/2, f. 93; Boswell, 439.

as Arthur Murphy and Hugh Kelly in both his notes and the *Human Wishes* fragment.[43] Beckett was certainly aware of, and interested in, Johnson's dynamic influence upon literary life in Ireland; in his notebooks, he reproduces a long excerpt from the letter in which Johnson encourages Charles O'Conor, a scholar of Gaelic and chief activist for Catholic emancipation, to carry out the groundwork necessary for a reappraisal of the history of Irish Gaelic.[44] Johnson's support of O'Conor's endeavor, as Thomas Curley points out, identifies him as "the first, and perhaps the only, major English author ever to champion Irish studies" (Curley, 135).

It is unsurprising that Beckett did not complete *Human Wishes*. Attempting to dramatize eighteenth-century literary history was akin to artistic suicide for an inexperienced playwright, and, particularly with regard to the figure of Swift, there were already too many precedents for the project to retain any originality. Charles Edward Lawrence, Lady Gregory's editor, had written an unsuccessful play on Swift's love life in 1926; this first foray into the subject prepared the ground for Yeats' *The Words upon the Window-pane*, a play which Beckett knew, and whose 1930 premiere at the Abbey he also may have attended.[45] Here, a Yeats by then routinely versed in the occult

---

[43] See Kelly, 30–31; *Human Wishes*, UoR MS 3461/2, f. 93.
[44] *Human Wishes*, UoR MS 3461/1, f. 31; Boswell, 804. The original letter from Johnson to O'Conor reads as follows: "What the Irish language is in itself, and to what languages it has affinity, are very interesting questions. Dr. Leland begins his history too late: the ages which deserve an exact inquiry, are those times (for such there were) when Ireland was the school of the West, the quiet habitation of sanctity and literature. If you could give a history of the Irish nation, from its conversion to Christianity to the invasion from England, you would amplify knowledge with new views and new objects." On the contexts shaping Johnson's intervention, see Thomas M. Curley, *Samuel Johnson, The Ossian Fraud, and the Celtic Revival in Great Britain and Ireland* (Cambridge: Cambridge University Press, 2009), 135–138.
[45] Richard Ellmann, "Samuel Beckett: Nayman of Noland," in *Four Dubliners: Wilde, Yeats, Joyce, and Beckett* (London: Hamilton, 1987), 100; Pilling, 28. David Richman notes that Yeats and Beckett faced similar problems but does not take the comparison further; see Richman, *Passionate Action: Yeats's Mastery of Drama* (Cranbury, NJ: Associated University Presses, 2000), 109.

revives Swift as a spirit during a séance of the Dublin Spiritualists' Association. Anticipating *Human Wishes*, in which Johnson's words are spoken through his female entourage, Yeats' Swift speaks through a medium, Mrs. Henderson, who alternately takes on the persona of Swift and the two women he loved, Stella and Vanessa.[46] As in *Human Wishes*, the stuff of drama in *The Words upon the Windowpane* grows from the leftovers of the tea party; the séance succeeds in entertaining the Dublin middle-class where tea and cakes fail to provide excitement. The play ends with Mrs. Henderson making a cup of tea after the end of the séance and suddenly reverting to Swift's voice ("Perish the day on which I was born!"), a terrifying vision which confirms the resilience of Swift's spirit in the drawing room that Stella once inhabited.[47]

Beckett's notes on Johnson's dabblings in demonology and superstitious attitude toward spirits suggest that he briefly considered following the same avenue as Yeats.[48] In later plays such as *Krapp's Last Tape* and *That Time*, the resurfacing of Johnson's shadow occurs in the context of the séance as evoked by Yeats—in the context of reviving, visualizing, and listening to a ghostly past and self. However, in the 1930s, Johnson's terror and close escapes from death seemed to open up greater imaginative potential for Beckett's naturalistic project, and he returns on two occasions in his notebooks to Johnson's account of an early life suspended close to death in his *Annals*: "I was born almost dead, and could not cry for some time [...] In ten weeks I

---

[46] C.E. Lawrence's failed play provided the initial inspiration for Yeats' play; see Mary Fitzgerald, ed., "Introduction," in W.B. Yeats, *The Words Upon the Window Pane: Manuscript Materials*, (Ithaca and London: Cornell University Press, 2002), xvii-xx.

[47] W.B. Yeats, *The Collected Plays of W.B. Yeats*, 2nd ed. (London: Macmillan, 1969), 617. Mrs Henderson's Swift, as Michael McAteer points out, ventriloquizes Christ's condemnation of Judas in the Gospel of Matthew, referring to Job 3:3 (McAteer, 164).

[48] *Human Wishes*, UoR MS 3461/1, f. 74; UoR MS 3461/2, f. 35; see also Piozzi, 125; Sir John Hawkins, *The Life of Samuel Johnson, LL.D.*, edited by Bertram H. Davis (London: Jonathan Cape, 1962), 131.

was taken home, a poor diseased infant, almost blind."[49] The passage certainly anticipates the equation between birth and annihilation which pervades much of Beckett's dramatic writing, as exemplified in Pozzo's assertion in *Waiting for Godot*, "[t]hey give birth astride of a grave," or in the opening line of *A Piece of Monologue*: "Birth was the death of him."[50] If *Human Wishes* does indeed look toward the spectral, it never fails to speak of unfortunate deaths and progressive disappearances with humor: "Let us not speak unkindly of the departed," says Mrs. Desmoulins (*Disjecta*, 161).

Like Beckett, who searched for analogies to Johnson's psychological "impotence" (in the figure of Rousseau, for instance), Yeats was fascinated by the dramatic potential opened up by Swift's difficult love life and absence of public commitment, an issue which he attributed to Swift's "madness."[51] "Swift haunts me; he is always just round the next corner," he wrote in his introduction to *The Words upon the Window-pane*, the first part of which immediately preceded Beckett's "Alba" in the *Dublin Magazine*.[52] Beckett might have concurred, for he later reminisced about a Yeats unable to let go of his reimagined Swift during their only meeting in Killiney, in 1932.[53] Beckett was, however, far more scrupulous and diligent than Yeats when researching his obsessions, possibly because Yeats' preoccupations remained at the level of Swift's political career, which he utilized in order to justify his own vision of a new Ireland led by the old intellectual aristocracy (*Explorations*, 357–358). Yet, ironically,

---

[49] Samuel Johnson, *Diaries, Prayers, and Annals*, edited by E.L. McAdam and Donald and Mary Hyde (New Haven: Yale University Press, 1958), 3, 5; *Human Wishes*, UoR MS 3461/2, f. 105; UoR MS 3461/3, f. 14.
[50] Beckett, *Waiting for Godot*, edited by Mary Bryden (London: Faber and Faber, 2010), 86; Beckett, *A Piece of Monologue*, in *Krapp's Last Tape and Other Shorter Plays*, edited by S.E. Gontarski (London: Faber and Faber, 2009), 117.
[51] *Human Wishes*, UoR MS 3461/1, f. 70; Yeats, *Explorations*, 361–363.
[52] Yeats, *Explorations*, 345; *Letters*, 152 n. 8.
[53] Emilie Morin, *Samuel Beckett and the Problem of Irishness* (Basingstoke: Palgrave Macmillan, 2009), 36.

Yeats' re-imagining of the golden age of the Ascendancy remained mediated by Johnson's "ponderous body."[54] Indeed, the fragment of Stella's poem to Swift which, in Yeats' play, is carved upon the window and sets the mood for the séance, was given to him by Lady Gregory, who took it from Samuel Johnson's *Works of the Poets of Great Britain and Ireland*, and he drew on Johnson's "sniffy" biographical essay on Swift when writing his introductory essay to *The Words upon the Window-pane*.[55]

* * *

The resonances between Yeats' play on Swift and Beckett's projected play on Johnson enable a reconfiguration of Beckett's interest in Johnson's distrust of philosophical systematization. For Beckett, Johnson's ethic of ceaseless self-observation proved to be an appropriate source for a non-systematic ontology predicated upon the incapacity of intellectual thought to comprehend the mind's workings—a failure also acknowledged by Fritz Mauthner, whose critique of language is predicated upon an acknowledgement that the complexity of language remains indomitable.[56] Beckett's notes emphasize Johnson's skepticism toward philosophical attempts to domesticate the sheer tedium of life and present as central to the Johnsonian worldview the "vacuity of life," as recorded by Mrs. Thrale: "Vacuity of life his favourite hypothesis. 'Such things as other philosophers attribute to X various and contradictory causes, appeared to him uniform enough:

---

[54] Yeats, *Explorations*, 359. In this essay, Yeats also refers to a story about Swift's *Drapier's Letters* as reported by Johnson in his biographical essay on Swift in *The Lives of the Most Eminent English Poets*.

[55] Lady Gregory, 1 October 1930, *Lady Gregory's Journals*, vol. 2, edited by Daniel J. Murphy (Gerrards Cross: Colin Smythe, 1987), 554. It is likely that the book Lady Gregory owned was Johnson's *The Works of the Poets of Great Britain and Ireland*, which contains a selection from Swift's poems and Johnson's short biographical essay on Swift.

[56] See, for instance, Fritz Mauthner, *Beiträge zu einer Kritik der Sprache*, vol. 3 (Leipzig: Felix Meiner, 1923), 641.

all was done to fill up the time, upon this principle.'"[57] Much of the fabric of society, Johnson suggests, develops from an inability to acknowledge and negotiate the intolerable emptiness at the heart of living. His theory of vacuity, as Charles Hinnant has argued, performs a radical interrogation of the principle of plenitude which had long sustained approaches to the metaphysical; it replaces the possibility of a generalized theory of metaphysics with an acknowledgement of the significance of a new set of scientific and social phenomena relating to the relation between matter and void (Hinnant, 9–10). Johnson's concerns find echoes in the *Dictionary*, where the threat of void permeates even that which is not void: the term "fully," for instance, is defined as "without vacuity."[58] The philosophical undercurrent which shapes such a definition also reflects Johnson's perception of his own intellectual endeavor with the *Dictionary*, in which, as he pointed out, he managed to make philosophical terms accessible to the wider public, by reflecting upon their resonances in popular terms and ideas.[59] More importantly, these considerations of the importance of void and emptiness exemplify Johnson's anti-systematic approach to the problem of being: indeed, vacuity stands as an astute demonstration of the fragility of philosophical analysis when tested against empirical observation.[60]

It is this aspect of Johnson's philosophical orientation that had an enduring influence upon Beckett: in particular, the Johnsonian concept of "impotence" in the face of vacuity finds powerful echoes in Beckett's statements about his own artistic endeavor, not least when he described the recognition of his own "impotence" and "ignorance" and the exploration of the literary terrain of "impotence" as

---

[57] *Human Wishes*, UoR MS 3461/1, f. 73; Piozzi, 99–100.
[58] Johnson, *Dictionary*, vol. 1, 849.
[59] Samuel Johnson, *The Rambler*, vol. 5, edited by W.J. Bate and Albrecht B. Strauss (New Haven: Yale University Press, 1969), 319.
[60] I am here referring to Charles Hinnant's illuminating essay on "Vacuity, Time and Happiness in Johnson's Moral Psychology"; in particular, see Hinnant, 4–5.

guiding his artistic concerns.[61] The Johnsonian principle of vacuity also finds many dramatic conversions beyond the *Human Wishes* project: indeed, Johnson's view of experience as a void needing to be filled finds powerful illustrations in, for instance, *Waiting for Godot*, *Endgame*, and *Happy Days*, which rest upon the preeminence of an inactivity that constantly demands a humble form of activity in order to be sustained. The preoccupation with that which defines an active intellect and an active memory, so salient in these plays, certainly finds a powerful precedent in Johnson's writings, for the qualities of activity imagined by Beckett can only be defined by means of an acknowledgement of the unavoidable presence of inactivity, whose resurgence constantly fails to be curbed.[62] The vulnerable Beckettian mind, only too aware of the difficult boundaries between activity and inactivity, finds its energies consumed in attempts to avert the promise of emptiness in concrete experience, rather than metaphysics.

Beckett's presentation of vacuity as the central principle of Johnsonian empiricism in his notes reflects his scholarly awareness of the complexities of Johnson's *oeuvre*, for the principle of vacuity operates as a bridge between many facets of Johnson's thought about philosophy, literature, and creativity. Indeed, the exposition of the mind to vacuity, in Johnson's writings, marks the point at which the creative life of the imagination, philosophical thought, and literary production coincide: all intellectual and creative faculties are kept in check by the preeminence of, and the exposition to, vacuity, as experience becomes subsumed under a desire for metaphysical fulfillment, which is itself necessarily self-defeating.[63] An awareness of the dan-

---

[61] Beckett, quoted in Israel Shenker, "An Interview with Beckett [1956]," in Lawrence Graver and Raymond Federman, eds., *Samuel Beckett: The Critical Heritage* (London: Routledge & Kegan Paul, 1979), 148. It is necessary to note, however, that the authenticity of the interview has been questioned.

[62] On this aspect of Johnson's understanding of vacuity, see Hinnant, 15.

[63] I am here indebted to Charles Hinnant's and Arieh Sachs' analyses of Johnson's moral philosophy. See Arieh Sachs, "Samuel Johnson on 'The Vacuity of Life,'" *Studies in English Literature, 1500–1900* 3, no. 3 (1963): 345–363.

gers inherent in such contingencies underlies Johnson's plea for the paramount necessity of self-examination and moral reflection: "Whatever philosophy may determine of material nature, it is certainly true of intellectual nature, that it *abhors a vacuum*: our minds cannot be empty; and evil will break upon them, if they are not preoccupied by good" (Boswell, 454). In turn, Johnson's view of the intolerable position of the soul, confined to contemplating its own metaphysical deficiency and at best barely able to shoulder "the burthen of life," shapes his reflection upon the necessity of maintaining some form of intellectual and moral diligence in order to avoid the "state of unruffled stupidity" generated by idleness; in *Rasselas*, for instance, ignorance, affiliated to idleness, is granted the status of "privation," of "a vacuity in which the soul sits motionless and torpid for want of attraction."[64] The *Sermons* also resort to the word "vacuity" to evoke the confrontation with the ephemerality of human activity; Johnson speaks of the event of death as bringing about "[a] gloomy vacuity, without any image or form of pleasure, a chaos of confused wishes, directed to no particular end, or to that which, while we wish, we cannot hope to obtain; for the dead will not revive."[65] Only intellectual humility and the pursuit of spiritual and moral knowledge, then, can provide hints at an escape from the void at the core of being, for against the continual deceptions and frustrations of living one can always uphold the promise of divine presence, revealed in the confrontation with death. Beckett was sensitive to the complexity of Johnson's views on death and the writing process: copying from Hawkins' biography, he remarks, for instance, that Johnson's grief at the loss of friends was often the trigger which stimulated him to write.[66] Never-

---

[64] Samuel Johnson, *The Rambler*, vol. 3, ed. W.J. Bate and Albrecht B. Strauss (New Haven: Yale University Press, 1969), 31; Samuel Johnson, *The Idler and The Adventurer*, ed. J. Bate, John M. Bullitt, and L.F. Powell (New Haven: Yale University Press, 1963), 96; Johnson, *Rasselas and Other Tales*, 49.
[65] Samuel Johnson, *Sermons*, edited by Jean Hagstrum and James Gray (New Haven: Yale University Press, 1978), 267.
[66] *Human Wishes*, UoR MS 3461/2, f. 51; Hawkins, 250.

theless, the satisfactions to be derived from writing are, at best, fleeting and not worth the effort that writing demands. Beckett's notebooks feature several witticisms on this topic: "No man but a blockhead ever wrote except for money"; "It has been said that there is pleasure in writing, especially in writing verse. I allow you may have pleasure from writing after it is over, if you have written well."[67]

Johnson's *Annals*, whose influence upon Beckett was formative, further suggest that intellectual thought and writing involve a coming to terms with a series of dreary repetitions of the same, which ultimately yield less than what their incremental addition initially promised (see Kelly, 36–41; Tonning, 116–7). The *Annals* offer an ongoing portrayal of a restless mind attempting to resist "the vacuity of life" and hoping to resist "[i]dleness intemperate sleep dilatoriness immethodical life" and "[t]o reclaim imagination"; "[t]o read good books"; "[t]o rise early"; "[t]o study the Scriptures"; "[t]o keep a journal" (*Annals*, 63, 71, 82, 267). Prayers and resolutions are juxtaposed to lists of sins committed, and, gradually, a complex system of spiritual and intellectual debts and repayments forms, one exceeding the possibility of reimbursement. Similarly, the intellectual process is portrayed as composed of tedium and reiteration, and frustrated wishes replace achievements. Various literary schemes, including projects to write histories of war, melancholy and memory, are no sooner evoked than dropped; Johnson also briefly toys with writing about "the study of philosophy, as an instrument of living" but immediately relents. Admitting defeat becomes an acknowledgement of the uselessness of philosophy to the dynamics of vacuity: "This study was not persued."[68]

The qualities that are now subsumed under the label of "the Beckettian" certainly exist in close proximity to the philosophical terror of idleness and annihilation portrayed in Johnson's *Annals*. John-

---

[67] Boswell, 730, 1234; *Human Wishes*, UoR MS 3461/1, f. 17; UoR MS 3461/2, f. 81.

[68] Johnson's planned history of melancholy might anticipate Beckett's "Journal of a Melancholic." Johnson, *Annals*, 71, 100, 119, 57.

son's portrayal of endless tedium and paralyzing awe in the face of the ticking clock impressed itself deeply upon Beckett; in a 1938 letter to MacGreevy, he compared his secluded life in Paris, away from the intellectual excitement offered by the city, to "the kind of life that filled Dr Johnson with horror. Nothing but the days passing over" (*Letters*, 606). Johnson's conception of human life as a succession of tedious confrontations with void and the potentiality of annihilation finds far-reaching philosophical echoes in Beckett's work, and acknowledging such an influence upon Beckett enables, in turn, a reconfiguration of his relationship to twentieth-century philosophy: indeed, the restless Johnsonian mind stands as a precursor of Heideggerian ontology and Sartrean phenomenology.[69] But Beckett certainly had many reasons to resort to Johnson's pessimism beyond the aborted birth of *Human Wishes*, for particular anxieties about the zones of interpenetration between the literary and the philosophical, which Beckett shared, are crystallized in Johnson's preoccupation with void, vacuity, and melancholy. These manifestations of interest in Johnson the author and thinker are important for yet another reason: indeed, the contents of the *Human Wishes* notebooks and the circumstances of the play's aborted genesis across Europe raise important questions about the mediated nature of Beckett's understanding of philosophical questions. For a Beckett clearly attuned to the political stakes facing Europe and eager to demarcate himself from the idealizations of the Enlightenment produced by his Irish contemporaries, reading about Samuel Johnson opened up new avenues for conceiving of the relationship between philosophy, politics, and literature. The raw notes contained in the archives bear testimony to the importance of such a mediation, revealing as much about Beckett's rich and complex relation to the history of Western philosophy and literature as they convey about his response to the immediate present of his fictional writings; as such, reading and borrowing from a Johnsonian philosophy of vacuity enabled Beckett to better understand the

---

[69] Max Byrd, "Johnson's Spiritual Anxiety," *Modern Philology* 78, no. 4 (1981), 377–378.

complex relation between philosophical and literary history, describing both a past far removed and the immediate concerns of contemporary life.

Beckett and Abstraction

Charlotta Palmstierna Einarsson
(University of Stockholm, Sweden)

This article explores Beckett's use of "abstraction." The concept of abstraction in Beckett's work has previously been considered by, to name only a few, Erik Tonning, who in *Samuel Beckett's Abstract Drama* delineates the complexity of Beckett's attitude to the concept; and by Pascale Casanova who in *Anatomy of a Literary Revolution* introduces Beckett *l'abstracteur* to suggest that Beckett's decision to write about the impossibility of writing is a formalist solution to a technical problem.[1] However, the phenomenological aspect of his solution has been relatively little discussed. In the postmodern context, we use our minds to construct and reconstruct the world and ourselves. In other words, the world is mere appearance and identity has crumbled to pieces that can never make up a whole. Whatever identity we may construct is a bricolage in which no "presence" may endure. To Beckett, however, the mind's grasp of reality is inherently fictive and the very concept of meaning is therefore blurred. What is thematized in Beckett's abstractions is not "reality" but "irreality,"[2] that is, not the "truth" about reality represented in language, but the

---

[1] See also Germaine Bree, "Beckett's Abstractors of Quintessence" (*The French Review*, 36 [1963], 572–576); Garin V. Dowd, *Abstract Machines: Samuel Beckett and Philosophy After Deleuze and Guattari* (Amsterdam and New York: Rodopi, 2007).

[2] The term "irreality" is here used in the sense introduced by Maurice Natanson in *The Erotic Bird: Phenomenology in Literature*. Drawing on Husserl's explication of eidetic intuition, Natanson refers to the manner in which the "reality" of the world appears to consciousness as "meant" only to suggest that these meanings are essentially fictive. What presents itself to consciousness in the natural attitude, does so "within what Husserl calls the 'irreality' of the world: the fictive universe of intentional consciousness, the world as meant". (*The Erotic Bird: Phenomenology in Literature* [Princeton: Princeton University Press, 1998], 20).

extent to which reality, as we perceive it, is frequently unintelligible, vague or unclear. To Beckett, abstraction is a methodological effort to overcome the problem of expression: a problem evolving out of the awareness of the role of perception in experience. More specifically, it is the thematization of experience and perception that allows Beckett's abstractions to appear. In effect, Beckett turns to abstraction as a "solution" to the problem of expression, well aware that the problem needs to be reformulated.

The problem of expression as it occurs in Beckett relates both to the problem of *mimesis* and to the spurious positing of the expression as a mediating entity between phenomena and the mind. Already in his 1934 review "Recent Irish Poetry," Beckett identifies a "rupture in the lines of communication" and suggests that "the artist who is aware of this may state the space that intervenes between him and the world of objects ... as no-man's-land, Hellespont or vacuum, according as he happens to be feeling resentful, nostalgic or merely depressed."[3] The problem of expression is here reformulated to concern not the problem of *mimesis,* not the identity of phenomena or meaning, but the meaning-making process itself.

Beckett's "solution" has a formal as well as a methodological dimension—formal, because language as the medium of expression in itself is form, and methodological because it concerns the mode of presentation more than the object of perception. It is Beckett's frustration with words that impels the effort to find a "solution" to the problem of expression. Although Beckett's explicit desire "to create a literature of the unword" (*Disjecta*, 173) may be understood as a desire to do away with words as such, this contribution to *Beckett/Philosophy* will go on to suggest that it is, rather, the belief in

---

[3] In the review "Recent Irish Poetry," Beckett identifies "the breakdown of the object, whether current, historical, mythical or spook" as the "new thing that has happened, or the old thing that has happened again," Beckett wrote this review under the pseudonym Andrew Belis. It appeared first in *The Bookman* in 1934, but has subsequently been reprinted in *Disjecta: Miscellaneous Writings and a Dramatic Fragment,* edited by Ruby Cohn (London: Calder, 1983), 70–76.

language as a shaping force that is sought to be dethroned in Beckett's fiction.[4] "Paradoxically," Beckett explains in an interview with Charles Juliet, "it is through form that the artist may find some kind of a way out. By giving form to formlessness."[5] The supreme task for the artist becomes, in Beckett's view, "to find a form that accommodates the mess."[6]

The term "abstract" generally refers to a concept derived from perception of the visible, concrete world. For example, the geometrical concept of a circle takes its departure from a tangible form in the world, i.e. a round thing. According to Michel Henry, "Mondrian's or Malevich's pure abstraction is precisely a geometrical abstraction, an abstraction which comes from the world and gets its nature from the world while at the same time seeking to formulate its essence."[7] By contrast, the object of Kandinsky's painting is not a concrete phenomenon of the world, but his own feelings.[8] To Kandinsky, the abstract content which art seeks to express is invisible because "[t]rue reality is invisible, [and] our radical subjectivity is this reality" (Henry, 21). Kandinsky's notion of the "abstract" therefore constitutes a break with traditional understandings of art by positing the abstract in

---

[4] Admittedly, language, since Saussure, is not only words but also includes other signs, such as for example, body language.

[5] Charles Juliet, *Conversations With Samuel Beckett and Bram van Velde*, translated by Tracy Cooke, Axel Nesme, Janey Tucker, Morgaine Reinl and Aude Jeanson (Champaign and London: Dalkey Archive Press, 2009), 24.

[6] Tom F. Driver, in "Columbia University Forum," in Lawrence Graver and Raymond Federman, eds., *Samuel Beckett: The Critical Heritage* (London: Routledge & Kegan Paul, 1979), 219.

[7] Michel Henry, *Seeing the Invisible: On Kandinsky*, translated by Scott Davidson (London: Continuum, 2009), 21.

[8] According to Henry, Kandinsky's notion of the abstract grew out of the combined influence of the intense aesthetic experience of "seeing Monet's haystacks at the 1896 Moscow exhibition," and the lesson learned from reading Niels Bohr, namely, that "the physical reality has no substance and in some way no reality; quanta of energy move in leaps without crossing through it" (15).

the subjectively experienced, affective realm of life, rather than in opposition to the concrete world (Henry, 12–21).

Like Kandinsky, Beckett recognizes that what is given in experience is something completely different from concepts and ideas. In an interview with John Gruen, republished in *Vogue* in December 1969 following the award of the Nobel Prize, Beckett claims to "perhaps" having found a way to escape the dilemma of mimetic presentation:

> I think perhaps I have freed myself from certain formal concepts. Perhaps, like the composer Schoenberg or the painter Kandinsky, I have turned toward an abstract language. Unlike them, however, I have tried not to concretize the abstraction—not to give it yet another formal context.[9]

While Beckett sympathizes with Kandinsky's project, he is also highly critical of its subjectivist stance: "[t]he problem with Kandinsky's art for Beckett lies in what he sees as the painter's incipient attempt to transcend the 'rupture of the lines of communication' between subject and object altogether, leading him to a plane of fantasy."[10] Despite the fact that abstraction in Beckett's work bears an affinity to the notion of the abstract in Kandinsky's work—both grasp the role of perception in aesthetic experience and both emphasize the breakdown of the object—unlike Kandinsky, Beckett's use of abstraction does not sustain belief in any kind of truth.

On the contrary, much of Beckett's work suggests that the human condition is inexplicable: "[w]e cannot know and we cannot be known."[11] For Beckett, "art has nothing to do with clarity, does not dabble in the clear and does not make clear" (*Disjecta*, 94). Clarity or

---

[9] Quoted in Lois Oppenheim, *The Painted Word: Samuel Beckett's Dialogue with Art* (Michigan: University of Michigan Press, 2003), 126.

[10] Erik Tonning, *Samuel Beckett's Abstract Drama: Works for Stage and Screen, 1962–1985* (Bern: Peter Lang, 2007), 67. The quotation is from *Disjecta*, 70.

[11] Samuel Beckett, *"Proust" and Three Dialogues With Georges Duthuit* (London: Calder, 1999), 66.

intelligibility, therefore, either of perception or expression, seemingly, is not the aim of Beckett's literary effort. In an interview with Tom Driver, Beckett speaks of an art that allows obscurity, suggesting that where ambiguity prevails art "is unexplainable, and there art raises questions that it does not attempt to answer" (Driver, 220).[12] However, in the light of Beckett's literary use of abstraction, the emphasis on ambiguity should not be taken at face value. Highlighting ambiguity does not necessarily mean that a work is obscure and unintelligible. Rather, as Beckett's own work testifies, ambiguity is as visible as any other phenomenon.

Beckett's literary thematization of perception bears a strong similarity to the phenomenological investigation of human experience.[13] The focus of the phenomenological attitude is to look *at* phenomena *as they appear to perception* from different angles, shades and aspects, in order to be able to see the manifold ways in which the phenomenon appears. The conviction that pervades the non-phenomenological or so-called "natural attitude" is "one of belief" (Sokolowski, 45). By contrast, the phenomenological attitude requires a suspension of belief. What is under scrutiny in the phenomenological attitude is *how* belief is constituted. Appearances, beliefs, practices, etc., are thematized and reflected on, not so as to deny them, but to clarify them. The thematization can be described as an "irrealization" or "reduction" (50) of the world of the natural attitude, which enables the phenomenologist "to preserve the reality of the thing itself [and] not turn the identity of the object into one of the 'mere' appearances"

---

[12] In the same interview with Tom F. Driver, Beckett contrasts the ambiguity of his work with the clarity found in the classical drama: "the destiny of Racine's Phèdre is sealed from the beginning: she will proceed into the dark. As she goes, she herself will be illuminated. At the beginning of the play she has partial illumination and at the end she has complete illumination, but there has been no question that she moves toward the dark" (220).

[13] "Phenomenology is the study of human experience and of the way things present themselves to us in and through such experience" (Robert Sokolowski, *Introduction to Phenomenology* [Cambridge: Cambridge University Press, 2000], 2).

(50). Implicit in this view is also a questioning of the philosophical understanding of consciousness as internal to the mind and meaning as subjectively constituted. Meaning is not a phenomenon in the mind, whether in the artist's or in the spectator's, but appears as an identity in the manifold ways in which a phenomenon appears to be perceived.

Beckett's introduction to phenomenology was mediated by his reading of philosophical overviews such as Jules de Gaultier's *From Kant to Nietzsche*, and Wilhelm Windelband's *A History of Philosophy*, which he read already in the beginning of the 1930s.[14] According to Matthew Feldman, Beckett's handwritten notes at the time hinged on "the question: '*the relation of knowledge to its object*, in what does it consist, and what does it rest?'" (cited in Maude and Feldman, 24–25).[15] However, Beckett was also aware of the work of contemporary phenomenological philosophers such as Sartre, whose work *The Psychology of Imagination* was published around the same time, and which also emphasized the role of perception as reinforcing the reality of phenomena as entities of the world rather than intrinsic to the subjective mind. It is with respect to the significance given to the many ways of appearing of phenomena and the thematization of perception that Beckett's phenomenological attitude is most obvious. Essentially, it is this phenomenological attitude that impels Beckett's literary use of abstraction.

According to Matthew Feldman, Beckett's writing underwent a "phenomenological turn" (Feldman, 14) starting with the postwar novel *Watt* and continuing throughout his career Beckett. In a manner similar to Watt, it seems that Beckett is not concerned with what a thing *is*, in reality, but with what it *appears to be,* in reality. Sitting at the train station, Watt perceives a figure in the distance, too far away

---

[14] Ulrika Maude and Matthew Feldman, eds., *Beckett and Phenomenology* (London: Continuum, 2009), 24.

[15] Feldman draws on John Pilling to explicate Beckett's interest in the relation between the "object and its representation" as demonstrated by jottings from the introduction to Gaultier's *From Kant to Nietzsche* near the end of the 1931–1932 *Dream* Notebook (24).

for him to be able to really discern with clarity "what it was, coming along the road," and whose approach Watt at first awaits impatiently, only to suddenly realize

> that it was not necessary, not at all necessary, that the figure should draw very near indeed, but that a moderate proximation would be more than sufficient. For Watt's concern, deep as it appeared, was not after all with what the figure was, in reality, but with what the figure appeared to be, in reality. For since when were Watt's concerns with what things were, in reality?[16]

The descriptions of Watt's "reality," in this case a vague perception of a distant figure, constitutes precisely what Beckett set out to find, namely a methodological solution within which to accommodate the chaotic and highly ambiguous and inexplicable aspects of being. In phenomenological philosophy, as in Beckett's literary abstractions, it is not the actual but the apparent that is at issue. Although not a philosopher, it would appear that Beckett owes a debt to phenomenology, both in terms of the understanding of perception and in terms of his use of abstraction as a methodological solution.

Essentially, Beckett's literary use of abstraction to thematize experience can be found in all of his writing. In all texts, there is a strong focus on the way things appear to be perceived by the characters. However, because of the limited scope of this article, I shall focus on one particular text that will serve as an example of Beckett's use of abstraction. The short story "One Evening" is a good illustration of Beckett's "phenomenological turn" and I have chosen to discuss one single text in greater depth instead of generalizing about several texts.

In "One Evening," an old woman's coming out at sunset is carefully crafted so as to describe what is given in experience—rendering both the "messy" quality of her perceptions and how these perceptions become tentatively meaningful to her, and to the reader. Coming out in search of yellow flowers, she stumbles on the body of a man

---

[16] Samuel Beckett, *Watt*, edited by Édouard Magessa O'Reilly (London: Faber and Faber, 2009), 196.

lying spreadeagled on the ground: "He was found lying on the ground. No one had missed him. No one was looking for him. An old woman found him. To put it vaguely. It happened so long ago. She was straying in search of wild flowers. Yellow only. With no eyes but for these she stumbled on him lying there."[17] The woman's experience of the world is a mixture of presence and absence—one where any actuality is consistently layered with many possible meanings, "[t]o put it vaguely" (119). The actual is thus only one contingent aspect within a temporal horizon of experience.

The event of the woman's finding the man is described as "the shock of her foot against a body" (121). The narrative description of her experience reflects the way in which phenomena appear to her. The woman does not see the body lying on the ground but notices this "fact" only as she experiences the *shock of her foot against a body.* The description underlines the way in which phenomena appear to the natural attitude. The woman experiences her own foot, her own body. The body of another, the man lying there, only provides the context within which her own body "dys-appears" as an irksome presence.[18] The woman's perception of the man, then, grasps directly the meaning of the experience in a precise way; her own body comes to the foreground. The narrative description of the woman's perception of the world constitutes a suspension or "bracketing" of the natural attitude, allowing the reader to see beyond the woman's experience of

---

[17] Samuel Beckett, "One Evening," in *Company/Ill Seen Ill Said/Worstward Ho/Stirrings Still*, edited by Dirk Van Hulle (London: Faber and Faber, 2009), 119.

[18] In *The Absent Body* (Chicago: University of Chicago Press, 1990), Drew Leder convincingly argues that while "in one sense the body is the most abiding and inescapable presence in our lives, it is also essentially characterized by absence" (1). However, although the body is absent from everyday performance of habitual acts, it nevertheless "dys-appears" when there occurs a disruption of sorts, as for example when a movement is dysfunctional or when we are in pain. The concept of "dys-appearance," thus, refers to the thematization of the body in "times of dysfunction or problematic operation" (85).

her own body, to take in also the sunset, the flowers and the body of the man on the ground as the context within which her body appears. Beckett's focus on the world as experienced reveals a phenomenological structure immanent to the formulation of its "coming to givenness."[19] For example, the notion of identity is given as a structure that prevails beyond the self's manifold ways of appearing. This can be seen in the way the woman's shadow "irks her. So much so that she turns to face the sun" (120). In order to escape the confusion of having "another" self, the old woman turns her face to the sunlight, trying to obliterate the irksome shadow which she cannot otherwise escape—similar to Buster Keaton's character in the Berkeleyan *Film*, scrabbling to avoid the camera—but she has to tread carefully because any movement away from the light means the obliteration of her transient freedom. Thus, she "moves with half-closed eyes as if drawn on into the glare," and "craves for sundown to end and to stray freely again" (121, 120). The thematization of presence means that the simple act of walking in the field at sunset stands out against the double background of self and non-self as represented by the body and its shadow. However, more importantly, it reveals the woman's recognition of her own identity through the various appearances of self. Identity is here shown "beyond the dimension of appearances, as something presented through them all, and through other possible appearances as well" (Sokolowski, 30). The manifold appearances of "self" now allow the vagueness and ambiguity of identity to appear in a way that approximates the phenomenological suspension of belief in reality, in order to "distinguish the object from its appearances" (Sokolowski, 50). Although this does not mean that Beckett is conducting a phenomenological investigation into the structure of consciousness, the description of the woman's perception of self is a thematization *in abstracto* of the structure of experience.

---

[19] The term "coming to givenness" should here be taken in the phenomenological sense, referring to the way in which the world presents itself, or appears, in and through perception.

What primarily concerns Beckett is not that "reality" is being misrepresented in literature, but that "reality," performed as it appears in perception, and as it is conveyed via language, is perceived in a state of utter confusion: "'The confusion is not my invention. We cannot listen to a conversation for five minutes without being acutely aware of the confusion. It is all around us and our only chance now is to let it in. The only chance of renovation is to open our eyes and see the mess. It is not a mess you can make sense of'" (Driver, 218). As Judith Dearlove has pointed out, "[i]nstead of absolutes, Beckett presents possible shapes and ideas."[20] Moreover, "his narratives are united less by stylistic, metaphoric, and thematic designs than by their unremitting efforts to find a literary shape for the proposition that perhaps no relationships exists between or among the artist, his art, and an external reality" (3). The literary description of the "mess" in "One Evening", then, should in this sense be seen as an aesthetic design to accommodate the ambiguity and vagueness of perceptual reality similar to a phenomenological description of the structure of experience..

The descriptions of the man on the ground and the woman poised beside him, in a manner similar to an abstract painting, foregrounds the colours and spatial relations of the tableau:

> He lay face downward and arms outspread. He wore a greatcoat in spite of the time of year. Hidden by the body a long row of buttons fastened it all the way down. Buttons of all shapes and sizes. Worn upright the skirts swept the ground. *That seems to hang together.* Near the head a hat lay askew on the ground. At once on its brim and crown. He lay inconspicuous in the greenish coat. To catch an eye searching from afar there was only the white head. May she have seen him somewhere before? Somewhere on his feet before? *Not too fast.* (119, emphasis added)

Despite the emphasis placed on the points and lines of the tableau, the narrator's comments—"*That seems to hang together ... Not too fast*"—intermittently suspend the flow of the story and consistent-

---

[20] J.E. Dearlove, *Accommodating the Chaos: Samuel Beckett's Nonrelational Art* (Durham, NC and London: Duke University Press, 1982), 12.

ly signal to the reader an awareness of the process of interpretation that a painting, perhaps, would not include quite as explicitly.

The narrative voice suggests that the man's actual position on the ground, hiding the long row of buttons fastened all the way down, seems to hang together with an imagined upright position, where the skirts of the coat would sweep the ground in a manner parallel to the woman's skirt. The description introduces a third dimension of perception to allow the long row of buttons, now hidden, as well as the length of the coat to appear. Again a blend of absence and presence prevails in the description of the situation, allowing the ambiguity of the presentation to appear. What can be made of the fact that the greatcoat, "fastened all the way down" with buttons of "all shapes and sizes" would sweep the ground if the man were in an upright position? Is the man dead or will he be able to continue walking? Is there a bond between the man and the woman, or does the imagined position of the man's coat sweeping the grass, suggest a memory of a different time? Rather than concretizing the expression, the thematization of the bodies' different positions is suggestive of the possibilities of interpretation that appear through the manifold ways of appearing.

Yet another perspective is included when the narrator introduces an *imagined* third party's perspective of the old woman standing next to the body on the ground, which also *seems to hang together*:

> Were a third party to chance that way theirs were the only bodies he would see. First that of the old woman standing. Then on drawing near it lying on the ground. *That seems to hang together.* The deserted fields. The old woman all in black stock-still. The body stock-still on the ground. Yellow at the end of the black arm. The white hair in the grass (120, emphasis added).

The introduction of "a third party" implies a perspective similar to the reader's. This can further be seen as an illustration of how presence and absence permeate our intuitive acts. As readers, we are now intending the fictive situation, the absence as presence, as well as the act of "intending"[21] this situation. We are reflecting *in abstracto* on the presentation. Clearly a "reduction" is taking place. Not, however, simply through a minimalistic emphasis on form and style, but in the sense that the reader is being asked to suspend belief in the "reality" of the fictive world described.

Similarly, the prescriptive yet ambiguous phrase, "not too fast," which is repeated twice in "One Evening" acts as a meta-textual signal that invites the reader to abide in the moment of description with its suggestion that all possibilities of meaning have not yet been satisfactorily recorded or explored. Each intermission becomes a discriminating moment, thematizing different objects of attention such as the woman or the weather:

> *Not too fast.* She was all in black. The hem of her long black skirt trailed in the grass. [...] *Not too fast.* The weather. Sky overcast all day till evening. In the west-north-west near the verge already the sun came out at last. Rain? A few drops *if you will*. A few drops *if you will* (119, 120, emphasis added).

The narrative voice's question and answer suggests that there is an ongoing process of evaluation, one in which the narrator assumes the reader's potential disbelief. The idiom "if you will" is ambiguous. It both allows the narrator to escape commitment and emphasizes the sense of a phenomenological "perhaps" in the text.

The blend of absence and presence that prevail in "One Evening" is shown through descriptions of the old woman's experience. Phrases like "[s]he remarks with surprise the absence of lambs in great numbers here at this time of year" (120) are further evocative of the woman's intuiting absence as a presence. Technically, the moment of experience cannot be considered in itself because an experi-

---

[21] In phenomenology, the concept of "intentionality" is central. "The core doctrine in phenomenology is the teaching that every act of consciousness we perform, every experience that we have is intentional: it is essentially 'consciousness of' or an 'experience of' something or other ... Every act if consciousness, every experience, is correlated with an object. Every intending has its intended object" (Sokolowski, 8).

ence cannot occur out of context (Sokolowski, 24). It is a moment existing "only as blended with [its] complementary parts" (Sokolowski, 24). Yet, the thematization of perception through language allows Beckett to discriminate and analyze aspects of perception otherwise taken for granted. The description of the old woman's experience thus blends with the description of the situation to indicate the divide between the *way* in which phenomena appear to be perceived and the manifold meanings they may present. The thematization of phenomena and situations, therefore, reflects the way the theme of "perhaps" permeates Beckett's creative work. The very same "perhaps," as Feldman points out, is central to the "methodology of phenomenological reduction."[22] If anything, then, Beckett's understanding and use of abstraction is phenomenological.

Ultimately, what Beckett seeks is a "new form" in literature, one that "admits the chaos and does not try to say that the chaos is something else" (Driver, 219). Beckett finds this "form" through the use of abstraction. Beckett's persistent exploration of the structures of perception should, however, not be seen as an effort to "explain" the world in terms of clear and precise representations. Instead, as Beckett himself suggested: "life is to be seen, to be talked about, [but] the way it is to be lived cannot be stated unambiguously but must come as a response to that which one encounters in 'the mess'" (Driver, 223). The power of Beckett's literature to present "the mess" lies precisely in setting the stage for potential meanings to appear.

Importantly, Beckett's presentations of the old woman's perceptions as experience, does not form a window through which we may perceive her world more clearly or "accurately." Nor do the descriptions of her experience reveal the "truth" about the reality of any kind of world—neither "the world" defined as the context in which the literary work is read or written, nor the literary work as a "world unto itself," providing its own context. Beckett does not present a phenomenological rendering of the woman's world; rather, his work

---

[22] Matthew Feldman, "I Inquired Into Myself: Beckett, Interpretation, Phenomenology?" in *Samuel Beckett Today/Aujourd'hui*, 12 (2002, 229).

converges with phenomenology in that the narrative experience of her world is constituted as *given in such and such a way*. Correspondingly, it is through his writing's positing of the world as *experienced* that Beckett evokes the irreal in the real. This is the way that Beckett finds to mock words with words, not by suggesting that they do not mean anything, but by showing how ambiguous and unreliable they are; and consequently, how ambiguous and unreliable any description of a perception must be, given that it coalesces with the natural attitude.

In Beckett's literary use of abstraction, it is the meaning-making process itself that is thematized. The abstractions we find in Beckett's work shed light on the extent to which our perception of the world is irreal. Irrealization, or thematization of the natural attitude, is in this sense, abstraction, and phenomena that are put into relief—for example, in "One Evening," the descriptions of the white head, the yellow flowers, the green coat, the body on the ground, the woman, her irksome black shadow, the sun, the weather, the rain, presence, absence, and so on — are thematized to show that meaning is not a phenomenon in the mind, whether in the artist's or in the spectator's, but appears as an identity in the manifold ways in which a phenomenon appears to be perceived. The thematization of the different phenomena also reveals how perception entails perceiving beyond the shades, aspects, or profiles of its multiple appearances. Although it may be argued that literature always seeks to illuminate the way we perceive the world, in Beckett's fiction the reality of the world is posited as inherently fictional. Perception of the world cannot convey "truth," or knowledge of truth no matter how "true" the perception is, but "the art of fiction may tell us the truth about the fictions natural to the mind."[23]

Paradoxically, it is language that enables Beckett to use the method of abstraction to reflect on human experience. It is by means of language that Beckett is able to describe the manifold ways in which phenomena appear to be perceived by the characters. The the-

---

[23] George Santayana, cited in Natanson, *Erotic Bird*, 4.

matization of experience allows the gap between perception and meaning to appear and the descriptive reflection on the characters' perceptual reality then constitutes moments of experience taken *in abstracto*. It is Beckett's essentially phenomenological effort to describe the structures of experience without falling prey to the fallacy of trying to explain that impels his abstractions. Rather than imparting some kind of truth about this world, therefore, Beckett's fictions and their descriptions make manifest that, since the mind's perception of the world is inherently artful, "truth" in the philosophical sense of the word is unattainable.

"I can't go on, I'll go on":
Beckett's Form of Philosophy

Kathryn White (University of Ulster, UK)

In *The Philosophy of Samuel Beckett*, John Calder examines the possibility, or probability, that Beckett's work will eventually be remembered, fundamentally, for its "philosophical and ethical message": "Voltaire considered himself to be a novelist, a poet, a dramatist and a writer of opera libretti, but we think of him today largely as a philosopher. The same *fate* may overtake Samuel Beckett, because what future generations can expect to find in his work is *above all* an ethical and philosophical message."[1] Calder maintains that this in no way detracts from the originality of the works and suggests that Beckett wrote with the purpose of "making us face, head-on, the realities of the human condition" (1). There is little doubt that Beckett provides an insight into the fundamental nature of reality and existence and provides a challenging depiction of the human condition: plagued with hardship and suffering, in a world awash with failure, Beckett can be surely said to present "humanity in ruins," one where "disimprovement" prevails. There is no denying that Beckett had, to use Shane Weller's expression, a taste for the negative. Yet one factor preventing Beckett from being classified as a nihilist, and enabled Theodor Adorno, Jacques Derrida and Maurice Blanchot to defend him against such a charge, is the indisputable reality that the characters, despite the chaos, are compelled to go on. Beckett, in a conversation with Gottfried Büttner, questioned why some people viewed him as a nihilist, claiming there was "no basis for that," and referred to Hamm's speculation in *Endgame,* that beyond the hills "[p]erhaps

---

[1] John Calder, *The Philosophy of Samuel Beckett* (London: Calder, 2001), 1 (emphases added).

it's still green,"[2] as counter to the nihilist interpretation.[3] As James Knowlson says, Beckett conveys a "view of life which sees birth as intimately connected with suffering and death and which sees life as a painful road to be trod."[4] And yet Beckett's characters keep treading that painful route—they persist. Is this Beckett's philosophy? Is this the philosophical message that Calder refers to and endorses? Put another way, is Beckett's "philosophy" encompassed within that now famous two-word formulation—"Nohow On"?

Beckett certainly engaged with philosophy in his own reading and his writing undoubtedly displays countless philosophical allusions, with Arthur Schopenhauer, Democritus and Arnold Geulincx featuring quite extensively. There is no doubt that philosophy influenced Beckett and, in turn, critics are now turning their attention to the ways in which Beckett has "influenced" the philosophers of the twentieth century: Maurice Blanchot, Jacques Derrida, Michel Foucault and Alain Badiou to name but a few. Anthony Uhlmann notes that

> the works *are* philosophical in that they have had and continue to have profound effects on philosophical discourse: both engaging with and influencing philosophers, and influencing and changing how western culture in general has come to think about particular problems. Yet questions concerning how we might understand this process are only beginning to come into focus. How do these works make us think? How have they changed our understanding of what it means to think and be in this world?[5]

Uhlmann also argues that Beckett's works have provoked those who read philosophy and, perhaps more importantly, those who write

---

[2] Samuel Beckett, *Endgame*, preface by Rónán McDonald (London: Faber and Faber, 2009), 25.
[3] See Gottfried Büttner, "Schhopenhauer's Recommendations to Beckett," in *Samuel Beckett Today/Aujourd'hui*, 11 (2002), 121.
[4] James Knowlson, *Damned To Fame: The Life of Samuel Beckett* (London: Bloomsbury, 1997), 2.
[5] Anthony Uhlmann, "Beckett and Philosophy," in S.E. Gontarski, ed., *A Companion to Samuel Beckett* (Oxford: Wiley-Blackwell, 2010), 93.

philosophy, but it remains an open question whether Uhlmann confronts what is surely the crux of the matter: "How *do* they make us think?"; perhaps not *how* have they changed our comprehension of what it means to exist in this world but rather, *have* they reshaped or altered our perception of existence? Furthermore, if Beckett's works do change our understanding of what it means to be in the world, does this necessarily entail his status as a philosopher, as Calder foresees? And would this disconnect him from the position of artist? Again the point is picked up by Uhlmann, who states in his "Introduction to Beckett's Notes to the *Ethics*" that "[i]t is clear that he [Beckett] is in no way apologetic for making use of philosophy in his own way: he is an artist, not a philosopher, and wishes to work with philosophy only insofar as it would add to his capacity as an artist."[6] It is clear from his essay, "Dante...Bruno.Vico..Joyce" that Beckett, right at the start of his writing career, confronts the issues of literature and philosophy and their corresponding association.

There has been a long-standing relationship between literature and philosophy and numerous questions have been asked, as John Cruickshank affirms in *The Novelist as Philosopher*, regarding the nature of this relationship. Cruickshank refers to Maurice Merleau-Ponty who suggested that "a simple story can present the world to us with as much "depth" and meaning as would a philosophical treatise."[7] And works such as *The Oxford Handbook of Philosophy and Literature* and the *Journal of Philosophy and Literature* convey the scholarly interest in examining the correlation between fiction and philosophy. Martha Nussbaum, in her book *Love's Knowledge: Essays on Philosophy and Literature,* claims that literature is a form of philosophy which "takes its bearings from Henry James's claim

---

[6] Anthony Uhlmann, "Introduction to Beckett's Notes to the *Ethics*," in Arnold Geulincx, *Ethics* With Samuel Beckett's Notes, edited by Han van Ruler and Anthony Uhlmann (Boston: Brill, 2006), 301, quoted here from Joanne Shaw, *Impotence and Making in Samuel Beckett's* Trilogy—Molloy, Malone Dies *and* The Unnamable—*and* How It Is (Amsterdam: Rodopi, 2010), 22.

[7] See John Cruickshank, ed., *The Novelist as Philosopher: Studies in French Fiction, 1935–1960,* (London: Oxford University Press, 1962), 9.

that the novelist's art performs a practical task [...] by expressing a 'projected morality' and an active 'sense of life,' and also from Proust's claim that it is only in a text having narrative form that certain essential truths about human life can be appropriately expressed and examined. At its core is the claim that literary form and human content are inseparable."[8]

Beckett was unquestionably a product of his time. The century in which he found himself was one plagued with war, unfathomable atrocities, poverty, selfishness, and cruelty: a humanity in ruins. Usually artists turn to art as an escape from the chaos—an escape from reality—but not Beckett; instead, Beckett created an aesthetic to confront the realities of existence, indeed to *affirm* these realities, perhaps in an attempt to comprehend or even interrogate them. The writing, which he referred to as a "bloody awful grind,"[9] signified existence itself, as Beckett confronted the necessity of writing life. In his essay "'Writing Myself into the Ground': Textual Existence and Death in Beckett," Mark Nixon explores "Beckett's poetics of going on, and not going on, through an examination of the convergence of text and existence, and looks at the way this convergence is established through the material act of writing."[10] As Henry James affirms in his essay, *The Art of Fiction*, the novel is, broadly speaking, an impression of life. Literature is therefore—at its most fundamental—an imitation of existence. But, how does one write life? How does a writer convey the intrinsic nature of existence—especially through the very words that Beckett deemed fundamentally ineffectual?[11]

---

[8] Martha Nussbaum, *Love's Knowledge: Essays on Philosophy and Literature* (New York: Oxford University Press, 1990), 289.

[9] See Samuel Beckett, *The Letters of Samuel Beckett, Vol. 1: 1929–1940*, edited by Martha Dow Fehsenfeld and Lois More Overbeck (Cambridge: Cambridge University Press, 2009), 157.

[10] Mark Nixon, "'Writing Myself into the Ground': Textual Existence and Death in Beckett," in *Beckett and Death*, ed. Steven Barfield, Philip Tew, and Matthew Feldman (London: Continuum, 2009), 23.

[11] Beckett details his approach to language in the oft-quoted letter to Axel Kaun, dated 9 July 1937. See "The German Letter of 1937," in Samuel Beck-

It is interesting that Beckett essentially wrote nothing new, as far as "philosophy" is concerned. Yet he very much endorsed Schopenhauer's theory that "[l]ife is a task to be worked off,"[12] a trial which must be endured until the endpoint; with no option to opt out or surrender.[13] The harshness of existence and the frailty of the human body reduce Beckett's characters to states of what can only be described as physical wreckage: suffering physically and, more often than not, mentally, they undergo a perpetual decline. And yet Beckett endows them with a propensity for propulsion. However, Beckett's view of life, his representation of existence and the intrinsic nature of man, essentially his "philosophy," remains, in essence, unaltered throughout his *oeuvre*—the only thing that fundamentally changes and evolves in the work is his form of writing. Beckett endeavored to find the form that would accommodate the "mess" of existence and perhaps, without the artistic innovation, the "philosophy" would have become redundant.[14] It is, to borrow David Hesla's expression, "the shape of chaos" that elevates Beckett's work above that of many of his contemporaries—he was not in effect saying anything different but he was saying it *differently*. It is here that the philosophy and artistic endeavor become inextricable, as philosophy becomes manifest in Beckett's imperative to create, despite the impossibility of creation[15]—that desire to find new ways of saying the "nothing new" and new methods of expressing "how it is"—in essence to fail again but

---

ett, *Disjecta: Miscellaneous Writings and a Dramatic Fragment*, edited by Ruby Cohn (London: Calder, 1983), 170–173.

[12] See *The Letters of Samuel Beckett*, 38.

[13] Beckett considered suicide an unacceptable form of surrender. See Knowlson, *Damned To Fame,* 569.

[14] In an interview with Tom F. Driver, Beckett discussed the need to find a form that would accommodate the mess. See T. F. Driver, "Beckett by the Madeleine," *Columbia University Forum*, IV (1961), 21–25.

[15] Anthony Cronin describes this as the artist's "special burden and torment." See Anthony Cronin, *Samuel Beckett: The Last Modernist* (London: Flamingo, 1997), 398.

only better, as the stoicism found within the characters permeates the words themselves.

Beckett's creative process is undoubtedly complex; as he discarded all that he deemed superfluous, the works became intricately crafted, each aiming to convey "lessness" and each a triumph of artistic creation. As conventional narrative is jettisoned, Beckett creates new genres and original dramatic experiences. His use of neologisms, and periodic abandonment of punctuation (as in the challenging novel *How It Is*), pushes language to the extreme, as Beckett struggles to do more and more with less and less, forcing language to the realms of metafiction where it becomes, to use Shimon Levy's term, "self-referential": self-conscious words commenting on themselves and acknowledging their own inadequacy. Beckett was stylistically more innovative than thematically inventive. Of course it can be argued that the world, and man's condition in it, are immutable, and therefore that it is understandable why the tropes remain unaltered. In this way, the paradoxical nature of the writing is acknowledged, while also recognizing a style that was continually evolving in its drive to illustrate concerns that remained unchanged.

Calder further suggests that Beckett's work illustrates the determination "to become nothing, desire nothing, expect and be nothing" (Calder, 4). This is very similar to what Geulincx advocates in his seventeenth-century tract, *Ethica*. I have elsewhere suggested that Beckett was attempting to write himself out of language,[16] referring to his words in *Proust* that "the artistic tendency is not expansive, but a contraction."[17] Due to the inadequacy of words it is best perhaps to eradicate them: "an assault against words in the name of beauty" (*Disjecta*, 173). But what if Beckett was not trying to write himself out of language, but instead wrote Nothing (affirming what he believed to be the reality of existence and adhering to Democritus' the-

---

[16] See Kathryn White, *Beckett and Decay* (London: Continuum, 2009), 109–152.
[17] Samuel Beckett, *"Proust" and Three Dialogues With Georges Duthuit* (London: Calder, 1965), 64.

sis) in an attempt to negate reality? The Nothing in literature differs from the Nothing in life, as words substantiate the void—turning it from Nothing into *Something*—thereby affirming its existence and destroying its concept. What if Beckett was not endeavoring to write himself out of words, but out of existence? In *What is Philosophy?* Gilles Deleuze and Félix Guattari, as Uhlmann asserts, propose that "a work of art reaches the infinite through the finite."[18] Beckett, as Uhlmann points out,[19] endorses this view in "Dante...Bruno.Vico..Joyce." Perhaps only through art can the void be illustrated and the emptiness of existence conveyed.[20] This is reminiscent of Lambert Zuidevaart's proposition that "[a]rt needs a philosophy that needs art."[21] Is it therefore impossible to completely detach philosophy from art? Or does aesthetic philosophy approach the problems of meaning, being and knowing in a more comprehensible way? "Where now? Who now? When now? Unquestioning."[22] Space, identity and time occupy Beckett's protagonists as they continually revolve the implications of existence. Thus, the Unnamable asks: "What am I to do, what shall I do, what should I do, in my situation, how proceed? By aporia pure and simple? Or by affirmations and negations invalidated as uttered, or sooner or later" (1). Creation and decreation, affirmation and negation, all pervade Beckett's language. *The Unnamable*—language evidently ineffective in providing a suitable title—or rather, the title effective in conveying the inadequacy of words—strives to articulate "I" in an attempt to bring closure to lan-

---

[18] Gilles Deleuze, and Félix Guattari, *What is Philosophy?* (New York: Columbia UP, 1994), 197, quoted here from Anthony Uhlmann, *Beckett and Poststructuralism* (Cambridge: Cambridge University Press, 1999), 7.
[19] Uhlmann, *Beckett and Poststructuralism*, 24.
[20] It is interesting, and worth noting, that in an interview with John Gruen, Beckett talks about turning toward an abstract language. See John Gruen, "Samuel Beckett Talks about Samuel Beckett," *Vogue* 154, No. 10 (December 1969), 210.
[21] See Richard J. Lane, *Beckett and Philosophy* (New York: Palgrave Macmillan, 2002), 2.
[22] Samuel Beckett, *The Unnamable*, edited by Steven Connor (London: Calder, 2010), 1.

guage and life concurrently. Theme and form are damned by affirmations and negations, as the inability to express is coupled with the impossibility to determine self. The desire to formulate an identity is unachievable because the words are incapable of describing "I." Hence, the voice is condemned to remaining "unnamable" while at the same time striving to find the right words to denote self and, consequently, to conclude the continual outpouring of language once and for all. Here theme and form merge, producing a text that challenges the nature of being and the essence of literature itself, progressing toward "unreadability."[23]

With reference to *The Unnamable*, Maurice Blanchot claims, "[p]erhaps we are not dealing with a book at all, but with something more than a book; perhaps we are approaching that movement from which all books derive, that point of origin where, doubtless, the work is lost, the point which always ruins the work, the point of perpetual unworkableness with which the work must maintain an increasingly initial relation or risk becoming nothing at all."[24] Perhaps, as Blanchot suggests, we are not dealing with a book but rather confronting a consciousness that requires words to provide confirmation of existence, unaware that neither (words nor existence) can be sustained. Words take precedence, not the conveying of a philosophical message; words are the subject in this text, coupled with the pointlessness of the creative process. This is not to suggest that *The Unnamable* is merely a mass of words conveying nothing apart from the inadequacy of language itself. As Blanchot argues, "the stories are still trying to survive" (118); that is, "the words continue, the wrong words, until the order arrives, to stop everything or to continue every-

---

[23] Leslie Hill suggests that Beckett's writing from the *Trilogy* onwards tends toward "unreadibility." See Leslie Hill, "Poststructuralist Readings of Beckett," in *Palgrave Advances in Samuel Beckett Studies*, ed. Lois Oppenheim (New York: Palgrave Macmillan, 2004), 74.

[24] Maurice Blanchot, "The Unnamable," in Lawrence Graver and Raymond Federman, eds., *Samuel Beckett: The Critical Heritage* (London: Routledge & Kegan Paul, 1979), 120 (first published in *Nouvelle Revue Française* [October 1953], 678–686).

thing, no, superfluous, everything will continue automatically, until the order arrives, to stop everything. Perhaps they are somewhere there, the words that count, in what has just been said, the words it behoved to say, they need not be more than a few" (*The Unnamable*, 85–86).

The Unnamable may be considered Beckett's most unyielding attempt at finding a language to accommodate the chaos of existence and words simultaneously. Although the stories are endeavoring to survive, they are gravitating toward failure, and it is evident that, from this point onwards, Beckett's "stories" increasingly become accounts of existence in ever decreasing words. This results in an artistic contraction and straining toward evanescence and extinction. Interestingly, Leslie Hill asks whether the voice of *L'Innommable* is basically the voice of literature itself (cf. Hill, 72). And the answer is both yes and no. It is the voice of literature because it is self-referential, questioning the implications and limitations of language and highlighting the difficulty of the creative process. But it is also the embodiment of Beckett's "philosophy" because, as the "prose becomes disjointed, leaping from topic to topic and switching pronouns at will,"[25] we recognize that, despite the impossibility of successful artistic expression—and even though they are predisposed to failure—Beckett's words, like his protagonists, go on. The spirit of stoicism is apparent in the words themselves—"you must go on, I can't go on, I'll go on" (*The Unnamable*, 134).

Following theories first supplied by Ferdinand de Saussure and later developed by Roland Barthes and Jacques Derrida, we have come to acknowledge that the very existence of narrative raises philosophical questions. This Linguistic Turn has highlighted the relationship between philosophy and language, a so-called "linguistic philosophy." Richard Rorty defines the latter: "linguistic philosophy, the view that philosophical problems are problems which may be solved (or dissolved) either by reforming language or by understanding more

---

[25] Lance St. John Butler, *Samuel Beckett and the Meaning of Being: A Study in Ontological Parable* (London: Macmillan Press, 1984), 117.

about the language we presently use."[26] Clearly, in his study, Rorty does not dissociate philosophy from the arts—language and philosophy are intrinsically linked. In Beckett's writing we witness the very thing Rorty calls for: a new understanding of language, an evolution of form. In his 1931 essay on Proust, Beckett states that "for Proust the quality of language is more important than any system of ethics or aesthetics. Indeed he makes no attempt to dissociate form from content. The one is a concretion of the other, the revelation of a world" (*Proust*, 88). Surely, this "acknowledgement" can also be applied to Beckett's own writing.

Yet Iris Murdoch, from the privileged position of being philosopher and writer of literature, feels that philosophy and literature are fundamentally different. In an interview with Bryan Magee,[27] she asserts that philosophy's aim is to clarify whereas literature's aim is to mystify; literature is written to entertain and the same cannot be said of philosophy. But is literature's function solely to entertain, and how does this accord with the writer's obligation to express? Beckett's works go beyond entertainment and the poignancy of his language helps us acknowledge that his work is, at its most fundamental, a depiction of humanity. "Beckett's works themselves offer important ways of understanding the world—that in some sense they offer us a kind of knowledge which might only come to light in the forms and through the processes Beckett creates" (Uhlmann, 92). Or as Malone has it in *Malone Dies*, "the forms are many in which the unchanging seeks relief from its formlessness."[28]

Even more than his earlier works, Beckett's late prose works demonstrate a severe linguistic contraction: conventional narrative is discarded and a new style emerges. These experimental fictions are

---

[26] Richard Rorty, *The Linguistic Turn: Essays in Philosophical Method* (Chicago: The University of Chicago Press, 1992), 3.

[27] This interview formed part of a series of interviews Bryan Magee conducted with various philosophers, called *Men of Ideas*, and was filmed by the BBC in 1978.

[28] Samuel Beckett, *Malone Dies*, edited by Peter Boxall (London: Faber and Faber, 2010), 23.

designed to capture the formlessness of experience and an increasing poetization resulting from this reductionism is evident. Language distinguishes us from animals; it confirms our humanity and structures experience. Wittgenstein studied the role of language in human thinking and life, claiming that if sentences are going to represent reality or states of affairs then there must be something in common between sentences and states of affairs. If humanity is fractured, then this reality must be, in turn, represented through a fractured narrative. Words are, as Heraclitus claimed, "fallible things" and language becomes a system that detracts meaning, an "incommunicable essence" (*Proust*, 65). As Calder notes, "the language, the metaphors, the visual aids and conceptual conceits and inventions which [Beckett] needed to turn the philosophy of negation, that he shared with many thinkers he had read, into a remarkable new literature [...] he found on his own" (Calder, 6). In this reading, Beckett's writing fundamentally articulates "how it is" to be alive. Especially in his later works, Beckett encapsulates existence from the moment of birth to the time of death (and indeed beyond), charting the process from "silence to silence"; his final texts express concisely the evanescence of language and life. In a similar vein, John Fletcher asserts that "Beckett has ranged freely among the writings of philosophers, where he has found confirmation and justification of the metaphysical obsessions that haunt his work."[29] How does an artist capture the futility and transience of existence in words—when how it is *said* becomes as fundamental as "how it is"?

What is often called Beckett's second "trilogy," entitled *Nohow On*—comprised of *Company*, *Ill Seen Ill Said* and *Worstward Ho*—comes close to capturing the void, and this two-word formulation contains the essence of Beckett's writing, both thematically and structurally: there is no possibility of successful expression, although the need to create forces the words onwards. Proust affirms that, for the writer, style is a question not of technique but of vision: style reveals

---

[29] John Fletcher, "Samuel Beckett and the Philosophers," in *Comparative Literature* Vol. 17, No. 1 (Winter, 1965), 55–56.

more than direct and conscious methods can.[30] Here, it may be said that Beckett's de-structured form fundamentally exemplifies the condition of humanity. John Pilling suggests that, for Beckett, the written word is not the medium able to absolve the crime of being.[31] But perhaps this is not its primary function—absolution is not required, only consternation. Beckett does not attempt to give meaning to existence, so those who turn to his work hoping to find enlightenment will be sadly disappointed; on the contrary, Beckett strives to capture the purposelessness of life. So there are no theories, no wonderful insights into why we are here, no explanations offered regarding our condition, no philosophy claiming that the world—or our position in it—will improve. Godot never comes and Malone dies on; Winnie in *Happy Days* remains incarcerated within the earth and *Footfalls*' May continues pacing, while the Unnamable strives to say "I." Issues are not resolved in Beckett's work—there is no message of hope, only a depiction of truth.[32] Calder suggests that the message that emerges most clearly from Beckett's work is that "one should do whatever is possible to alleviate the suffering of others, and where possible prevent it, while ignoring one's own problems" (Calder, 129). Instead, what Beckett presents are depictions of isolation, especially as the work progresses and the couplings tend to evaporate. Isolated in their suffering, the characters found in the late works exude a deep longing to be gone; and yet, termination appears to elude them, as human suffering is presented in new forms.

For example, *Ill Seen Ill Said*, Beckett's late prose poem, is best approached by way of its central images rather than through any expectations about narrative. Maurice Merleau-Ponty's phenomenology

---

[30] See Marcel Proust, *Remembrance of Things Past*, vol. 2 (Hertfordshire: Wordsworth Editions, 2006), 1169.
[31] See James Knowlson and John Pilling, *Frescoes of the Skull: The Later Prose and Drama of Samuel Beckett* (London: Calder, 1979), 184.
[32] Weller points out that Geneviève Bonnefoi, in her March 1956 review of *Nouvelles et Textes pour rien*, argues that the "I" in the prose texts exhibits an "extreme exigency of truth." See Shane Weller, "Beckett and Ethics," in *A Companion to Samuel Beckett*, 119.

of perception, which is similar to Beckett's own, can help in understanding this text; as Ulrika Maude points out, Beckett's interest in the "embodied nature of perceptual experience was central to the formation of his aesthetic."[33] As this suggests, Beckett's language offers no explanation of existence, only depiction and, as the writing progresses, words are eliminated, resulting in minimalist works which, above all, depict an image, as language evolves into "art." As Lois Oppenheim has argued in *The Painted Word,* Beckett essentially paints with words, a thesis supported by Fionnuala Croke's (ed.) *Samuel Beckett: A Passion for Paintings* and John Haynes and James Knowlson's *Images of Beckett.* This is what remains when everything has been pared down—the creation of the visual, as the philosophy becomes manifest in the aesthetic. Hence, in *Company,* the narrative is structured around an image of the figure on his back in the dark; a picture of the boy walking home with his mother, formulating questions about the distance of the sky; an old man "plodding along a narrow country road"[34]; a beggar woman "fumbling at the gate" (9); a young boy contemplating taking the plunge into the Forty Foot; Mrs. Coote taking tea with the wafer-thin bread and butter; and a hedgehog, dead in an old hat box. The words striving to articulate these images—pictures of isolation, fear, guilt and death—attempt to be the very articulation of life itself, not through dense prose but rather through a style transcending convention, one that struggles onward despite Beckett's aesthetics of failure.

Perhaps more than any other of his texts, *Ill Seen Ill Said* most succinctly conveys Beckett's "philosophy": an image of human life at "the inexistent centre of a formless place" (45–46), on the brink of inexistence, "railing at the source of all life" (45). Denied termination,

---

[33] Ulrika Maude and Matthew Feldman, "Introduction," in *Beckett and Phenomenology,* ed. Ulrika Maude and Matthew Feldman (London: Continuum, 2009), 6. For an insightful analysis of Beckett's treatment of perception, see Ulrika Maude, "'Material of a Strictly Peculiar Order': Beckett, Merleau-Ponty and Perception," in *Beckett and Phenomenology,* 77–94.

[34] Samuel Beckett, *Company/Ill Seen Ill Said/Worstward Ho/Stirrings Still* (London: Faber and Faber, 2009), 8.

the narrative's "old so dying woman" (53) is condemned to a lingering dissolution as she habitually makes the journey from her cabin to the gravestone and back again. She is continually "ill seen," and the narrator finds it difficult to express her condition, thereby conveying a narrative which is therefore "ill said." A sense of illness pervades the "story" no less than the words that tell it, as the content becomes wholly encompassed in the form. Language becomes reduced, meticulously crafted, and a series of images, or snapshots, are presented that may qualify as cinematic: pictures of the cabin, the buttonhook, the clock, the hands viewed from above—successive "photographs" of an empty existence. The eye's quest to perceive the woman is captured in a language struggling to describe the process—"long this image till suddenly it blurs" (52)—the process of seeing and saying conjoined. Seen in her cabin, seen in the pastures, seen from behind, a picture of waiting emerges, and readers are similarly condemned to wait, denied the image of her face until, seen from below, it finally consents—"Calm slab" (56)—the image of a death mask. This text, like many of Beckett's works, contains false endings and so the reading of it mimics the slowness of dying and the deceleration of the body in old age. The eye (or "I"), through which articulation is made possible, however poorly, wants the commenting to cease, perhaps aware that all is futile—"Nothing else. Contemplate that. Not another word. Home at last" (60). Home, where words are no longer required to depict or qualify life; but while there is continuance, and the characters go on, language persists in its quest to make manifest the illness ascribed to both itself and humanity. It is not clear whether the characters go on because words deny them termination; or instead, if the words go on in an effort to depict their condition. Inextricably linked, Beckett's protagonists—and the language used to describe them—endure a perpetual worsening, the breakdown of narrative reflecting corporeal disintegration. If language is used to reflect meaning, it therefore fails in its primary function as a means of communication; and to return to an earlier point, what if Beckett *was* trying to write himself out of language, but not out of communication?

It may be suggested that, in his late works, Beckett was using "worsening words" (*Worstward Ho,* 93) to facilitate the breakdown of narrative: "Say for be said. Missaid. From now say for be missaid" (81). Words are to be "missaid" so as not to give language the primary position, but to instead reserve this for the image that the words produce. *Worstward Ho,* a masterpiece of literary inventiveness, continues to explore Beckett's phenomenology of perception, as the text returns to images viewed by the skull. Forcing failing language to create, the words eventually call forth a body, albeit pained, assembling it from bones and urging it to its feet—vertical, it stands with "[c]lenched staring eyes" (83), ready to survey the dim void. Slowly, the image of an old man and child comes into focus, only to fade, followed by an old woman, back bowed. Yet she too cannot be sustained, as the image blurs and all that remains is "[t]hree pins. One pinhole" (103). Was Beckett essentially working towards signs and symbols (pictures), a form of hieroglyphics perhaps, where the failure of the human condition could be conveyed through a medium which, unlike language, is not plagued with the same "illness"?[35]

Following the eradication of the man, boy and woman, giving precedence to the void, language and image vie for supremacy, as language ensures that this text, following *Ill Seen Ill Said,* will be "worse seen," and "worse said," thus ensuring that the ontological image is in fact a truer expression of existence. The images which appear to be external and perceived by the skull become gradually reduced and deconstructed. By the dimness of the final paragraph, perception is denied almost entirely. The ultimate pinhole is perhaps bored through the skull, transforming it into a lightproof box, a simple camera without lens in which to capture the image but, without light to pass through the pinhole, the image cannot be projected and is therefore lost—this is why the skull cannot register the image and why the language declares in conclusion: "Enough."

---

[35] In the letter to Axel Kaun, dated 9 July 1937, Beckett compares the nature of words to the elements found in the arts of painting and music. See Beckett, *Disjecta,* 172.

Anthony Uhlmann states that, when it comes to these philosophical impressions, "images are projected from bodies and then 'screened' by the brain in two senses. Firstly, they are projected on to the brain as if it were a cinema screen. Secondly, they are filtered or 'screened' by the brain, so that material considered not of interest is ignored, while material considered of immediate interest is brought into focus."[36] This accurate summation of Beckett's application of phenomenological perception and the perceiving eye (or "I") throughout his *oeuvre* succinctly sums up the *modus operandi* used to select the required image. Moreover, it also encapsulates Beckett's technique of "filtering" or "screening" language so that everything which is deemed superfluous is discounted. It is interesting that the final words in *Worstward Ho* are not "nohow on" but, instead: "Said nohow on." "Said," functioning as the past participle of "say" and therefore not requiring a new utterance but reinforcing the already-stated command—"nohow on". This suggests that there is nothing new which can be said: "no" confirms the unwillingness; "how" questions the means; and the "on" undermines both by demanding continuance, thus conveying the fundamental condition of existence and language concurrently. In discussing Vico's treatment of language more than a half century earlier in "Dante...Bruno.Vico..Joyce," Beckett had already claimed that "the root of any word whatsoever can be traced back to some prelingual symbol" (*Disjecta*, 25). Was the artistic contraction, the gravitation toward minimalism—this attack on words through the medium of language- therefore an attempt to transcend conventional narrative in order to fail better? This raises the crux of Beckett's artistic philosophy, already announced in his first essay from 1929—"form and content are inseparable" (25). The aesthetics of failure subsequently embraced by Beckett enabled him to convey the reality of the human condition, coupled with his propensity for continuance, in a language whose structure mirrored its content. With reference to Joyce's aes-

---

[36] Anthony Uhlmann, *Samuel Beckett and the Philosophical Image* (Cambridge: Cambridge University Press, 2006), 148.

thetic Beckett stated, "[w]hen the sense is sleep, the words go to sleep. When the sense is dancing, the words dance" (27). And as ultimately achieved by Beckett's so-called "late trilogy," when the sense is failure, the words fail.

Thus in many respects Calder is right to suggest that future generations are likely find an ethical and philosophical message in Beckett's work. Yet this "philosophy" will not be the *raison d'être* that sets it apart, for the thematics has been—and surely will continue to be—discussed by many other artists. Rather, it is the packaging of his "philosophy" that will be of most interest; Beckett's aesthetics, the fundamental form. Only through artistic inventiveness was Beckett successfully able to narrate existence, as the language taken to extremes, compelled to worsen and yet still "ooze on" (*Worstward Ho*, 98) could truly reveal the reality of existence. It is this aesthetics of failure, seamlessly inscribed into his content, which future generations may find the most significant in Beckett's form of philosophy.

Beckett and the Refusal of Judgment: The Question of Ethics and the Value of Art

Mireille Bousquet
(Université Paris-8—Vincennes—Saint-Denis, France)

The acknowledgement that a fundamental indecision characterizes Samuel Beckett's oeuvre is one of the stumbling blocks of criticism and is indicative of how language and art operate in his work. Georges Bataille was among the first to align himself with this position and uses the term "indifference" when speaking of a book which "explores with an unflinching irony the extreme possibilities of indifference and misery."[1] In particular, he analyzes the workings of the author-reader relation as one of attack:

> This frantic progress toward ruin that animates the book, which, being the author's attack on the reader, is such that not for an instant is the latter given the leisure to withdraw into indifference–could it have been produced if so persuasive a conviction did not originate in some powerful motive? [...] Certainly, here all reasonable *hopes* and plans are engulfed in indifference. (64, 65)

The analysis unfolds by way of the question of meaning and touches one of the most eminently problematic points of Beckett's work: "the only meaning in all this lies in the fact that nonsense in its own way makes sense; a parody of meaning, perhaps, but finally a distinct meaning, which is to obscure within us the world of significations" (64).

---

[1] Georges Bataille, "Georges Bataille in 'Critique,'" in Lawrence Graver and Raymond Ferderman, eds., *Samuel Beckett: The Critical Heritage* (New York and London: Routledge & Kegan Paul, 1979), 64.

Once this indifference is extended to the whole of the work, inclusive of the author,[2] and even his readership, the stakes are truly of an ethical order. Bataille concludes logically: to such a "limping, imperfect indifference, how can one after all not be indifferent?" (67). If the indifference that carries the work overwhelms the reader and elicits the same attitude in return, it becomes truly a matter of surprise that this limit-work should still find an audience! Doubtless it is because the force of this generalized indifference has the power to create its own capacity for regeneration.

Bruno Clément's findings in *L'Oeuvre sans qualités* apply with equal validity to the assertion of indifference and to the refusal to choose. The figure of epanorthosis, which, for Clément, characterizes Beckett's work, is capable of figuring that which would be simultaneously form and movement, while, on the other hand, it carries a certain value, that of the absence of choice:

> In effect, epanorthosis is selected not because it allows, at almost each of its moments and places, the work to summon terms whose existence and relevance it would recognize and between which it would never have to choose, but because the poles that it names without disdain are for the work nothing more than empty places for dead objects.[3]

According to Clément the effect produced by the work is one of hesitation:

> Of course the statement of the question imposes, simultaneously with the question, the terms in which it is posed. Above all, through the play of alternatives, it imposes its skillfully constructed ambiguity. Thus it says: either the sketch is the reflection of its object or it betrays the incapacity [...] of the subject. [...] Yet all that counts is the object produced by the text: hesitation. (421)

---

[2] It is moreover to this excess of indifference that Bataille attributes the comic base of the narrative: "An author writing while consumed with indifference to what he writes might seem to be acting out a comedy" (67; translation modified).

[3] Bruno Clément, *L'Oeuvre sans qualités: rhétorique de Samuel Beckett* (Paris: Seuil, 1994), 242.

Clément concludes his analysis with the state of perplexity of the reader (necessarily his lot):

> ... nothing is as we thought. There is certainly someone, something, this moment is probably datable, this place locatable and there is well and truly a text. But we know nothing more. (425)

Clément thus draws attention to the process of unlearning that Beckett induces in the reader. But this process of apprenticeship in reverse leads the reader to confront the interrogation to which the text gives rise. The old certainties are truly undone, but nothing comes to replace them. If hesitation is in fact the sole object produced by the text, then it must be conceded that critical and interpretive reading reflects its own questions, as in a game of mirrors: only hesitation responds to the reader's interrogation. This surely accounts for a good part of the fascination that Beckett's work exercises, and poses a significant problem for criticism to the extent that the latter claims to formulate answers. So it is hardly surprising that, generally speaking, the critical gesture comes to the conclusion of indifference.

Let us take up, as another case, the example of Leslie Hill, whose study of Beckettian discourse leads to the same conclusion of indifference. According to Hill, the indetermination of which he gives an account constitutes an aporia,[4] and his reading arises out of a careful examination of philosophies of language that take the side of the unnamable, thereby treating language as a problem of nomination, and looking for a way out:

---

[4] "In Beckett, aporia is usually signalled by devices such as the careful rhetorical balancing of contradictory periods, the repeated use of terms like 'd'un côté' or 'd'un autre côté,' 'peut-être,' and the fondness for unanswerable rhetorical questions" (Leslie Hill, *Beckett's Fiction: In Different Words* [Cambridge: Cambridge University Press, 1990], 62).

> Beckett's work pursues one end, which is the end of language. The end of language, however, never comes. Or rather it has always already taken place. Beckett writes in the name of something which has no name, but to which he struggles to give a name. That something is what throughout this book, for my part, I have named: indifference. Yet indifference is not stasis. It is the infinity of difference, the erasure of identity and the still turbulence at the centre of language and the body [....R]epeatedly [...] the writing refuses to allow itself to be read as some form of coded message [...] it does this in part by denying its own binary logic and stability. (62)

The problem here is of knowing whether it is Beckett's writing that refuses to be decoded, as if this were implicitly a function of all language, or whether we are dealing with a dubious conception of language, which the work itself criticizes. Additionally, Hill's conclusion broods over the question of negativity in Beckett, a negativity that is first of all tied to a conception of language—even if Hill's reflection on indifference is very strong, particularly when he speaks of an "infinity of difference," it raises genuine questions while analyzing the ambivalent character of a work that invites interpretation even as it refuses it:

> What is left is a binary opposition which invites or solicits interpretation, yet refuses any contextual framework for interpretation. The contrast becomes crucial and indeterminate, significant yet devoid of meaning. (62)

How, in the end, is this negativity a problem? Perhaps because, in the last instance, everything that can be regarded as critical discourse leads to the assertion, which is to say the impasse, of aporia? Perhaps also because one senses here a kind of critical impotence, a renunciation that compels an exit from the work, to take the air as it were? From this point of view, Hill's conclusion is remarkable:

> Negativity in Beckett's work does not allow redemption; the issues it raises cannot be resolved by dialectical decision, by the covert imposition of a body of beliefs or doctrines. The force of indifference in Beckett's writing cannot be incorporated. That is its definition. This is why, for this book at least, there is no exit from the labyrinth.
> The heavens, however, continue to gleam and one may still get a sight of the sun and the other stars. (187)

Happily consolation is possible, but it is to be sought outside of the work, in the real world.

Despite or alongside this force of indifference, another force is continuously at work, the *on*: "I must go on." For Shane Weller, the undecidable character of the work is tied to this necessity of going on, to this imperative that draws in its wake a questioning of ethics. Against this conception, Alain Badiou sees the continuousness and force of "on" as having a purely ethical essence; and Stanley Cavell sees "[s]olitude, emptiness, nothingness, meaninglessness, silence" as "not the *givens* of Beckett's characters but their goal, their new heroic undertaking."[5] Weller suggests that Beckett's "on" constitutes a mute or opaque moment in the work, that no attempt at interpretation can deny, simultaneously forming the very condition of the possibility of the ethical and of its absence:

> each and every clarification of the imperative to go on, each and every attempt to make sense of it in terms of a meta-discourse, be it ethical, aesthetic, philosophical, political, religious, or psychoanalytic, serves to negate the possibility that the 'il faut' is simply a blank at the very heart of Beckett's *oeuvre*, a very specific nothing around which that *oeuvre* is painstakingly constructed.[6]

This is what leads Weller to describe as "anethical" a work whose fundamentally indecisive character resembles neither the ethical nor its opposite, but the negation of a possible difference or dis-

---

[5] Stanley Cavell, "Ending the Waiting Game: A Reading of Beckett's *Endgame*," in *Must We Mean What We Say? A Book of Essays* (Cambridge: Cambridge University Press, 2002), 156.

[6] Shane Weller, *Beckett, Literature and the Ethics of Alterity* (New York: Palgrave Macmillan, 2006), 193.

tinction between the two: "The anethical is to be understood, then, as neither an ethics nor an alternative to ethics, but rather as a failure either to establish or negate the difference between the ethical and the unethical, nihilism and anti-nihilism, philosophy and literature, thought and action, the terminable and the interminable" (194–195). Here, Weller testifies to the concern to maintain the work outside of judgment—ethical, aesthetic, political—without losing sight of the resistant character and the force of indecision that the work carries. But this refusal of judgment poses the problem of a possible ethical reading of the work.

It is well known that Beckett steadfastly refused to deliver any interpretation whatsoever of his work. In a letter to Alan Schneider, Beckett refrains from commenting on *Endgame*: "My work is a matter of fundamental sounds (no joke intended) made as fully as possible, and I accept responsibility for nothing else. If people want to have headaches among the overtones, let them. And provide their own aspirin. Hamm as stated, and Clov as stated, together as stated, nec tecum nec sine te, in such a place, and in such a world, that's all I can manage, more than I could."[7] This resistance to interpretation is not necessarily indicative of a kind of aporia, despite some interpretations of Beckett's criticism. And yet the work is not given over to the absurd. Consequently, it is necessary to view the work's undecidability as a new regime of meaning and not its annihilation. Two alternatives offer themselves for establishing the readability of Beckett's strategies to escape from the finality of judgment. The first is to recover the primary elements of reflection produced by Beckett himself. If he has not theorized much about his own work, he has nevertheless delivered some reflections regarding his conception of literature as a teacher at Trinity College, Dublin. The other path necessitates a close inspection of the indetermination to which the work's enunciative process is submitted.

---

[7] Samuel Beckett, *Disjecta: Miscellaneous Writings and a Dramatic Fragment*, edited by Ruby Cohn (London: Calder, 1983), 109.

During his years of teaching at Trinity College, of which he retained only the worst memories,[8] Beckett made a deep impression on one of his students, Rachel Burrows. The lecture notes that she took in 1931 were bequeathed to the University of Dublin. These were seldom remarked by critics, with the notable exception of Lawrence E. Harvey, who mentions them in *Samuel Beckett: Poet and Critic*, until the recent appearance of the book by Brigitte Le Juez, *Beckett Before Beckett*, which transcribes the essential parts. Her patient labor of transcription of barely legible manuscript notes throws a new light on Beckett's views of French literature. The notes reveal the assertiveness of Beckett's ideas. It is interesting to observe which aspects Beckett privileges in his lectures and what qualities he admires in the writers of whom he surveys. These reports sketch out a number of paths and reveal influences that were to mark his work. His interest in the complexity and obscurity of certain works is significant—these are the elements that will be rediscovered in his own.

Le Juez reports that Beckett "criticises the Naturalists' 'forced unification (Zola, etc)' and the presence of a system of reference based on a single idea, a single attitude, from which complexity is excluded. Outlining Gide's literary background, Beckett describes the Romantics and the Naturalists as artificial, and the pre-naturalists as authentically complex" (31). Le Juez adds: "The 'authentic complexity,' underlined in Rachel Burrows' notes, is a recurrent criterion in Beckett's literary judgments" (25). Beckett denounces the logical character of Balzac's work, the counter-example *par excellence*. In a 1982 interview, cited by Le Juez, Rachel Burrows reported:

---

[8] "According to his friends, his distaste of having to stand in front of an audience of giggling girls provided him with an excuse to drink excessively on the eve of his lectures so as to forget momentarily what awaited him the next day. In front of his students, however, he gave the best of himself" (Brigitte Le Juez, *Beckett Before Beckett*, translated by Ros Schwartz [London: Souvenir Press, 2008], 20).

> He hated Balzac, of course. He hated what he called the snowball act, which means that you do something that has causes, causes, causes, causes so that it's all perfectly consistent. (28)

The caricature of this type of logic will later be exploited in the crazy combinations of *Watt* and the endless ratiocinations of *Molloy*. The influence of Racine, which has perhaps never been accorded the importance that it had for Beckett, is here brought to light in a radical way. In the lecture on Gide, Beckett says: "Corneille/Balzac abdicate as critics vs [unlike] Racine" (55). Complexity is therefore one of the key values of modern literature for Beckett, who specifies that "Gide [is] preserving [the] integrity of incoherence" (44), concluding: "his material can't be stated or valued or related to any valuable cause: [the] incoherence of it alone can be stated" (32). Taking a step back, certain of his remarks are revelatory with regard to characteristics of Beckett's own work, among them those relating to the unfathomable, to mystery, to indetermination. Beckett told his students: "You can either respect a cavern or go about it with an electric torch as Stendhal or Balzac" (40). The quality of *clair-obscur* has its origins in the influence of Dostoevsky, whom Beckett compares to Rembrandt: "Dostoevsky composes a picture in which the most important consideration is the question of light ... But in Dostoevsky's books, as in a Rembrandt portrait, the shadows are the essential. Dostoevsky groups his characters and happenings, plays a brilliant light upon them, illuminating one aspect only. Each of his characters has a deep setting of shadow, reposes on its own shadow almost" (39). It is impossible not to think of the characters in the late plays, barely visible in the midst of a scene plunged in shadow. Another argument is well-analyzed by Le Juez: "What interested Beckett above all in Racine's plays is that little happens" (52). This consideration prefigures the situations in *Endgame* and *Waiting for Godot*, which rest on the absence of events. "The essential aspect of Racine's modernity remains, in Beckett's view, '[the] explicit statement of [the complex]'" (60). One of the qualities on which Beckett insists the most, visibly, and on several occasions, is what he calls "the *'complexité problématique'* [problematic complexity]" (36). So, some elements that characterize Beckett's work find their influence very early on in writers in the French tradition, as Brigitte Le Juez's painstaking analysis of Rachel Burrows' notes makes clear.

Beckett's stated desire, in the lectures, to render an account of the complexity of things will be translated into a labor on language and enunciation which will recompose the motifs of signification [*signifiance*] to the point that the latter might be seen as confusion. In reality, meaning is recomposed in the here and now of a statement that no longer refers to anything outside of the work. This can be noticed in the decomposition-recomposition of the series "thing," "nothing," "something" operative in *Endgame* or *Happy Days*, where the enunciative process works upon these terms to such an extent that they become a stumbling block to any solidarity of meaning.

If the only way to speak of nothing is to speak of it as though it were something,[9] then the importance of the "nothing" cannot be completely understood without its pendant, "something." When "nothing" passes or happens, it is something, or the "it" that haunts *Endgame*. The close proximity of "something" and "nothing" is stated by Winnie in the same sentence: "Yes, something seems to have occurred, something has seemed to occur, and nothing has occurred, nothing at all ..."[10] To be sure, the something concerned remains mysterious and uncertain. In *Happy Days*, the uncertainty regarding the origin of Winnie's acts is signaled by the indefinite marker "something": "Something says, Stop talking now ..." (23). By the same logic, the imperative that Winnie gives herself—"Do something!" (24)—declares the object to be inaccessible. "Doing" is opposed to "saying," operating as a cliché, but shifted in Beckett, for whom "saying" often constitutes the only action possible. Further-

---

[9] "For the only way one can speak of nothing is as though it were something" (Samuel Beckett, *Watt*, edited by C.J. Ackerley [London: Faber and Faber, 2009], 64).

[10] Samuel Beckett, *Happy Days*, preface by James Knowlson (London: Faber and Faber, 2010), 22.

more, the formula, "stop talking and do something for a change" (23), is charged with irony and particularly unhappy for a character no longer able to move.

Whatever the "something" may cover can only be an object of conjecture. It is probably of the same order as the "I have things to do"[11] spoken by Clov in order to go back to his kitchen. "Things," "something"—these insist to the very end, without the least possibility of the semblance of an action or realization, on the extreme insignificance that must characterize any project. The cohabitation in the same sentence of "that," "thing," "something," associated with repetitions of "or," characteristically contributes to the effect of indecision, of self-cancellation, of unproductive discourse on the plane of determination and designation, which characterizes Beckett's manner:

> Then it goes and I see it's not that, but something else, difficult to grasp, and which I don't grasp, or which I do grasp, it depends, and it comes to the same, for it's not that either, but something else, some other thing, or the first back again, or still the same, always the same thing proposing itself to my perplexity, then disappearing, then proposing itself again, to my perplexity still unsated, or momentarily dead, of starvation.[12]

The "not that," like the "something else," participate, even as they oppose each other, in the same unknown universe, one accessible only in the head of the narrator, the true dramatic space of the work, to which they return: "always the same thing." The command, "[l]eave all that," hurled in Text III of the *Texts for Nothing* establishes the mode of indetermination and self-reference: "[l]eave, I was going to say leave all that" (11). "All that" relates to the narrator's unknown world and marks the very strong subjectivization of the Texts. Yet its reference must remain deeply mysterious for the reader. This phenomenon permeates all of the Texts. Deictics are thus turned away

---

[11] Samuel Beckett, *Endgame*, preface by Rónán McDonald (London: Faber and Faber, 2009), 7.

[12] Samuel Beckett, *Texts for Nothing and Other Shorter Prose, 1950–1976*, edited by Mark Nixon (London: Faber and Faber, 2010), 40.

from their normative usage; their only contribution is to indicate a referential gap. The "something" that remains unknown to the reader, but also perhaps to the narrator himself, participates in the undefined action, thereby reinforcing the policy of "nothing" that animates the work. Whatever the "something" is that troubles the minds of the characters or narrators, it provides the passing semblance of an objective in making the time pass (the inventory of material possessions is one of the principal variants of this), but it is never "it." Things fill up space and supply an immediate object. Malone says, "I think I shall be able to tell myself four stories, each one on a different theme. One is about a man, another about a woman, a third about a thing and finally one about an animal, which is probably a bird. I think that is everything."[13] The "thing" is placed on the same plane as "man," "woman" and "animal," and concludes by recapitulating "everything," thereby assimilating the entire list to "things."

The insistence with which the inventory is described as a "thing," when the inventory is itself a list of "things," produces, beyond the effect of the bizarre, the image of a world in flux, a world of indeterminable things:

> For then I shall speak of the things that remain my possession, that is a thing I have always wanted to do. It will be a kind of inventory. In any case that is a thing I must leave to the very last moment, so as to be sure of not having made a mistake. In any case that is a thing I shall certainly do, no matter what happens (*Malone Dies*, 5).

The systematic repetition of "thing" is not innocent. It is not for nothing that, in the French version, the writing project concerns a thing qualified as "any" [*quelconque*]: "Je pense que je pourrai me raconter quatre histoires, chacune sur un thème different. Une sur un homme, une autre sur une femme, une troisième sur une chose quelconque ..."[14] The word "thing" allows one to express while naming nothing (or, more precisely, while implicitly naming the "nothing"),

---

[13] Samuel Beckett, *Malone Dies*, edited by Peter Boxall (London: Faber and Faber, 2010), 5.
[14] Samuel Beckett, *Malone meurt* (Paris: Minuit, 1951), 10.

creating an indistinct referential environment. Franck Neveu has amply demonstrated the value of the word "thing" in Beckett's work, precisely for its quality of indistinct designation: "The interest of the word resides above all in its semantic quasi-vacuity and in its great contextual adaptability, which make it a very effective auxiliary designator in the indistinct deixis constructed by 'it.'"[15]

Of course the thing also allows the signaling of the ordinary unnamable of discourse and the everyday, which is never very far from horror:

> HAMM: Have you not had enough?
> CLOV: Yes! [*Pause.*] Of what?
> HAMM: Of this ... this ... thing [....]
> HAMM: [*Anguished.*] What's happening, what's happening?
> CLOV: Something is taking its course. (*Endgame*, 7, 12)

The use of things is especially well summarized at the end of the first act of *Happy Days*, where their impact on temporality is clearly revealed. Even more than space, it is time that things occupy: "I used to think—I say I used to think—that all these things—put back into the bag—if too soon—put back too soon—could be taken out again—if necessary—if needed—and so on—indefinitely—back into the bag—back out of the bag—until the bell—went. [*Stops tidying, head up, smile.*] But no" (26). Ideally, things should last indefinitely. Yet this illusion is itself a snare, as Winnie's "[b]ut no" soberly confirms. Winnie's universe is populated by things, things which punctuate a beginning and an end (first thing, last thing) in time and which age as she does herself: "prayers perhaps not for naught—[*pause, do.*]—first thing—[*pause, do.*]—last thing [...] Old things. [*Pause.*] Old eyes. [*Long pause.*]" (7). But they also function to return Winnie to her involuntary passivity because, whatever she may do to rid herself of them, the things return:

---

[15] Franck Neveu, "Sur la relation partie:tout et la désignation indistincte dans *Fin de partie*—Référence et contexte au théâtre," in Franck Neveu, ed., *Faits de langue et sens des textes* (Paris: SEDES, 1998), 286.

> I take up this little glass, I shiver it on a stone—[*does so*]—I throw it away—[*does so far behind her*]—it will be in the bag again tomorrow, without a scratch, to help me through the day. [*Pause.*] No, one can do nothing. [*Pause.*] That is what I find so wonderful, the way things ... [*voice breaks, head down*] ... things ... so wonderful. (22–23)

In this last passage, the reference to "things" bestows on them a quasi-metaphysical and unfathomable quality. The "thing" allows passage from horror to wonder because it can qualify either, alternatively, indistinctly. It is this same quality, or absence of quality, that confers its disquieting strangeness.

Even if it appears absurd and contradictory from the point of view of the statement, Beckett's work systematically points to the possible relationship, even identity, of "nothing," "thing" and "something," thus obviating every possibility of judgment on the basis of the statement. The material absence of referential marks on the stage no more allows the identification of what "it," "things," or "nothing" designate—as Franck Neveu demonstrated in the case of *Endame*—than is possible in the strictly verbal universe of the fiction. Designation without referent, or with a vague and confused reference, is a good description of Beckett's manner beyond the genre divisions of the work. It is thus, in the survey of the attempts to state an indeterminate, that the blockage of all possibility of judgment gets organized for a reading only able to conceive of itself as resistance.

If the work worries this problem of differentiation and the recomposition of signification, outside of any moral bias, does this mean that it elevates itself, solitary and indifferent in the midst of the world? A gesture that would imply a view of art as severed from the world and humanity? It is on this ground, in my view, that debate must be engaged. It is therefore the question of meaning that raises itself: what meaning is to be given to what is read, how to attribute this meaning, how is it constructed? And what kind of meaning? This is not a new question. Roland Barthes raised it in *Criticism and Truth*: "Does the work have meaning literally or else symbolically—or again, in Rimbaud's phrase, 'literally and in every sense'?"[16] The theoretical approach, particularly that of a theory of language, effectively induces a reading. Either the work does what it says (it speaks of indifference and adopts the same posture, which is to attribute to the discourse of a narrator or character the intentions of the author) or what the work does, its signification (or *signifiance*, in Henri Meschonnic's sense), is not to be found in its statement. Questions of value and ethics find themselves involved with the problem of meaning.

Charles Juliet reports a conversation with Beckett during which Beckett spoke of his refusal to judge, implicitly castigating critics who all too easily assigned his work to the theater of the absurd:

> Cautiously, I explain that I believe that an artist's work is inconceivable without a strict ethical sense.
> A long silence.
> "What you say is true. But moral values are inaccessible. And they cannot be defined. In order to define them, you would have to pass a value judgment, which is impossible. That's why I could never agree with the notion of a theater of the absurd. It involves a value judgment. You cannot even speak about truth. That's what's so distressful. Paradoxically, it is through form that the artist may find some kind of a way out. By giving form to formlessness. It is only in that way, perhaps, that some underlying affirmation may be found."[17]

This refusal of judgment in favor of form, even if it would be formless, as the sole affirmation possible for the artist, clearly involves an ethical consideration, but one exclusive to art: the invention and creation of internal value. The "you must go on" declared in *The Unnamable*, but also the "[b]esoin d'avoir besoin" [need to need] (*Disjecta*, 55), constitute the only declaration(s) possible, the imperative of the creative faculty whose value lies outside morality and

---

[16] Roland Barthes, *Criticism and Truth*, translated by Katrine Pilcher Tody (London: Continuum, 2007), 16.

[17] Charles Juliet, *Conversations With Samuel Beckett and Bram Van Velde*, translated by Tracy Cooke, Axel Nesme, Janey Tucker, Morgaine Reinl and Aude Jeanson (Champaign and London: Dalkey Archive Press, 2009), 23–24.

judgment. In this, Beckett comes close to Gilles Deleuze, who also wishes to wrest philosophical thought from the tyranny of judgment, above all when he challenges the apparatuses of power (including Marxism, psychoanalysis and linguistics) and pleads for a philosophy that would integrate "nomadism, the war-machine, becomings, nuptials against nature, captures and thefts, interregnums, minor languages or stammering of language."[18] Deleuze's reflection involves a construction of language which would get rid of the official language of the State—the notion of a correct idea:

> ... thought borrows its properly philosophical image from the state as beautiful, substantial or subjective interiority. It invents a properly spiritual State, as an absolute state, which is by no means a dream, since it operates effectively in the mind. Hence the importance of such notions as universality, method and question and answer, judgement, or recognition, of just correct, always having correct ideas ... Philosophy is shot through with the project of becoming the official language of a Pure State. (*Dialogues*, 13)

Deleuze rebels against the disease that he calls interpretosis, and searches for an art or a thought freed from the necessity of signification: "Since the 'signifier' has been invented, things have not fallen into place. Instead of language being interpreted by us, it has set about interpreting us, and interpreting itself. Signifiance and interpretosis are the two diseases of the earth, the pair of despot and priest" (13). Henri Meschonnic also declares, rather provocatively, that "meaning is the last thing that matters." To wrest writing, whether artistic or philosophical, from the draining of signification, from the identity of the Ego, and from all determinations—this is a project common to Deleuze and Beckett:

---

[18] Gilles Deleuze and Claire Parnet, *Dialogues*, translated by Hugh Tomlinson and Barbara Habberjam (London: The Athlone Press, 1987), 14.

> We are always pinned against the wall of dominant significations, we are always sunk in the hole of our subjectivity, the black hole of our Ego which is more dear to us than anything. A wall on which are inscribed all the determinations which fix us, put us in a grille, identify us and make us recognized, a hole where we deposit—together with our consciousness—our feelings, our passions, our little secrets which are all too well known, our desire to make them known. Even if the face is a product of this system, it is a social production ... Our societies need to produce the face. (45).

Refusal of the face, that is, of the subject given over to the determinations of an identity, instead of a subjectivity generated from alterity. Behind form as sole affirmation, there is life: "la vie des lignes et des couleurs," "la seule vie qui compte" ["the life of lines and colors," "the only life that matters"] (*Disjecta*, 119), as Beckett says of the canvas. Deleuze suggests:

> Let there be just fluxes, which sometimes dry up, freeze or overflow, which sometimes combine or diverge ... On lines of flight there can no longer be but one thing, life-experimentation. One never knows in advance, since one no longer has future or past. (*Dialogues*, 47)

The line of flight invented by Deleuze allows us to speak of the rootedness of art in life:

> The great and only error lies in thinking that a line of flight consists in fleeing from life; the flight into the imaginary or into art. On the contrary, to flee is to produce the real, to create life, to find a weapon. (49)

The exhaustion that characterizes Beckett's work, and which passes through a search for the impersonal,[19] for effacement, for a response to the question "[c]omment représenter le changement?" ["how can change be represented?"] (*Disjecta*, 129) is perhaps quite close to the project of becoming-imperceptible that is, for Deleuze, the enterprise of writing: "The aim, the finality of writing? Still way

---

[19] "[T]he aim of writing is to carry life to the state of a non-personal power" (Deleuze, *Dialogues*, 50).

beyond a becoming-woman, a becoming-Negro, a becoming-animal, etc., beyond a becoming-minority, there is the final enterprise of the becoming-imperceptible" (*Dialogues*, 45; translation modified).

One problem is to determine whether the undecidable is actually a value of the text, or the result of subjectivism, a critical incompetence, as Henri Meschonnic and Gérard Dessons explain:

> The undecidability of a reading is of two orders: either it is the work of incompetence or it belongs to the text itself. In the latter case, it must be apprehended and recorded as a value of the text and not cut away in favor of an arbitrary personal interpretation. An uncertainty may even affect a language category, giving rise to a categorical blinking, which is a blinking of speech ... There is no "choice" to be made if the text has not already "chosen."[20]

The question of the undecidable must be approached as a problem of meaning, but so that to make a critique of meaning. This approach, then, does not consist of proposing an interpretation, but of liberating the critical force of the poem, which is infinite. The assertion that we cannot make a choice because the work does not choose is perhaps a declaration of the failure of criticism, if one believes that criticism (or the work) must provide answers. This position is tied to one that envisages the operation of the work as a search carried out on the side of the message (to explain, to understand) and not on the side of the invention of value. Does this approach leave criticism in a position of weakness, or at any rate in one of little power, since it is no longer a question of affirming a truth, of finding the solution to a problem, but more modestly of bringing out the questions asked by the text, to us, to the society in which it is bound up indefinitely? To escape definitions, determinations, is what matters here, and constitutes a project common to the work of Samuel Beckett, Gilles Deleuze and Henri Meschonnic:

---

[20] Gérard Dessons et Henri Meschonnic, *Traité du rythme: des vers et des proses* (Paris: Dunod, 1998), 188.

> Poetry without answers, since poetry begins in the escape from every definition, every place, every question of origin or inscription. It escapes from the verb "to be." It is the figure of language itself. Why it is a question, not an answer. And, as a question, it is without answer. Except that its reflection, as unstable as itself, constitutes each time the "answer," in displacing, language-story to which it is correlated, something of the conditions of discourse.[21]

All three examine the relations between art, life and the subjects that populate this space, collective and political. In *Le Monde et le pantalon*, Beckett had already precisely formulated the essential relation between art, life, and the gaze:

> Achevé, tout neuf, le tableau est là, un non-sens. Car ce n'est encore qu'un tableau, il ne vit encore que de la vie des lignes et des couleurs, ne s'est offert qu'à son auteur. Rendez-vous compte de sa situation. Il attend, qu'on le sorte de là. Il attend les yeux, les yeux qui, pendant des siècles, car c'est un tableau d'avenir, vont le charger, le noircir, de la seule vie qui compte, celle des bipeds sans plumes. (*Disjecta*, 119)
> [Finished, brand new, the canvas is there, a non-sense. For it is still but a canvas, it still lives but the life of lines and colors, is offered to none but its maker. Consider its situation. It waits for us to bring it out. It awaits eyes, eyes that, for centuries to come, since it is a canvas of the future, will charge it, darken it, with the only life that matters, that of featherless bipeds.]

That which traverses the work of art, like literature, philosophy or critical thought, manifests itself first of all in the form of expectation—of an unknown, of an interrogation. It is necessary to see the work of art as a process, the monstration of a construction, an awareness and hold on life, but without answer, as it returns first of all to the autonomy, the solitude of the reader, the only judge incapable of judging. It is perhaps in the awareness of this impossibility of judgment that the radical force of Beckett's work is found. Where all is thrown into question, because it is alive. It is this that Beckett began to formulate in "Le Monde et le pantalon" in opposing the doubts of

---

[21] Henri Meschonnic, *Poésie sans réponse* (Paris: Gallimard, 1978), 11.

the amateur to the possibility of aesthetic judgment: "Il n'y a pas de peinture. Il n'y a que des tableaux. Ceux-ci, n'étant pas des saucisses, ne sont ni bons ni mauvais. Tout ce qu'on peut en dire, c'est qu'ils traduisent, avec plus ou moins de pertes, d'absurdes et mystérieuses poussées vers l'image, qui'ils sont plus ou moins adéquats vis-à-vis d'obscure tensions internes" [There is no painting. There are just canvasses. These, not being sausages, are neither good nor bad. All that can be said is that they translate, with more or less loss, some absurd and mysterious thrusts toward the image, that they are more or less adequate to some obscure inner tensions] (*Disjecta*, 123). Beckett explicitly puts forward the process of artistic creation as the invention of value internal and peculiar to the work, forever to be discovered.

Conclusion: Beckett in Theses

Karim Mamdani

As the essays in this collection make abundantly plain, the question of Beckett and philosophy remains very much relevant, in spite of having been asked and explored repeatedly for decades. Its persistence can only partly be explained by the obscurity attaching to the many scattered allusions to philosophers in Beckett's works—and of which Matthew Feldman has provided a sample sketch in his Introduction to this volume—as the debate surrounding the allusions might be counted on to lose its attraction with the passage of time and the tedium of argument. Are Beckett's philosophical references serious or ironic? Or, as Dirk Van Hulle perceptively suggests in his treatment of Fritz Mauthner in *Rough for Radio II* (in) may an explicit reference contain elements of misdirection at the same time as confession? Does this vacillation or indeterminacy capture something of what occurs in Beckett's texts at a literary, non-philosophical level, allusion thus giving the critic something to fasten upon in the search for a broader accounting? Perhaps, as Laura Cerrato says, it is best to think of the relation between Beckett and philosophy as inherently *difficult*.[1]

Cerrato believes that Beckett's readings of philosophy are best seen as active misreadings, not as passive or fortuitous encounters, but quarrelsome, ironic, skeptical engagements with the tradition of Western philosophy (120). She speaks of "Beckett and the philosophers" rather than of Beckett and philosophy,[2] but it is possible to accommodate a more explicitly differentiated role for the latter by add-

---

[1] Laura Cerrato, "Samuel Beckett y los filósofos: una difícil relación," in *Beckett: El Primer Siglo* (Buenos Aires: Ediciones Coihue, 2007), 107–120.

[2] Is it possible to engage a philosopher without the philosophy? This is what Matthew Feldman has provocatively and engagingly suggested is the case with Descartes; see Matthew Feldman, *Beckett's Books: A Cultural History of Samuel Beckett's "Interwar Notes"* (London: Continuum, 2008), 41–57.

ing a second distinction. The poet J.H. Prynne, applying the following conceptual pair to poetry exclusively, has defined a difference between obscurity and difficulty: "When poetry is *obscure* this is chiefly because information necessary for comprehension is not part of the reader's knowledge ... and finding out this information may dispel much of the obscurity. When poetry is *difficult* this is more likely because the language and structure of its presentation are unusually cross-linked or fragmented, or dense with ideas and response-patterns that challenge the reader's powers of recognition."[3] The distinction may then be adapted so that "obscurity" refers to the philosopher, while "difficulty" belongs to the philosophy. This distinction should not be seen as absolute—"[t]he danger is in the neatness of identifications," as Beckett's first published essay from 1929 warns[4]—and, as Prynne says, it is perfectly possible to find the two working together in the same text or text-fragment, as in Beckett's aforementioned allusion to Mauthner. Yet some real weight must be given to this distinction in approaching the "empirical turn" evident in the majority of the contributions to this issue, and which marks one of the most interesting and exciting developments in the study of Samuel Beckett.

Certainly one of the recommendations implied by the examination of the "Interwar Notes" kept by Beckett in his self-imposed study of philosophy is the weight of corroboration that it lends to claims of influence or inheritance. The disadvantage, for the non-specialist

---

[3] J.H. Prynne, "Difficulties in the Translation of 'Difficult' Poems," *Cambridge Literary Review*, 1/3 (Easter, 2010), 160 n. 1. It may be thought abusive to apply Prynne's pairing to Beckett, who was not exclusively a poet; however, as Beckett's late works are not infrequently described as prose poems, the application seems valid. See, for instance, on *Ill Seen Ill Said*, Marjorie Perloff, "Between Verse and Prose: Beckett and the New Poetry," in *The Dance of the Intellect: Studies in the Poetry of the Pound Tradition* (Chicago: Northwestern University Press, 1996), 135–154; and, more recently, the Special Issue "Samuel Beckett as Poet," ed. Philip Nikolayev, *Fulcrum, An Annual of Poetry and Aesthetics*, 6 (2007): 442–624.

[4] Samuel Beckett, "Dante...Bruno.Vico..Joyce," in *Disjecta: Miscellaneous Writings and a Dramatic Fragment*, edited by Ruby Cohn (London: Calder, 1983), 19.

reader with limits to access, is that this research is largely carried out in specialized archives in Britain, Ireland and the US, and thus not available to many scholars. In consequence of this work, it is no longer a matter of the educated guess (Descartes) or the philosophical hypothesis (existentialism), based on textual suggestion, but a labor of manuscript research and cross-checking of primary sources. If this de-democratizes or narrows the interpretive field, however, the price may be one a majority of readers would still be willing to pay—especially given the sometimes arbitrary identification of Beckett with a given philosopher, as though in the conduct of an experiment, which seems to add rather than remove obscurity for the study of more persistent difficulty.

The value of this work is felt keenly in the study of Beckett. Witold Gombrowicz left his readership a brief and witty study of philosophy, *A Guide to Philosophy in Six Hours and Fifteen Minutes*; Jorge Luis Borges explicitly included philosophy in his *ficciones*; Vladimir Nabokov was very free with his opinions; even Fernando Pessoa, whom it would be very interesting to treat in comparison with Beckett, left the occasional explicit philosophical hint—albeit relativized by being delivered by a heteronym. By contrast, Beckett's reticence in the matter of philosophy is notorious:

> I never read philosophers.
> Why not?
> I never understand anything they write.[5]

No great effort is needed to show that these statements are false, but what kind of falsity is at work in them? Is it the same kind that readers encounter in the novels? "It is midnight. The rain is beating on the windows," concludes *Molloy*, before immediately adding: "It was not midnight. It was not raining."[6] Clearly, something other than

---

[5] Gabriel D'Aubarède, "Interview With Samuel Beckett," in Lawrence Graver and Raymond Federman, eds., *Samuel Beckett: The Critical Heritage* (London: Routledge & Kegan Paul, 1979), 217.

[6] Samuel Beckett, *Molloy*, edited by Shane Welller (London: Faber and Faber, 2009), 184.

irony or defensiveness appears involved. Beckett's overt rejection of philosophy, in favor of a more affective logic, is thus unconvincing—even if it is not possible to reject this rejection completely. This situation is oddly like the chiaroscuro Beckett described to Tom F. Driver,[7] which compels one to continue examining the inscrutable, and which the slash in *Beckett/Philosophy* tries to convey.

Before turning to a brief synopsis of the preceding contributions to this volume, however, it is worth noting another gravitational pull on scholarly trajectories with respect to Beckett and philosophy. If empirical approaches collectively seek to ground philosophical attributions by demonstrating Beckett's awareness of the sources named—and so brings philosophy into the orbit of Beckett's own experience—the treatment of Beckett by philosophers themselves is understandably free of any such considerations: Stanley , Theodor W. Adorno, and, more recently, Gilles Deleuze and Alain Badiou have all taken up Beckett as an important, occasionally central figure in their respective philosophies. In each of these cases, the philosopher's reading has itself become the subject of a critical, second-order consideration—to the point, indeed, that entire books can be found devoted to these new hybrid subjects.[8] Yet such studies run the risk of

---

[7] Tom F. Driver quotes Beckett: "If there were only darkness, all would be clear. It is because there is not only darkness but also light that our situation becomes inexplicable" ("Interview With Samuel Beckett," in *Samuel Beckett: The Critical Heritage*, 220).

[8] On the relation between Deleuze and Beckett, see Isabelle Ost, *Samuel Beckett et Gilles Deleuze: cartographie de deux parcours d'écriture* (Brussels: Facultés universitaires Saint-Louis, 2008). For more on Badiou, see Andrew Gibson, *Beckett and Badiou: The Pathos of Intermittency* (Oxford: Oxford University Press, 2006). Even Derrida's well-known ambivalent dodge has provoked a book-length study; see Asja Szafraniec, *Beckett, Derrida, and the Event of Literature* (Stanford: Stanford University Press, 2007). In this unlikely context there is still some small "empirical" support to be had. André Bernold reports that he acted as intermediary between Derrida and Beckett, but this seems to have been confined to getting Derrida to agree that Bernold should deliver Derrida's texts on Joyce to Beckett. Bernold also records Beckett asking questions about Derrida and Deleuze; once again, however, this interest seems a bit abstract and (it is hard to judge from Bernold's hagi-

making Beckett little more than a privileged exhibit in the exposition of the philosopher's system.[9] What is significant for the present survey is that, alongside the possible extinction of poststructuralism as a force in the study of literature, these confrontations are framed in philosophical terms that no longer take refuge in abstract "theory."

Bruno Clément has observed that philosophers writing about Beckett can be divided into two groups, corresponding to two different moments. The first, which he identifies above all with Maurice Blanchot, he calls "mimetic criticism." In this type of text, the philosopher is ventriloquized by Beckett's work and adds nothing foreign. A second moment leaves behind this kind of conceptual paraphrase and becomes "philosophical criticism (which sometimes gives the impression of making Beckett's work say something other than what it says)."[10] It is in this latter camp that Clément numbers Deleuze and Badiou, the two philosophers whose relatively recent interventions into Beckett Studies have witnessed the greatest response. Their work marks the moment that a philosopher's pronouncements on Beckett are integrated into that philosopher's broader concerns—with all the promises and obvious dangers this entails.[11]

---

ographic style) may have been simple politeness on Beckett's part; see André Bernold, *L'Amitié de Beckett 1979–1989* (Paris: Hermann, 1992), 84–85.

[9] It must be said that Isabelle Ost, more than most, avoids this trap, and constructs a very detailed set of readings of Beckett.

[10] Bruno Clément, "Ce que les philosophes font avec Samuel Beckett," in *After Beckett/D'après Beckett, Samuel Beckett Today/Aujourd'hui* 14 (2004), 221.

[11] Jean-Jacques Lecercle has drawn attention to Badiou's odd willingness, in seeming contradiction to his own definition of art as non-philosophy, to treat *Worstward Ho* as "a short philosophical treatise"; see Alain Badiou, *On Beckett*, edited and translated by Alberto Toscano and Nina Power (Manchester: Clinamen, 2003), 80. As Lecercle adds, "[t]his paradoxical method of reading raises serious problems: Beckett risks being taken for a proto-Badiou"; see Jean-Jacques Lecercle, *Badiou and Deleuze Read Literature* (Edinburgh: Edinburgh University Press, 2010), 134. Lecercle concludes that, while more original, Badiou's reading of Beckett is finally not as compelling as Deleuze's more fastidious treatment of the work (154).

On the other hand, the empirical approach on offer here can be regarded as an attempt to escape the perils of "dogmatic" assertions and ungrounded speculation—both based in concepts rather in documentary evidence. However, if this empiricism has wakened criticism from its complacent slumbers, it does not, and cannot, account for the more general, truly critical question: What is a *philosophical* reading of Beckett? This is the question that the last few essays included in this collection begin to address, if not to answer, remaining in their own way faithful to the abiding difficulty recorded in Beckett's interview with Tom F. Driver: "art raises questions that it does not attempt to answer" (Driver, 220).

* * *

Donald Phillip Verene's essay presents an unusual and sometimes forgotten Beckett; it gives us a portrait of the artist as a young man, but a young man caught in the magnetic fields of aesthetics and philosophy, sketching out a theory that elevates artistic practice over abstract conceptualization—a practice of art, however, not his own. This is another "Beckett before Beckett" to be added to the one uncovered by Brigitte Le Juez.[12] Yet where Le Juez presents a Beckett assembling a mobile and polemical canon of novels, Verene's Beckett is more a developing philosopher than an artist in genesis. To the Beckettian, perhaps more than to the Joycean, this asymmetry seems ill-formed, maybe even malformed, another difficult birth to ponder in and before the work. Yet if Beckett's later insistence on the antithesis between himself and Joyce suggests that Vico was discarded along with other burdensome influence, Verene reminds us of a tenuous and difficult continuity, one without solution, in Bruno's "coincidence of contraries." The conclusion to be drawn is not that maximum (Joyce) and minimum (Beckett) can be identified in some new

---

[12] Brigitte Le Juez, *Beckett Before Beckett*, translated by Ros Schwartz (London: Souvenir Press, 2008). See above for Mireille Bousquet's extensive consideration of the relations between this early Beckett and the "mature" artist who had developed or invented his own aesthetic.

and yet to be conceived literary space. Consider in this regard the conclusion to F.K. Stanzel's *A Theory of Narrative*, whose climactic and surprising final pages both fulfill the typological circle of narrative situations and suggest symmetrical ways in which it may be exceeded—centrifugally through the surging operations of *Finnegans Wake* and centripetally by the implosive dehiscences of Beckett's "Ping."[13] This is the circle, whose mutations in both Joyce and Beckett are well-documented, as a new type of cycle. Yet we should note that if contraries seem in this way to share a similar end, it is a (late) Beckettian lesson that it is only the asymptotic approach to zero that makes it the infinite.

An early and deeply personal influence on Beckett is the subject of the first essay in this collection, Erik Tonning's "'I am not reading philosophy': Beckett and Schopenhauer." Near the beginning of a volume largely devoted to Beckett's reading of philosophy, Tonning's title may strike an ironic note; but it conveys the important insight, which the essay brilliantly pursues and elaborates in multiple directions, that Beckett's adoption of philosophy is never systematic, but a complex matter of personal disposition, artistic convenience, and formal exercise. The influence of Schopenhauer on Beckett's only academic monograph, the 1931 *Proust*, has often been noted and the broader relevance of Schopenhauer's pessimism is a common motif in Beckett criticism. However, Tonning draws attention to a number of Schopenhauerian specifics (the "veil" of the German letter of 1937, the pensum and original sin, mysticism and asceticism) that, as Tonning wryly observes, threaten to multiply for the attentive observer to the point that they suffuse the whole of Beckett's work, making it look like "a ludicrously extended argument for a certain metaphysics." What militates against any sameness of content, more importantly, is not simply the resistance to some of Schopenhauer's notions, regarding music and harmony, or even hope, for example, but Beckett's resolutely writerly and artistic manipulation of philosophy, trans-

---

[13] F.K. Stanzel, *A Theory of Narrative*, translated by Charlotte Goesche (Cambridge: Cambridge University Press, 1984), 235–236.

lating the conceptual into the aesthetic in an abstract drive that refuses the rest of Schopenhauer's artistic consolation. Yet Tonning convincingly demonstrates the degree to which Schopenhauer, more than any other philosopher, remained a kind of interlocutor throughout the decades of Beckett's artistic practice; a "conduit," as Tonning says, for many other influences and developments, even more than a single, influential source.

David Addyman's "'Speak of Time, without Flinching ... Treat of Space with the Same Easy Grace': Beckett, Bergson and the Philosophy of Space" offers an equally provocative thesis: Bergson, the philosopher of time, was instrumental in the development of Beckett's sense of the primacy of space. The first part of Addyman's essay is devoted to a fascinating bit of detective work, assessing the evidence for Beckett's having read Henri Bergson prior to the writing of *Proust*, something that most readers have taken for granted but which, thanks to Addyman's painstaking review of the evidence, seems much less straightforward. Indeed, in one sense, Addyman's essay elaborates upon Tonning's, suggesting that the "temporocentrism" of Beckett's reading of Marcel Proust is more indebted to Schopenhauer, perhaps, than to the author of *À la recherche du temps perdu*. A similar disappointment meets readers who imagine Bergson to be a looming presence in *Endgame*, as the much more likely source is to be found in early Greek philosophy. These are interesting and necessary details in order to establish—with any degree of certainty—Beckett's actual reading of Bergson, and therefore the kind of influence that might be suggested. The real surprise, however, is the degree to which the opposite is revealed. Not Bergson, but Proust turns out to be the real influence; moreover, an appropriated Proust, emancipated from the strictures of time into the lived locality of *place*. Addyman convincingly argues that, although he was the first modern philosopher whom Beckett read in the original, Bergson was less an influence than a vehicle, perhaps not entirely conscious, for Beckett to develop his own very different stress on space (as in the famous "closed space" works such as *The Lost Ones*) but, like Tonning's discussion of Schopenhauer, the number of locations quickly multiply and threaten to overrun the body of work. If Bergson has relevance, it is in the manner described above by Laura Cerrato: an "interlocutor," to use Addyman's word, and not a conceptual source.

Going beyond the explicit Sophist presence in *Endgame*, Peter Fifield's "'Of being—or remaining': Beckett and Early Greek Philosophy" clarifies the very great extent to which the early Greeks were a formative influence on Beckett. Fifield's discovery of a new source for Beckett's notes on early Greek philosophy—along with Fifield's explanation for his reluctance to use the term "pre-Socratic"—is of invaluable help in the removal of "obscurity." What emerges from his elegant and meticulous essay, however, is the sense in which obscurity persists and compounds itself with difficulty. Some sources may now be known more precisely, but the diffuse inheritance of the early Greeks, their "ill-heard" fragments—whose formal character as much as their philosophical content likely appealed to Beckett—makes the analysis and isolation of concepts almost impossible to accomplish. Yet by way of micro-study, Fifield carefully reads "Imagination Dead Imagine" as evincing an Anaximandrean logic. Yet no such stable logic can be found in early Greek philosophy as a whole, with its famous oppositions (Parmenides and Heraclitus), and its poetic, non-systematic character. Fifield shows that this inheritance must now be counted as equal in importance to the Christian and psychoanalytic bases normally accepted as key influences upon Beckett, and also that the latter's turn to these ancient sources propels him into a new and unsuspected modernity, one shared by Heidegger, Derrida and others.

Matthew Feldman is an important impetus behind the "empirical turn" in the study of Beckett, and his "Samuel Beckett, Wilhelm Windelband and Nominalist Philosophy" provides abundant documentary evidence, judiciously applied to Beckett's artistic work, for the under-perceived influence of nominalism. In *Beckett's Books: A Cultural History of the "Interwar Notes"*, Feldman had previously demonstrated the immense importance for Beckett of Wilhelm Windelband's *A History of Philosophy*, the central source for his self-inflicted apprenticeship in philosophy. In this essay, Feldman especially focuses upon the trope of philosophical nominalism, above all in its relation to language and the "Nominalist irony" Beckett held up as a stage on the way to a "literature of the unword" in his "German Letter of 1937."[14] Feldman astutely analyzes the workings of nominalism in Beckett's *Watt*, a novel that seems to explore the limits of a nominalist vocabulary, and in which every generalizable entity or event threatens to break down into the comedy of its particulars. As Feldman concludes, however, there is no reason to believe that the influence of nominalism ended with *Watt*; its presence may be less immediately apparent in the later works, but it is evident nevertheless— in *Ill Seen Ill Said* and *Worstward Ho*, for example—the particulars now themselves trembling and afflicted by a new transformation, demanding a new expression. In more philosophical terms, Feldman demonstrates that a general medieval philosophy, like that of the early Greeks, can have a far-reaching influence, and combine with other sources; in this case, as Feldman shows, with the work of Schopenhauer and Fritz Mauthner. And once again, as a writer Beckett happily refashions his source, reading against the grain of Windelband in order to extract the "absurdities" of nominalism from their neo-Kantian presentation in *A History of Philosophy* and elsewhere.

    C.J. Ackerley's extraordinarily detailed study of the presence of Leibniz in Beckett's work is the first hint of a "post-Cartesian" Beckett in this collection. In his "Monadology: Samuel Beckett and Gottfried Wilhelm Leibniz," there is the surprising genesis of *Murphy* out of monads and their persistence, with a shift in emphasis, from the doomed search for freedom in the microcosm to establishing a harmony with the macrocosm, in *Watt*. Ackerley's close readings reveal not only the presence, but also the ironic problem presented by Leibnizian philosophy; namely, the insufficiency of reason generating new paradoxes instead of affording a descriptive constant. Yet, equally, Ackerley demonstrates how Leibniz recurs as an opaque reference in Beckett—from the attraction of the monad and its *petites*

---

[14] Samuel Beckett, "German Letter of 1937," in *Disjecta*, 173.

perceptions, to the conduit between philosophy and psychology, onto which there is added skepticism for the theodicy and the pre-established harmony. This is philosophical engagement as artistic agon.

Steven Matthews' "'The Books are in the Study as Before': Samuel Beckett's Berkeley" also provides a post-Cartesian setting, but one famously concerned with perception. Matthews wisely does not discuss *Film* at length, the work in which Beckett adopts *"esse est percipi"* as a motto—but without granting it any truth—and instead concentrates on less commonly perceived affinities. These range from the ironic reference to the "idealist tar" in *Murphy*, where Berkeley seems more a figure of fun than a potential source of aesthetic ideas, to what Matthews identifies as the imaginative possibility, made at least partly possible by the ever-present danger of solipsism, which Beckett was to explore in the works of the post-war period. It is in the works starting with *Watt* that the notion of perception, by self and others, grows into one of the mutable constants of Beckett's artistic microcosmos. This aesthetic value, Matthews suggests, occupies both Beckett's art and his writing about art—as Berkeley's famous dialogues between Hylas and Philonous become the model for Beckett's 1949 *Three Dialogues With Georges Duthuit*, and as Berkeley's solutions to the dilemmas of mind and matter may be seen as provoking Beckett to transform them into new and paradoxically productive impasses.

Arnold Geulincx is both obscure and difficult and David Tucker is to be thanked for bringing clarity to both his philosophy and its place in Beckett's work. "Beckett's 'Guignol' Worlds: Arnold Guelincx and Heinrich Von Kleist" returns again to familiar post-Cartesian problems (in this case regarding interactions of mind and body), but in the specific form given them by a thinker who perhaps rivals only Schopenhauer in Beckett's esteem. Tucker not only traces Geulincx's cherished statement *ubi nihil vales, ibi nihil velis* [wherein you have no power, therein you should not will] and its appearance in *Murphy*—demonstrating again another influence at work in that very crowded novel—but draws equal attention to Geulincx's view of action in his philosophy. If being and having are two fundamental questions, in philosophy as well as in Beckett, Geulincx pays more attention to doing—to action as it relates to an agent. Geulincx's profound Occasionalism led him to deny that any action could belong to its agent, but only to God, for any agent needed to be able to rationally explain everything involved in the action (the lifting of one's arm, for example)—and, as ever, something escapes. Tucker admirably demonstrates how this notion of action appears in Beckett's novels as well as his plays, complicating the usual mind-body division by this unique epistemic constraint. Beckett's assimilation of this notion of action to puppetry also finds, fascinatingly, an echo in the work of Heinrich von Kleist, whose famous essay on the marionette theater, as Tucker shows, had a great impact on Beckett. Tucker outlines the difference between the miserable entrapment of Geulincx's suffering agents, aware of their suffering but not of their action, and the spontaneous lightness of Kleist's puppets, aligning the former with the "behaviorist-like" manipulations in Beckett's *Act without Words I*. It is in his reading of "Still," however, that Tucker suggests something like an autonomous grace in a frozen figure, a trembling tension, once again, between philosophy and image.

With "Beckett's Critique of Kant," P.J. Murphy leads us out of rationalism and Occasionalism and into a philosophical context not commonly associated with Beckett. Yet Murphy demonstrates that Kant's three great questions—What can I know? What ought I to do? What may I hope?—all recur in serious or ironic form in Beckett's work. Murphy documents both Beckett's note-taking from his secondary sources on Kant, as well as the extraordinary purchase of Kant's entire works in the late 1930s (which he later gave to his friend, the painter Avigdor Arikha). Not only, then, is there evidence for the kind of interest that Beckett applied to other philosophers, but a remarkable investment in Kant's works themselves. For Murphy, it is Kant's critical insight that the objects of possible experience are given by the subject that most deeply affected Beckett. This raises a kind of a subjectivism different from that of the post-Cartesians, and at the same time points forward to phenomenology. Murphy carries his demonstration of Kant's presence into readings of *Watt*, the postwar Trilogy (*Molloy, Malone Dies* and *The Unnamable*) and *How It Is*. Among the most interesting suggestions is that the Trilogy forms a kind of fictional counterpart or answer to Kant's three Critiques—but with the telling difference that *The Unnamable* would not be concerned with the faculty of judgment, qualifying instead as a *Critique of Pure Imagination*. Here again, the limit of philosophy's application to Beckett is raised, with particular reference to the Critique that Kant regarded as the lynchpin of his system, and which Beckett converts into an expansive aconceptual productive imagination threatening a new kind of mathematical sublime.

Dirk Van Hulle's "'Eff it': Beckett and Linguistic Skepticism" is another break in chronology, propelling us into the twentieth century and into the little-known work of Fritz Mauthner. It recalls Matthew Feldman's treatment of nominalism, except that it moves from the general to a skeptical particular. Van Hulle's rigorous and thorough examination covers a great number of tendencies in a short space—not only German and Austrian philosophies of language, but also a backward look at Bacon's idols through Hugo von Hofmannsthal's famous "Chandos Letter"; a disquisition on contingency and the avoidance of anthropomorphism; in addition to, quite provocatively, a section on the "cognitive functions of writing." The latter includes a brief account of Daniel Dennett, who famously rejected the notion of consciousness as a "Cartesian theater" in favor of a "multiple drafts model" of recursive (and parallel) processes having no center. Most surprisingly, there is the suggestion that Beckett's well-known inclusion of the creative process in his texts is a kind of allegory of this new model. Of all the rejections of Cartesianism in this collection, and indeed perhaps elsewhere, this is the most extraordinary. Van Hulle deals with language and thought through the lens of this neo-empiricism and its unfamiliar denial of the difference between the sensible and the intelligible.

Emilie Morin's "Beckett, Samuel Johnson and the 'Vacuity of Life'" points to another unusual edge between philosophy and non-philosophy. Johnson is in no sense a traditional philosopher, as Morin points out, and would not be included in familiar lists of canonical philosophers; in fact, Johnson's famous "refutation" of Bishop Berkeley is often offered as a pure example of non-philosophy. Beckett's inclusion of Johnson, however, in Lucky's monologue in *Waiting for Godot*, promotes him to the same level as Voltaire and Berkeley. It is thus possible to extend Morin's insight that, for Beckett, this meant that a "non-sytematic philosophy of experience" held equal rank with the philosophers clearly occupying his attentions elsewhere. Perhaps this poses a scenario such as that described by Gilles Deleuze, in which philosophy needs non-philosophy; without which it cannot exist. Johnson's non-philosophy is such that it is a necessary complement to Beckett's immersion in the philosophers, and perhaps reveals its greatest power in Johnson's preference for an eternity of torment to "positive annihilation." The psychological motives that drove Beckett to attempt the abortive fragment of *Human Wishes*—a biographical study of Johnson with the central figure forever just off-stage, which Morin reveals in a wealth of detail—transcend their origin, leaving Johnson's shadow to fall across post-war works ranging from *Waiting for Godot* to *A Piece of Monologue*.

Lotta Palmerstina Einarsson's "Beckett and Abstraction" clearly marks a break from the preceding essays. No longer are demonstrable philosophical influences or allusions to philosophers under scrutiny here. Einarsson provides a philosophical reading *of* Beckett, a reading that discovers the phenomenological dimension of abstraction, not in any conceptual or historical appropriation, but through the intense attention to textual detail, the results of which are impressively displayed in her reading of "One Evening." In this respect, Einarsson's approach differs from those she identifies as her precursors in the study of abstraction—Erik Tonning, whose study involves the use of "Beckett's Leibniz" (i.e., the Leibniz that can be reconstructed from Beckett's reading notes), and Pascale Casanova, who uniquely gives a

Bourdieu-inflected reading of abstraction as pure non-representation. For Einarsson, the phenomenological approach best captures the process of textual construction, while emancipating the work from the realist snares of both mimesis and expression.

Kathryn White's "'I can't go on, I'll go on': Beckett's *Form* of Philosophy" continues by posing the necessary question: precisely what is Beckett's philosophy? In doing so, she draws attention to the manner in which this question has been elided by those most obviously engaged in the study of Beckett and philosophy. White demonstrates how, with respect to an artist, the question of philosophy cannot be framed in terms of concepts, since philosophical concepts can never remain such in the work of art, but must be sought at the level of statement or belief. Framed in this way, the situation is similar to that presented by Morin's discussion of Samuel Johnson. White presents a Beckett steeped in both philosophy and non-philosophy simultaneously. It is the very great strength of her reading that she captures the motion of aesthetic ideas in Beckett's purely formal exercise. Readers may not be left with a single philosophical "message," as John Calder believed, but White presents Beckett's form of philosophy as a new philosophy of form.

Mireille Bousquet's "Beckett and the Refusal of Judgment: The Question of Ethics and the Value of Art" takes a different view of philosophy in Beckett, by absenting it almost completely from consideration. Instead, Bousquet implies, there are strategies at work in Beckett's art—rhetorical, ethical, aesthetic—which bring his work close to that of philosophers—above all to the work of Gilles Deleuze—yet without ever identifying itself with them. This is itself a philosophical interpretation, but one that does not extract philosophy from the work; instead it investigates the way in which the work makes any easy demarcation impossible. In a kind of anti-Kantianism, there is a refusal of judgment developed across Beckett's writings. Yet this is not in order to bring thought to a terminus; this refusal is an ethical gesture, the only one capable of liberating thought from inherited conditions. In the final chapter in this volume,

Bousquet thus both discovers a purely aesthetic Beckett and situates him within a wider cultural movement, one which is perhaps the most unexpected of all: an alliance between art and philosophy.

* * *

Finally, can we claim to any kind collective statement to bind all of these theses together? Obviously not: there is no way these varied and not always compatible approaches to Samuel Beckett could be "cooked to give unity."[15] Yet this is one longstanding way of keeping faith with Beckett, of refusing to impose a single method or to insist upon a single methodological approach. If there are occasional and important differences, it is hoped that these will provoke further inquiries into this fascinating, if difficult, subject matter. For now, at least, literature and philosophy may sit side by side, like a pseudo-couple in one of Beckett's postwar works, mostly companionably.

---

[15] Samuel Beckett, "Proust in Pieces," in *Disjecta*, 65.

Information about the Authors and Editors

Prof. Chris Ackerley is Professor of English at the University of Otago, New Zealand.

Dr. David Addyman is a Research Fellow with the 'Modernism and Christianity' project at the Universtity of Bergen, Norway.

Dr. Mireille Bousquet is a member of Polart—Poétique et politique de l'art group—and is librarian in charge of acquisitions at the Bibliothèque Sainte-Geneviève, Place du Panthéon, Paris, France, EU.

Dr. Lotta Palmstierna Einarsson is a postdoctoral researcher at the University of Stockholm, Sweden, EU.

Prof. Matthew Feldman is Professor in the History of Modern Ideas at the University of Teesside, United Kingdom, EU.

Dr. Peter Fifield is a Lecturer in Modern Literature at the University of Birkbeck, United Kingdom, EU.

Prof. Alexander L. Gungov is Professor of Logic and Continental Philosophy at Sofia University, Bulgaria, EU.

Karim Mamdani in an independent scholar residing in North American and Europe. He is the Reviews Editor of *Sofia Philosophical Review*.

Prof. Steven Matthews is Professor of English at the University of Reading, United Kingdom, EU.

Dr. Emilie Morin is a Lecturer in the Department of English and Related Literature at the University of York, United Kingdom, EU.

Prof. Peter Murphy is a Professor of English at Thompson Rivers University, Canada.

Prof. Erik Tonning is the Director of the 'Modernism and Christianity' project at the University of Bergen, Norway.

Dr. David Tucker is a Visiting Research Fellow at the University of Sussex, United Kingdom, EU.

Prof. Dirk Van Hulle is a Professor of English Literature at the University of Antwerp, Belgium, EU.

Dr. Donald Phillip Verene is Candler Professor of Metaphysics and Moral Philosophy at Emory University, Atlanta, Georgia, USA.

Dr. Kathryn White is a Researcher with the Ulster-Scots Poetry Project at the University of Ulster, United Kingdom, EU.

Index of Names

A

Adorno, Theodor W. 27, 27 n. 7, 273, 275 n. 31, 341, 382

Aristotle 26, 26 n. 6, 46, 64, 134, 137, 141, 155, 158, 159 n. 19, 160, 162, 168 n. 38, 177, 178, 180, 181, 281

B

Bachelard, Gaston 18

Bacon, Francis 65, 65 n. 28, 273, 280, 286, 287-289, 297, 391

Badiou, Alain 27, 27 n. 7, 48, 342, 363, 382, 382 n. 8, 383, 383 n. 11

Ballmer, Hans 95 n. 46, 208, 209

Balzac, Honoré de 365, 366

Bataille, Georges 359, 359 n. 1, 360, 360 n. 2

Bauman, Zygmunt 18, 19

Beethoven, Ludwig van 90, 95, 96, 97 n. 50, 163

Bentham, Jeremy 18

Bergson, Henri 32, 103-126, 189 n. 19, 386, 387

Berkeley, Bishop (George) 26, 26 n. 6, 32, 54 n. 8, 97, 97 n. 53, 153, 176, 176 n. 48, 197, 211-234, 303, 304, 304 n. 18, 310, 310 n. 32, 311, 312, 333, 389, 392

Biely, Andrey 274, 274 n. 30, 275

Blanchot, Maurice 27, 341, 342, 348, 348 n. 24, 383

Borges, Jorge Luis 64, 64 n. 27, 65 n. 29, 192 n. 27, 381

Burke, Edmund 310, 312

C

Camus, Albert 18

Cassirer, Ernst 261, 262, 263, 273

Cavell, Stanley 363, 363 n. 5

Cézanne, Paul 95 n. 47, 121 n. 55, 122 n. 58

Cixous, Hélène 27, 27 n. 8, 48

Corneille, Pierre 119, 366

Critchley, Simon 31 n. 19, 276 n. 37, 277, 277 n. 40

D

Dante 36 n. 2, 66, 72, 155, 161, 186 n. 5, 210 n. 59, 258 n. 52

Darwin, Charles 283-286

Deleuze, Gilles 27, 27 n. 8, 48, 347, 347 n. 18, 373, 373 n. 18, 374, 374 n. 19, 375, 382, 382 n. 8, 383, 383 n. 11, 392, 393

Democritus 97, 127-149 *passim*, 188, 342, 346

Dennett, Daniel C. 291, 292 n. 22, 391

Derrida, Jacques 27, 28, 28 n. 10, 341, 342, 349, 382 n. 8, 387

Descartes, René 18, 25, 28, 30, 104, 127, 157, 158, 158 n. 18, 180, 189, 193, 196, 210 n. 59, 237, 245, 291, 379 n. 2, 381

Dostoevsky, Fyodor 113, 115, 118, 242 n. 17, 366

E

Eliot, T.S. 24, 24 n. 3, 214, 240

F

Fichte, Johann Gottlieb 18, 90 n. 33, 262

Fielding, Henry 213

Foucault, Michel 31, 40, 342

Freud, Sigmund 98, 99, 99 n. 58, 99 n. 59, 210 n. 59

G

Geulincx, Arnold 25, 26 n. 6, 32, 33, 97, 127, 153, 161, 193, 200, 235-259, 342, 343 n. 6, 346, 389, 390

Gide, André 118, 196, 365, 366

Goldsmith, Oliver 310, 311, 311 n. 35, 312

Gombrowicz, Witold 381

H

Habermas, Jürgen 31, 40

Hegel, George Wilhelm Friedrich 14, 18, 19, 20, 55, 67, 68, 68 n. 36, 90, 148, 177

Heidegger, Martin 18, 31, 37, 40, 41, 148, 149, 149 n. 36, 245, 276, 276 n. 35, 322, 387

Henry, Michel 327-328

Hofmannsthal, Hugo von 280, 285-287, 391

Hume, David 68, 177, 266, 266 n. 17, 305

Husserl, Edmund 18, 276, 325 n. 2

I

Ionesco, Eugène 16

J

James, Henry 343, 344

Johnson, Samuel 25, 32, 100, 100 n. 64, 127, 225, 226, 299-323, 392, 393

Joyce, James 13, 25, 42, 43, 43 n. 16, 45, 51-73, 188 n. 19, 240, 261, 268, 268 n. 19, 269, 279, 287, 289, 356, 382 n. 8, 384, 385

Jung, Carl Gustav 99 n. 59, 210 n. 59

K

Kandinsky, Wassily 327-328

Kant, Immanuel 18, 19, 25, 26 n. 6, 32, 55, 113, 161, 177, 181, 182, 193, 245, 261-278, 390, 391

Kierkegaard, Søren 28

Kleist, Heinrich von 235-359, 390

Kristeva, Julia 15

L

Leibniz, Gottfried Wilhelm 26 n. 6, 32, 97, 98 n. 54, 130, 153, 185-210, 290, 388, 392

Locke, John 68, 177, 193, 216, 217, 226

M

Malebranche, Nicolas 26, 36, 300, 237, 311

Mauthner, Fritz 26, 26 n. 6, 32, 97, 97 n. 53, 103, 155, 172, 178-184, 273, 276, 279-297, 304, 317, 317 n. 56, 379, 386, 388, 391

Merleau-Ponty, Maurice 106, 122, 122 n. 57, 343, 352

Meschonnic, Henri 372, 373, 375, 375 n. 20, 376 n. 21

N

Nabokov, Vladimir 381

Nietzsche, Friedrich 31, 93, 148, 152, 169, 282, 282 n. 5, 283, 285

Nussbaum, Martha 343, 344 n. 8

P

Pessoa, Fernando 381

Plato 65, 79, 118, 133, 134, 162, 164, 168 n. 38, 177, 178, 180, 181, 281

Popper, Karl 39, 40 n. 11, 41, 41 n. 13, 296

Pound, Ezra 188 n. 19

Pre-Socratics [Presocratics, pre-Socratics, early Greek philosophy] 29 n. 12, 116, 117, 118, 127-149, 156, 157, 387

Proust, Marcel 75, 76, 78, 82, 103-126 *passim*, 188 n. 19, 240, 261, 344, 350, 351, 322 n. 30, 386

R

Racine, Jean 329, 366

Rembrandt 366

Rimbaud, Arthur 97 n. 50, 118, 372

S

Sade, Donatien Alphonse François, Marquis de 99, 100 n. 62, 274

Sartre, Jean-Paul 18, 30, 37, 103, 106, 106 n. 15, 148, 287, 330

Schelling, Friedrich Wilhelm Joseph 90 n. 33, 177

Schiller, Friedrich 90 n. 33

Schlegel, Friedrich 90 n. 33

Schoenberg, Arnold 328

Schopenhauer, Arthur 25, 28, 32, 42, 75-101, 104, 106, 113, 115, 115 n. 43, 116, 127, 172, 172 n. 45, 172 n. 46, 181, 192, 193, 272, 281, 281 n. 4, 282, 292, 342, 345, 385, 386, 387, 388, 389

Socrates 132, 159 n. 19, 169, 180

Spinoza, Benedict de 176, 188, 188 n. 18, 189, 193, 194, 265

Stendhal 366

Swift, Jonathan 310, 310 n. 33, 311, 312, 314-317

V

Vico, Giambattista 13-14, 18, 21, 25, 43-47, 51-73, 311, 356, 384

W

Wittgenstein, Ludwig 28, 293-294, 351

Y

Yeats, Jack 120, 122 n. 58

Yeats, W.B. 215-216, 310 n. 32, 311-312, 314-317

Z

Žižek, Slavoj 27, 27 n. 8

ibidem-Verlag

Melchiorstr. 15

D-70439 Stuttgart

info@ibidem-verlag.de

www.ibidem-verlag.de
www.ibidem.eu
www.edition-noema.de
www.autorenbetreuung.de

Zeitfracht Medien GmbH
Ferdinand-Jühlke-Straße 7,
99095 - DE, Erfurt
produktsicherheit@zeitfracht.de